MONITORING THE MOVIES

The Fight over Film Censorship in
Early Twentieth-Century Urban America

JENNIFER FRONC

University of Texas Press

AUSTIN

Requests for permission to reproduce material
from this work should be sent to:
Permissions
University of Texas Press
P.O. Box 7819
Austin, TX 78713-7819
utpress.utexas.edu/rp-form

♾ The paper used in this book meets the minimum requirements of
ANSI/NISO Z39.48-1992 (R1997) (Permanence of Paper).

LIBRARY OF CONGRESS CATALOGING-IN-PUBLICATION DATA

Names: Fronc, Jennifer, 1974– author.
Title: Monitoring the movies : the fight over film censorship in early
twentieth-century urban America / Jennifer Fronc.
Description: First edition. | Austin : University of Texas Press, 2017. |
Includes bibliographical references and index.
Identifiers: LCCN 2017012642| ISBN 978-1-4773-1379-4 (cloth : alk. paper) |
ISBN 978-1-4773-1393-0 (pbk. : alk. paper) | ISBN 978-1-4773-1394-7
(library e-book) | ISBN 978-1-4773-1395-4 (nonlibrary e-book)
Subjects: LCSH: Motion pictures—Censorship—United States—History—
20th century. | Motion pictures—Moral and ethical aspects—United
States. | Censorship—United States—History—20th century. | National
Board of Review of Motion Pictures (U.S.)
Classification: LCC PN1995.62 .F76 2017 | DDC 363.310973—dc23
LC record available at https://lccn.loc.gov/2017012642

doi:10.7560/313794

CONTENTS

ACKNOWLEDGMENTS

WHEN I MOVED TO RICHMOND, VIRGINIA, IN 2005, MY dear friend Brent Spencer took me to the historic Byrd Theater, a 1928 movie palace that is still in operation to this day, complete with live performances on the Mighty Wurlitzer. Then John Kneebone, my colleague in the History Department at Virginia Commonwealth University, mentioned that Virginia had had a state motion picture censorship law until the 1960s. My curiosity was piqued. I met with Ray Bonis, in Special Collections and Archives at the James Cabell Branch Library at VCU, who introduced me to the fascinating and complicated history of moviegoing and Progressive reform in early twentieth-century Virginia.

During the years of research for this manuscript, I have been fortunate to work with excellent and helpful people at a number of libraries and archives, including the Library of Virginia and the State Records Center in Richmond; the General Federation of Women's Clubs Women's History and Resource Center in Washington, DC; the James G. Kenan Research Center at the Atlanta History Center in Atlanta, Georgia; Manuscripts and Special Collections at the New York State Library in Albany, New York; and Special Collections and University Archives at the University of Massachusetts (UMASS) at Amherst. Special thanks to the New York Public Library's Manuscripts and Archives division, especially Thomas Lannon, Tal Nadan, John Cordovez, and Nasima Hasnat.

Kate Schmitz, my research assistant in Richmond, did meticulous work in Virginia newspaper archives. Brooke Parziale, my research assistant at UMASS, mastered Zotero and several databases. Thank you both for being dependable, responsible, and fun to work with. The students in my "History of Censorship in the United States" seminars during the fall 2013 and fall 2015 semesters advanced my thinking on the cultural and legal issues surrounding censorship and asked important questions about censorship and new technologies, such as video games and social networking platforms. My graduate students and teaching assistants have all been an important part of my work life at UMASS—Marwa Amer, Dan Chard, Andy Grim, Felicia Jamison, Michella Marino, Laura Miller, and Gina Talley deserve special recognition.

A short-term research fellowship from the New York Public Library and a Faculty Research Grant/Healey Endowment Grant from the Office of the Vice Chancellor for Research and Engagement at UMASS provided financial support for this project. The Dean's Office and History Department granted course releases for writing. My colleagues at UMASS and the Five Colleges, especially Chris Appy, Frank Couvares, Dan Czitrom, Jennifer Guglielmo, Barbara Krauthamer, Daniel LaChance, Ted Melillo, Chantal Norrgard, Dawn Peterson, Khary Polk, Liz Pryor, Anna Taylor, and Rob Weir, have provided intellectual support and important feedback.

I am fortunate to have good friends who also happen to be talented historians and scholars. Libby Garland read and commented on multiple drafts over the years—thank you for being an incisive critic and steadfast friend. Andrea Odiorne also read multiple iterations of this project, and was always willing to talk film and feminist theory. To those who have motivated and supported my intellectual development over the years—Jeffrey Adler, Betsy Blackmar, Shannan Clark, Jim Downs, Megan Elias, Ann Fabian, Kathy Feeley, Tim Gilfoyle, Elena Gorfinkel, Pippa Holloway, Seth Kamil, Alice Kessler-Harris, John Kneebone, Cindy Lobel, Ted McCormick, Wilbur Miller, Sharon Paradiso, Annie Polland, Matthew Raffety, Sam Roberts, Bill Sutton, Jeffrey Trask, Theresa Ventura, and Yücel Yanikdağ—thank you.

The University of Texas Press has been a pleasure to work with. Robert Devens, my acquisitions editor, is brilliant and hilarious. Thank you for your support over the years. Sarah McGavick has my gratitude for shepherding the manuscript as it made its way to the production process. The readers for the press provided extraordinarily detailed and valuable reports—special thanks to Matthew Bernstein and Kathryn Fuller-Seeley.

Finally, I thank my parents, Don and Maryann, and my sister, Andrea, for their unwavering support. Now, as my grandmother Rita Kusztelniak Fronc used to say, "Let's go to show!"

MONITORING THE MOVIES

INTRODUCTION: THE ORIGINS OF
THE ANTICENSORSHIP MOVEMENT

IN 1917 THE DIRECTOR IVAN ABRAMSON'S LATEST FILM, AN educational "purpose play" about premarital sex and abortion, debuted during an ongoing debate as to the legal merits of motion picture censorship. *Enlighten Thy Daughter* (Ivan Films, 1917) was an educational film with popular appeal; Abramson cast the silent film star Zena Keefe as Lillian Stevens, a sheltered young woman raised not to "know too much," and the Vitagraph favorite James W. Morrison as Lillian's love interest, Harold, "the pampered son of a wealthy widow."[1] Lillian's mother, portrayed by the stage and screen actress Marie Shotwell, "enjoys the wilder phases of life." She passes her days "gambling, flirting and spending" rather than tending to Lillian, "allow[ing] her daughter to grow up in ignorance." In a pivotal scene, a thunderstorm forces Lillian and Harold to seek shelter in an abandoned barn, and they succumb to desire. A whole "host of woes entwine" the characters; Lillian becomes pregnant and dies at the hands of "an unscrupulous physician" after a botched abortion, all resulting from "ignorance, neglect, [and] the failure of a mother to properly enlighten her daughter."[2]

The *New York Telegraph* declared Abramson's motion picture one of the best of the year, and several ministers endorsed this educational photoplay. The *New York Times* reviewer was less enthusiastic; although he expressed no moral objection to the film, he did dismiss it as another "inept and melodramatic variant" of a familiar plot. Readers were advised to keep their daughters away from the film; if they were childless, they should "do the next best thing and advise some other man's daughter not to waste time on the picture."[3] Yet *Enlighten Thy Daughter* became a box-office success. Was the success attributable to Abramson's ability to relay an important message with sensitivity, or to the titillating and controversial subject matter?

In an effort to better gauge public opinion on *Enlighten Thy Daughter*, the National Board of Review of Motion Pictures (NB) hosted a screening and

FIGURE O.I. Enlighten Thy Daughter *advertisement*,
Motion Picture News, *1917*

discussion at Wurlitzer Hall in New York City. The group in attendance—
volunteer reviewers from a variety of Progressive organizations, settlement
houses, and municipal agencies selected for their perspective and wisdom—
grappled with the implications of Abramson's film being exhibited to the public. One audience member described the picture as "excellent," but warned
that exhibiting it "indiscriminately, before very young children, is not wise
and not justified." Another audience member concurred, adding that it was
not "wise to put all things where all people can reach them [because] poor
mothers have not the time or knowledge to exercise control over what shows
their children attend." Several more chimed in, extrapolating from the example of *Enlighten Thy Daughter* that the only way to protect children from the
corrupting influence of objectionable motion picture content was for the government to censor movies prior to public exhibition. New York State, these
viewers insisted, needed to establish a state motion picture censorship board
to discern which motion pictures were suitable for public consumption.[4]

W. D. McGuire Jr. became exasperated with the discussion; after all, as executive secretary of the National Board, he had spent the previous eight years
trying to debunk the claim that motion pictures posed a threat to children.
Moreover, the governor of New York had just vetoed a state censorship bill

in 1916. So McGuire jumped in and critiqued the reasoning used by censorship's supporters—that, like child labor laws or building codes, state censorship would somehow protect the vulnerable from harm. Instead, he insisted, enacting censorship legislation was akin to telling great motion picture producers: "Because little Mrs. Smith hasn't any brains and doesn't know how to bring up her children, you must present only fairy tales." He then proceeded to cite surveys finding that children constituted only 15 percent of motion picture audiences; therefore, he said, censorship was "legislation for that 15%," or "legislation for foolish parents." He concluded by asking, "What would have happened to literature had it been confined to that sort of thing? If the motion picture is going to amount to anything it must get out of the fairy tale stage!" Swayed by McGuire's passion or logic, the audience responded with applause.[5]

AS THEY DID ON MANY OTHER ISSUES DURING THE LONG Progressive era, Americans debated the merits of regulation, and the role of state and private actors, in seeking solutions to the "motion picture problem."[6] Some reformers identified the spaces in which motion pictures were exhibited as dangerous to public health and safety; others focused on movies' content and mimetic power, calling for government intervention to prevent public exhibition of obscene or otherwise objectionable material.[7] Still other activists recognized the artistic and educational potential of movies and identified government censorship as a real threat to their future.[8] Neighborhood movie theaters were springing up on every corner in the nation's burgeoning cities. Should municipal, state, or federal authorities step in to control what people could watch when they went to them? Or, if motion pictures were not a matter for government decision-making, should some other type of entity—voluntary boards populated by trusted civic leaders and professionals, for example—step in to safeguard public morals?[9] Were motion pictures, as the newest medium of expression, similar enough to the printed word to qualify for First Amendment protections, or were they something else entirely? These are but some of the questions that animated the motion picture censorship movement during the first two decades of the twentieth century.

In 1915, the US Supreme Court affirmed the constitutionality of state censorship of motion pictures.[10] In January, the justices heard arguments in *Mutual Film Corporation v. Industrial Commission of Ohio*, and on 23 February they issued a unanimous ruling rejecting the "free speech for the movies" concept. Writing for the Court, Associate Justice Joseph McKenna noted that motion pictures were not "regarded, nor intended to be regarded by the Ohio Constitution . . . as part of the press of the country, or as organs of public opinion." Furthermore, because motion picture exhibition was "a business, pure and simple, originated and conducted for profit," motion pictures fell outside the protections of the First Amendment. Thus, the *Mutual* decision concluded, in establishing censorship boards to protect public morals, states were acting within the ambit of their constitutions.[11] Supporters of censorship were empowered by this decision, and by 1916, Ohio, Kansas, Pennsylvania, and Maryland all had state boards of censorship. Congressional hearings related to the creation of a federal censorship board had been held twice, in 1914 and 1916.

In the following pages, I explore the history of the movement against legal motion picture censorship from the perspective of the National Board of Review of Motion Pictures, its allies, and its traveling organizers. Founded in 1909 by a coalition of Progressive social activists, the NB emerged from the midst of a struggle for police censorship in New York City that was spearheaded by influential ministers and moral reformers. Under its original name, the National Board of Censorship, it advocated for voluntary motion picture regulation and established a tripartite system to carry it out. First, it conducted prerelease reviews of motion pictures by its in-house "model" audiences and publicized those decisions in its widely distributed weekly *Bulletin*. Second, it created (and updated annually) a set of "Standards" that served as a "code of ethics" for motion pictures. Third, it designed and implemented the City Plan for Voluntary Motion Picture Regulation, a model ordinance adopted by more than eighty cities by 1918 in lieu of legal censorship (see the appendix).

The NB took the position that the real "motion picture problem" was the "un-American" specter of legal censorship; in fact, its members agreed, the "recognition of the screen's right to freedom" was "fundamental in the theory" of the NB.[12] The board changed its name in the wake of the *Mutual* decision and increasingly linked its efforts to the First Amendment rights of motion picture producers. Throughout its history, the National Board walked a fine line, philosophically and logistically, around the issues of censorship and free expression.[13] It rejected the notion of giving politically appointed censors, police officers, or other agents of the state the authority to review content or require producers to excise frames prior to exhibition, defining this as prior restraint on speech. Indeed, it rejected any claim that it was engaged in censorship; rather, it screened motion pictures from the standpoint of "public opinion," which was "the only competent judge of the screen."[14]

The NB, comparing its role to that of a newspaper editor, asserted that its Review Committees "approximate[d] public opinion," and therefore were justified in exercising "the blue pencil"—or, in this case, scissors—to remove anything they deemed objectionable in service of "the public good and the screen's welfare."[15] The board argued that its system was thorough—so thorough as to preclude the need "for a separate Board or Bureau of Censorship

FIGURE 0.2. *National Board of Censorship seal*

... in any community."[16] By 1916, with the creation of its affiliated National Committee on Better Films, the NB was functioning as the national chaperone for motion pictures, and it seemed as if it had established a bulwark against the rising tide of support for state censorship. And yet, in 1917, twenty of the nation's forty-eight states considered censorship legislation, often backed by the powerful General Federation of Women's Clubs (GFWC).[17]

IN FEBRUARY AND MARCH OF 1917, *MOTION PICTURE NEWS* carried several advertisements for *Enlighten Thy Daughter* aimed at exhibitors, not consumers. One advertisement, addressed to "Mr. Foreign Buyer," touted the picture as a "sensational sex drama"; another boasted that the film was "a positive magnet to women—a sure fire matinee booster." The latter also prominently featured an endorsement from the editor of the *General Federation of Women's Clubs Magazine*, Mrs. Haryat Holt Dey, who confirmed that *Enlighten Thy Daughter* "handles a very delicate subject with great adroitness" and was "not in the least salacious."[18]

Mrs. Albert E. (Florence J. Breck) Bulson, president of the Michigan Federation of Women's Clubs, disagreed with Dey and organized her own screening and discussion of *Enlighten Thy Daughter*. She objected to the motion picture's depiction of "the criminal practice indulged in by the doctor," as well as the mother, a "supposedly respectable society woman," who drinks, smokes, gambles, and shows "absolute disregard of the marriage relation." *Enlighten Thy Daughter*, Bulson cautioned, would not "exert a wholesome influence" on the "young men and women who witness[ed]" it; therefore, she advocated for Michigan to create a state censorship board, preferably one staffed by mothers of discerning taste.[19]

During the Progressive era, women pro-censorship activists, wielding a "maternalist rhetoric," succeeded in keeping the issue of motion picture censorship on the political agenda at both the state and federal levels. Beginning in the late nineteenth century, women increasingly laid claim to temperance, antiobscenity, and similar moral reform campaigns by emphasizing their status as mothers and their ability to speak on behalf of children and other vulnerable figures, asserting a right to be political actors even in the absence of the franchise. The sociologist Theda Skocpol has argued that this "maternalist *rhetoric*" was "surprisingly effective with civic leaders and legislators" because it "appeared to rise above narrowly partisan considerations." As such, women's demands became "hard to ignore."[20] In the case of state censorship, governors often promised that appointments to the boards would go to the maternalist activists who helped bring them about. The boards therefore opened up new positions of political power for women before the passage of the Nineteenth Amendment in 1920.[21]

The powerful Women's Christian Temperance Union (WCTU), founded in 1873, exemplified this maternalist position, employing a rhetoric of "home protection" to bring about state and federal prohibition of alcohol. The maternalist reformers of the WCTU also found a number of powerful allies for their "second noble experiment"—federal motion picture censorship legislation.[22] In 1914, the WCTU's Department of Purity in Literature and Art announced its support for the Smith-Hughes Motion Picture Censorship Bill, which proposed the creation of a Federal Motion Picture Commission. The historian Alison Parker has written about the WCTU's pro-censorship campaign; much like its early temperance campaign, it was "both a tool for women's political empowerment" and a way for women to fulfill their most traditional responsibilities to the nation's children.[23] In 1916, the General Federation of Women's Clubs announced its intention to address the "motion picture problem." The organization formed a committee to study the issue, and two years later, it passed a resolution in favor of state-by-state censorship legislation.[24] With its roughly 2 million members, the GFWC emerged as the NB's greatest opponent in the fight over film censorship.

The National Board did not object to women's political activism per se, or to their presence on review boards; however, it did object to the maternalist mandate that the state screen motion pictures to protect children. NB executive secretary W. D. McGuire's correspondence, in particular, revealed his deep dislike of women pro-censorship supporters. In a letter to filmmaker D. W. Griffith, he described clubwomen as "repressionists by nature," "the very element whose natural type of mind was in favor of censorship." He wondered if there was any point in trying to find common ground with them:

"Seek[ing] their cooperation in the fight against censorship" would be "like attempting to engage Satan for the distribution of Holy Water."[25]

Despite these misgivings, McGuire recognized the collective power of the club's members and decided to organize them to support the NB's "voluntary regulation" system. He devised an ambitious scheme, funded in part by D. W. Griffith and Southern Enterprises of Paramount Pictures, to hire GFWC members to work as traveling organizers on behalf of the board's National Committee for Better Films. These organizers were to encourage the women of local clubs to adopt methods of local control and abandon legal censorship campaigns.[26] McGuire may have been surprised to find that many women were prepared to join forces with the NB so long as they maintained a significant amount of power locally.

Between 1916 and 1922, three women—Mary Gray Peck, Louise Connolly, and Mary Mason Speed—traveled extensively on behalf of the NB and the Better Films movement. In the ensuing chapters, I follow these women through Virginia, Florida, Georgia, and Alabama, relying on their extensive field reports to illuminate the concerns that animated supporters of censorship in the urban South. The correspondence and reports from these traveling lecturers and their local informants offer a new perspective on the most popular leisure space in urban American—the movies—and on the regional differences that divided Progressive social activists during the first two decades of the twentieth century.

Despite the months of travel these women took on and the hundreds of speeches they delivered, the GFWC's members remained among the staunchest opponents of the National Board's goals. After 1922, the GFWC embraced the Motion Picture Producers and Distributors of America (MPPDA) and its new president, Will H. Hays, who had an "open door policy" and an ambitious plan for industry self-regulation. By 1924, with the creation of the Hays Code, the GFWC declared the motion picture censorship issue "moot."

Although the NB failed to maintain its position as the national "clearinghouse for the movies," it did construct and operate a viable alternative to state censorship in the 1910s and 1920s. The NB then retreated from politics and turned its focus to encouraging the production of excellent photoplays, an undertaking that continues to this day.[27] Ultimately, the following account addresses some of the most significant concepts and tensions in US history: free speech versus censorship, civil liberties and civil rights, and state power in a democracy. As such, the film censorship debate has had ramifications felt throughout American society.

1 / THE LESSER OF TWO EVILS:
DEBATING MOTION PICTURE CENSORSHIP,
1907—1912

THE UNWRITTEN LAW: A THRILLING DRAMA BASED ON the Thaw/White Case (Lubin, 1907) depicts a dramatic true story: the death of the famous architect and playboy Stanford White at the hands of Harry K. Thaw, who murdered White in revenge for an incident involving Thaw's wife, Evelyn Nesbit, six years earlier. Hers was a famous face; she had worked as an artist's model, most notably for Charles Dana Gibson, who found inspiration in her voluptuous figure and dark, wavy hair. As a youth, Nesbit had graced the covers of women's magazines and appeared in advertisements for everything from life insurance to Coca Cola.[1] In 1901, at the age of seventeen, she had successfully transitioned to a stage career, becoming a popular chorus girl who partied with the smart set in Manhattan, where she attracted White's attention. *The Unwritten Law*, in which Nesbit plays herself, re-creates Nesbit and White's first meeting, as well as a subsequent meeting in which White allegedly drugged and sexually assaulted her; her marriage to Thaw; and Thaw's act of revenge, when he shot White in front of an audience at Madison Square Garden's rooftop theater. The film debuted in March 1907, during Thaw's first trial for murder.

Lubin Manufacturing, a silent-film production company, was attempting to capitalize on the public's fascination with the trial of the century. Daily, throngs of people "swarmed" the Criminal Courts building in Manhattan, congregating in the streets "in the idle hope of [catching] the merest glimpse" of the prisoner as police escorted him across the Bridge of Sighs to the Tombs Prison. Inside the courthouse, observers filled the "mezzanine galleries" until they resembled "the balconies of a crowded theater."[2] To direct *The Unwritten Law*, pioneering American motion picture producer Sigmund Lubin searched the newspapers to identify the trial's most "sensational points," according to *Variety*, and then assembled them "into a fairly complete exposi-

FIGURE 1.1. *Evelyn Nesbit*

tion of Mrs. Harry [Evelyn Nesbit] Thaw's testimony."[3] In order to reassure exhibitors familiar with the salacious details of the trial that the film was acceptable, the Lubin company issued a statement saying that the motion picture dramatization "contain[ed] absolutely nothing objectionable and may be shown in all theatres."[4]

Despite these assurances, *The Unwritten Law* raised serious questions about the morality of motion pictures, the newest mode of entertainment and expression. The *Chicago Tribune* reported that when *The Unwritten Law* was exhibited in April 1907, bookings were concentrated at the "downtown 5 cent theaters," and the audiences were packed with "school-girls." Unlike the adult women in the audience, who walked out in disgust, the *Tribune* reported, the girls "remained sometimes for two or three views of the pictures."[5] Shortly thereafter, in November, the Chicago City Council adopted police censorship of motion pictures, requiring licensing of all exhibition spaces and prohibiting the exhibition of "immoral or obscene" motion pictures to the public.[6]

Moving Picture World, an industry trade journal established that year, blamed the problem on "the five-cent theaters." It was the small theaters, or nickelodeons, that held a special danger for young people, the journal said.

And according to *Moving Picture World*'s editors, "the remedy for the evils of the five-cent theater is the same as that successfully employed in many other cases—the substitution of the wholesome and harmless for the unwholesome and hurtful."[7] Criminals, it was thought, could lurk in the shadows, and the solution was for exhibitors to improve the physical conditions of their buildings to discourage this and make their theaters safer places, and thus assuage some of the reformers' fears.[8] In terms of content, *MPW* encouraged exhibitors to reach out to community members to enlist their help in selecting high-quality shows. They shouldn't be "pandering to the lowest tastes." This phrase reflected an image that the motion picture industry had been trying to shake since its inception. The *MPW* asserted that *The Unwritten Law* had caused "more adverse press criticism than all the films manufactured before, put together, have done." Motion pictures had suddenly become "the cause of action" for "birds of a feather"—that is, the police and other authorities as well as "church, children's, purity, and other societies."[9] *The Unwritten Law* launched a burgeoning movement to monitor the movies, one that presented nothing less than an existential threat to the new industry—producers and exhibitors alike.[10]

As a business venture, moving picture exhibition had proved so successful by the time of *The Unwritten Law*'s release that entrepreneurs were moving beyond makeshift exhibition spaces to open dedicated venues; in cities, they often occupied storefront spaces. Called "nickelodeons" because of their modest five-cent admission price, these small theaters offered hours of entertainment by combining moving pictures with live entertainment—sing-alongs, comedy and musical acts, burlesque performances—all at a lower price than a vaudeville ticket.[11] A broad audience flocked to the five-cent theaters, and nickelodeons quickly incorporated families and women into the culture of moviegoing. By 1910, approximately 10,000 nickelodeons were in operation in the United States throughout the year, and considerably more during the summer months.[12]

The Unwritten Law, and numerous other motion pictures produced during the nickelodeon era, literally projected the anxieties of this moment onto the screen. Increasing numbers of women and children were flocking to the larger-than-life images dancing across the screen, a development that alarmed many onlookers.[13] This was the peak of immigration to the United States, with 1.2 million people entering the country in 1907 alone, and a corresponding moral panic arose about "white slave traffic" and women adrift in the city. The Mann White Slave Traffic Act, passed in 1910 in response to anti-immigrant sentiment and an alleged international "traffic in women," made it a federal crime for unmarried couples to travel across state lines together; it also significantly expanded the power and purview of the newly established (federal) Bureau of Investigation (BI), the agency which later became the Federal Bureau of Investigation (FBI). The BI's enforcement of the Mann Act policed women's sexual choices and worked to uphold "parental authority over daughters."[14] In the first two decades of the twentieth century, young women were recast as possible victims of suave playboys (a notion that disregarded women's sexual agency) or vulnerable to foreign kidnappers, and therefore in need of protection.[15]

However, the nickelodeons also emerged as a popular form of family entertainment, particularly in immigrant and working-class neighborhoods. These audiences made the moviegoing experience a participatory one—they were rowdy and chatty, cheering heroes and booing villains. If viewers disliked a particular reel, they might clamor for the projectionist to alter its speed, which quickly turned drama into comedy. Movies helped immigrants learn English and introduced them to American customs; working-class mothers sometimes relied on the neighborhood nickelodeon not only as a cheap form of entertainment for their children but also as a kind of daycare.[16]

The history of the movement to censor and control motion picture content can only be understood in the much larger context of American battles over vice, morality, and obscenity. These battles had already been raging for decades by the time the earliest moving pictures were screened to American audiences in the late 1890s. The organizations that appointed themselves to police the proliferation of "vice" in the nation's burgeoning urban centers in the late nineteenth century believed fiercely in the power of civic associationalism, and they combined this advocacy with deep fear of the decade's social and demographic shifts. They were especially concerned about trends that were remaking the urban landscape—such as immigration, urbanization, and mass consumption.

The history of the early movement to monitor motion pictures involved a number of factions: pro-censorship activists; Progressive social activists, who countered with an anticensorship stance; and the motion picture industry, which tried to respond to public concern. At stake was whether motion pictures should be censored by the state or other politically appointed bodies in order to protect children from the putative destructive power that movies had on their development. Pro-censorship activists favored a protective stance on behalf of "vulnerable viewers," arguing for strict policing of motion picture content and the places in which they were exhibited. Central to their argument was protection of children, based on the presumption that motion pictures could produce a mimetic response in vulnerable viewers.[17] Anticensorship activists proposed other types of measures, such as audience segmentation by age, and argued against blanket measures in which agents of the state mediated motion picture content.[18]

In late nineteenth-century cities, well-placed men—ministers, business leaders, academics, and the like—formed a variety of private organizations to directly intercede on behalf of the innocent and vulnerable.[19] The mainstays of these organizations—who were mostly Protestant—believed the battle for public morality was over more than just the quality of Americans' individual characters. They perceived the decline in the nation's moral fiber as an imminent threat to the health and safety of society: low morals, they believed, were directly linked to higher crime rates. This theory of criminality lined up neatly with the tendency of the native-born members of vice societies to believe that their urban neighbors—the poor, the foreign-born, and the non-white—required strict policing.[20] It also conveniently overlooked the socioeconomic factors—and the sheer population density—that contributed to a perceived spike in juvenile delinquency and urban crime rates in the late nineteenth century. Speaking from their positions of moral authority, these moral reformers, as part of their broader efforts to protect the vulnerable, warned against motion pictures, marshaling causal arguments about children's malleability to justify the call for increased government control over motion picture content.[21]

Vice societies—such as infamous moral crusader Anthony Comstock's New York Society for the Suppression of Vice—identified corrupt police officers and politicians as important components of urban decline. These corrupt officials, they complained, were allowing brothels and gambling parlors to operate with impunity. Moral reformers also founded and joined what historian Timothy Gilfoyle referred to as "preventive societies." The first of these were formed in New York City and Boston, including the Society for the Prevention of Cruelty to Animals (SPCA) in New York in 1866 (an outgrowth of an English organization founded in 1824). The Society for the Prevention of Cruelty to Children (SPCC) emerged from the SPCA's work in New York and became an organization unto itself in 1875.[22] Often, these groups assumed roles that the municipal and state governments did not prioritize—especially roles that involved policing vice and protecting the vulnerable from harm. In return, some states and cities, including New York City, granted powers of investigation and arrest to these organizations, which could act as agents of the state in court in cases of obscenity convictions, child abuse, and animal cruelty.[23] States and municipalities relied heavily on the labor of these private organizations to enforce new protective legislation against obscenity and cruelty.

Anthony Comstock became a leading figure in the fight against vice and obscenity in all of its manifestations. Raised in a strict New England Puritan household, he joined the Union Army during the Civil War and later settled in the booming metropolis of New York City. Initially a dry goods merchant, he became involved in the Young Men's Christian Association (YMCA) when it began to advocate for state and federal legislation to criminalize "obscene" material. Comstock became the secretary and chief agent of the YMCA-affiliated New York Society for the Suppression of Vice (SSV) in 1873.[24] In March of that year, Congress passed the Suppression of Trade in, and Circulation of, Obscene Literature and Articles of Immoral Use Act, colloquially referred to as the Comstock Act, which made it illegal to transport "obscene, lewd, or lascivious" material through the US mail. Twenty-four states followed suit, passing similar laws.[25] Comstock was subsequently appointed federal postal inspector, and in that position he kept zealous watch over what passed through the mails, expanding his reach over what Americans could produce, distribute, and consume.

The public and the courts actively debated and redefined the term "obscenity" in the late nineteenth century, partly as a result of the actions of Comstock and his SSV. Because "obscenity" functioned as the line between constitutionally protected and unprotected speech, how it was defined would have far-reaching implications. Comstock and other private actors wielded enormous power in shaping that definition by selectively seizing materials and targeting certain subjects. The courts frequently sided with Comstock and with his judgments on the appropriateness or inappropriateness of the material in question, yielding significant legal precedents.[26] For instance, two of the men Comstock arrested in the late nineteenth century for distributing obscene material through the mails ended up being the subject of US Supreme Court decisions that prevailed until the mid-twentieth century.

D. M. Bennett was the publisher and founder of *The Truth Seeker*, a "free thought" publication that supported women's suffrage, birth control, labor reform, and "free love" (that is, it opposed traditional monogamous marriage). Comstock kept Bennett on his watch list for years, first arresting him in 1877; he arrested him again in 1879 for using the US mail to distribute Ezra Heywood's free-love pamphlet "Cupid's Yokes: Or the Binding Forces of Conjugal Life." The Supreme Court upheld Bennett's obscenity conviction, thereby establishing the constitutionality of the Comstock Law.[27] In 1896, Comstock arrested New York City publisher Lew Rosen for distributing "Tenderloin Number, Broadway" through the mail. The cover image featured a horse with a cab and driver and "the figure of a female," captioned *Tenderloineuse*, suggesting that she was a prostitute. During Rosen's obscenity trial, the Court refused to even allow descriptions of the pamphlet to be entered into the record, as these "obscene, lewd, and indecent matters" would be "offensive" and "improper to spread upon the records of the court."[28]

To decide *Rosen v. United States*, the justices adopted the "Hicklin Test," a legal test already in use by the British court system stipulating that any material that had *the tendency* to deprave or corrupt fragile minds was obscene and could be legally banned on those grounds.[29] The Hicklin Test remained the standard by which the US Supreme Court judged obscenity until 1957, when *Roth v. United States* revisited the definition of obscenity. With *Roth*, the justices affirmed that obscenity would remain outside "the area of constitutionally protected freedom of speech or press," but a new, more representative test would be used to identify it. The new test applied "contemporary community standards," and the justices would ask whether "the average person" would find "the dominant theme of the material" to appeal solely to "prurient interests." If so, the material would be classified as obscene, and therefore beyond the protections of the First Amendment.[30] Nevertheless, for more than half a century, the standard the Supreme Court sought to uphold was rooted in late nineteenth-century ideas about protecting children and other "vulnerable viewers."[31]

"Cupid's Yokes" and "Tenderloin Number, Broadway" were not the same genre of obscene material, but Comstock increasingly wielded a broad definition of obscenity that conflated sex education, birth control, and marriage manuals with prurient material. By the early twentieth century, Comstock and his agents were pursuing birth-control advocates, radical free thinkers, and proponents of free love on the same grounds that they were pursuing sellers of pornographic postcards and erotic short stories, and it created a chilling climate for publishers and producers of this content. One of Comstock's targets was Ida C. Craddock, a women's rights activist and sex educator who had distributed educational manuals through the mail, including one titled *The Wedding Night* and another called *Right Marital Living*.[32] In 1902, a New York jury found her guilty of violating the Comstock Law, and rather than serve the five-year prison sentence, she committed suicide. Craddock left a note blaming Comstock, deriding him as nothing more than "a paid informer."[33] At the behest of Harry K. Thaw, Comstock even rented a room in Madison Square Garden, next to Stanford White's apartment, to try to gather enough evidence to arrest White for sexually abusing girls.[34]

Antiobscenity activism was not just a New York City phenomenon; concerned citizens in all of the nation's growing urban centers formed similar organizations to "clean up" their cities. New York City's preventive societies found allies and correspondents across the country, most notably in Boston. In 1878, Comstock traveled to Boston to address an audience at the Park Street Church regarding the city's moral climate. The assembled men, like their counterparts in New York City, had barred women from the proceedings, deeming the subject matter too "delicate" for their sensibilities.[35] By the end of his speech, Comstock had successfully organized the first branch of the SSV outside of New York—the New England Society for the Suppression of Vice (NESSV).[36] The earliest members of the Boston group were members of the city's elite. They included Edward Everett Hale and Phillips Brooks, who were described as "revered and beloved figures—the most prominent ministers in Boston—and considered to be Progressive and enlightened."[37] Rev. Frederick Baylies Allen, assistant minister of the Episcopalian Trinity Church, served as the organization's first president. His son, historian Frederick Lewis Allen, later described him as "the most beloved man in Boston," "equal parts moralist and social worker."[38]

Like New York City, Boston had been in the throes of a major demographic shift since the late nineteenth century, partly owing to immigration from Europe. After decades of chain migration—in which immigrants from a particular town or village followed in the footsteps of other immigrants from that location to settle in the same city—Boston emerged as a preferred destination for Irish (and, to a lesser extent, Italian) Catholics.[39] By 1890, immigrants constituted 68 percent of the city's population, with particularly large concentrations in the North End and South End neighborhoods. Boston's moral reformers became increasingly concerned about young men and women adrift in the city, complaining that they were hanging out on the streets without supervision and mingling promiscuously in cheap theaters. The changes they were noticing contributed to a "sense of alienation" on the part of Boston's elite, and their fears were compounded by the fact that, in the city proper, political power had recently transferred to the Irish political machine—and from Republicans to Democrats (although state offices remained largely Republican).[40] Unlike New York City elites, who were being lured steadily north by real estate speculators, and were largely ceding Lower Manhattan to immigrant and working-class populations, Boston's Brahmins maintained their elegant residences in Back Bay, Beacon Hill, and other centrally located neighborhoods.[41] As the nearby North End developed into an immigrant boardinghouse district, replete with saloons, dance halls, and cheap theaters, the native-born elites had a front-row seat to the changes being wrought by immigrant, working-class culture.[42]

Moral reformers in Massachusetts could rely on long-standing legal traditions in the Commonwealth related to regulating obscenity. Many ordinances, such as those concerning Sunday closings and the moral character of public amusements, dated back to the Puritan colony of the seventeenth century. The Massachusetts state legislature regularly took strong positions against materials deemed threatening to public morality; an 1880 law had banned printed materials that "contained language obscene, indecent, or impure." Empowered by this history, the NESSV did not have to resort to the kind of "stunt raids" that characterized Comstock's work in New York City. Instead, its inaugural campaign openly targeted two areas of concern: obscene literature and stage plays in Boston. By 1882, the NESSV had changed its name to the New England Watch and Ward Society (NEWWS), which its members adapted from the name of "an unofficial police force" previously used by the Massachusetts Bay Colony, and could claim all six states in the region as its territory; it shortened the name to the Watch and Ward Society (WWS) in 1891.[43] WWS agents were legally empowered to suppress all books and stage plays that contained "obscene" material.[44]

Boston emerged as a lucrative stop on national vaudeville and burlesque circuits, and its theater district boomed in the first two decades of the twentieth century. The *Boston Globe* regularly ran display advertisements for the city's burlesque houses, "legitimate" theaters, and moving picture shows side by side—entertainment available at every price point.[45] For instance, in January 1904, it ran an advertisement from the Boston Theater, which boasted of "high class attractions at fair prices." Eminent English stage actor Charles J. Warner starred in the well-regarded temperance drama "Drink." On the same page, the Paris Theater, "home of burlesque," announced that Weber's Parisian Windows Burlesquers, for whom "grief and worry appear as a crime," would come to Boston to "gavotte about the stage like yearlings."[46] Burlesque and cheap vaudeville theaters combined several forms of entertainment to provide a full evening's entertainment—including minstrel performances, *tableaux vivants*, slapstick comic acts, fire breathers, performing animals, and ribald women telling bawdy jokes and offering "leg dances." This new world of entertainment gave the film industry a boost: as film historian Richard Abel found, "the growing market for moving pictures was closely tied to the expansion of vaudeville."[47] After 1900, theater managers increasingly incorporated short motion pictures into their bills because audiences demanded them. The earliest films, termed the "cinema of attractions" by film scholar Tom Gunning, featured short subjects and were often only about a minute long.[48] Popular themes included speeding trains shot from the perspective of the viewer; animal spectacles—such as Professor Welton's boxing cats; and women performing the "hoochie coochie" and other exotic "muscle dances."[49] The Watch and Ward Society took notice and began policing screens along with stages in Boston. After 1909, the Office of the License Commissioner joined the WWS in its quest to clean up Boston.

Back in New York City, the Society for the Prevention of Crime (SPC) also became in involved in the campaign against motion pictures, casting them as a troublesome development that would encourage criminality, particularly among juveniles. Rev. Charles Parkhurst, pastor of the Madison Square Presbyterian Church—who had assumed leadership of the SPC in 1891—argued that rampant graft and corruption in the New York Police Department and City Hall were responsible for the growth in brothels and disorderly saloons in the city: they were being allowed to run "wide open" and had become big business. So dedicated to exposing the "vice trust" was Parkhurst that he once hired an undercover investigator to take him on a guided tour of New York City's underworld. Drawing on his horrifying (and eye-opening) experience underground, he delivered a damning sermon in 1892 that indicted corrupt police and politicians for the dens of iniquity that flourished in the immigrant and working-class districts of Lower Manhattan. Parkhurst's incriminating sermon was no mere rhetoric; his condemnations resulted in the New York State Senate's Lexow Committee Inquiry into police corruption in 1894, which ultimately revealed the extent to which Tammany Hall and the New York Police Department were colluding to protect organized crime and vice.[50]

The SPC regularly employed detectives and undercover investigators to keep abreast of New York City's moral environment. These agents went into the streets to gather information on tenement house prostitution, gambling, and the like, along with any supporting acts of municipal and police corruption. At the same time, the cheap moving-picture shows of the nickelodeons were rising in popularity, and the SPC identified them as a likely source of crimes against children and an especially dangerous place for young women. In early 1909, the city granted SPC agents the legal authority to enforce the statute that required Sunday closings of the nickelodeons. They were also authorized to enforce the prohibition of children under the age of sixteen from attending movies during school hours. SPC agents regularly attended motion picture shows to monitor them for "obscene" content.[51]

Canon William Sheafe Chase, rector of the Episcopalian Christ Church in Brooklyn and a prominent member of the SPC's board of directors, emerged as the leader in the fight for legal censorship of motion pictures in New York City. Rev. Parkhurst by this point had embraced the possibility that motion pictures could serve the causes of education and reform (he had even appeared in a couple of "problem plays" himself). Canon Chase took a harder line and regularly appeared before state legislatures and Congress to appeal for legal censorship on behalf of children. As a driving force in New York's pro-censorship coalition, Chase fought for censorship for the city in 1911–1912; backed New York State's Christman-Wheeler censorship bill in 1916, which the governor vetoed; and assisted New York State Senator Clayton Lusk in writing a successful censorship bill in 1921 (discussed in chapter 6).[52] In 1914 and 1916, Chase also regularly appeared as an expert witness before Congress during hearings about whether to establish a Federal Motion Picture Censorship Commission; he and Rev. Dr. Wilbur F. Crafts of the International Reform Bureau had contributed to the drafting of the bill that would have authorized such a commission. Neither bill received enough votes.[53] Chase was an outspoken opponent of the National Board, and he traveled far and wide to encourage good Christians to reject its appeals, working into the 1920s to warn of the organization's ties to the motion picture industry.[54]

A TRUE THEATER OF THE PEOPLE:
THE PROGRESSIVE RESPONSE TO MOTION PICTURES

In New York City, *The Unwritten Law* debuted in mid-1907, to the dismay of the Children's Aid Society, which contended that many children had seen this movie containing a drugging, implied rape, and murder.[55] Shortly after its release, Police Commissioner Theodore A. Bingham began enforcing Sunday blue laws and age limits for theaters. He also urged Mayor George B. McClellan Jr. to "follow the line of prohibition and cancel the licenses for most nickelodeons and arcades," which were breeding grounds, he said, for vice and crime.[56] In December 1908, McClellan gave in to pressure from his police commissioner, as well as influential moral reformers affiliated with the Society for the Prevention of Cruelty to Children, the Society for the Prevention of Crime, and, as the *New York Times* reported, "the rectors and pastors of practically all the Christian denominations in the city." McClellan convened a public hearing on the motion picture problem on 23 December, and some of those who spoke expressed their fear that moving picture theaters presented physical and moral dangers to the public—children in particular. Two of the men who inspected exhibition spaces across the five boroughs testified that physical conditions were "inadequate, at best, especially in regard to fire exits."[57] The fire chief agreed, remarking that celluloid film itself was extremely flammable.

Based on "the serious opposition presented," Mayor McClellan revoked all motion picture house licenses on 24 December, arguing that his action had "avert[ed] a public calamity" in the City of New York. Before they could reopen, the theaters would have to be inspected, and licenses would only be reissued for houses that agreed in writing that they would not open on Sundays. Mayor McClellan reminded exhibitors that he could revoke their licenses "on evidence that pictures . . . which tend to degrade or injure the morals of the community" had been shown.[58]

Despite McClellan's 1908 order, which he himself described as "a sop to the reformers," many Progressives were not appeased.[59] After all, many of the era's more optimistic reformers had lauded the nickelodeons, which were challenging the dominance of the saloons, and, by extension, machine politics.[60] Saloons served as gathering places for corrupt ward politicians, who often bought rounds of drinks in exchange for votes, and served to separate working men from their families (and paychecks).[61] Jane Addams, for example, who ran Hull House, a "settlement house" serving the working class that she cofounded in Chicago, suggested that "instead of suppressing" nickelodeon theaters, the government should place them "under proper supervision and regulation." Addams believed that the public wanted to see "clean and wholesome" shows.[62] Cheap motion picture theaters, "rightly conducted," could become "a benefit, not a menace, especially to the poorer classes."[63]

In an effort to prevent New York City from adopting a police censorship scheme similar to Chicago's, a group of exhibitors approached the director of the People's Institute (PI), Charles Sprague Smith, in 1908, asking him to bring together "representatives of various social and civic organizations" to "form a censor board, to protect them from the erratic action of unjust Mayors," as one National Board member put it.[64] The PI sponsored a variety of cultural events for the city's residents; part of its mission was to make such events available and affordable for all. Smith and other PI members were already advocates of the small exhibitors in the immigrant districts of Manhattan. The institute believed that access to leisure and recreational opportunities was foundational to democratic society, and it had issued a comprehensive survey of "cheap amusements" that January and concluded that despite any drawbacks, motion pictures were a positive social force.

Smith, a descendent of the Smiths who had endowed Smith College in Massachusetts, had been educated at Amherst College and was very much an idealist. Earlier in life, he had been a professor of modern languages and foreign literature at Columbia University. Frustrated with the confines and class strictures of the traditional university setting, he left academia in 1891, and in 1897 he founded the PI to facilitate interactions across social and economic class lines. Smith emphasized working together as "the people" to bring about solutions to the problems of urban, industrial society—including the problem of recreation in the city. The PI maintained that city government was the most representative democratic institution in the nation, as it most directly reflected the will of local people.[65] Headquartered at the Cooper Union— another public educational institution for "the people"—the PI organized a free lecture series in the Great Hall; popular topics in the lecture series included the single tax, home rule for New York City, and municipal ownership of utilities. The institute also offered theatrical and musical productions in the Great Hall at rates affordable to wage earners, and it sponsored a Wage Earner's Theater League and a People's Orchestra; many of the members were recent immigrants who had been virtuosos in their home countries. The PI promoted open access to culture by creating community centers and hosting noncommercial dances and other amusements.[66] Its members believed that nurturing family-centric pastimes could supplant saloons as gathering places, which would have the side benefit of reducing political corruption.[67]

In contrast to the vice societies, which sought to protect genteel women from exposure to the city's dangers, Smith and the PI worked closely with women, especially settlement-house workers, social workers, and nurses. On the motion picture problem, the institute partnered with the Women's Municipal League (WML) in early 1908. The WML had been founded in 1894 in New York City by prominent women reformers in response to Tammany Hall corruption. Lillian Wald, a Henry Street Settlement House headworker and nurse; sociologist Sadie American; and Josephine Shaw Lowell, commissioner of the New York State Board of Charities, founder of the New York Charity Organization Society and the New York Consumers League, and "grande dame of . . . social reformers," were among the WML's founding members.[68] According to Lowell, the problems facing late nineteenth-century New York City were "moral and not political"; therefore, they were as much "the concern of women as of men." By the early twentieth century, the WML had expanded its membership and emerged as an important force for "good government" reform in New York City. It encouraged women to develop an "interest . . . in the subject of the government of our city," even in the absence of the right to vote.[69]

The PI's survey of the motion picture industry was conducted with the WML's help in late 1907. The project had been directed by Josephine Redding, secretary of the WML, and John Collier and Michael M. Davis of the PI. Redding was a founding member of the WML and had also been a *Vogue* magazine editor; she was a passionate animal rights activist, a member of the Messiah Social Service League, and a prominent suffragist.[70] Davis was a paid social worker for the People's Institute and later worked for the Russell Sage Foundation; he also later authored several leading studies of commercial amusements, including *The Exploitation of Pleasure: A Study of Commercial Recreation in New York City* (1911) for the Russell Sage Foundation, in which he asserted that "moving-pictures themselves provide in the main a wholesome form of recreation."[71]

John Collier, the lead author of the PI study, began his career in the early twentieth century working with immigrants in New York City. Raised in Atlanta, where his father was a successful banker and former mayor, and educated at Columbia University, upon graduation in 1902 he had worked as a reporter in the style of muckraking journalists Hutchins Hapgood and Lincoln Steffens. Investigating and exposing the plight of immigrants moved Collier to social activism, and by 1908 he was working full time for the People's Institute, conducting studies on factors confounding children's attempts at play, establishing neighborhood social centers in Hell's Kitchen and the Lower East Side, and training other social workers. Collier also frequented Mabel Dodge's Greenwich Village salon, along with figures such as anarchist Emma Goldman, "Big Bill" Haywood of the Industrial Workers of the World, and the birth control pioneer Margaret Sanger.[72] Collier served as the executive secretary of the National Board until 1915, at which point he resigned following a disagreement over the direction the board was taking (see chapter 3).[73]

For the joint study, Collier, Redding, and Davis hired "field secretaries to investigate the whole subject, from the films to the picture houses." These field workers provided them with a comprehensive picture of New York City's ever-expanding commercial entertainment offerings. The resulting study, "Cheap Amusement Shows in Manhattan: Preliminary Report of Investigation," issued in January 1908, was abridged for publication in April in a social activist periodical, *Charities and the Commons*, under the title "Cheap Amusements."[74] The authors agreed with Canon Chase and other pro-censorship reformers that recreation had changed dramatically over the preceding decade, with the motion picture show emerging as the "most popular yet least regulated" form of urban entertainment.[75] Unlike Chase and his followers, however, Collier and his colleagues regarded the motion picture show as a potentially positive social force. "Cheap Amusements in Manhattan" thus presented a new perspective on the motion picture problem.

Collier, as lead investigator, explained that "the tremendously expansive nickelodeon" had edged out cheap vaudeville theater as the most popular of the cheap amusements; however, he conceded that its rapid growth— "from nothing to more than six hundred [venues]" within a few years—had also made it "the least regulated" form of entertainment in the city. Nickelodeons, when "considered numerically . . . entertain[ed] from three to four hundred thousand people daily, and between seventy-five and a hundred thousand children." Unlike censorship's supporters, Collier argued that the movies could become an educational and uplifting force—with the right kind of regulation.[76]

"Cheap Amusements" thus posited an alternative to pro-censorship supporters' main claim—that motion picture content threatened children's physical and moral development. Instead, Collier described the nickelodeon as "a family theater."[77] He regarded moving picture shows as a positive social development because they were a counterweight to homosocial spaces, such as saloons and political clubs, that caused the fabric of the family to fray. They could be educational, and they provided affordable entertainment for immigrant and working-class families. Presenting a far different picture of the five-cent theaters than the *Chicago Tribune* had when *The Unwritten Law* was playing, Collier remarked that, in nickelodeons:

> One sees history, travel . . . farce-comedy which at worst is relaxing, innocuous, rather monotonously confined to horseplay, and at its best is distinctly humanizing, laughing with and not at the subject. . . . At one show or another a growing number of classic legends, like "Jack and the Beanstalk" or "Ali Baba and the Forty Thieves," can be seen any night. The moving picture repertoire amounts to tens of thousands, and is amazingly varied. . . . In addition to the moving-picture, the nickelodeon as a rule has singing, and almost invariably the audience joins in the chorus with a good will. Thus has the moving-picture-show elevated itself.[78]

Collier concluded the "Cheap Amusements" study by noting that "all the settlement [houses] and churches combined do not reach daily a tithe of the simple and impressionable folk that the nickelodeons reach and vitally impress every day." He and his colleagues at the People's Institute argued that motion pictures were "a new social force . . . and an instrument whose power can only be realized when social workers begin to use it."[79]

Following the release of the "Cheap Amusements" study, the People's Institute partnered with the Motion Picture Patents Company (MPPC) to form the National Board of Censorship of Motion Pictures. The MPPC, founded in 1908 as the successor to the Edison Film Trust, at first supported the NB financially as part of its overall bid for greater legitimacy, but soon withdrew its funding in order to avoid the appearance of impropriety. Industry members continued to provide screening-room space to the NB'S Review Committees, however, and the two organizations enjoyed a close working relationship.[80] In March 1909, the executive board of the People's Institute selected the first fourteen members of its new National Board, which functioned as an official department of the PI until 1922, when it became an independent organization focused on supporting and recognizing excellence in filmmaking.[81]

The NB's founding members agreed that, with proper regulation, motion pictures could become the "true theater of the people." The group included prominent Progressive educators, activists, and clergy as well as social workers and settlement-house workers. Upon Charles Sprague Smith's death in 1910, John Collier became the board's chairman; Frederic Clemson Howe succeeded Collier as chairman in 1912, although Collier continued on as the executive secretary of the PI for a few more years. Howe was a well-known and respected Progressive reformer. He had earned a PhD from Johns Hopkins University in 1892 and had served on the City Council of Cleveland, Ohio, as part of a municipal reform agenda. He had moved to New York City in 1910, and had been serving as director of the People's Institute since 1911; he would stay in that post until 1914, when he was appointed commissioner of immigration for the Port of New York at Ellis Island.[82] Howe shifted the NB's agenda to focus "on the political nature" of the question of censorship. In that effort, as one historian later explained, he "defined leisure activities as an entitlement to which all citizens should have equal access."[83]

William D. McGuire Jr. joined the NB in 1909 as review secretary and quickly rose through the ranks of the board's executive branch. A graduate of Williams College and the School of Philanthropy at the New York School for Social Work at Columbia University, he became the organization's executive secretary upon John Collier's departure in 1915; in that post, he crafted many of the organization's policies and procedures until his sudden death in 1923.[84] McGuire fully embraced a First Amendment defense of motion pictures, advocated coalition politics in the fight against legal censorship, and, to that end, forged an important collaboration with Samuel Gompers and the American Federation of Labor. But McGuire also cultivated secretive, behind-the-scenes relationships with motion picture producers in order to prioritize the free-speech rights of filmmakers, particularly in the face of civil rights activists' calls for protection through liberal censorship of racially inflammatory content.

The NB selected three hundred of New York City's "best citizens" to serve on its Review Committee and inform its judgment. Members—more than half of whom were women—hailed from the fields of philanthropy, social work, settlement-house work, education, and prison reform. These individuals had "no connection with the motion picture industry," but were selected for "their active interest in the welfare of community life" and their "willing[ness] to share in the task of review without compensation."[85] As they were not paid, and sought simply to serve "in the public interest," in theory they had no interest "in the possible effect of their decisions on the industry."[86]

Two members in particular represented the viewpoint of parents on the Review Committee—Miriam Sutro Price and Birdie Stein Gans. Both women were from middle-class Jewish American families, and both were cousins of Gertrude Stein.[87] Price was a member of the Public Education Association and a prominent New York City philanthropist. Gans had earned degrees from Columbia University, the New School for Social Research, and New York University; she was also a member of the National Council of Jewish Women and the NAACP. Price and Gans were both active members of Dr. Felix Adler's Ethical Culture Society, which was interested in education of the young. At Adler's urging, Gans and a small group of women from the Ethical Culture Society had founded the Society for the Study of Child Nature in 1888, which changed its name to the Federation for Child Study in

1898. Gans remained president of the federation until 1933.[88] The federation maintained that parenthood was a "vocation" and that it had to be learned: "Mere parenthood brings neither wisdom nor understanding" of the problems modern children encountered, it asserted in its materials, and because "life is too complex," solutions could not be "accomplished . . . through the mother's instinct alone." Children's problems could only be solved once mothers engaged in objective and scientific studies of the factors influencing children and their development—which included everything from literature and school curricula to motion pictures.[89] The federation, through Birdie Stein Gans, worked closely with the NB on questions about how motion pictures influenced children.

Other prominent Review Committee members included the social worker Grace Abbott; the "art connoisseur and decorator" Mrs. Florence Hines-Cox; the settlement-house worker Mrs. I. F. Beal; Lucy P. Eastman, a settlement-house worker and suffragist; Dr. James P. Warbasse, a founding member of the NAACP and founder of the Cooperative League of the USA; Dr. Burdette Lewis of the New York Department of Corrections; Lester F. Scott of the National Council of Camp Fire Girls; and Louis Rouillon, an advocate for technical education and the director of the Franklin Union in Boston and the Mechanics Institute in New York City.[90] Drama critics, children's book authors, poets and playwrights, actors, and artists rounded out the NB's volunteer audiences, along with experts in the nascent "art of the photoplay" at Columbia University and New York University, namely, Victor O. Freeburg and Frederic Thrasher.[91]

The NB believed its review process was superior to that of state censorship boards because it incorporated different voices and perspectives and therefore better represented public opinion. Its Review Committees classified every motion picture they screened as "passed, passed subject to elimination, or rejected." When a Review Committee passed a film "subject to elimination," it identified which scenes needed to be removed or replaced prior to distribution and exhibition. All motion pictures, and their classifications, were then listed in the NB's weekly *Bulletin*. Notably, an entire section of the *Bulletin* was devoted to "Cutouts." The scenes identified for removal varied in intensity: they included, for example, an orgy scene in *St. George and the Dragon* (Edison, 1910); gambling and race-track betting scenes in *Red Bird Wins* (unknown); scenes of blood transfusions in *Scars of Possession* (Essanay, 1914); and a scene in Charlie Chaplin's *Those Love Pangs* (Keystone, 1914) showing a man "with trousers falling down."[92]

By 1911, the NB had secured agreements with nearly all forty of the film production companies headquartered in the United States along with thirty foreign ones that distributed motion pictures or were otherwise doing business within the nation's borders. The agreement stipulated that the companies would submit all of their motion pictures to the board for prerelease review; that they would each pay a small reviewing fee to support the ongoing voluntary work of the board; and that they would abide by the Review Committee's decisions, including making recommended changes to content and to title cards prior to distribution and exhibition. The industry cooperated with the National Board as the lesser of two evils, as the board was offering to prescreen movies for the entire nation for one reviewing fee, and the alternative, state-by-state censorship, would be expensive and complicated. After only two years in existence, the NB boasted that it had "caused the destruction" of 2 million feet of "objectionable films," which "represent[ed] a value of $200,000."[93] The board regularly declared that its Review Committee was screening "more than 99 per cent of the photoplays shown for entertainment purposes" in the United States prior to their release.[94]

For their part in attempting to give movies a better reputation, motion picture entrepreneurs made greater investments in their exhibition spaces, adding proper screens and fireproof projection booths. Many also invested in additional projectors to limit the wait time between reel changes. The small theaters had become permanent fixtures in urban neighborhoods, and local theater owners invested in prefabricated theater facades featuring "plaster relief decorations"—such as classically inspired columns and statuettes—to assert their respectability.[95] Production companies such as Vitagraph and Universal increasingly produced narrative motion pictures, often adapted from novels or stage plays, to try to attract a more "respectable" audience (increasingly defined as white, middle-class women).[96] Even while continuing in these efforts to draw in a broader audience, however, the industry courted more complaints about motion picture content.

In fact, Canon Chase and his political allies revived the campaign for legal censorship in New York City in 1911, this time targeting "the small houses," which were defined as those seating up to three hundred people. Chase charged that these theaters were "shamefully overcrowded," and that the city had "no requirements for lighting, ventilation, fire exits, fireproofing, window spacing, courts about buildings, or structural materials." The Board of Aldermen promised Chase and his allies that they would investigate "the situation pertaining to motion pictures," focusing on "the abuses of overcrowding in the little theatres, of the admission of unaccompanied minors, and, especially, the menace of such conditions to young girls," all of which were "matters of complaint."[97] As the moving picture show grew in popularity among women and children, moral reformers became increasingly interested in regulating these spaces.[98]

At about this time, the Women's Municipal League suddenly announced its withdrawal from the anticensorship coalition, throwing its support behind an official board of censors for New York City instead. Newly elected WML president Mrs. Gilbert Holland (Amy Angell Collier) Montague maintained that "the moving-picture films are by no means all censored by the National Board of Censorship," and the "suggestions for the elimination of objectionable films are not always obeyed and cannot be enforced." Moreover, she claimed to have an old letter signed by the late Charles Sprague Smith in which he admitted to a financial connection between the industry and the National Board, but had said that it was "to be kept secret." Because the NB was "paid in part . . . by the very corporations whose movies they must pass," the WML questioned the validity of its motives and decisions, no matter how many people served on its Review Committees. These allegations of close ties to the industry would stalk the NB throughout its political campaigns into the 1920s—and rightly so.[99]

On 1 December 1911, hearings on the matter began, with Alderman John J. White—who had a personal financial stake in vaudeville theaters—presiding. The Board of Aldermen's Special Committee proposed following Chicago's lead and adopting police censorship of motion picture content as well as police regulation of exhibition spaces with a capacity of fewer than three hundred seats. Over two hundred "small exhibitors" attending the hearings protested the proposed ordinance, which would "work hardship on them." Because the ordinance "distinctly" favored vaudeville venues "doing a moving-picture business" and "houses already in existence," if the proposal passed it would effectively shift motion picture exhibition to "legitimate" theaters in Midtown and vaudeville theaters downtown. Small exhibitors viewed this as an effort by Alderman White to "curtail the expansion of the business" in immigrant and working-class districts.[100]

Henry Moskowitz, president of the East Side Civic Club, future husband of social reformer Belle Lindner Israels, and a respected Progressive activist in his own right, spoke on behalf of the National Board and its constituents. He argued that "these moving-picture places are the local theaters of the family," and therefore, the city "should be careful not to work injustice" against them. Other opponents of the proposal included License Commissioner James Wallace, who stood to lose a significant amount of his own power and influence if motion picture regulation passed to the police department; and Police Commissioner Rhinelander Waldo, who expressed concern about the police having to screen all the motion pictures slated for exhibition in New York City. There was little enough time already for the police to carry out their duties, and it would be an added burden: "The eye-strain alone, it was said, might cause blindness," reported the New York Times. No one present opposed "those parts of the ordinance that reenact[ed] the present provisions for the physical safeguard of persons entering motion picture halls," which included regulating the buildings and prohibiting children under the age of sixteen without a parent or guardian.[101]

At an impasse, Alderman Ralph Folks, who was also a member of the NB's General Committee, proposed a compromise measure, which became the focus of debate in 1912. The Folks Ordinance, as it came to be known, proposed fire codes and other "structural" requirements to address the immediate safety issues for motion picture houses, but remained silent on content censorship.[102] By June, Alderman Folks's "structural ordinance" was still held up in hearings, in no small part because Canon Chase opposed it, demanding instead a bill that provided for both censorship of content and structural regulations.[103] Six months later, the Folks Ordinance was finally scheduled for a vote. Several important "churchmen and philanthropic leaders" sent a letter to every alderman urging them to support the Folks Ordinance regardless of their position on content censorship—signees included Frederic C. Howe, director of the People's Institute and the National Board; Rev. Orrin G. Cocks, secretary of the Federation of Churches (and later the NB's advisory secretary); and Dr. Luther H. Gulick, director of Child Hygiene for the Russell Sage Foundation. The letter argued that political corruption continued to put New Yorkers at risk, as "thousands of citizens" were being exposed "to the serious risks" presented by "small, badly ventilated, unsafe theaters" every day: "Some of them are causing sickness. Some of them are breeding immorality. Panic or fire in many of them would cause an awful loss of life." The Folks Ordinance could immediately make theaters "safer and cleaner" without having to wait for agreement on content censorship. Finally, the letter's signatories advocated for "concentrating responsibility for clean, wholesome picture houses in the Bureau of Licenses; [and] providing a report to the Mayor on the moral character of performances, leaving with him the power to revoke or suspend licenses." In essence, the signatories urged New Yorkers to back the NB's City Plan for Voluntary Motion Picture Regulation.[104]

Although the People's Institute, the City Club, the East Side Local Needs Association, "and many more great bodies existing solely for the common good," including "representatives of 800 churches in the city," supported the Folks structural ordinance, as did thousands of citizens who signed petitions in support of the measure, two more months passed, and still no compromise could be reached in New York City.[105] The New York City Aldermanic Committee on Laws and Legislation held yet another public hearing on the motion picture problem. This time, four ordinances were under consideration—the Folks Ordinance; the Morrison Ordinance, which addressed structural issues and content censorship in one bill; a new ordinance proposed by Tammany alderman (and vaudeville investor) John J. White; and another that emerged from the committee's Minority Report. White led the fight against the Folks Ordinance, arguing that it "meant that the moving-picture business would be put in the hands of the so-called 'film trust,'" again alluding to the NB's connections to the industry.[106] Canon Chase also opposed the Folks Ordinance, but on the grounds that it did nothing for "the real welfare of the children."[107] He endorsed the Morrison Ordinance. The hearing dragged on for hours and was marked by verbal altercations and accusations. The meeting adjourned without a vote when one alderman threatened to throw his colleague out of the nearest window.[108]

In rejecting paternalist and maternalist arguments for censorship, the National Board began constructing an approach to motion pictures that was fundamentally different from what the moral reformers and antiobscenity activists—censorship's early supporters—were demanding. From its founding in 1909 through 1912, the NB sought to present its plan as a reasonable approach to the motion picture problem; it established rules and procedures to govern motion picture review on its end, and provided constructive feedback to motion picture producers to help them understand what public opinion would tolerate. The motion picture industry largely shared the National Board's interest and early efforts. But the film industry was undergoing rapid change, and the issues surrounding censorship were changing, too. The NB, and the film industry, would continue to face new challenges.

2 / "CRITICAL AND CONSTRUCTIVE": THE NATIONAL BOARD'S "STANDARDS" AND CITY PLAN FOR VOLUNTARY MOTION PICTURE REVIEW, 1912–1916

IN NOVEMBER 1915, FOX FILMS RELEASED *CARMEN*, BASED on the 1845 novella by Prosper Mérimée, starring the bewitching Theda Bara in the title role. The Swedish silent-film actor Einar Linden debuted as Don José, a young Spanish soldier who first meets Carmen at the tobacco factory where she works. He attempts to arrest Carmen after she attacks a coworker with a knife, but she distracts him with a kiss and escapes. Don José is court-martialed and sent to prison; Carmen reappears and breaks him out, and they escape to the Andalusian mountains, where they live together as lovers among a gang of murderers and thieves. Carmen eventually leaves Don José for another man, and the narrative culminates in a dramatic bullfight scene, during which Don José stabs Carmen and then rides his horse off a cliff to his death.[1]

Charles M. Farrer, the president of the Seattle Humane Association, wrote to the National Board to protest *Carmen*, but not because of Bara's controversial "vamp" persona. The "moral issues" raised by the movie were of "trifling importance," in Farrer's opinion, when "compared with the degrading and inexcusable horrors and brutalities" of the bullfight scenes.[2] The assistant secretary of the National Board of Censorship, Wilton Barrett, reassured Farrer that typically, the "presentation of a pure bull-fight . . . would be ruled against by the National Board," but in this case, the Review Committee agreed that the scene was "legitimately a part of the drama" and that it was therefore "advisable to pass the production as it stood." In closing, Barrett thanked Farrer for his letter, emphasizing that "the ideas of people outside of the work" of motion picture review were "valuable to the Board, very often informing its policies and correcting its point of view."[3]

By 1915, after five years of reviewing motion pictures for the public, the NB began strategically co-opting the concerns of its collaborators (and opponents) in the service of building a broader anticensorship coalition. It positioned itself as the national clearinghouse for information on motion pictures as well as the

FIGURE 2.1. *Theda Bara as Carmen*

main node of communication between the motion picture industry and "public opinion." The board courted the public's complaints and suggestions in order to discover what viewers found distasteful or worthy of censorship, and it incorporated those views in subsequent revisions of its "Standards" document; this level of responsiveness often served to pacify certain single-issue censorship supporters. In an effort to suppress pro-censorship sentiment and absorb more activists into its system of voluntary regulation, the NB also distributed its *Bulletin* and related publications to interested parties outside the industry—to parent-teacher associations, mothers' clubs, women's clubs, churches, schools and universities, and concerned individuals—all of whom the NB also invited to participate in the voluntary regulation of motion pictures in their communities.[4] It even included forms like the one below in mailings to community organizations in order to learn more about people's perspectives on motion pictures and inform its work of appraising them:

Gentlemen:

As a correspondent of the National Board of Censorship, I wish to call to your attention the fact that eliminations were not made as requested by the Board in the picture (name and number of reels): _____

Produced by (Name of company or brand): _____

And seen by me at the (Name of theatre): _____

At (Give address, City, and State): _____

On the _____ day of the ___ month 19__

This Picture is listed on the Bulletin of the Board for (give date) _____ 19__

The eliminations requested in the above picture were not made in the following particulars:

(Discuss in detail those parts of the picture which were not properly cut, making reference to the eliminations listed on the bulletin.)[5]

Citizen correspondents frequently alerted the NB to subject matter that was controversial regionally, which allowed the board to work proactively with those constituencies. The board regarded its role, in part, as shielding the motion picture industry from interference, so that producers and directors could focus on making higher-quality productions, not answering a litany of complaints. Certain themes arose frequently as these methods of handling film content developed. Two of these—the issue of animal cruelty and the treatment of matters of concern to organized labor—can serve as case studies in how the National Board of Review operated and negotiated with various constituencies while trying to prevent legal censorship. Racial issues also began to emerge around this time in censorship-related discussions. Because of regional differences on these and other issues, the NB ultimately devised its City Plan for Voluntary Motion Picture Regulation.

"A CODE OF ETHICS" FOR MOTION PICTURES

The National Board's "Standards" represented its attempt to construct and represent the point of view of an adult motion picture viewer—over the age of sixteen, "reasonable," and not easily offended or influenced. Rather than relying on the notion of a vulnerable viewer who needed to be protected, the NB constructed a narrative based on a new conception of the motion picture viewer, one who expected the screens to be free from obscenity, but who also believed that motion pictures deserved the same protections granted to artists and journalists.

The board rationalized its review process and issued its first official "Statement of Standards" in 1912. This document was to serve as a guide for its Review Committees, for production companies, and for citizen correspondents in the field.[6] The timing of this document's release coincided with a shift in motion picture production and exhibition. As film historian Douglas Gomery has argued, "the movie house had become a permanent part of the American scene by 1910."[7] Nickelodeons and small storefront theaters were being joined by "modern moving picture theaters."[8] American film production picked up at roughly the same time in order to meet exhibitor and consumer demand for more new movies. Film historian Richard Abel found that, by the fall of 1912, most of the movies screened in the United States were, for the first time, domestic productions. Multiple-reel films had become the norm, and popular subjects included serialized sensational melodramas, westerns, and war films. Women, children, and families had become the target audience, and the industry continued to strive for middle-class respectability.[9]

John Collier, the author of the original "Statement of Standards," expressed the board's utmost appreciation for motion pictures; the cinema had become America's "main theatre, one of our main newspapers, one of our main forums of public discussion." They were "drama, book, newspaper and oration; they are art. They are free speech," he wrote. "Their development has only begun; they are going to be some kind of public problem for decades, perhaps for centuries." Collier dismissed any criticism that the National Board was engaged in "prior restraint" censorship; rather, he pointed out that since the NB was a voluntary organization, its decisions were not legally binding, and therefore it was engaged in "selection, not censorship."[10] The "Standards" enumerated the principles that guided the National Board's voluntary review of motion pictures and served as "a code of ethics for the film."[11]

Collier's "Standards" established three main principles to guide motion picture review. First, the National Board would not act as "a censor of taste, unless it is clear that the question of taste is an essentially moral question." To this end, the NB would not permit obscene, lewd, or lascivious material, but it could not eliminate lowbrow jokes or slapstick physical comedy. This principle remained a contentious issue for the NB, one fraught with individual and regional interpretations through the 1920s. Second, the NB would not function "as a censor of accuracy" on historical, literary, or scientific interpretations, "unless the inaccuracy in question . . . will result in some concrete disaster as to the person whom the inaccuracy misleads." Collier clarified with the example of a film that might claim "patent medicines" could cure tuberculosis or other diseases; the board would reject such spurious claims to safeguard the public. Third, Collier established that the board would not "judge films exclusively from the standpoint of children, of delicate women, of the emotionally morbid or of any one class of audience." The Review Committees would watch films from the viewpoint of a reasonable adult, not from a position of moral or maternalist authority on behalf of vulnerable viewers.[12]

For decades, the "Standards" represented the NB's "constructive" effort to give motion pictures greater respectability. In part, they were designed to assure the industry as well as the general public that Review Committee members did not just impose their "own views of what is desirable or right" on motion pictures; instead, they were instructed to "judge as to the real effect of each film on the composition audience which will witness it." After a Review Committee reached consensus on that point, Collier explained, its members should "act on behalf of the general conscience and intelligence of the country, in permitting or prohibiting a given scene or film."[13] The NB updated the document annually, and the changes reflected negotiations with interest groups concerned with filmic representations.

In addition to functioning as a rubric for the Review Committees' assessments, the "Standards" gave advance warning to producers and directors as to which topics raised censorship sentiment. For example, although the NB "[did] not forbid all representation of crime in motion pictures," crime was not to be shown in a positive light.[14] To cast a broad net forbidding all portrayal of crime, the NB claimed, would "exclude the dramatic element and . . . involve the prohibition of most of the classics and most of the Bible," in addition to "depriv[ing] the motion picture art of its potential moral influence."[15] Censorship advocates routinely contended that motion pictures influenced vulnerable viewers, causing them to mimic what they saw on-screen. The NB's compromise was to warn against showing crime "in such a detailed way as may teach the methods of committing crime"; however, it reserved the right to discern the difference between acceptable and potentially harmful portrayals.[16] Scenes identified by Review Committees for removal under the rubric of "crime" included images of people stealing, committing murder, threatening police, threatening girls and women, and committing kidnappings.[17] For *The Sheriff's Reward* (Selig, 1914), for example, a Review Committee requested the elimination of three scenes of cattle branding and another involving the abduction of a girl.[18] Another film, *Mother's Darling Boy* (Pathé, 1914), was rejected in toto because it "portray[ed] a series of crimes committed by children."[19]

Perhaps because ministers and other clergy tended to be involved in pro-censorship activism, the "Standards" also warned that blasphemy was often grounds for a film's rejection.[20] Collier defined blasphemy as "the careless or wanton or unnecessary offence against religious susceptibilities of any large number of people in the country."[21] An early example comes from *Pieces of Silver: A Story of Hearts and Souls* (Helen Gardner, 1914), which the Review Committee cut to soften what it saw as "an attack on religion." Helen Gardner was a silent film actress as well as a motion picture industry pioneer. After leaving Vitagraph in 1912, she opened her own production studio, Helen Gardner Picture Players. As a producer, she was an early adopter of multireel, narrative motion picture features, and she was a staunch proponent of the film industry.[22] Her early filmography as an actor and producer included *Cleopatra* (Helen Gardner, 1912) and *A Sister to Carmen* (Helen Gardner, 1913). Gardner was a forerunner to the "vamp" figure that Theda Bara popularized a couple of years later; one film scholar noted that Gardner was a "wonderfully expressive and sensuous actress for her day," which can be "seen in the dynamism of her facial expressions, the beauty of her moving hands, and the undulations of her body." In fact, censors in Rockland County, New York, removed Gardner's "death dance" from *Cleopatra* (Helen Gardner, 1912) because it was "entirely too raw."[23]

Pieces of Silver begins when a dying man decides to bequeath his fortune to his niece, played by Helen Gardner, on one condition—she must marry immediately or lose the estate to her aunt. The aunt conceals the terms of the will from the young woman and convinces her to embrace religious life and join a convent. The young woman's beau, heartbroken by the news, joins the seminary himself and takes a vow of celibacy. The aunt, on her deathbed, reveals her betrayal to her niece, who is soon faced with a throng of suitors. The young woman, realizing that because her one true love has become a devoted priest, she can never marry, forsakes her fortune and returns to the convent, taking her own vows of initiation and celibacy, and emerging as Sister Berenice.[24] It is unclear from the NB's records what, precisely, may have been perceived as an "attack on religion" in *Pieces of Silver*. Perhaps the reviewers objected to the film's presentation of Catholic religious life as an option to romantic disappointments, and not a sincere calling. The movie may have depicted "inappropriate" longing and sexual tension between the priest and Sister Berenice. It could even have been images or scenes ancillary to the main narrative, or simply the sensuous way that Gardner moved, that raised concern among reviewers. The film was released in March 1914 with unknown changes to its content.

The Review Committee also rejected a cautionary tale about a drunkard's fall, *Across the Continent* (Pilot, 1913), after four screenings and extensive feedback. In the film, a married man, George, falls under the sway of a manipulative saloonkeeper, John Adderly, and quickly becomes an alcoholic. George spends his wages and free time at the saloon rather than providing for his wife, Agnes, and their two young children. Agnes visits Adderly at the saloon and begs him to stop serving her husband; instead, he invites Agnes to join him in a toast. Agnes, accepting the glass, foretells that Adderly's son, John Jr., will "live to curse his father." The narrative flashes forward twenty years, to a scene in which John Jr. robs his father of all his money, "leaving the old man blind and heartbroken." After being captured and imprisoned for his crimes, John Jr. curses his father from his jail cell.[25] *Across the Continent* still "show[ed] four murders, numerous gambling scenes, jail breaking, robbery, abduction, suicide, and delirium tremens."[26]

Although Collier intended for the "Standards" to reflect public opinion, they also helped to shape it. The "Standards" functioned to create an internalized, self-censoring mechanism among cooperating producers, filmmakers, and Review Committee members, influencing content production in the early years of motion pictures even as the National Board was fighting to protect motion pictures from more egregious interference—such as legal censorship. The NB executive committee revised the "Standards" document annually so that it would reflect the rapidly changing spirit of the times. In 1914, Chairman Frederic Howe described the board as "a human institution" that "reflect[ed] a public opinion which constantly varies." As "society formulates intelligent theories and principles of conduct, [the NB] must inevitably alter its decisions," Howe explained. "The Board freely grants differences of opinion to various classes and to various constituent parts of the Nation."[27] However, as the NB's correspondence with certain constituencies reveals, the "Standards" were also adapted to please noisy and powerful groups. An examination of its interactions with these groups—namely, animal cruelty groups and organized labor—illuminates how the NB worked with its political allies and opponents.

"OUR DUMB ANIMALS": ANIMAL WELFARE AND MOTION PICTURE CENSORSHIP

In June 1914, letters from local humane societies, branches of the Society for the Prevention of Cruelty to Animals, and the American Humane Association started pouring into the National Board's New York City office. The Humane Society of Berks County, Pennsylvania, wrote to "strongly protest against the exhibition of motion pictures wherein the suffering of animals are depicted; thereby causing a false impression as to the treatment of animals in the minds of the spectators." The Humane Society of Sioux Falls, South Dakota, opposed "the practice . . . among the makers of moving pictures to permit gross cruelty to animals for the purpose of producing thrilling and exciting pictures." They argued that it "should be stopped," not only because it was "cruel and inhuman to the animals themselves," but also because it was "demoralizing to the persons who view[ed] the pictures."[28]

Animals were considered the most vulnerable of creatures and therefore the most deserving of protection. Many animal welfare activists set themselves up as advocates for animals and attempted to speak for them—to become the voice of creatures that could not speak for themselves. This concept is reflected most acutely in the title of the first magazine published in the United States by humane societies, *Our Dumb Animals*, started by the founder of the Massachusetts Society for the Prevention of Cruelty to Animals, George T. Angell.[29] Executive board members of humane organizations tended to be white men "of privilege, property, wealth, and influence," as the authors of a book analyzing child welfare practices in the United States noted in 1996. These men were predominantly Republican and Protestant, and many of them were "manufacturers, merchants, bankers, owners of railroads and mines, and lawyers." They often belonged to charitable and private organizations simultaneously (like the SPC, SSV, and ASPCA), and their networks could sway legislators on a variety of issues, including motion picture censorship.[30]

Collectively, the humane societies argued that any depiction of cruelty toward animals should be banned from motion pictures. For example, the president of the New York Anti-Vivisection Society, Diana Belais, reasoned that if the NB "cut[s] out" anything related to crime "and matters of that sort," then it was "a logical and exact parallel that no pictures of cruelty to animals be permitted." Children had an "instinctive" understanding that it was not right to steal, Belais argued, but there was "little instinctive appreciation or understanding of the immorality or wrong-doing contained in acts of cruelty" toward animals. Therefore, she concluded, Americans would benefit from "the strictest censorship against pictures which show cruel acts and familiarize the youthful and even adult mind with the sufferings of animals."[31]

In the summer of 1914, the Motion Picture Exhibitors League (MPEL) was to hold its annual convention in Dayton, Ohio, and the humane societies sent letters timed to arrive in the National Board's office shortly before that. They also planned to present a petition against animal cruelty to the MPEL at the convention, and sought the support of the National Board. In response, the NB took up the cause and modified its "Standards" accordingly, expanding its definitions of cruelty and obscenity in the process.

As part of an attempt to forge coalitions with these powerful humane organizations and to prevent them from throwing their significant influence behind campaigns for legal censorship, in 1914 the National Board hired Rev. Orrin G. Cocks to serve as an advisory secretary. An ordained minister in the Presbyterian Synod of New York, Cocks had previously served as the secretary of the Student Branch of the YMCA in New York City. He was active in Progressive Christian campaigns against prostitution and was known for his passionate advocacy of community motion picture regulation, and these credentials allowed him to make important connections on behalf of the board with other ministers, religiously affiliated organizations, and women who were engaged in maternalist reform efforts. Cocks assumed an influential role as liaison between the motion picture industry, the humane associations, and the NB.

Cocks contacted the Motion Picture Exhibitors League on behalf of the animal welfare organizations, persuading its members to take a stand against cruelty toward animals in motion pictures. He pointed to the "great cruelties" that motion picture producers had been depicting in their "thrilling stories," westerns in particular, "such as throwing animals over cliffs, letting lambs, etc., be torn to pieces by wild animals, [and] other scenes in which our silent partners are subjected to undeserved ill treatment." Cocks urged the MPEL, "as an organization," to condemn these "reprehensible" practices, emphasizing that "cleaning up their own industry of this unnecessary cruelty" would certainly "help stem the calls for censorship."[32]

The pressure that Cocks and the humane societies brought to bear on the MPEL paid off. At its 1914 annual meeting, the MPEL passed a resolution "pledging the moral support of the League to the humane and other social agencies that are opposing cruelty to animals as inflicted in the production of certain films." The terms of the resolution asked exhibitors "not to display pictures depicting cruelty to animals."[33] The NB updated its "Standards" to reflect this agreement as well. The question, however, remained: If one did not show cruelty to animals, did that mean it must not occur on set, during production, as well?

John Collier's original 1912 "Standards" had included language that prohibited the "unnecessary elaboration or prolongation of scenes of suffering, brutality, violence, or crime."[34] Implicitly, this clause referred to human actors. But after being lobbied extensively by animal welfare organizations and humane associations in 1914, the National Board expanded its definition of suffering, brutality, and violence to include animals. In the contemporary debate over the meaning of "obscenity," sexual content received the most attention, particularly from moral reformers like Comstock or the Watch and Ward Society. As the language of the Hicklin Test specified, anything that might have "the tendency to deprave or corrupt those whose minds are open to such immoral influences" should be censored. For members of humane societies, cruelty and violence toward animals qualified as "obscene," and they argued for its suppression based on its "tendency" to corrupt weak-minded individuals.[35]

Despite the NB's proactive work on behalf of animals, animal welfare activists continued to find objectionable content across genres. In August 1916, the ASPCA forwarded a letter to the board about *Hulda from Holland* (1916), the latest Mary Pickford vehicle, which was supposed to be an unobjectionable tale expressly designed for a general audience.[36] "Miss Mary" plays Hulda, a newly arrived immigrant from Holland. The saga begins when her wealthy uncle, Peter, is knocked unconscious on his way to meet her ship; she then has to proceed through a variety of plot twists to the film's happy ending and her wedding.[37] *American Club Woman Magazine* recommended *Hulda from Holland*, calling it "a beautiful story, with heart appeal," particularly appropriate for "older children."[38] Yet a viewer named Mrs. A. C. Christianson found *Hulda from Holland* so objectionable that she contacted the ASPCA.

According to Christianson, *Hulda from Holland* contained a scene in which "a goat appears and is supposed to have taken the paint from a pail standing near, and the goat apparently dies." She wondered if the producers had filmed "the picture of the dying goat . . . while in agony," because it "does not appear to do the act of a trained animal, but of a poisoned animal." She asked the ASPCA to investigate, but concluded that the producers would "no doubt . . . say this act is that of a trained animal, but anyone viewing the picture will be convinced to the contrary."[39] The ASPCA superintendent, J. F. Freel, forwarded her complaint to the National Board, which acted promptly on it—testimony to the collective power and influence of the humane societies. Wilton Barrett, the board's review secretary, replied to Freel that the Review Committee had eliminated "the whole scene where the goat is kicking around" because it was "quite a prolonged view." Furthermore, Barrett noted, "it would be hard to determine whether the animal in this picture was drugged or simply tied in such a way that it appeared to be dying."[40] Eliminating a scene after production, however, did nothing about abuse the animal may have already endured on set.

In 1916, as a result of persistent lobbying by the animal welfare organizations, the NB issued a special bulletin on the issue of animal cruelty; it announced that the "Standards" had been updated: henceforward, it would be "contrary to the standards of the National Board to pass any picture in which cruelty to animals is shown." This included "horses, cattle, and all domestic animals in ordinary motion picture productions." No animal could be used in motion picture production in "any way that will conflict with ideas of humanity and fair treatment," and any "apparent cruelty to animals" was to be avoided. "The American public" found cruelty toward animals to be offensive, and the Review Committees would "continue to be watchful for incidents in pictures which indicate that animals have been ill-treated." It would "never pass any films that so much as suggested cruelty."[41] *Hulda from Hol-*

land demonstrated that even camera tricks and clever editing could create public outcry.

Although the National Board's members may not have shared the humane societies' passion for animal welfare, they understood the strategic necessity of accommodating their point of view. Doing so served the board's intertwined goals of giving motion pictures more respectability and protecting them from legal censorship. But one genre—nature films, which were popular for children in the 1910s—brought the NB's principles into direct conflict with those of the animal welfare organizations, and the board was unwilling to compromise. The board classified "hunt films" as educational or documentary, and thus exempted them from its screening process. However, motion pictures about animals, using animal actors, were not passively filmed; they were staged and manipulated to produce a narrative arc—to provide comedy, drama, and pathos. Moving pictures in the hunt film genre featured an animal as the villain, often one that was encroaching on domestic agriculture or the built environment, and a hunter and his companion animals as the protagonists. Hunt films end with the capture, and sometimes destruction, of the animal.[42] The NB typically exempted nature films from review, but hunt films created significant controversy.

One seemingly innocuous nature documentary in the hunt film genre was *A Badger Hunt* (Pathé, 1915), which starred a "rapacious little badger," according to *Motography*. A Review Committee screened *A Badger Hunt* and it was "passed subject to eliminations."[43] The picture opens with a glimpse of the badger "slink[ing] away at the first streaks of dawn," while a furious farmer, his "wrath" provoked by "the mischief committed by the badger during his nocturnal visits," rages at the destruction of his crops. The farmer proceeds to release his hunting dogs, which trail the badger to its underground "hiding place." The farmer then carefully selects which dog he will send in to "attack the badger in its tunnel retreat." The crafty badger continues to elude the farmer and his dogs; after another scene of struggle and retreat, the farmer finally "catches the badger around the neck and lifts him, struggling, to the surface." The victorious farmer holds "the frightened animal, blinking but still fighting," up to the camera, and then deposits it "alive and unhurt in a heavy bag."[44] The Review Committee recommended the removal of two scenes prior to public exhibition: one showing "a badger being pulled by the ear," and another of a "hunter holding badger with pincers around neck."[45]

Despite the National Board's accommodations to the animal welfare activists on other issues, hunt films threatened their temporary coalition. In 1917, Sydney Coleman, president of the American Humane Association, complained about *A Badger Hunt*, an unedited version of which was being exhibited near Albany, New York, and arousing concern among AHA members.

Coleman cited *A Badger Hunt* as more evidence of the need for legal censorship, exclaiming in his letter to the National Board, "There is enough necessary pain in the world without inflicting it upon dumb animals for the entertainment of the theatergoing public." He suggested that the NB eliminate "hunt pictures" from domestic distribution altogether, arguing that children "should be shielded from such influence."[46] The NB patently disagreed, ultimately leading Coleman and the AHA to withdraw from the National Board's coalition when the question of legal censorship reemerged in New York State in 1921.

"AMERICAN INSTITUTIONS":
ORGANIZED LABOR AND MOTION PICTURES

In 1914, Éclair released the railroad melodrama *Strike at Coaldale*, featuring silent film favorites Stanley Walpole and Mildred Bright. *Strike at Coaldale* is a love story set against the backdrop of a fictional railroad strike; the peak of action comes when the young railroad engineer, played by Walpole, steers a train across a burning railroad trestle to win the strike and the woman he had been courting—the boss's daughter. The production cost "many hundreds of dollars," in part because an actual trestle was burned during filming.

In 1916, the Ohio State Board of Censors condemned *Strike at Coaldale*, preventing its exhibition in their state. The National Board's executive secretary, W. D. McGuire, puzzled over the Ohio board's decision, noting that "the story itself certainly does not warrant condemnation on the ground of immorality," and the picture "did not purport to be an actual portrayal of any specific strike." However, there was a rumor circulating "among the film men" that the Industrial Commission of Ohio, the department in which the Board of Censors was housed, was "not enthusiastic over having pictures shown in which strikes were apparently successful."[47] For McGuire, it was an example of rank political censorship—and a sign of what was to come, should more state censorship boards be established.

Before World War I, Ohio was already home to a number of steel mills and railroads for transporting materials, and steel mills increased production during the war years. Although employment rose, the economic benefits never trickled down to the rank-and-file, many of whom were immigrants. In December 1915, five hundred steelworkers in East Youngstown, Ohio, went on strike against Republic Iron and Steel Company, demanding higher wages. With the support of the Industrial Workers of the World (IWW) and other local unions, the strike quickly spread, and by early January 1916 more than 16,000 workers in the region were out on strike. Republic Iron and Steel, as well as other local operations, hired armed guards to protect the mills. The private police and strikers clashed on 7 January, when guards opened fire on the picket line. Protesters and strikers responded by marching into East Youngstown and setting fire to the central business district in retaliation. The Ohio National Guard was called in to put down the conflagration. In the wake of the strike, steel mill operators raised wages to head off future conflicts.[48]

It was in this context that the Ohio State Board of Censors considered *Strike at Coaldale*. McGuire suspected that because *Strike at Coaldale* was such "a powerful appeal to the labor man," the Ohio board had condemned it for that reason alone. Perhaps its exhibition would have been interpreted as tacit approval of the strike as a labor action. McGuire warned that Ohio's condemnation of *Strike at Coaldale* "demonstrates how censorship will work out if it is allowed to progress," and claimed that the evidence from Maryland, Kansas, and Pennsylvania boards provided "many [more] examples of the censorship of pictures without regard to the interest of labor."[49]

Following the decision in *Mutual Film Corporation v. Industrial Commission of Ohio* in 1915 and congressional hearings on the creation of a Federal Motion Picture Censorship Commission in 1914 and 1916, censorship's opponents increasingly placed First Amendment issues front and center. In 1915, Samuel Gompers, president of the American Federation of Labor, joined the National Advisory Committee of the National Board. Typically, organizations appointed luminaries like Gompers to their advisory boards as honorifics, or for public relations purposes. But Gompers became actively involved in the fight against the legal censorship of motion pictures, and he worked closely with McGuire to shape labor's image on-screen, in fiction films as well as in newsreels.

At its annual convention in August 1916, the AFL passed a resolution condemning any government censorship of motion pictures. Echoing Collier's language, the AFL resolution stipulated that motion pictures had emerged as a "public agency for education and the dissemination of current information comparable in many respects to the daily press and public forum." Therefore, the movies "must be protected by the same guarantees of freedom that have been bestowed upon oral utterances and the press." The AFL opposed "government censorship of expression of opinion in any form" and affirmed that the "freedom of expression, freedom of opinion, freedom of speech, and the freedom of the press and motion pictures are the palladium of free institutions."[50]

In November 1916, the NB and the AFL jointly issued the text of the resolution as a pamphlet titled "Against Government Censorship." The frequent references to Americanism in the pamphlet reflect the larger domestic climate of World War I: many Americans of the time not only opposed the antidemocratic institutions abroad, but also the battering of civil liberties and civil rights at home in the name of national security. Gompers was also working closely with a variety of organizations behind the scenes to protect the gains of moderate labor and to suppress radical sentiment among workers.[51] In addition to working with the National Civic Federation, he served on the National Council of Defense, to which he had been appointed by President Woodrow Wilson.

The NB mailed "Against Government Censorship" directly to AFL members' homes in an effort to expand the anticensorship message and coalition. AFL membership passed 2 million in this period, and it now represented an important demographic in American politics. Gompers, meanwhile, continued to bring the AFL into closer alignment with the Democratic Party.[52] Moreover, AFL members' wives were likely interested in the issue of motion picture censorship, and may have been members of mothers clubs, parent-teacher associations, or the General Federation of Women's Clubs. "Against Government Censorship" was as much an appeal to AFL families as it was an expression of the AFL's principles.

However, in 1917, the NB/AFL coalition foundered in coal country, when the Pennsylvania Central Trades and Labor Council (CTLC) passed a resolution urging the Pennsylvania State Federation of Labor and the American Federation of Labor to support legal censorship of any motion pictures that misrepresented organized labor, the right to strike, or the role of state police in labor conflicts. The CTLC wrote its resolution in response to unidentified "moving picture companies" using northeastern Pennsylvania's Wyoming Valley as a set.[53] According to local informants tracking the production, the "working class" was depicted "acting as lawless mobs and the State Police used as the guardians of the peace, thereby creating the wrong impression in regard to the actions and aims of organized labor and its members." Fred Dorward, the secretary of the CTLC, believed that these motion pictures were being made solely "for the purpose of creating a public opinion in favor of these Cossacks," referring to the state police.[54]

The Wyoming Valley of Pennsylvania—home to Scranton, Hazleton, and Wilkes-Barre—was an important anthracite coal–mining region with a violent labor history. In 1897, a multiethnic coalition of miners marched into Lattimer, Pennsylvania, under the American flag, demanding their right to assembly. The sheriff and his deputies were waiting for the marchers and responded with a hail of gunfire, killing 19 men.[55] Five years after the Lattimer Massacre, the protracted Anthracite Coal Strike of 1902 rocked the region. In May of that year, John Lewis, president of the United Mine Workers (UMW), called his members out on strike against Pennsylvania's anthracite mine operators. Approximately 100,000 workers went on strike; in response, the mine operators hired 5,000 men to serve as their private Coal and Iron Police, to whom the Pennsylvania state legislature granted official police powers. For months, striking miners faced off against scabs, local and private police, and the Pennsylvania National Guard. After months of conflict, President Theodore Roosevelt, in order to prevent a coal famine (and, more importantly, social unrest in this immigrant-dominated region), intervened to mediate a solution between capital and labor. The settlement was widely regarded as a victory for labor, and UMW and AFL unions expanded in the years following. In 1914, the anthracite mining industry set an employment record in Pennsylvania. Three years later, production reached a record high, but mine operators had cut thousands of jobs in an effort to retain more profits.[56] The United Mine Workers responded by waging an extensive, and often contentious, organizing campaign during this period in an effort to protect workers' modest gains.

This conflict informed the Pennsylvania CTLC's censorship resolution—an effort to protect organized labor's image on-screen. Instead of appealing to the existing Pennsylvania State Board of Censors, Dorward asked Gompers to use his influence to "have the National Board of Review cut out the parts objectionable to organized labor," and to have this as yet unfinished moving picture banned "in States where an effort is being made to establish the State Police as strikebreakers," including Pennsylvania, West Virginia, and New York.[57] When NB executive secretary McGuire replied to the Pennsylvania CTLC, he assured them that the NB was sincerely "interested in organized labor," but offered an alternate interpretation of the unreleased motion picture being filmed in the Wyoming Valley. "Suppose . . . that the Labor Unions were shown active in their legitimate pursuits but being hounded and disrupted by the State Police?" McGuire suggested that such a motion picture could turn out to be "distinctly favorable to organized labor on account of the fact that it might show the abuse of power of the State Police." Nevertheless, to placate this large and important constituency, McGuire promised to contact the production company; he was certain either he or Gompers "could present to them arguments which would lead them to revise the story."[58]

This film caused strain between the National Board and the American Federation of Labor. Gompers, after receiving Dorward's communication, "emphatically protested" to McGuire against the NB passing "any motion picture . . . which has for its purpose placing the wage earners and the toilers of the country in the position of appearing to act as a lawless mob or . . . as violators of the law."[59] If Gompers parted ways with the anticensorship coalition, he would take millions of AFL members with him. So McGuire assured Gompers that the NB would conduct "an investigation to determine, if possible, what company is making this picture."[60] The next day, Gompers brought his men into line with strongly worded telegrams to both the Pennsylvania and West Virginia State Federations of Labor, emphasizing that "any attempt to pass a law establishing governmental censorship of moving pictures is an invasion of free expression." He conceded that the NB's "voluntary censorship" had been "ineffective" on some points in the past, but maintained that it was "better that occasional lapses may occur than encounter the danger of governmental censorship or denial of free expression."[61]

The situation in Pennsylvania strained, but did not sever, this partnership. Gompers and the AFL continued to provide support to the National Board's political agenda during crucial moments of pro-censorship activism. In 1919, when state censorship bills came before the legislatures in Illinois, Michigan, Nebraska, North Carolina, and South Dakota, McGuire wired Frank L. Morrison, secretary of the AFL, and asked him to "contact labor men" in those states to voice their opposition to the proposed legislation. Incidentally, these were also states where Federations of Women's Clubs supported censorship legislation—most urgently in Illinois and Michigan, where the measures were ultimately vetoed by the governor and defeated in the legislature, respectively.[62]

McGuire continued to hold the high-minded ideal that "education, opportunity and social justice" were not "compatible with censorship."[63] However, he was not above striking backroom deals in support of what he understood as the National Board's first principle—protecting motion pictures from political censorship. As he revealed in a February 1917 telegram to Gompers, D. W. Griffith had been "cooperating" with the NB behind the scenes "in opposing state censorship."[64]

"TREATMENT OF A RACE THAT IS UNDULY LIBELOUS":
THE "STANDARDS" AND RACIAL REPRESENTATIONS

The National Board of Review's "Standards" on race and racial representations were not as clear as those relating to animal cruelty or labor. Collier's original 1912 "Standards" warned that any "treatment of a race [that] is unduly libelous" often caused "the question of censorship" to arise in response, and thus should be avoided.[65] For an organization that was careful enough to require elimination of all close-up shots of postage stamps and currency to prevent counterfeiting, the NB's relative silence on negative portrayals of African Americans during a period of racial hostility and extreme violence is puzzling, on its face. The only suggestion offered in the "Standards" is vague: "Do not libel any class, race, religious institution, etc."[66]

In 1914, when the board conducted its annual revision of the "Standards," it warned motion picture producers that "many of the criticisms of motion pictures and their censorship have their foundation in local prejudice."[67] Although the NB claimed that it would require the elimination of any material likely to incite violence or riots, it would defer to "local public opinion" to make, or avoid making, the final decisions on racial ridicule. McGuire used the case of *At the Cross Roads* (Select, 1914) to contrast the NB's perspective on motion picture content with that of the Ohio State Board of Censors, suggesting that the NB's method resulted in a more acceptable product. *At the Cross Roads* was a popular melodrama adapted from famous playwright and stage and screen actor Hal Reid's 1902 play about murder and miscegenation.[68]

In *At the Cross Roads*, a southern minister, Rev. Thornton, hires Parepa Mendoza, a formerly enslaved "creole" woman, as his live-in domestic servant. Thornton's son Dayton regularly abuses Parepa and eventually rapes her. Dayton later murders a man, and he kidnaps Parepa during his escape. He "soon tires" of Parepa and kicks her out, even though she is pregnant with his child. Desperate, Parepa returns to Rev. Thornton and tells him her tragic story, and he commands Dayton to marry her. After the wedding, Dayton and Parepa move north to live as a white couple, and following the birth of their daughter Annabelle, Parepa's relationship evolves into that of domestic servant. Annabelle grows up not knowing that Parepa is her mother. When the Thorntons return to the South, Dayton drunkenly reveals that Parepa is Annabelle's mother, and that Parepa is actually a black woman. Dayton narrowly escapes being killed by a mob of angry African Americans, only to be murdered by Parepa. During her trial, it is revealed that she is "actually a white woman of Spanish heritage." With this revelation, which clears the air on the question of miscegenation, Parepa's actions are justified as a white woman protecting herself, and the judge releases her.[69]

The NB's Review Committee initially rejected *At the Cross Roads* "because this picture has a tendency to disturb the public peace and shows a series of criminal acts including several murders, arson, gambling, race riots between Negros [*sic*] and whites and other objectionable scenes."[70] When Select resubmitted the edited version, the Review Committee still required extensive cuts, including changing the "wording of subtitles to eliminate the word 'nigger'" throughout. The Review Committee also required elimination of the "part where Drayton [*sic*] pulls Creole woman [Parepa] down on the couch." Of the rape scene, one Review Committee member wrote, "Nothing could have been more suggestive." The board advised Select to cut the entire scene and only show Dayton and Parepa "standing and talking in the room." Whether the audience was confused about Annabelle's parentage because of this cut is unknown. The Ohio State Board of Censors, by contrast, eliminated an extended bar fight and a shooting scene, in addition to a title card that read, "I swear to avenge the death of my father."[71] It made no mention of the rape scene or the racial slurs in the title cards.

The New Governor (original title: *The Nigger*, Fox, 1915) also provides insight on the National Board's efforts to address racially libelous content. Based on a 1909 play by Edward Brewster Sheldon, *The Nigger* was released within a week of *The Birth of a Nation*; it is about an upstanding young white man from an old southern family, Philip Morrow, played by William Farnum, who is convinced to run for governor by a political boss and whiskey distiller, Cliff Noyes. After Morrow wins the election, Noyes blackmails him, threatening to go to the newspaper with proof of Morrow's African American ancestry if he signs a prohibition bill into law. Governor Morrow is shocked to discover that he is not white, but he sticks to his principles and signs the bill enacting statewide prohibition. He then resigns from office and moves north to start a new life as "a negro," dedicating himself to improving the condition of "his people."

Playwright Edward Sheldon maintained that his play was a temperance tale about the dangers of alcohol; in particular, he believed that the "negro problem" in the American South was "due largely to bad whiskey." Because alcohol was the underlying cause of "the 'usual crimes' of the Southern negro, for which the penalty is usually lynching," Sheldon reasoned that states should pass prohibition laws. Sheldon intended for his play to make the case that if liquor were removed from the South, "the race problem would cease to be one." After all, Sheldon noted, "the negro is naturally primitive. Alcohol brings the worst in him to the surface. It makes him worse than the brutes."[72]

The NB Review Committee required the title of the film to be changed to *The New Governor* prior to distribution. In addition, it required elimination of a title card that stated "an impossible gulf exists between the white and black races." Much as they did with a similar scene in *The Birth of a Nation* (to be discussed in chapter 3), the Review Committee required extensive eliminations from a scene in which a drunken black man meets a white girl in the woods and attacks her; the ensuing manhunt and lynching scenes were also eliminated. McGuire noted that the Review Committee had found "a number of objectionable scenes in the picture," including "one where a nigger is burned at the stake."[73] His casual use of the racial slur in his correspondence with John M. Casey, the Boston license commissioner, belied his real sentiments toward African Americans, and his belief that censorship to protect them encroached on white filmmakers' freedom of expression.

The National Board surmised that "many of the criticisms" that erupted in response to racial and ethnic representations had "their foundation in local prejudice." Although "the people of the United States are practically uniform in most of their ideas—political, social and moral," the "Standards" of 1914 noted that "certain striking differences" remained, and "these differences naturally are much in evidence in the comments on motion pictures."[74] In the wake of the *Mutual* decision and the controversy over *The Birth of a Nation*, as will be covered in the next chapter, the NB embraced a free speech position that prioritized "history" over any possible harm that might be caused by racially libelous content, and deferred to local public opinion to make those distinctions. On the whole, the board rejected any claims to "liberal censorship" to prevent negative racial representations, even though there was a long history of banning those caricatures from the stage at the local level.[75] Thus, in an effort "to adhere as closely as possible to the rationally conceived principles for which it stands, and yet pay significant regard to popular prejudice," the NB developed its model ordinance—the City Plan for Voluntary Motion Picture Regulation—which allowed local committees to selectively edit films for regional differences.[76]

THE CITY PLAN FOR VOLUNTARY MOTION PICTURE REGULATION

The City Plan called for the creation of "an unpaid motion picture commission" in any community where citizens wished to exert influence over local motion picture bookings. Under the City Plan, the responsibility "to prohibit . . . any 'obscene, indecent, licentious or immoral film, or any picture which would have a harmful influence on the public,'" fell to the local commission, and any "violation of any provision of the ordinance, whether with reference to previously filed applications, statement of fact, or the ignoring of the commission's orders," would be a misdemeanor for the exhibitor, punished by fines or revocation of license.[77] The city's license commissioner or police department would be vested with responsibility for enforcing the commission's decisions and levying fines. The Office of the License Commissioner was relatively new, a part of the Progressive overhaul of cities in the early twentieth century, and not tainted by a history of corruption, graft, or a long-standing relationship with local political machines.

Anyone who "propose[d] to exhibit motion pictures" to the public was required to notify the local commission "three days, or a reasonable time, in advance of the first exhibition." Exhibitors were to include a brief synopsis of each film and had to indicate "whether it ha[d] been reviewed by the National Board of Censorship." The local commission cross-referenced exhibitors' lists with the NB's weekly *Bulletin* to determine the status of motion pictures proposed for local exhibition.[78] The unpaid commission would not rescreen motion pictures intended for exhibition in its jurisdiction, but could preview those films whose synopses "indicate[d] moral damage" might result from public exhibition.[79] If the commissioners found that the NB's required edits had not been made prior to distribution, the City Plan empowered the local commission to physically remove those scenes and retain the excised scraps of film as contraband.[80]

For example, when World Film Corporation's *A Square Deal* (1917) arrived in Bridgeport, Connecticut, the film still contained an objectionable title card—one which the NB's Review Committee had singled out for elimination prior to exhibition. *A Square Deal* tells the story of three friends—writer Mark Dunbar, newspaper reporter Doris Golden, and artist Hugh Eltinge. Mark, newly successful on the literary scene, meets and falls in love with a beautiful "gold digger" named Ruby, played by the popular silent-film actress Muriel Ostriche. Blinded by her charms, Mark marries her, and he only learns of her "true nature" as she makes increasingly extravagant purchases as the new Mrs. Dunbar. Hugh, concerned about his old friend Mark, disguises himself as a millionaire and woos Ruby away. Mark divorces Ruby and later recognizes the value of a true friend.[81] In one controversial scene, Ruby's mother is shown grooming her; the original title card accompanying the scene read: "For it is a woman's beauty that appeals to men; not her brains." The Review Committee had requested elimination of all title cards in that scene, "for the reason that . . . the action at this point where the mother is dressing the girl would be quite proper without any subtitle inserted."[82]

Bridgeport, Connecticut, used the NB's City Plan, and its police department was responsible for local enforcement. So Police Lieutenant George Fox notified the board's membership secretary, W. M. Covill, about the errant title card, and Covill immediately contacted the World Film Corporation on Fox's behalf. Ever mindful of the NB's position on freedom of expression, Covill allowed: "If, however, you feel that some subtitle should be inserted at that point we would suggest that you use one similar to . . .'You must do your best to catch him.'"[83] World's representatives responded quickly to Covill: "Your instructions have been complied with, and the title suggested—'You must do your best to catch him'—has been substituted, as per your request." The letter ended with a phrase common in the NB's correspondence with the industry: "assuring you of our desire to heartily co-operate with you."[84] World—and other production and distribution companies—worked with the NB because it was ultimately in their best interest to do so.

The City Plan constituted a large part of the NB's "constructive" work, serving as both a model ordinance and a system that allowed for "all of the forces seeking the improvement of the photoplay both dramatically and socially" to cooperate at the local level.[85] Commenting on the City Plan, McGuire declared not only that it was "good business for the manufacturer to

FIGURE 2.2. *The "Boston Plan" cover*

have such an efficient service," but that it acted "as a satisfactory check in preventing pictures being exhibited which are harmful to the morals of the public," as distributors and exhibitors far from New York City frequently tried to skirt the NB's orders.[86] The City Plan allowed communities to tailor films to local needs; after all, as one NB board member noted, "a film that would be favorably received in New York City might be completely repudiated in Centerville, Iowa."[87]

The first city to adopt the NB's City Plan was Boston, in 1909. Massachusetts mayors already had the authority to "grant licenses for all amusements in the city 'under whatever terms and conditions [they] may deem reasonable.'"[88] Boston mayor George Albee Hibbard (1908–1910) required that all moving picture houses be licensed by the city, and all motion pictures exhibited in Boston had to bear the seal of the National Board. The license commissioner thus became responsible for policing the screen, in addition to burlesque and "legitimate" theater houses, and was authorized to close obscene or immoral establishments.

In the same year, Boston adopted a new city charter, replacing the bicameral city council with a single-chamber council and reducing the number of councilors from eighty-seven to nine, elected at large instead of by ward.[89] In addition, the heads of the city departments would no longer be elected, but appointed by the mayor; nominees were to be "recognized experts in the work which they supervise," and selected "regardless of party affiliation and without confirmation by City Council." Boston's new city charter made it a leader in municipal reform, but it was also an effort to diminish the power of the Irish American political machine.[90] Nevertheless, Irish American politicians continued to win mayoral elections in Boston, notably John F. "Honey Fitz" Fitzgerald (1910–1914) and James Michael Curley (1914–1918). As Irish Catholics, they shared the same aversion to "obscenity" as the Watch and Ward Society's constituents.

John M. Casey served as Boston's official censor from his appointment as license commissioner in 1904 until his retirement in 1932. He banned bare legs on stage, and he declared that "nothing should be placed upon the stage of any theater anywhere to which you could not take your mother, sweetheart, wife, or sister."[91] As bureaucrat-in-chief, he aided and abetted the WWS's censorship campaign against literature, stage plays, and controversial motion pictures through the 1910s and 1920s.[92] Casey vocally supported the City Plan throughout his career, writing several pamphlets about its benefits; he fervently believed that the National Board, "by the decisions of its reviewers, more nearly voices public sentiments than has been given by any other method."[93]

The NB benefited from this relationship and frequently pointed to Boston as an example of a successful partnership. The board used the example of Boston as an organizing point in its correspondence with activists and municipal officials nationwide. In 1914, McGuire boasted that in Boston—a city renowned for its Puritanical streak—"no picture which has not been passed by the National Board can be shown at all."[94] Within a year, however, the National Board faced its first significant challenge to the City Plan, and to the tenuous consensus against legal censorship, in Boston, and it was triggered by D. W. Griffith's *The Birth of a Nation* (1915).

3 / "AN HISTORICAL PRESENTATION":
THE BIRTH OF A NATION AND THE CITY PLAN,
1909–1917

ON 9 APRIL 1915, THE FIFTIETH ANNIVERSARY OF GEN-
eral Robert E. Lee's surrender to General Ulysses S. Grant at Appomattox,
The Birth of a Nation (Griffith, 1915) debuted in Boston.[1] Audience members
were "prepared for the unusual" the moment they entered the Tremont Theatre. After "a young man in evening dress and a silk hat" took tickets, "two
young women in flounced hoop skirts and with long curls" gave "a sort of
graceful minuet bow" and handed out programs. Flanking the aisles were
"soldiers 'on guard' in the Civil War uniforms of the North and South"; another costumed young woman ushered people to their seats.[2] As the film pro-
jector flickered to life, a title card issued an important caveat to the audience:
"This is an historical presentation of the Civil War and Reconstruction period and is not meant to reflect in any way upon any race or people of today."[3]
D. W. Griffith did not write this title card, however; the National Board had
inserted it to head off protesters and signal its commitment to filmmakers'
right to freedom of expression.

D. W. Griffith's *The Birth of a Nation* was based on Thomas Dixon's 1905
novel *The Clansman: An Historical Romance of the Ku Klux Klan*. The book,
subsequent stage play, and film depicted the struggles of two fictional families in the aftermath of the Civil War—the northern family, the Stonemans,
headed by an abolitionist congressman named Austin Stoneman (loosely
based on Thaddeus Stevens, R-PA), and the Camerons, a family of elite South
Carolinians whose lives become radically transformed by the upheavals of the
Civil War and Reconstruction. A black militia ransacks the family home during the war, and they lose two sons in battle. The surviving son, Ben Cameron, founds the Ku Klux Klan to bring about home rule.[4]

For weeks prior to the film's Boston debut, the National Equal Rights
League and the local chapter of the NAACP lobbied the license commissioner
to prevent its exhibition. The president of the NERL, William Monroe Trot-

ter, who was also the editor of the *Boston Guardian*, a nationally circulated African American newspaper, and a cofounder of the Niagara Movement—a civil rights group that had first met at Niagara Falls in 1905—had led a successful campaign to ban Thomas Dixon's play *The Clansman* from the stage in Boston five years earlier. Trotter characterized Griffith's motion picture as "a libel on the race" and "an incentive to great racial hatred."[5] Yet the National Board's ten-member Review Committee that screened *The Birth of a Nation* on 20 January 1915, failing to find anything objectionable, obscene, or likely to generate controversy in the motion picture, "voted unanimously to pass the picture as presented."[6] Griffith was thus free to book the film into theaters, and prints of *The Birth of a Nation* would bear the NB's seal. Any dispute arising from its exhibition was now a question for local officials.

That same month, the NAACP launched a campaign to have *The Birth of a Nation* banned from screens nationwide. Mary Childs Nerney, secretary of the NAACP's executive board, contacted Frederic Howe, chairman of the National Board's executive board, to register a formal objection to Griffith's motion picture, asking for it to be suppressed in order to protect African Americans from defamation and possible violence as a result of the film's content and message. Significantly, the NB and the NAACP both had their offices at 70 Fifth Avenue in Manhattan, and the organizations shared several executive board members. Judging by the limited extant correspondence between these two organizations across several archival collections, it seems likely that the bulk of the negotiating over Griffith's controversial motion picture took place face-to-face in the offices, stairwells, and meeting rooms.

In response to the NAACP's request, Howe overturned the initial Review Committee's decision and ordered the General Committee to rescreen the film. On 1 March, the NB's General Committee assembled to watch it and voted "to pass the first part of the picture subject to minor changes," but "condemned" sections in the second half that the committee felt "might create race hatred and prejudice."[7] According to the NB's executive secretary, W. D. McGuire, those scenes included one in which "the old lady smells of the colored boy and waves him away at account of his odor. This indicates that the whole colored race is odorous." In addition, a scene depicting "a violent fight in the saloon where the negroes are beaten up" was removed.[8]

The NB's General Committee also expressed concern over the "chase scene." In this infamous scene, Griffith's favorite young actress, Mae Marsh, portrays Flora Cameron, or "the little pet sister," the youngest daughter of the Cameron family and a symbol of white southern womanhood. Flora wishes to go down to the spring alone, against the objections of her mother and older sister. She skips merrily along, giggling at a squirrel and greeting birds. Suddenly, Gus, a "renegade negro, a product of the vicious doctrine spread by

FIGURE 3.1. *Flora from* The Birth of a Nation

FIGURE 3.2. *Gus from* The Birth of a Nation

carpetbaggers," appears, foaming at the mouth and ogling Flora. NAACP cofounder Mary White Ovington, describing Gus's character, later said, "It was enough to make a Bostonian on Beacon Hill double-lock his door at night."[9] Playing Gus was Walter Long, a white silent-film actor in blackface.

As Gus chases Flora deeper into the forest, a title card flashes, saying, "You see, I'm a captain now, and want to marry." Flora begins to run, and Gus lurches behind her, the title card announcing: "Wait, missie, I won't hurt yeh!" She reaches a precipice; her face contorts with anguish as she realizes Gus is fast approaching. Weighing her options, Flora chooses to jump to her death rather than risk being raped. The following prolonged shot shows her body bouncing down the cliff's face before she lands, crumpled like a rag-doll. Later in the film, a white-robed vigilante mob dumps Gus's dead body on Lieutenant Governor Silas Lynch's doorstep as a warning. The character of Lynch, the "mulatto protégé" of a northern abolitionist politician, is also portrayed as a lecherous rapist throughout the film.[10]

Howe feared *The Birth of a Nation* "would cause race riots in the South" and "postpone solution of the race problem." General Committee members Dr. James P. Warbasse, Dr. Burdette Lewis, Miriam Sutro Price, and Birdie Stein Gans agreed; all four condemned it. Significantly, all four were also members of the NAACP.[11] Jane Addams, who was not only a member of the NAACP but also on the NB's National Advisory Committee, decried the film as a "pernicious caricature of the Negro race" that "appeal[ed] to race preju-dices upon the basis of conditions of half a century ago, which have nothing to do with the facts that we have to consider today." "Even then," she said, "it does not tell the whole truth." Of the claim that *The Birth of a Nation* was a historical presentation, Addams noted, "You can use history to demonstrate anything when you take certain of its facts and emphasize them to the exclu-sion of the rest."[12]

New York City mayor John Purroy Mitchel, a respected Progressive, agreed to hold a special hearing on whether to allow continued public exhi-bition of *The Birth of a Nation*.[13] According to the *Baltimore Afro-American*, which provided extensive nationwide coverage of the campaign against the film, more than two hundred citizens came to Mayor Mitchel's meeting. In attendance were representatives from the National League on Urban Condi-tions Among Negroes as well as "the colored and white ministry of Greater New York, the Citizens Club of Brooklyn, and the Northeastern Federa-tion of Women's Clubs." Dr. William H. Brooks, pastor of St. Mark's M. E. Church; Fred R. Moore, a prominent Black Republican and editor of the *New York Age*; Oswald Garrison Villard, a prominent journalist and a cofounder of the NAACP; W. E. B. DuBois, another NAACP cofounder as well as the director of the NAACP's Publications and Research branch; and Rabbi Stephen Wise of the Free Synagogue, who was also an NAACP cofounder, were also present. Rabbi Wise, in asking Mayor Mitchel to prevent further exhibition of *The Birth of a Nation* in New York City, said that the film had come at a particularly bad time, "when we [are] witnessing in Europe the frightful effects of the breedings of hate and prejudice," and he feared that *The Birth of a Nation* "might perhaps incite to breaches of the peace" domestically. All present "urged upon" Mayor Mitchel "the importance of suppressing the moving picture play."[14] At Mayor Mitchel's request, Griffith voluntarily removed two scenes, but *The Birth of a Nation* continued to run in New York City.[15]

Howe and other prominent members of the NB agreed with the NAACP and the civil rights activists that *The Birth of a Nation* should be suppressed in the service of racial harmony. W. D. McGuire, however, rejected that position. He believed that African Americans' claims for protection through censorship were directly at odds with filmmakers' right to expression, and were therefore illegitimate. Moreover, he maintained, as *The Birth of a Nation* was "a historical presentation," it was "hardly just to condemn it entirely."[16] After all, the "Standards" clearly stated that the National Board was not "responsible for the historical, geographical, or scientific accuracy of films."[17] What most concerned McGuire was "the Colored Association," whose members "said that they were going to make trouble in every city where it [was] shown."[18]

Indeed, as opposition to *The Birth of a Nation* mounted in Boston, License Commissioner John M. Casey contacted the National Board for guidance after he received "protests . . . from all classes of people," including a number of city councilors and "some of the best lawyers (white)." Casey claimed that *The Birth of a Nation* had "stirred up the greatest opposition it has ever been my lot to encounter" in the six years he had been enforcing the National Board's City Plan for Voluntary Motion Picture Regulation in Boston.[19]

McGuire reassured Casey that he had "talked with a number of prominent people about the picture, particularly some fine people on the New York Board of Education, who think it is very fine."[20] He emphasized that *The Birth of a Nation* had been greatly "toned down," as a "number of scenes where a colored fellow was chasing a woman and comes in close view to the camera frothing at the mouth" had been removed, in addition to the "big fight in the saloon in which several fellows were shot"—specifically, "the shooting of the colored people."[21] While "some scenes . . . may be considered distasteful to colored people," McGuire maintained, "there [was] nothing immoral in the picture," and therefore no reason to suppress it.[22] He asserted that "the only ones taking exception" to the edited version of *The Birth of a Nation* were members of the NAACP, which he dismissed as an "Association [that] believes in intermarriage of the races" as part of its "propaganda."[23] Moreover, under the "Standards," *The Birth of a Nation* was classified as a historical presentation, which he felt required the use of different standards from the ones used with fully fictional motion pictures. In reality, McGuire was relying on the distinction to shirk responsibility for allowing the exhibition of racially defamatory portrayals.

McGuire never shared the text of the eliminated title cards with Casey, although he claimed their removal had produced a "toned down" version of the film. The excised cards read: "Pious Puritans blessed the traffic," and "Having profited by the trade and having no use for slaves themselves, the traders of the 17th century became the abolitionists of the 19th century."[24] These revisions revealed the National Board's sensitivity to white audience members—particularly in Boston with its proud abolitionist history. The NB did not want to anger Bostonians—or anyone else—who could influence politicians to adopt censorship legislation. McGuire did not prioritize protecting black audiences from libelous portrayals of their race; nor did he accept the premise that *The Birth of a Nation* would move Americans, white or black, to racial violence.

Boston mayor James Michael Curley was not as dismissive of African Americans' concerns as McGuire. Although African Americans represented only 1.8 percent of Boston's population in 1890, and 2.1 percent in 1900, they constituted an important swing constituency for Curley's Democratic machine. Under Boston's new at-large voting system, no one could afford to alienate constituencies, so Curley attempted to balance the interests of Catholics, immigrants, and African Americans.[25] On 8 April 1915, Curley held a public hearing after Trotter and "many colored citizens" warned that exhibition of *The Birth of a Nation* in Boston would "incite race hatred." Curley asked Griffith to further shorten the chase scene and eliminate any suggestion of lynching to ensure that "the fullest possible measure of justice" would be "accorded the colored citizenship of Boston."[26] Curley was satisfied that the amended version of *The Birth of a Nation* that would be exhibited in Boston would provide justice to the "colored citizens" while honoring other Bostonians' rights to attend this motion picture.

However, the print of *The Birth of a Nation* exhibited the next day at the Tremont Theatre had not been cut according to Curley's specifications. The manager claimed he had not been given enough time to complete such a large job; although he had exhibited the NB-approved print on Saturday, he intended to make the mayor's edits on Sunday. But the damage had been done.[27] According to the *Globe*, "the colored population of Boston," which had "vainly protested" against *The Birth of a Nation* for months, finally "gave free vent to their feelings" on 17 April. Inside the Tremont, audience members threw rotten eggs and "exploded stinkpots" to protest the ongoing exhibition of the unedited version of Griffith's film, while more "disturbances" occurred outside. The box-office manager, fearful that Trotter would "fill the house with negroes" who would "destroy the films and stop the play," called the police. "As a racial demonstration," the *Boston Globe* estimated, "nothing like it has been seen in Boston since before the Civil War."[28]

Despite these protests, *The Birth of a Nation* continued to play in Boston for weeks. "Crowds thronged the matinee and night performances," including a "large attendance of women," many of whom were "drawn to the film's dramatic and romantic aspects." Others were driven to the Tremont by sheer "curiosity," turning out to see the film because it had "caused so much discussion." The audience, estimated in the thousands, exhibited "a lack of nervousness over the reports of opposition and disturbances."[29]

Civil rights activists in Massachusetts turned to Governor David I. Walsh (D), urging him to support more expansive censorship legislation. In May, with his backing, the Massachusetts General Court approved the Sullivan Bill, which created a three-member board of censors for the city of Boston composed of the mayor, the police chief, and the chief justice of the municipal court. This board was legally empowered to "revoke or suspend" licenses for public entertainments, but Boston continued to rely on the National Board's City Plan as its first line of defense.[30]

D. W. Griffith, for his part, attacked Boston's new censorship board as "threaten[ing] the freedom of the stage and the press." He condemned the "underhanded and un-American methods" used to achieve political support for the measure, claiming that "the negroes who are promoting the intermarriage of blacks and whites in this country" had forced Governor Walsh to act. Notwithstanding all of the efforts "to suppress or alter the film," Griffith boasted, *The Birth of a Nation* had "passed over every legal barrier placed in its way by the negro intermarriage societies opposed to its presentation in New York, Boston, Los Angeles and San Francisco and has been sustained in every instance." He also reminded readers that the film had earned "the sanction of the National Board of Censors"—although with this statement he was misrepresenting the meaning of the organization's seal.[31]

In the wake of the crisis, McGuire was anxious to maintain Boston as a City Plan city; therefore, he selectively notified Casey in advance of motion pictures that the NB had passed that were still likely to cause controversy in Boston. One such film was *Whom the Gods Destroy*, a Vitagraph production of 1916 loosely based on Ireland's Easter Rising of that year, in which Irish nationalists declared the founding of the Irish Republic and staged an armed rebellion against the British government. In the movie, a young Irish woman, Mary O'Neil, played by prolific silent-film star Alice Joyce, refuses to marry until the "Irish question" is settled. One of her suitors is Sir Denis Esmond,

FIGURE 3.3. *Alice Joyce, 1917*

modeled on Sir Roger Casement, an Irish nationalist and anticolonialist leader of the Easter Rising. The British government had tried and executed Casement for treason in 1916, yet in this retelling, the benevolent king pardons Esmond in service of the love story.

The British Board of Censors banned *Whom the Gods Destroy* for its pro-Irish nationalist sentiment and the likelihood it would cause disturbances.[32] In New York City, Irish immigrants protested the movie for its pro-British interpretation of the Easter Rising. The newly founded Friends of Irish Freedom (FOIF) officially objected to *Whom the Gods Destroy* for taking "liberties with history," challenging its depiction of "Irish rebels as a disorganized mob, armed with sticks and stones instead of rifles," and its "attempt to make the American people believe Sir Roger Casement was pardoned by a kind king instead of put to death," which was "a historic lie." The FOIF condemned the film and encouraged a boycott. Vitagraph claimed that the FOIF provoked riots in movie theaters across the city—including one in Brooklyn that resulted in arrests—in an effort to prevent further exhibition of *Whom the Gods Destroy*. But according to the *New York Times*, "many theaters . . . canceled the picture" because "hundreds had walked out during its presentation." In one case, an audience member had "taken his stand by the screen" in a Brooklyn theater and "told the true story as each incident was shown, to the huge enjoyment and approval of his audience."[33] Vitagraph's suggestion of mob violence may have been an attempt to generate controversy to boost box-office sales.

Although the NB's Appeals Committee expressed "sympathy with the movement for Irish freedom," its members concluded that it was "entirely out of their province" as a "reviewing body" to "take adverse action on this picture merely for the reason that it might prove offensive to loyal Irishmen."[34] McGuire, whose brother was a founding member of the FOIF, wrote to Casey to alert him and to let him know that a large number of Irish immigrants in Boston might protest its local exhibition.[35] He explained to Casey that, much like *The Birth of a Nation*, "which offended the negroes," the Irish would have to deal with being offended, too, in service of the greater good—freedom of expression.[36]

Following the controversy around *The Birth of a Nation*, fault lines emerged among Progressives. Some recognized the value of a liberal censorship to protect black Americans from racially libelous portrayals and foster civil rights; others gave more weight to the civil liberties argument on behalf of filmmakers. Mary White Ovington of the NAACP wrote a scathing letter to the National Board to confront McGuire about the organization's decision regarding *The Birth of a Nation*: "It may interest the board that sent the Scenario under its approval to know that it has caused the murder of an innocent lad."[37] She informed McGuire that a young man named Henry Brocj, immediately after seeing *The Birth of a Nation* in Lafayette, Indiana, "walked out on the main street . . . and fired three bullets into the body of Edward Manson, a Negro high school student, fifteen years old. The boy died to-night. There was no provocation for the tragedy and Brocj is in jail under charge of murder."[38] The implication of the article, and Ovington's letter, was that everyone was wrong to think that this particular film would not incite racial violence.

John Collier, who also became disillusioned with the direction the National Board was taking, contacted fellow Progressives, urging them to reconsider their membership in the organization entirely. Perhaps surprisingly, Collier was not protesting *The Birth of a Nation*; he was more immediately concerned about the City Plan, which he believed represented a shift in the National Board's "philosophy regarding the legal control of films." NB General Secretary Collier explained that, "fundamentally," the National Board had long held the position that "it would be dangerous precedent to establish legal, compulsory, pre-publicity censorship, either through paid or unpaid local officials." However, with growing emphasis on the City Plan, Collier warned, it would be more "dangerous to have the National Board statutorily created

[as] the local censor." Were the City Plan "widely enough adopted," the National Board would no longer be "a cooperative, voluntary arrangement, but a compulsory one, forced upon the motion picture art by statutes existing in cities more or less numerous and important." As such, the City Plan was nothing more than "an insidious means of introducing a legal, compulsory, pre-publicity censorship principle into American public laws." Moreover, the plan "incapacitate[d] the National Board," rendering it unable to fight "against legal, compulsory, pre-publicity censorship on grounds of principle."[39] Collier himself discontinued his work with the National Board in late 1915, and he moved to Los Angeles the following year. Frederic C. Howe also quit the National Board in the aftermath of the battle over *The Birth of a Nation*.

Following the departures of Collier and Howe, McGuire assumed more power over the direction of the organization. McGuire supported the City Plan, noting that his correspondence "show[ed] no indication that where the City Plan has been in operation a year and a half, that any injury has been reported either to the development of the motion pictures or to the public at large." The City Plan, he said, offered "enlightened regulation through local groups expressing local public opinion and backed by . . . civic authority," and such groups would "most speedily develop a social conscience which will permit complete freedom of expression."[40]

Perhaps most indicative of this shift to McGuire's perspective was the organization's name change in 1916. Following the Federal Motion Picture Commission hearings in January of that year and the New York State legislature's debate over the Christman-Wheeler motion picture censorship bill in April, the NB's executive board voted to change the name from "National Board of Censorship" to "National Board of Review of Motion Pictures." As McGuire explained to the Boston license commissioner, Casey, the name change was expressly to "eliminate the word 'censorship.'" As lobbyists, McGuire explained, members of the NB had "found it very difficult in various states to put over the idea as to why we were opposed to state censorship when we ourselves were carrying on censorship." McGuire assured Casey that "our work will remain the same, yet we will be in a better psychological position" to battle legal censorship.[41]

MOTION PICTURES:
THE CHIEF AMUSEMENT OF THE ADULT PUBLIC

The New York State Assembly passed the Christman-Wheeler censorship bill in April 1916 following much debate. As it sat on Governor Charles Seymour Whitman's desk awaiting his signature or veto, activists organized a series of publicity events in Albany in an effort to influence the governor's decision. The National Board hosted a talk by its new chairman, Rev. Cranston Brenton, a professor of English at Trinity College in Hartford, Connecticut, to "explain some of the vagaries of the working of the various state boards."[42] Doris Kenyon, a popular "picture actress," traveled to Albany to present Governor Whitman with a petition signed by 100,000 New Yorkers, including "many men prominent in the industry," asking him to withhold his signature from the bill. Supporters of the Christman-Wheeler bill included Canon Chase and "clergymen of all denominations," the Women's Christian Temperance Union, and the American Humane Association, all of which maintained that "state supervision was essential for the proper protection of the morals of the young."[43] Governor Whitman vetoed the bill, but pro-censorship sentiment remained strong in New York State.

The NB also released a pamphlet, titled "State Censorship of Motion Pictures—An Invasion of Constitutional Rights," that reflected recent changes in the board's personnel and ideology. It relied heavily on the constitutional argument in the wake of the decision in *Mutual Film Corporation v. Industrial Commission of Ohio* and the Federal Motion Picture Commission hearings: "Motion pictures have arisen since the framing of the Constitution," the pamphlet noted, and are "obviously a means whereby opinion is expressed," and as such, they were "entitled to the same right of liberty as is accorded speech and press." State censorship boards represented nothing less than "the fastening of this designing, ignorant, irresponsible tyranny upon our free institutions." The pamphlet also forcefully attacked the "chief reason advanced for state censorship"—that "ordinary shows are unfit for children to attend." The NB maintained that "no censorship" could create "a commendable entertainment for children," and furthermore, "nobody has any business trying to do this." Over the course of their development, motion pictures had emerged as "the chief amusement of the adult public," and "any attempt to standardize it as a child's entertainment is as intolerable as it is impossible."[44]

Simultaneously, the National Board actively engaged the child question, bringing together a coalition of civic organizations to "provide children with special programs." The collaborative National Committee on Better Films emerged out of a meeting called by Birdie Stein Gans, who was a member of both the NB and the Federation for Child Study; it was held at the Woman's City Club in June 1916, and the attendees "discuss[ed] the formation, principles and methods of work of a National committee interested in selected films." Those present included General Federation of Women's Club members Louise Connolly and Helen Varick Boswell; magazine features writer Helen Duey; Lester F. Scott, secretary of the Camp Fire Girls; and W. D. McGuire and Rev. Orrin Cocks of the National Board. Gans proposed a committee that would "discover" what kinds of motion pictures "appeal[ed]" to children and young people; encourage "the production and use of children's pictures and programs"; and function as "a clearinghouse of information on successful work in various places and to develop cooperation with various existing agencies." After discussion, those assembled decided to create such a committee, which they thought "should have close affiliation" with the NB.[45]

The Better Films Committee (BFC) emphasized working in cooperation with theater owners in local communities and assisted local organizations in requesting "finer pictures" from exhibitors. In theory, this work would "build up" local audiences for finer films, making "unprofitable the mediocre or questionable productions," and "vice versa."[46] Committee members hoped that supporters of censorship would be drawn to the work of the BFC as well. Rev. Orrin G. Cocks assumed leadership of the Better Films Committee, and the work was conducted out of the NB's offices. He cultivated support for the committee among prominent organizations, such as the National Congress of Mothers, the New York Federation for Child Study, the Minneapolis Women's Co-operative Alliance, the Southern Co-operative League, and parent-teacher associations in Connecticut, Pennsylvania, and Colorado, among others.[47]

According to the industry trade journal *Motion Picture World*, the earliest adopters of the Better Films Committee were clubwomen in Ohio, where state censorship already existed. Miss Bertelle Lyttle, chairwoman of the Civics Committee for the General Federation of Women's Clubs, reported that it was "the failure of censorship [that] started the better film movement" in Cleveland.[48] By September, Blanche McDonald had reported in *American Club Woman Magazine* that Ohio women were organizing "to have the official power of censorship stricken from the statute books." McDonald asserted that "a decided change of sentiment" had occurred around "the regulation of motion pictures" since the founding of the Ohio Board of Censors. "The decisions of the official censor boards" in Ohio, Pennsylvania, Kansas, and Maryland, she noted, were "in many cases extremely unreasonable and not infrequently ridiculous." Ohio, for instance, had prohibited "show[ing] snakes upon the screen, even in cartoons." Increased study, she added, had "convinced thoughtful people that political regulation is not a solution; it simply does not accomplish results." Therefore, many clubwomen "and others who have thought carefully about the matter," were electing to cooperate with the National Board, "which, more than any other organization, stands for clean pictures."[49]

McGuire openly supported the work of the BFC while also cultivating a behind-the-scenes relationship with D. W. Griffith. In May, McGuire contacted Griffith to express "a great deal of interest" in his recently published booklet *The Rise and Fall of Free Speech in America*, which on its cover featured "a photogravure of Miss Liberty being bound by film censors with a reel of film."[50] Griffith warned in the booklet that "every time you enter a moving picture theater where films are subject to censorship . . . your inalienable right of freely selecting your photodrama, your literature, your philosophy, your knowledge of life, has been slyly taken from you."[51] By October, according to NB financial statements, Griffith's Wark Producing Company and Epoch Producing Company had donated hundreds of dollars to the NB to create a temporary "Speakers Bureau," which dispatched women to certain areas of the country to carry out an active campaign against legal censorship.[52] McGuire staffed the Speakers Bureau with anticensorship activists, many of them affiliated with the General Federation of Women's Clubs, and focused their efforts on locations where state censorship campaigns appeared.

Mary Gray Peck was the Speakers Bureau's first hire. A former English professor at the University of Minnesota, she had become prominent in the women's suffrage movement, working as secretary to National American Woman Suffrage Association (NAWSA) president Carrie Chapman Catt. Peck was also an active member of the General Federation of Women's Clubs and served on its Motion Picture Committee, which was established in June 1916 (see chapter 5).

Through late 1916 and into 1917, Peck traveled extensively on behalf of the NB. While traveling, she avoided any mention of her connections to the NB so she would not "be subjected to the same type of criticism to which [it] is often subjected." Instead, she stressed "the importance of selecting pictures for children's performances as one solution of the motion picture problem as far as children are concerned," and emphasized that "any thought that children are protected through censorship is entirely erroneous."[53] During an eight-week tour of the Midwest, Peck observed that censor boards had "not made pictures any better in quality than those seen elsewhere." She pointed to Cleveland, in particular, where the public and exhibitors had joined forces to create a local Better Films Committee.[54] Peck believed "beyond doubt" that the recurrent campaigns for state censorship boards were not related to the quality of motion pictures, but to the fact that "children all over the country are going to adult shows." The "obvious remedy" was to schedule special shows for children and families "on regular days," so that the character of the films exhibited "would not be in doubt." Special programs for children would provide "a comfortable grave for the legal censorship idea."[55]

4 / "IS ANY GIRL SAFE?":
WHITE SLAVE TRAFFIC FILMS AND
THE GEOGRAPHY OF CENSORSHIP, 1914—1917

WHEN THE NATIONAL BOARD'S REVIEW COMMITTEE FIRST
screened *Shackled Souls* (Dragon, 1914), its members agreed: "This picture
should not be publicly exhibited in its original form." *Shackled Souls* tells the
tragic story of a naïve young woman, Elsie, who is seduced into a life of prostitution by a man named Burton and his friend Mr. Johnson, a "white slave
trafficker." The Review Committee required Dragon to make several eliminations prior to distribution, including "any reference [in] the subtitles to any
of the characters being white slavers." Once the "white slavery" narrative was
edited out of the title cards, *Shackled Souls* became a sanitized romance, and
Dragon was free to distribute it bearing the NB's seal.[1] The review secretary
directed Dragon to resubmit *Shackled Souls* after editing "for final action" by
the committee before proceeding with bookings and distribution.[2] Dragon
failed to respond, and the board subsequently listed *Shackled Souls* in the *Bulletin* as "condemned."

The NB promptly alerted its regional correspondents to the fact that an un-
edited "white slave traffic" picture might be circulating in their jurisdictions.
The board also directed local committees to make the following cuts from
Shackled Souls prior to exhibition, listing them as follows:

1. Eliminate any reference in the subtitles to any of the characters being
   white slavers.
2. By means of subtitles, show that Burton has become infatuated with Elsie through the description of Johnson, who introduces Burton to her.
   Change the character of Johnson from that of trafficker to that of simply a friend of Burton. In other words, eliminate the idea that this man is
   mixed up in any white slave traffic.
3. Eliminate the scene showing close up view in the hack where Johnson
   discloses his identity [as a white slaver].

4. Insert the subtitle to the effect that Burton persuades Elsie to attend the garden party and supplies her with the necessary clothes.[3]

Mrs. Reed Finley, secretary of the Dallas Board of Censors, notified NB executive secretary W. D. McGuire when an unedited copy of *Shackled Souls* appeared in her jurisdiction; she would make the edits, as Dallas did not permit exhibition of any motion pictures condemned by the National Board.[4] She also informed McGuire that she had been disappointed in the NB's actions recently on "white slave" pictures; the Dallas Board of Censors had started rescreening all films in the genre, including those passed by the NB.[5] The Dallas board had adapted the City Plan to meet local needs and was now rejecting any motion picture that showed "the inside of houses of ill repute." Finley noted that the action had been well received by the local branches of the YMCA, YWCA, Women's Christian Temperance Union, General Federation of Women's Clubs, Camp Fire Girls, and mothers' clubs as well as by "pastors, businessmen, doctors and lawyers."[6] Although Dallas residents were pacified, Finley warned McGuire that white slave traffic pictures were stirring up support for legal censorship in other Texas cities—Fort Worth and San Antonio, in particular.

As a genre, "white slave traffic" pictures exploded in popularity after Universal's enormously successful *Traffic in Souls* (1913). In that film, two Swedish immigrant sisters, Mary and Lorna, work in a "fashionable confectionary" in Manhattan. One day, handsome Bill Bradshaw comes into the shop and invites Lorna on a date. Lorna wakes up the next morning in a locked room in a brothel; Bill, whom she had naïvely taken to be "nice" and "mannered," had drugged her the night before, and he is in fact a procurer of prostitutes. In a scene at the police station, a cub reporter overhears the officers saying that Lorna has been kidnapped; he publishes a scoop under the headline "Young Girl Disappears. Foul Play Suspected." The newspaper article, functioning as a title card in the film, reads: "A pretty little girl, employed in a well known candy store, reported last night as possibly having fallen into evil hands. Is it possible our candy stores can be used as a market for this infamous trade?"[7] When the owner of the candy store reads the article, he fires Mary "on account of her sister's disgrace."[8] Fortunately, the "wife of the man higher up" offers Mary a secretarial position at her "pet charity," the Purity and Reform League, to protect her from encountering the same fate as her sister. Once Mary is at her new job, she answers a phone call and recognizes the voice of the man who abducted her sister; she realizes that the reformers "must be in league with the infamous traffickers."[9] *Traffic in Souls* takes aim at John D. Rockefeller, who is represented by one of the characters from the Purity and Reform League. Rockefeller had recently supervised a grand jury investigation into the alleged traffic in women in New York City, and some observers regarded the reports that came out of those investigations, such as George Kneeland's *Commercialized Prostitution in New York* (1913), as obscene material.[10]

Much like muckraking journalists, who believed that investigative journalism could be wielded in the fight against government corruption, some earnest reformers embraced the popular new medium of motion pictures as a tool for educating audiences about the alleged traffic in women. But as film historian Shelley Stamp has argued, "white slave traffic" films presented "risqué subject matter under the guise of upright instruction for the nation's young women."[11] Universal advertised *Traffic in Souls* as a "truthful picture-sermon," saying it offered "a lesson to young and old."[12] The genre coincided with a nationwide moral panic over immigration, urbanization, and women's increased presence in the paid labor force. Film historian Eric Schaeffer understands "white slave traffic" films as a precursor to the better-known "exploitation films" of the Production Code era, which exploited the boundaries of the Motion Picture Production Code by showing everything from drug use to sex to kidnapping in a moralistic framework in the guise of an instructional film.[13] During their height of popularity, from 1913 until the National Board's prohibition on new productions of films in the genre in 1917, white slave traffic films exploited not only the bounds of good taste, but also the emerging geographic boundaries of censorship.

White slave traffic pictures emerged during a pivotal moment in the development of the motion picture industry. In the pre-studio era of the 1910s, motion pictures were typically distributed in one of two ways: by the "road-show" method or by the "states' rights" method. In the road-show method, with its origins in the legitimate theater, the distributor contracted directly with theaters and booked a film for a set length of time in exchange for a set percentage of box-office receipts.[14] During the period of the white slave traffic film, from roughly 1914 to 1917, the motion picture industry was undergoing dramatic changes in terms of distribution. Paramount Pictures was created by merging several exchanges (film rental bureaus) to become the first nationwide distributor of feature films; it kept 35 percent of box-office returns "as a distribution fee," and the producer received the remainder of the profits.[15] This emerging system of "distributor-financed film production" and control proved to be a symbiotic relationship for producers and distributors. By 1916, new studios, including Famous Players, Fox, and Universal, were playing a significant role in creating new distributors and exchanges. Distributors loaned money to independent producers to cover their production costs, giving them financial freedom to focus on creating high-quality films, and handled distribution through its network of exchanges and theaters. This system also aimed to eliminate the states' rights market, which existed beyond the control of the rational system of distribution and threatened profits for the studios.

In the states' rights method, individual exhibitors purchased exclusive distribution and exhibition rights for a motion picture in a particular territory during a specified time period; states' rights exhibitors could also purchase motion pictures outright from the releasing company. They then traveled with the reels, booking the title into local movie theaters—as well as into other exhibition venues, such as legitimate and vaudeville theaters, church basements, or lodge halls.[16] Itinerant exhibitors showed their reels until they physically deteriorated, keeping controversial material in circulation for extended periods of time.[17] They threatened the motion picture industry and its efforts at gaining respectability for film as an educational and uplifting medium while exploiting tensions around race, rape, urban disorder, a shadowy international "vice" trust, and the perils faced by white women adrift.[18] Exploiting the boundaries of good taste and the geography of censorship, states' rights exhibitors posed a threat to established local exhibitors, many of whom were struggling to be accepted as legitimate business operators invested in the welfare of their communities.

In 1913, the National Board updated its "Standards" document to include a new clause. It noted that, henceforward, the organization was "forbidding scenes or films which, because of elements frequently very subtle which they contain, have a deteriorating tendency on the basic moralities or necessary social standards."[19] This language was an opaque reference to the white slave pictures, or any scene in any other film that featured "the buying and selling of girls and women for the purposes of prostitution."[20] Until 1917, when the NB banned white slave traffic films altogether, its Review Committees attempted to distinguish films that exploited the white-slave-traffic trope as a means to present nudity and lewd behavior from those that were serious attempts to address social problems or provide sex education.

"IS ANY GIRL SAFE?"

Rev. Charles Parkhurst, unlike Canon William Sheafe Chase, his former colleague from the Society for the Prevention of Crime, had embraced "the possibilities of motion pictures as an instrument of history," and he partnered with Anti-Vice Motion Pictures to produce his own white slave traffic film, *Is Any Girl Safe?* (Anti-Vice Motion Pictures, 1916). *Is Any Girl Safe?* opens with Parkhurst delivering "a sermon against the dangers which beset young girls in a big city," and then the point of view shifts from Parkhurst's pulpit to "graphically" represent the urban dangers Parkhurst has just described.[21]

Bill Kerns, a young man embarking on his career as a procurer of prostitutes, sells factory worker Jean into "white slavery." Bill later discovers his own sister Marjorie in the arms of a "white slaver," and suddenly awakens to the immorality of his profession. His sister is on the verge of falling into the trade, but he rescues her and vows to "join the reformers" in the crusade against it. Bill stages a dramatic search for Jean, and when he finds her, he marries her. Bill even convinces Marjorie's pimp to make an honest woman of her, and everyone lives happily ever after.[22]

In its bid for legitimacy, *Is Any Girl Safe?* features leading figures in the fight against vice in New York City—in addition to Parkhurst, New York Police Department lieutenant "Honest Dan" Costigan of the Vice Squad also appears, as does District Attorney Edward Swann. As a condition of his sentencing, a notorious underworld figure, Yushe Botwin, cooperated with the filmmakers. Botwin had spent more than twenty years as the mastermind of a vice syndicate that connected New York City to upstate New York as well as New Jersey; his procurers trawled movie theaters, schools, and other places where naïve and "foreign" girls congregated.[23] Eschewing older techniques, like drugging "ignorant young girls," Botwin's cadets "simply [took women] to gay restaurants and dance halls . . . about town in automobiles, and . . . dazzle[d] them with the 'possibilities' of a life beyond their homes," easily seducing them into prostitution in the process.[24] *Is Any Girl Safe?* tapped into ongoing fears about women adrift, but the moral panic indicted consumer culture as much as it did lecherous men.

The NB Review Committee screened *Is Any Girl Safe?* in late 1916, during a period of intense scrutiny of white slave traffic films. The NB Review Committee that screened *Is Any Girl Safe?* acknowledged that the picture largely dealt with "the subject of white slavery," but did not find "any scenes of a sensuous character or that are suggestive or that would tend to degrade moral standards." As there was technically "nothing objectionable" about the film, the Review Committee passed it, even though the reviewers unanimously agreed it was "a worthless exhibition which had no education value." The distributors were free to book *Is Any Girl Safe?* bearing the NB's seal.[25]

Soon after the movie opened in New York City, License Commissioner George Bell sought an injunction to prevent future exhibition. He justified his decision by pointing to the fact that *Is Any Girl Safe?* was a "white slave" film, a genre that produced "a thoroughly bad effect."[26] Justice John Cohalan of the New York State Supreme Court agreed, preventing its further exhibition in the city. Although the film contained title cards defining (and defending) its contents as "literally a picturized sermon," Judge Cohalan argued that it "offend[ed] public decency and tend[ed] to the injury not only of the young of the community, but of all persons who witness it." Cohalan's decision formed the "basis for action" for Bell to move against controversial motion pictures in the future.[27] The decision, coming from the NB's backyard, also lent credence to the criticism that the board was too lenient in screening motion pictures for objectionable content.

Anti-Vice Motion Pictures, which was distributing *Is Any Girl Safe?* through the states' rights method, promptly withdrew the film from New York City and booked it for exhibition at the Majestic Theatre in Boston.[28] A week after the New York City showings ended, the *Boston Globe* reported that the "vice crusade film that created something of a sensation in New York City" was coming to Boston. *Is Any Girl Safe?* promised "startling revelation of the horrible truths of an abhorrent practice, presented with dramatic force, yet shorn of vulgar or repulsive details." According to the *Globe*, the film would educate parents about the "methods employed by vultures of society in drawing innocent and unsuspecting young girls into their nets," thereby helping them guard their daughters from procurers.[29] A couple of days later, the *Globe* gave the film an exemplary review, commending its "impersonal and purely objective" approach to the topic of white slavery and lauding its framing "device"—the detached, documentary-style telling of the fall of women. It had presented the subject, according to the *Globe*, "without any of the vulgarity which might easily dominate such a film."[30]

In an effort to preempt controversy over the film in Boston, McGuire contacted John M. Casey, the city's license commissioner. Despite Rev. Parkhurst's top billing, McGuire warned, the picture did exploit the boundaries of good taste; he suggested that Boston's new censorship board supplement the NB's review with one of its own "to determine whether the opinion . . . is in line with local sentiment." After all, McGuire said, he did "not wish to be placed in the position in regard to this picture of having His Honor feel that the National Board has made an error."[31] However, Boston's mayor, James Curley, permitted the exhibition without a supplemental screening. Soon after the film's debut, he received several complaints about it, however, and he revoked the Majestic Theatre's license. The next day, the three-member Boston Board of Censors screened the film and unanimously upheld the license suspension, "thereby automatically remov[ing] the film from presentation in Boston." The theater manager called the decision "an outrage."[32]

Casey contacted McGuire about *Is Any Girl Safe?* and warned him that the Boston censors thought the National Board had become "quite lax in their duties and should tighten up." In particular, they had objected to a scene in which "the colored maid in the house of prostitution" takes a "vial from her pocket, pulls the cork from it with her teeth and pours the contents in the cup." Casey could not believe the Review Committee had allowed the picture to include "an actual act of drugging," as he "was of the impression the Board never approved" such things.[33] The Motion Picture Exhibitors League of Massachusetts supported the Boston board's decision, arguing that the "transient exploitation of sex problem pictures" that "haunt[ed] the very borderline of obscenity" should not be shown publicly. In making this statement, the MPEL was clearly trying to curry favor with the public and the censors and shift the blame for the controversy to itinerant exhibitors, who were not members of the MPEL.[34]

In response to all of this, the National Board conducted a survey on the topic of white slave traffic pictures in the communities of "representative exhibitors throughout the country from Maine to California and from Minnesota to Louisiana," and "nearly five-sixths of the responses showed that the patrons . . . did not want such films." In response to the question, "Do you approve of the exhibition of white slave films?," many respondents used phrases such as "'Never,' 'I most assuredly do not,' 'Positively no' and 'Not in our houses.'" To better reflect public opinion, and in an effort to avoid further public criticism of its methods and integrity, the NB's executive board announced a ban on the genre to take effect in January 1917. It issued a special bulletin announcing that "no picture hereafter will be passed by the National Board which is concerned wholly with the commercialized theme of 'White Slavery,' or which is so advertised as to give the impression that it is a lurid 'White Slave' picture."[35] Despite the ban, itinerant states' rights exhibitors kept white slave traffic titles in circulation, leaving enraged viewers and pro-censorship sentiment in their wake. These exhibitors functioned outside of the emerging disciplining systems of major studios, exploiting sensitive topics and the emerging geographical boundaries of motion picture censorship for profit.[36] For the National Board, the threat was not so much about morals as about the danger that states' rights exhibitors traveling with white slave traffic pictures posed to the fragile consensus against legal censorship, particularly in the South.

THE ATLANTA BOARD OF CENSORS

At the dawn of the twentieth century, Atlanta emerged as "the melting pot" of the South. In the demographic shifts that took place during Reconstruction, the "Gate City" had attracted rural dwellers in search of economic and social opportunities. As a destination for black and white migrants alike, it saw a rise in population from 89,000 in 1900 to 150,000 in 1910. Most of the new arrivals were single men and women between the ages of eighteen and twenty-five, and the black population increased to nearly 40 percent of the total by the early twentieth century.[37]

Along with Atlanta's changing racial demographics came new class distinctions and changes in the composition of the labor force. The number of white women working outside the home grew at an unprecedented rate—increasing from 2,381 in 1890 to 9,352 by 1910. This growing reliance on wage work among white women added to the perception among white men that they were losing social status; they could no longer afford to be their family's sole breadwinners. As further evidence of the eroding racial hierarchy, according to the historian David Godshalk, white Atlantans needed only look to the Five Points neighborhood in the city center, "where 'fallen women' lived in bordellos and cheap houses of assignation, where visibly drunk women walked the streets, and where unescorted daughters and wives might appear and disappear among large crowds." Around Decatur and Peachtree streets, more interracial, working-class socializing occurred. Saturdays were particularly busy, as it was payday, and Atlanta's black and white working class took advantage of the city's amusements, such as "mean" saloons and cheap theaters. Rural dwellers also came to the city for weekly errands and city pleasures. Godshalk argued that "these twin images of white women and 'strange' black men adrift became powerful metaphors for the social disruptions and cultural dislocations wrought by Atlanta's growth."[38] Elite Atlantans responded by enacting increasingly segregationist measures and allowing the white working class to mete out physical violence.

Racial tensions only increased during the first decade of the twentieth century. In 1905, a fight broke out among black and white audience members during a production of Thomas Dixon's stage play *The Clansman*. Following the lynching scene, black audience members booed and hissed with disapproval; the police were called to the theater and arrested a black audience member.[39] Local newspapers frequently fanned the flames of racial animosity.

With the city already on edge, on 22 September 1906 the newspapers reported four alleged attempts by black men to rape white women, and mobs of white men and boys responded by beating and stabbing black Atlantans in the streets. Walter White, who would later become executive secretary of the NAACP, was thirteen years old when the Atlanta race riot occurred. In his autobiography, he recalled that "the inflammatory headlines in the *Atlanta News* and the more restrained ones in the *Atlanta Constitution* which reported alleged rapes and other crimes committed by Negroes" had become more frequent in the weeks leading up to the riot.[40] The riot also occurred in the context of an inflammatory gubernatorial race in which one of the candidates, Hoke Smith—who would later cosponsor federal motion picture censorship legislation—proposed disfranchising black men as part of his platform.

In the aftermath of the riot, Atlanta's white city fathers decided the solution to "the negro problem" was the segregation of all public accommodations.[41] The public library, department stores, restaurants, schools, hospitals, and movie theaters, "like all aspects of life in Atlanta," would now exclude black participation.[42] As Siobhan Somerville has argued, the racial segregation of movie theaters "acted as an imagined defense against the powerful myth of black men's sexual threat to white women."[43]

White slave traffic films could be viewed from multiple perspectives, including subversive ones. Young women in northern cities may have found the melodrama and danger overblown and amusing, whereas white southern audiences may have found the films attractive because they identified with the idea that young white women needed to be protected from danger. The controversy over the white slave traffic genre coincided with the emergence of the so-called "girl problem" in Atlanta in the 1910s, according to historian Lee S. Polansky: to add to the frequent allegations of black men raping white women in Atlanta's newspapers, there had been a spate of stories about "young girls behaving in rebellious ways"—sneaking out to the movies, meeting boys, necking in public, and dancing in juke joints, for example.[44] Historian Natalie J. Ring noted that the term "white slavery" was also used to describe the deplorable conditions in which young white children often worked. In the early twentieth-century South, cotton was "king," and the one-crop culture enslaved many poor white farmers in debt peonage; other poor whites worked in the cotton textile mills and factories of the New South, which was no better.[45] The risks that factory work posed to young white women included sexual violence, as the murder of a thirteen-year-old pencil factory worker, Mary Phagan, made clear to Atlantans in April 1913.[46] In the South, white slave traffic pictures echoed the fears and the narrative structure of rumors that often preceded a lynching: a young, innocent white woman sexually sullied by a dark man—Jewish or African American. Southerners had an insatiable demand for such pictures during this period of riots, lynchings, and the legal fortification of white supremacy in the 1910s and 1920s.

Ultimately, worries about "race suicide" and white sexual degeneracy intersected with concerns about motion picture theaters and content in Atlanta—particularly as young white women were supposed to produce and educate future generations and exposure to controversial motion pictures might taint them in this role.[47] Pro-censorship sentiment in Atlanta emerged out of, and spoke to, impulses that were similar to those of Prohibition—the main goals being to protect white women and children from harm and to assert the dominant status of white men as controlled, temperate patriarchs.[48] The preoccupation of Atlanta's censors with sexual content both reflected and reinforced the fears of white racial degeneracy. In July 1913, the Atlanta City Council passed an ordinance "penalizing obscene pictures, lewd songs and like entertainments in moving picture theaters." It also "prohibit[ed] and penaliz[ed] the exhibition of obscene, immoral and indecent pictures and pictures unapproved by Censors of motion pictures" and prohibited the performance of "immoral, lewd or suggestive songs, dances, or like entertainment in electric or motion picture theaters." The newly empaneled Atlanta Board of Censors (ABC), coterminous with the Carnegie Library Board of Trustees, assumed responsibility for policing the city's screens.[49]

The secretary of the Atlanta Board of Censors, J. W. Peacock, contacted the National Board almost daily for assistance. After serving in the position for two years, he became frustrated that Atlanta-based distributors and exhibitors were still refusing to comply with his directives. The tools available to him, he complained, still did not allow for the disciplining of states' rights exhibitors.[50] Throughout Peacock's correspondence with McGuire, he expressed bitterness about movies that exploited sexual themes.[51]

Theda Bara's movie *The Serpent* (Fox, 1916) was one of the pictures that stirred up controversy in Atlanta for its sexually charged content. Directed by Raoul Walsh, the melodrama stars Bara as Vania Lazar, a young peasant woman in Russia. When a grand duke rapes Vania and murders her fiancé, his actions transform her into a bloodthirsty woman who desires to execute a revenge plan spanning the continent against him and his entire family. In the end, Vania awakens from her dream—much to the surprise of the audience. Walsh used the narrative device of the dream to show Bara's character engaged in a sexual and violent revenge fantasy.

The National Board required "seven eliminations to be made" on *The Serpent* prior to exhibition.[52] However, when *The Serpent* opened in Atlanta, "none . . . had been made," according to Peacock. The Atlanta board then contacted the local Fox exchange and "demanded" that the eliminations be made, "which resulted in a heated controversy with the Fox office." Rather than make the eliminations, the Fox representative told Peacock that the film "would be replaced" in Atlanta; Fox would send *The Serpent* to Birmingham, Alabama, instead.[53] McGuire promised Peacock he would address the issue with Fox's main office in New York City, "so that [the manager] can get in communication with his branch offices and see that such incidents do not recur in the future." As for the more immediate problem in Atlanta, McGuire advised Peacock to make the cuts himself and to keep the physical scraps he cut in his possession. Because Fox had entered into an agreement "to make all eliminations asked by the National Board," McGuire explained, "when such eliminations have not been made before the actual exhibition of the film, . . . this makes the eliminations themselves contraband." If Peacock kept the scraps, it would "make the reinsertion of such parts by the branch managers impossible," he said, "and save us considerable correspondence with other cities which are asked to inspect the pictures passed subject to eliminations."[54]

A month later, another film arrived in Atlanta with its offensive scenes still in place. *He Fell in Love with His Wife* (Paramount, 1916), directed by popular silent-era actor and director William Desmond Taylor, stars talented actress Florence Rockwell as Alida Armstrong, a young wife who discovers that her husband is a bigamist and a murderer. She leaves him and lives in a poorhouse until a man named James Holcroft hires her to work as his domestic servant. Before she will accept the job, Alida requires James to marry her, so as to not incite gossip about an unmarried couple cohabitating. Initially, the marriage is strictly a business arrangement, but they develop real feelings for one another. One day, Alida's estranged husband reappears, and James throws him off a cliff after a fight. Alida and James live happily ever after as a "real" married couple.[55]

The NB *Bulletin* listed several eliminations from *He Fell in Love with His Wife* prior to distribution, including the scene "in which the man is killed." Local exchange managers were instructed to "eliminate the actual shooting by the bigamist . . . from the point where he draws the gun to the point where the man staggers and falls," which "applies likewise to the flash back of this scene in the last scene." Peacock, discovering after the fact that distributors and exhibitors in the region had failed to comply with his directives, contacted McGuire. McGuire again contacted the noncompliant distribution company on Peacock's behalf, reminding its agents of the required eliminations.[56]

When McGuire learned that another film circulating in Atlanta, *The World Against Him* (Paragon, 1916), had "not [been] properly revised in accordance with the request of the National Board submitted recently," he sent a telegram to World Film Corporation, the distributing agent for the motion picture.[57] *The World Against Him* is about a cowboy, Mark West, who lives on a ranch with his disabled sister, Mary. Violet Ridgeway, an "Eastern socialite," visits the ranch, and Mark falls in love with her. In an effort to find happiness, Mark toils long hours to earn the money for an operation for his sister, so that he might be free to pursue Violet. During her surgery, Mary dies at the hands of the unscrupulous doctors, one of whom is engaged to Violet. After an "evil" Indian, a kidnapping plot, and a fight for Violet's heart, Mark and Violet flee over the Canadian border together to live happily ever after.[58]

The NB's Review Committee found *The World Against Him* to be unnecessarily violent; it featured several fight and murder scenes—not to mention a graphic and prolonged scene in surgery. McGuire asked World to "issue at once telegraphic instructions to the exchanges" to shorten a scene in the first reel "that showed the doctors getting ready to operate" on Mary, and the scene in the second reel in which Mary is shown slowly dying. In addition, McGuire asked World to issue instructions for "eliminat[ing] the actual shooting of the doctor by [Mark], cutting from the point just after the doctor seizes the gun. The doctor may then be shown lying in the chair with [Mark], gun in hand, standing by him."[59]

William Kelly of World Film's executive offices in New York City responded to McGuire saying that he had notified all of his branches to immediately make the edits to *The World Against Him*. He included a copy of the precise instructions he sent to exchange managers.[60] The instructions guided the technician to the "very end" of the first reel, "following the subtitle 'THE OPERATION,'" where "the scene of the two doctors preparing to operate must be cut in two." Kelly's instructions noted: "Remove a few feet from the beginning of this last scene." In reel two, the instructions asked the technician to locate the title card "THE VALLEY OF THE SHADOW," near "the center of the reel," and then "remove 7 feet of the beginning of the following scene." For the objectionable shooting scene, Kelly's instructions noted:

THE CUT IS MADE AS FOLLOWS:
Scene #3—*The first 6 inches of this scene*, where the gun is actually being fired, must be removed entirely. Two feet of the beginning of scene #4— where the nurse runs to the door, must be placed between scenes 2 and 3 where the six inches was removed.
CONTINUITY WILL RUN AS FOLLOWS:
SUB: "I'm going to give you the same chance for your life that you gave her."
Sc. 1—Lincoln and man standing back of table—talking.
Sc. 2—C.U. gun on table—hand reaching for it.
Sc. 3—Nurse runs to the door
Sc. 4—Man falling back in chair, smoke disappearing from gun
(THE ACTUAL FIRING OF THE GUN WAS REMOVED)
Sc. 5—Nurse standing at door—starts to open
Sc. 6—Lincoln standing in foreground—nurse enters.[61]

An exchange manager or local exhibitor in Atlanta may have looked at such lengthy and involved instructions and decided to leave the scene in, planning to feign ignorance of the instructions if Peacock became aware of the offense. Many considered Peacock to be incompetent, at best, and exhibitors in Atlanta may not have much cared about removing a shooting scene to please strangers in New York City. McGuire was not surprised; he confided to William Percy of Atlanta (a member of the NB's National Advisory Council) that people frequently took "exception to New Yorkers trying to suggest ways of handling a local situation, though they may have the best intentions in the matter."[62]

At this point, it dawned on McGuire that a trend was developing among exchange managers and exhibitors in the South. Given the fact that requested eliminations had not been made in *The Serpent, He Fell in Love with His Wife*, or *The World Against Him*, and when they were made, "the parts of the film eliminated" were not "turn[ed] over to Mr. Peacock," McGuire concluded that there must be "a desire to reinsert these parts" for exhibition elsewhere.[63] Exhibitors screened unedited films in one city, generating controversy around particular titles, and followed the publicity to get bookings in neighboring cities, only excising the NB-identified scenes when local authorities caught them in the act of showing the films still intact and required them to carry through with the cuts. This was not just happening around Atlanta; McGuire observed a similar pattern emerging in Tennessee, where the City Plan had been adopted in Memphis, Nashville, and Chattanooga. He told one manager that if the film companies wanted to encourage the establishment of local government censorship boards, "the right way to go about it" would be "to send out pictures not revised in accordance" with the National Board's recommendations.[64] But according to film scholar Max J. Alvarez, the issue of damaging motion pictures with permanent excisions was a "sensitive and explosive topic" for exchange managers, theater owners, and projectionists. Exchange managers "blamed theater owners for clipping out scenes for personal use or to add to their own film collections" before returning the reels, "rendering many pictures incomprehensible to audiences."[65] In addition, theater owners, projectionists, and even exchange managers may not have had the technical acumen to handle the kinds of editing jobs being requested by the NB and their home offices.

By August 1916, the Atlanta City Council had expanded the Atlanta Board of Censors' powers to include an enforcement mechanism. It had also adopted a "City Ordinance for a Motion Picture Commission," modeled on the NB's City Plan. The Atlanta ordinance "prohibit[ed] and penalize[d]" the exhibition of any "obscene, immoral, and indecent" motion pictures, as well as any "pictures unapproved by the [National] Board of Review of Motion Pictures."[66] The new law imposed harsh penalties on exhibitors, with fines of up to $200 or a sentence of public works service for up to thirty days for violations.[67] Mayor J. G. Woodward approved the measure on 10 August.[68]

Six months after Atlanta adopted the City Plan, Peacock discovered that a "local firm" was planning to exhibit *Warning! The S.O.S. Call to Humanity* (Photodrama, 1916), a movie the National Board had condemned.[69] Promotional materials for *Warning!* touted a script cowritten by Hal Reid, an acclaimed silent-era director, and an endorsement by Rev. Charles Parkhurst, who also "appear[ed] in an introduction to the film." It was intended as an educational film, and promotional materials claimed that the "strong theme" of white slavery was "handled with force and dignity." *Warning!*, the descrip-

FIGURE 4.1. *Rev. Charles Parkhurst*

tion said, showed "pure-minded and happy school girls . . . tempted by keepers of candy stalls near the gates of the very establishments which are supposed to be fitting them for the stern duties of life." Its moral lessons "should strike home in every household."[70]

The NB Review Committee that first screened *Warning!* disagreed with this assessment and sent the film to the General Committee for further review.[71] The NB review secretary, W. M. Covill, noted that the last two reels of the film dealt with the issue of white slave traffic, showing the "methods by which innocent victims are trapped," such as "selling candy on the street, peddling of drugs, and fake hair dressing establishments."[72] The General Committee voted to condemn *Warning!* in full because members did "not believe that any good [would] be accomplished" through public exhibition of such a film. "On the contrary it will constitute a pandering to morbid curiosity."[73]

The Photodrama Company appealed the NB's decision and submitted an edited version of *Warning!* for rescreening in December 1916. Rev. Parkhurst personally appeared before the General Committee on behalf of the film. Several of the reviewers noted that they felt uncomfortable having Parkhurst present, but that did not stop them from denouncing his latest motion picture. Robert Crosby, the head worker of the University Settlement Society in New York City, described *Warning!* as "a mighty poor sermon" that presented "muddled, confused issues." The superintendent of schools for New York City, Henry E. Jenkins, rejected Parkhurst's claim that "the picture was intended for the protection of young people in the slums." In fact, "the picture disgusted me—disgusted me absolutely," Jenkins admitted. E. A. Moree, director of the Atlantic Division of the American Red Cross, agreed; after working as a "police court reporter for some years" in Manhattan, he had learned that "a whole lot of this stuff about poison candy, poison needles and the sale of girls is the result of very fervid imaginations"—and usually, "hysteria." The National Board upheld its original decision, and in its January 1917 *Bulletin* listed *Warning!* as condemned.[74]

Within two weeks, an exhibitor in Atlanta requested permission from the ABC to exhibit Parkhurst's film. McGuire contacted the Photodrama Company of New York on Peacock's behalf, but its representatives denied that *Warning!* was in circulation anywhere. Mr. Savini, the Atlanta exhibitor requesting permission to show the film, claimed that the motion picture in his possession did not feature Parkhurst, but was "a different picture" entirely. Peacock asked Savini to submit a "synopsis of picture," which revealed that the version of *Warning!* in his possession was, in fact, Parkhurst's picture. Peacock again sought McGuire's guidance. McGuire explained that *Warning!* had been condemned and that the NB would "not see its way clear to reconsider its action."[75] He shared a theory: "Personally I think that they are just trying to show the picture to the Board in any old shape in order that we pass it and then they are going to . . . afterwards put in parts of the film."[76] In other words, McGuire believed that unscrupulous exhibitors would agree to make any changes suggested by Peacock, and leave in—or reinsert—the offending scenes and title cards. McGuire became increasingly concerned that moving pictures with sexual content, in particular, would leave significant pro-censorship sentiment in their wake, particularly among religious southern audiences.

Meanwhile, Savini wired Peacock "requesting action," saying that he intended to immediately release Parkhurst's film across the South. The Atlanta Board of Censors "declined approval" for the exhibition based on the synopsis that had been provided and the NB's earlier condemnation. Savini advertised in the *Atlanta Herald* anyway, touting *Warning!* as "a white slave film." Additionally, according to Peacock, *Warning!* was already "in circulation in this section of the country (but not in Atlanta)." Dan Webster, a states' rights exhibitor, was booking *Warning!* "in Birmingham and vicinity" and had "just returned from a tour of the Carolinas."[77] Atlanta's adoption of the City Plan may have cleaned up exhibitions within the city limits, but it pushed states' rights exhibitors into the rest of the southern market. They looked for audiences wherever they could in their attempt to profit within the emerging geography of censorship.

In response, McGuire issued a preemptive strike and contacted his southern allies, excluding exhibitors and exchange managers through a mass mailing. Municipal officials and activists in Alabama, Georgia, North Carolina,

Tennessee, Virginia, West Virginia, Kentucky, and Mississippi received a letter explaining that *Warning!*, which "was recently condemned" and "deals with white slavery," was in circulation in their jurisdictions. Correspondents were asked to notify the National Board and, more importantly, complain to the local exhibitor if they encountered *Warning!* in their area. States' rights exhibitors could awaken audiences to the need for legal censorship, but the National Board could try to preempt that, and invited citizens to adopt its methods or invoke its name.

As the industry continued to strive for respectability, major studios exploited the states' rights method. Motion pictures that the NB's Review Committee had rejected as controversial, or that required significant edits, might be sold on the states' rights market rather than distributed nationwide. Production companies like Lasky and Paramount did not want to besmirch their own good names with controversial material, but as businesses, they did want to recoup their investments. *A Mormon Maid* (states' rights, 1917) is one such example. Although the film claimed to be "based on the authentic records of the practices of Mormonism," it was little more than a thinly veiled attempt to exploit polygamy and anti-Mormon sentiment for profit.[78] At the beginning of the film, elder Darius Burr and his adherents save John Hogue, his wife, and their daughter Dora from attack by "savage" Indians. Burr and his sect, the Avenging Angels, sport costumes emblazoned with an "all-seeing eye" that resembles those worn two years earlier in *The Birth of a Nation* by characters who were playing members of the Ku Klux Klan.[79] According to film historian Tom Rice, *A Mormon Maid* was advertised in Kansas as a sequel to *The Birth of a Nation*, and "reviews suggested that the reuse of the Klan costume from *Birth* . . . provide[d] 'added interest'" for audience members, and that "with 'intelligent use' of the costume in advertisements, which often featured a robed rider on top of a horse, 'exhibitors could do a lot of business.'" Indeed, said Rice, in their efforts to capitalize on the success of *The Birth of a Nation*, producers and exhibitors were employing Klan imagery in "ever more unusual contexts."[80] After the Hogue family joins Darius Burr's community, Dora (played by Mae Murray, the girl with the bee-stung lips) falls in love with Burr's acolyte Tom Rigdon. However, Burr decides he wants Dora to become one of his many wives, and unless she agrees to marry him, her father will be forced to take a second wife. Dora consents to the marriage, for her family's sake, but "tells the assembled group that she cannot marry the Apostle" because she isn't a virgin.[81] Burr forces her father to take a second wife, and her mother subsequently commits suicide. After several convoluted plot twists, Dora, Tom, and her father are finally freed from the clutches of the Mormons.[82] Because the risk of offending Mormons and drumming up pro-censorship sentiment outweighed any possible profits, both Paramount and

Lasky decided not to distribute the film. Lasky pulled out of the deal so late that some prints of *A Mormon Maid* bore his company's name even though it was distributed on the states' rights market.[83]

D. W. Griffith received a telegram from an executive at the Swanson Theatre Circuit in Salt Lake City, Utah, warning about the support being generated by *A Mormon Maid* for censorship legislation in Utah and Colorado. Griffith became involved in the effort to suppress *A Mormon Maid*, perhaps because it copied his Klan uniform's aesthetic, or drew unfavorable connections between Mormons and the Klan. Just as likely a reason was that Utah was home to a large and profitable theater circuit (with several large theaters in Salt Lake City, two in Ogden, and one in Provo) that was frequented by the large immigrant and working-class populations of the nearby mining communities. Salt Lake City was also a major distribution point for motion pictures exhibited in the West; after running in Salt Lake City, films were shipped to smaller cities and towns in Utah as well as in Arizona and Colorado. Furthermore, the Utah state legislature and Salt Lake City's City Council were both considering punitive motion picture censorship legislation. The state-level proposal would have created an official board of censors, which would have been authorized to charge exhibitors a reviewing fee of $2 per reel. That would have amounted to fees of more than $10 a day for theater owners.[84] Salt Lake City's exhibitors, who regarded this amount as an unfair economic burden, contacted Griffith and the National Board for assistance.

McGuire dispatched traveling lecturer Mary Gray Peck to Utah following the alarm raised by *A Mormon Maid*. She discovered that two prominent local GFWC members, Mrs. George M. (Isabel Gerry Dame) Bacon and Mrs. John Malick, opposed legal censorship: "They believe[d] that in cooperation with the National Board of Censors the several cities [in Utah] are equipped to deal with the matter more effectually than is the state." They had already protested a bill in Salt Lake City's City Commission, convincing Mayor W. Mont Ferry to "obtain the free bulletin service of the National Board . . . and cooperate with the National Board in the matter."[85] The clubwomen had also appeared before the state legislature "opposing the bill . . . providing for the appointment of the state superintendent of public instruction as official censor." Malick presented a letter from Mayor Ferry and the city commissioners to the state legislators, who were "of the unanimous opinion . . . that municipal cooperation with the National Board of Review will result in ample protection against the exhibition of motion pictures which are inimical to good morals." Mayor Ferry and the commissioners concluded that "it is unnecessary, therefore, that any state legislation be enacted upon the subject." Shortly thereafter, the NB sent a letter to Mayor Ferry confirming Salt Lake City, Utah, as an official "City Plan" city.[86]

Ferry was Presbyterian, originally from Michigan, and formerly the head of the anti-Mormon American Party in Utah. When serving on the City Council, he and his bloc voted in the American Party's interests. Ferry was also president of American Silver Producers, a significant economic interest in the region. Salt Lake City and nearby Ogden were hubs of the silver industry as well as of cross-country train transportation. Silver industry executives supported motion picture amusements for their miners and workers. Motion pictures lured workers away from the saloons, and they did not harm workplace productivity the way a hangover did. Mrs. Malick was the wife of Rev. John Malick, the Unitarian minister in Salt Lake City; Mrs. Bacon was Protestant and a member of Salt Lake City's elite, often appearing in the society pages. They opposed motion picture censorship in part to keep the issue out of the hands of Mormon politicians, who supported the aforementioned punitive legislation.

Mr. L. Marcus, owner of Notable Feature Films, a Salt Lake City–based division of Paramount Pictures, reported to McGuire on the successful campaign to quash censorship in Utah. With the help of Malick and Bacon, he had earned "the approval of the Screen Club of Salt Lake City, the Film Exchange Managers' Association of Salt Lake City, and the Home and School League."[87] Together, they cooperated on selecting matinees, children's shows, and family shows for his theater chain. As a businessman reliant on his community for his income, he found this arrangement to be mutually beneficial. McGuire regarded Salt Lake City as a model of community cooperation: if more "local motion picture men should cooperate in giving [clubwomen] this voice," he wrote, "then you will have less cries for censorship on the part of the women's clubs throughout the country."[88]

Maternalist reformers were beginning to have a greater impact on the conversation about the censorship and regulation of motion pictures, and the industry was paying attention. By requesting special titles from local exhibitors and attending children's matinees and family programs in their communities, women—as reformers and consumers—had made their influence known to the motion picture industry. According to *Motion Picture World* in July 1916, Pathé had announced a new Gold Rooster program, which was expressly designed to generate more movies suitable for general audiences. Filmmakers were invited to make motion pictures for the new series.[89] Among the new productions were *Little Mary Sunshine* and *The Shine Girl*, which both became representative of the industry-wide effort to increase the respectability and appeal of motion pictures to middle-class audiences.

Little Mary Sunshine (Balboa, 1916) was a sentimental temperance film starring three-year-old Marie Osborne in the title role. Little Mary hides in a stranger's automobile after witnessing her alcoholic father beating her mother

FIGURE 4.2. *Gladys Hulette*

to death. Soon thereafter, the stranger, Bob Daley—who is also "addicted to the devil brew"—is thrown out of his own house by his fiancée. He stumbles to his car, where he discovers Little Mary, who is sleeping peacefully. Bob is so affected by Mary's story that he takes her home and lovingly cares for her, becoming a devoted father—and a teetotaler in the process. His fiancée even returns, and the three become a happy family. The film therefore shows the temperate life in a positive light and reinforces the sanctity of marriage.[90]

Also new to the Gold Rooster program was *The Shine Girl* (Thanhouser, 1916), which Pathé advertised as "just the type of picture for which the Women's Clubs have been asking and will undoubtedly be used as an example of the right sort of picture by those who are preaching 'better pictures without sex appeal.'"[91] Gladys Hulette, "five feet of cheerfulness," stars as the Shine Girl, an orphan who polishes shoes and tries to appease "grouchy and brooding souls" with her cheerful demeanor and beautiful smile. When she steals a loaf of bread to help her sick and impoverished neighbor, however, she is caught and taken to Children's Court. The young judge who hears her case, deeply moved by her story, pardons her. He even takes her to his family's country home upstate, "where she can have some real sunshine," and arranges for a kind couple to adopt her. In the meantime, the judge reconnects with his childhood sweetheart, who is unhappily married. The Shine Girl learns that they are planning to run away together, and she "bravely sets out" to stop the couple. When she finds them at the train station, she reminds the judge of his own words at her trial: "It isn't square to steal what belongs to someone else." The judge realizes the Shine Girl is right and returns to the city, lonely and unhappy. At the "next apple blossom time," he returns to the country and finds the Shine Girl "budding into womanhood." Despite the difference in age and status, the two fall in love, and the Shine Girl "promises to be his 'for keeps.'"[92]

In San Antonio the Texas Women's Club "arranged for a private showing" of *The Shine Girl* for prominent members of their community. After the screening, members raved about the film, telling a reporter that *The Shine Girl* was "'the cleanest, sweetest picture' they had ever seen." They wanted "more pictures of the sort" to be produced to "bring sunshine into people's lives."[93] Although women's club members were charmed by the May/December romance in *The Shine Girl*, however, boys and girls tended not to be interested in "clean" and "sweet" pictures. Victor O. Freeburg, a professor of the photoplay at Columbia University and NB Advisory Committee member, explained that "most girls are good," but "good girls do not want to see other good girls upon the screen. There's no interest, no fascination, in that for them." Freeburg cited Theda Bara's success as an example of this axiom: Bara's characters showed audiences "something different, vastly different, from the life they know." The medium of film allowed viewers to "do her deeds and live her life. Their emotions are enriched by that much."[94] Having vicarious experiences would not drive young women to rebel, or to run away from home, Freeburg asserted; rather, motion pictures offered a healthy release and taught viewers empathy. Nevertheless, maternalist reformers and pro-censorship advocates continued to dispute that position.

5 / "WHETHER YOU LIKE PICTURES OR NOT": THE GENERAL FEDERATION OF WOMEN'S CLUBS AND STATE CENSORSHIP LEGISLATION, 1916–1920

"MOST CLUBWOMEN DO NOT LIKE PICTURES," MRS. AMbrose N. (Frances) Diehl, chair of the newly formed Committee on Motion Pictures of the General Federation of Women's Clubs, announced at the organization's biennial meeting in June 1916 in New York City. But it had become women's "business to be interested in them." The Daughters of the American Revolution were already "interested in this big problem," as was the Women's Christian Temperance Union and parent-teacher associations nationwide. Diehl informed her audience that "whether you like pictures or not," they were "of vital importance to our community."[1]

Rev. Cranston Brenton, the new chairman of the National Board of Review, also addressed the clubwomen assembled at the GFWC Biennial. A professor of literature at Trinity College in Hartford, Connecticut, and a minister in the Episcopal Church, Brenton acknowledged that discerning viewers' "taste" might be offended by the "vulgarity, low comedy and grotesque humor" found in popular motion pictures, but said that was insufficient reason to advocate for censorship legislation. "The whole matter" was "not the problem of the manufacturer, not the problem of legalized censorship, but the problem of the community," he opined. If vulgar shows and low comedies played in neighborhood theaters, it was because demand existed for them: one simply needed to stop attending those shows, and they would disappear from the screens. Brenton urged the clubwomen to adopt a stance of "community cooperation" with their local motion picture exhibitors, aided by the National Committee on Better Films. He maintained that motion pictures constituted "the greatest single potential educational factor in the world, bringing life, education, amusement and cheer to a community." And the Committee on Better Films was "the only way to success." A "rapid question and reply" followed, during which the clubwomen pressed Brenton on everything from the legal principle of censorship to the allegedly corrupt relationship between the

NB and the motion picture industry. Through it all, Brenton maintained that "the basic principle of legalized censorship is undemocratic."[2]

Clubwomen were deeply divided on the issue of motion picture censorship, as women were not a unified force in this period, politically or socially.[3] For instance, Mrs. Charles W. Cartwright from Minnesota, the chairwoman of the Drama Committee and a member of the GFWC Special Committee on Motion Pictures, opposed legal censorship, arguing that it did "not protect sufficiently, according to reports of delegates from states where legal censorship now operates." Cartwright supported local control of motion pictures because "people in small towns are 'shocked' differently from people in cities. For this reason the same pictures cannot be selected for all communities."[4] Miss Helen Varick Boswell of New York City, chairwoman of the GFWC Special Committee on Motion Pictures, agreed. Instead of fostering "antagonism" toward the industry, she advocated "concerted action and cooperation" on the part of clubwomen and exhibitors to produce results that addressed "the immediate needs of the boys and girls." Boswell supported the National Board and urged clubwomen to join the NB or form local Better Films Committees.[5]

Next on the biennial program were presidents of State Federations of the GFWC with established motion picture programs. Mrs. Albert H. Hildreth, from Syracuse, New York, president of the New York State Federation, explained how her club had "urged" Governor Whitman "to sign the bill putting [motion picture] censorship under the Board of Regents" earlier in the year. (He vetoed it.) She assured the audience that women "have something to say as to what pictures our children shall see," and therefore, should be involved in the political conversation. Mrs. J. W. Allen, president of the South Carolina Federation, reported that her club endorsed the idea that "something must be done to encourage the showing of pictures that will not be harmful and degrading in their influence on young people." However, "just how to accomplish these things is not yet clear."[6]

Diehl announced that her Committee on Motion Pictures planned to conduct "a survey to 'see what it was all about.'" To approach this enormous task, she requested that local clubs begin "organization work." The Committee on Motion Pictures' plan required each State Federation to appoint a state motion picture chairwoman, district chairwomen, and individual club chairwomen. Once that structure had been created within the GFWC, Diehl's committee would begin distributing lists of films "to everybody who asks for them, to every Chairman, and, in fact, to everyone interested in better pictures." Diehl's "organization work" would replicate the National Board's work, but with clubwomen in positions of authority.[7]

The GFWC motto, "Unity in diversity," often remained more of an aspiration than a reality. An important distinction existed between GFWC clubs that identified primarily as "volunteer clubs" and those that identified primarily as "cultural clubs."[8] Volunteer clubs predominated in northern cities and tended to have a younger, pro-suffrage cohort that supported a variety of causes. The Oregon Federation of Women's Clubs exemplified this model. Professional women, many of whom were single, composed its membership; many of them worked in municipal government and state agencies. One member of the Oregon Federation was Millie R. Trumbull, for example, who was also the secretary for the Oregon Child Labor Commission.[9] Influential cultural clubs included the Richmond (Virginia) Woman's Club and the Atlanta Woman's Club. Both had been founded in the late nineteenth century as all-white, elite women's spaces, counterparts to private men's clubs such as the Commonwealth Club in Richmond. The buildings in which these clubs met functioned as important public gathering places for white urban women, and they regularly convened in them for lectures, art exhibits, and afternoon teas accompanied by live entertainment.[10] The Richmond Woman's Club focused on programs for its members' own enrichment—for example, lectures from distinguished professors, reading and study groups, and art lessons and opportunities to perform in drama clubs.[11] Depending on the social and political context in their hometowns, cultural clubs with older members might be reluctant to take on seemingly political work—such as motion picture censorship issues.

Throughout its history, the GFWC had maintained that it was not a political organization and would not become "a playground for political parties."[12] The organization refused to take an official position on women's suffrage before passage of the Nineteenth Amendment. Some GFWC members were directly involved in the campaign for the federal suffrage amendment and members of the National American Woman Suffrage Association (NAWSA), but opinions on suffrage varied widely among clubwomen. Southern women tended to oppose the federal amendment but sometimes supported state suffrage amendments.[13] Many older members refused to discuss the issue at all, insisting that politics were not women's concern. By 1920, when women received the right to vote, there were approximately 40,000 clubs in the GFWC, representing 2 million members—rivaling the size of the American Federation of Labor.

At the close of the 1916 biennial, Mrs. Percy V. (Anna) Pennybacker, president of the GFWC, noted that the motion picture issue had not been resolved, and that state clubs remained "divided as to the best approach." She suggested that clubwomen return home and "make a survey of the question of the motion picture, and report what seems to be the wisest plan of action." They would reconvene at the 1918 biennial, to be held in Hot Springs, Arkansas. In the interim, members of the Committee on Motion Pictures would file their report and issue their recommendations to the executive board at its 1917 meeting in New Orleans.[14]

"MOTION PICTURES NOT GUILTY": THE NATIONAL BOARD CONFRONTS THE GFWC

Following the 1916 GFWC Biennial, an industry publication, *Motion Picture News*, carried the headline, "Women's Clubs Go on Record Against Censorship." In a tone of palpable relief, the article explained that although "censorship is twice mentioned" in the GFWC's report, "in neither instance is it apparently looked upon by the clubwomen with much favor." "A national demand for better conditions is evident," the magazine reported, but that demand was based on "the peculiar danger to the adolescent of a large percentage of the films now being displayed upon the screen." The article concluded that "a great opportunity" had emerged "for a better understanding between the club women of the country and the motion picture producers as to the immediate needs of the boys and girls."[15] The National Board was not as optimistic about the new development with the GFWC as *Motion Picture News* was. It responded to GFWC members' claim that motion pictures caused delinquency and criminality by continuing to promote its Better Films Committee and commissioning another in-depth study to debunk those causal claims.[16]

The NB had already conducted numerous surveys of the motion picture problem since its founding study in 1909, "Cheap Amusements." In 1915, members of the board conducted a survey of students at Horace Mann, the laboratory school associated with Columbia University's Teachers College. The survey included fourth-, fifth-, and sixth-grade boys and girls as well as girls in their first year of high school. The questionnaire asked: "How often do you attend motion picture shows?"; "What kind of pictures do you like best?"; "Which do you prefer, motion pictures or vaudeville?"; and "Would you like to have a children's motion picture house in your neighborhood?" The results revealed that fourth-graders preferred "war pictures," whereas fifth-graders liked "comic pictures." Sixth-graders enjoyed "scenes of adventure," and first-year high school girls preferred "historical pictures." The respondents also indicated an overwhelming preference for the movies over vaudeville, as "about half of the students surveyed attended a movie once a week or once a month." Most significantly, the NB concluded from the data that the movies had not caused any aberrant behavior in children. However, the board failed to account for the survey's small sample size, or the fact that results may not have been replicable in other regions—or even another neighborhood in Manhattan, for that matter.[17]

The NB's desire to convince—or silence—its opponents in the GFWC guided its research agenda. In early 1917, after the GFWC launched its nationwide survey, the NB commissioned a comprehensive investigation of motion pictures and nickelodeon theaters to study their influence on rates of juvenile delinquency, focusing on New York City. The executive board hired Edward Barrows, an investigator for the People's Institute, to lead this research. Barrows's résumé included work for the National Child Labor Council, the Russell Sage Foundation, and the West Side Recreation Committee.[18] He and John Collier had coauthored *The City Where Crime Is Play* for the People's Institute in 1914, for which he "had occasion to look into the part the movie theatres played in the annals of juvenile crime." Barrows explained that although "policemen, judges and reformers" often held the movies responsible for "the commission of crime" by children, in his own investigation he had identified "only a very few cases" in which that connection could be sustained "by any actual facts." Although he had uncovered "a number of cases in which the children [admitted] in court that they got their ideas from the movies," upon further investigation Barrows had concluded that the connection had been "put into their heads" either by "the arresting officers or adult acquaintances." The children themselves, Barrows noted, were not "keen enough analysts to know whether or not they really were so influenced" by motion pictures.[19]

Barrows conceded that boys, particularly those who were "weak-minded and impressionable, and possessed a lawless instinct," could be adversely influenced by exposure to "melodramatic, garish motion picture dramas dealing with crime, burglary, and other situations heroic to youth." However, he also acknowledged that "if the movies were abolished to-day, the same erratic children that are led to crime through the movies would be influenced by the next most sensational thing which existed." Therefore, he reasoned, "you cannot make a case against bad movies without thereby making a case of equal strength for the good movie."[20]

Barrows therefore confirmed the NB's suppositions about the relationship between motion picture content and juvenile delinquency in New York City. Next, the board conducted a nationwide survey of probation officers and juvenile justice officials working in Children's Courts. The survey asked a series of questions about the effect that respondents believed motion pictures had on juvenile crime in their jurisdiction.

The NB survey began by asking if local records "show[ed] any cases where the delinquency of the young person can be directly attributed to the influence of any particular motion picture film." If so, the survey clarified, this did not refer to "attendance at a particular theatre, but the direct influence of a particular film." The NB acknowledged that, "in some cities . . . children are allowed indiscriminate attendance" at theaters where "the films themselves may be entirely unobjectionable, but the physical surroundings . . . may influence them toward delinquency." Therefore, the survey requested that the official identify other possible contributing factors in the child's development, such as "the realm of heredity, environment, etc." that may be responsible for delinquent acts. Finally, the survey asked respondents to compare the "number and character of juvenile offences" prior to the "advent of motion pictures," to the past twelve months, "point[ing] to any conclusions as to the effect of motion pictures on the conduct of young people." The compiled results were distributed as a pamphlet, "Motion Pictures Not Guilty." Unbeknownst to the respondents, all of the questions were iterations of the same claims made by ministers, clubwomen, and other pro-censorship activists.[21]

After assessing the evidence and compiling the responses, the NB confidently denied that any connection existed between motion picture content and the alleged rise in juvenile delinquency. "Motion Pictures Not Guilty" declared that, after "an extensive investigation as to the effects of pictures on young people . . . only five probation officers stated that . . . motion pictures were to blame for juvenile delinquency." Moreover, "two out of those five cases were in states where there is state censorship."[22] If motion pictures were responsible for juvenile delinquency, then this evidence clearly proved that legal censorship was not the solution to the problem.

Despite the NB's surveys and efforts to debunk causal claims with regard to children and the movies, sensational cases continued to provide evidence that motion pictures did, in fact, provoke aberrant behavior in children. In August 1917, a twelve-year-old Brooklyn boy named Morris Cohen nearly died imitating a scene from *The Heart of a Hero* (World, 1916), a dramatization of Nathan Hale's role as a traitor during the Revolutionary War. The *New York Times* reported that after Morris and several friends saw the film, they decided to "re-enact [it] on the roof of a tenement house." Morris volunteered to "play the traitor." The boys set up a makeshift gallows, with the rope hanging over the cornice of the three-story building. The *New York Times* noted that if the rope had broken, death would have been certain. Morris would have fallen "sixty feet to the ground."[23]

The boy, who reportedly placed the rope around his neck himself, lost consciousness while dangling over the street. He had "carried out the sentence of the court with such impressiveness that [his playmates] ran in fear. Even the 'physicians' who had been assigned to feel his pulse could not stand the ordeal." A janitor spotted Morris's body and became so frightened that he, too, fled the scene. The speed with which he took off attracted the attention of

Morris's mother and neighbors, who rushed to the roof to see what was going on. The building's "janitress" rescued Morris, and he regained consciousness in the hospital. The police were waiting bedside to interview him. Because he refused to give up the names of his friends, they charged him with juvenile delinquency.[24]

The NB quickly hired an investigator, Frances Benzecry, to look into the matter, hoping there might be a counternarrative in the sensational Morris Cohen case. Benzecry, a member of the NB Review Committee, had previously worked as the sole female investigator for the New York County Medical Society; going by the pseudonym "Belle Holmes," and working undercover, she had sought treatment from "metaphysicians," naturopaths, and Christian Scientists who were suspected of practicing medicine without a license. For the NB's case, she started by interviewing Morris's mother, who disclosed that Morris "was a very wild boy." The neighborhood grocer confirmed the mother's assessment. Benzecry then visited the neighborhood movie theaters, where she confirmed that "shortly prior to Morris' escapade," three films containing war scenes had been exhibited. Upon Morris's release from the hospital, Benzecry interviewed Morris himself. He claimed to have been playing alone on the roof when he decided to place a rope around his neck the way he had seen it done in *The Heart of a Hero*. While adjusting the rope, he said he had "tripped and didn't remember anything further until he was in the hospital," reported Benzecry. She concluded her report with testimony from adults in Morris's life—"the janitress said that Morris was always in some kind of mischief, but was not really a bad boy." Morris's teacher "thought [he] was mentally defective as he was always doing what he ought not to do."[25] Benzecry exonerated *The Heart of a Hero* of any blame in this case.

The NB also dispatched Benzecry to investigate the case of three twelve-year-old girls who had been arrested for theft. In their case, police spotted one of the girls reaching into "a lady's handbag and taking some money out." She handed the money to her friend, who "ran away a short distance" before she was caught by a police officer and arrested. Benzecry interviewed all three of the girls for the NB: Ethel Brown, Diana Chaplin, and Eleanor Karppinen. Ethel told Benzecry that she rarely went to the movies, and when she did, her mother accompanied her. Benzecry concluded that Ethel was a very "bright girl" who had simply been in the wrong place at the wrong time.[26]

Diana, the girl who had been caught with the money, had initially told the police that she had never seen "a little girl or woman in the pictures steal from another person," but she later confessed to an officer that she had, in fact, seen such a picture, but she "didn't remember the name." Diana told Benzecry that she and Eleanor had seen a motion picture in which "a thief opened a woman's handbag, took something out of it and ran away," and Eleanor corroborated that story. According to Diana's parents, their daughter was "incorrigible," "crazy about the pictures," and frequently sneaked into nickelodeons "by the side door." She was already on probation from the Children's Court for an indefinite period of time, and her parents were attempting to place her "in a Jewish institution." When Benzecry interviewed Eleanor, she also admitted to sneaking into the theater through the side door when she did not have the price of admission. Just four weeks earlier, Eleanor had been arrested for "snatching a pocketbook containing one dollar from a small child." The judge had "censured" Eleanor and allowed her to go home with her mother. Benzecry discovered that Eleanor's mother was "ill in bed under a physician's care," and the Children's Court had already ruled that the home "was not the best place for her." According to Benzecry's sources, Eleanor would likely be "placed in a Catholic protectory."[27]

Unlike Ethel, Benzecry concluded, both Diana and Eleanor were girls "of the incorrigible type resulting from lack of proper guardianship." These girls had "a generally bad reputation" in the neighborhood; both had used "the excuse of having seen a robbery in a picture six months previously" to justify their pickpocketing scheme. Benzecry noted that children with "proper parental control and guardianship," like Ethel, "do not get into trouble."[28] Perhaps Ethel had lied—to her mother, the police, and Benzecry—about her role in the theft to preserve her own access to motion pictures. Perhaps Diana and Eleanor had felt intimidated during their police interviews and agreed with the suggestion that the "movies made them do it" when it was offered as an explanation for their behavior. Working-class children and families had complicated relationships to the police, social workers, and "friendly visitors" in the early twentieth century, with some parents inviting these agents into their homes to frighten their wayward children into behaving, or to take an incorrigible teenager off their hands for a few years.[29]

Despite the evidence presented by the NB in "Motion Pictures Not Guilty," the general public remained convinced that motion pictures were responsible for child crime, especially when they could cite stories of young neighbors like Morris Cohen or Diana Chaplin who had seemingly been corrupted by them. The NB executive secretary, W. D. McGuire, increasingly expressed frustration in his correspondence that he still had to debunk claims about the impact of motion pictures on children's moral, physical, and social development. After all, the NB had engaged and tested the question in several social scientific studies over its eight-year existence, all of which had been issued as pamphlets to individuals, organizations, and newspapers nationwide. None of those investigations had uncovered compelling evidence to support the causal power attributed to motion pictures. Would data ever be enough to win over those who suspected a causal relationship between motion pictures and juvenile delinquency—especially the clubwomen in places where they embraced maternalist authority, which was their entrée into the political realm in the first place?

When the GFWC's executive committee convened in New Orleans in 1917, the ad hoc Motion Picture Committee presented its interim study to the members. Mary Gray Peck attended the meeting; in addition to traveling on behalf of the NB, she had also helped the GFWC conduct its survey, "visiting a large number of cities, interviewing officials and various organizations." She had arrived at "the very definite conclusion that censorship was a bad proposition."[30] Peck recommended to the committee that the organization cooperate with the NB, rather than support legal censorship of any kind. Helen Varick Boswell, who chaired the Motion Picture Committee, agreed; she suggested that GFWC members form local Better Films Committees to implement children's programs locally and encourage improvements in the motion picture industry generally. Peck assured McGuire that "the [final] report of the committee," to be presented to the general membership at the upcoming GFWC Biennial in 1918, "was *opposed* to legal censorship."[31]

However, when the GFWC assembled in Hot Springs, Arkansas, in May 1918 for the biennial, Mrs. Albert E. Bulson, representing the Motion Picture Committee, advocated for the GFWC to support legal censorship. In her appeal, she told the audience the story of two boys, "habitués of the lowest theatres," who had allegedly "learned the techniques of crime" from *The Hidden Hand* series (Pathé, 1917), which dramatized "Jesse James and men of his ilk." One night, while being escorted home by two clubwomen, one of the boys had "eluded" his guardians and proceeded to "rob a grocery and a candy store, also another business place, cracking a safe and securing $8.53." After the clubwomen located him, they had "the Binet-Simon test made" on the two boys' "mentality" and arranged to have them both "sent to the Lapeer Home for the Feeble-Minded," where they may have been subjected to Michigan's eugenic sterilization policy.[32] She claimed that once the NB received word of the movement for state censorship in Michigan, "telegrams and letters came pouring in . . . with offers of speakers who would present the matter from the standpoint of the producer." She confessed that "the effort put forth by the National Board of Review of Motion Pictures to spread a propaganda against any kind of censorship helped to accomplish my conversion," and she had become an ardent supporter of legal censorship. While at the biennial, Bulson received word that "the police commissioner of Detroit" had "recently awakened to the fact that some sort of censorship is necessary and is having the police censor the movies." Bulson did not know at the time of her announcement that the Detroit Police Department had signed on with the NB.[33]

Mrs. Guy Blanchard, of the Chicago Women's Club, also presented at the

Hot Springs biennial, drawing on evidence from a report that had been prepared by the GFWC Department of Civics and Education, "What the State Surveys Have Revealed." The Illinois, Michigan, Arkansas, South Dakota, Rhode Island, West Virginia, and New York Federations had all completed surveys, and in aggregate they had revealed that "25% of the pictures shown were vicious and demoralizing and 46% were 'not worth while.'" Moreover, "criminal acts and questionable conduct . . . figure[d] in more than a third of the film stories." Rather than addressing the fact that only seven states had contributed to the survey data, Blanchard invited Miss Lutie E. Jackson of the Kansas State Censorship Board to join her on stage. Jackson "pleaded for the work of the women" in agitating for state censorship laws, because once "the protected area" was "widened," "the future of the children [would be] ensured against the stream of filthy suggestion constantly flashed from the uncensored screen."[34]

Finally, Bessie Leach Priddy of Michigan, chairwoman of the GFWC's Civics Department, reminded the assembled women that Frances Diehl's original Committee on Motion Pictures, which had been convened in 1916, had been temporary, and when its tenure had lapsed in 1917, the motion picture work had passed to her department. She then introduced Dr. Ellis P. Oberholtzer, the secretary of the Pennsylvania State Board of Censors, who urged the clubwomen to support state censorship legislation. He followed up his plea by exhibiting a reel of "cut-outs," featuring offensive scenes he had personally excised from popular motion pictures. Following these presentations, the attendees of the GFWC Biennial of 1918 were presented with a resolution "in favor of state censorship of motion pictures." By a show of hands, they voted unanimously to pass the resolution. It might have been difficult for some members to object under those circumstances.[35]

At least McGuire thought so; he remained convinced that the majority of clubwomen did not actually support legal censorship, and therefore could be easily organized to oppose it once they were back home. In a letter to the secretary of the Conference of Mayors of the Cities of New York, McGuire pointed out that neither Mary Gray Peck nor Frances Diehl had been able to attend the biennial meeting. Thus, the Committee on Motion Pictures had been represented "chiefly by Mrs. Blanchard of Chicago who had been fighting tooth and nail for state censorship in Illinois, and did not want the handicap of an adverse report" from the GFWC. Peck and the other GFWC members who opposed legal censorship had promptly resigned from the committee.[36]

McGuire may not be the most reliable narrator in this instance. In the absence of more detailed minutes or caches of personal letters, it is hard to say. It is interesting to note, however, that at the GFWC Biennial in June 1920, one of the proposed—and defeated—resolutions was on the "Censoring of Motion Pictures." According to the minutes, the resolution "request[ed] that the Congress of the United States provide for the proper censoring of all films before releasing them to be shown in any community for public entertainment," but "the motion LOST." McGuire had spotted an opportunity in this schism among organized women—if he could arrange funding, he could send more anticensorship clubwomen—ones with opinions like Mary Gray Peck's—to travel the country and organize their peers into Better Films Committees. In this way, the NB might be able to expand its own geographical coverage and prevent legal censorship from taking hold in the states.[37]

CENSORSHIP SENTIMENT IN VIRGINIA

Virginia was a battleground state for the National Board for over six years, beginning in May 1916, a month before the thirteenth GFWC Biennial. A. M. Gunst, a Richmond city councilor and a press representative for the Wells Theatre, alerted the NB to a growing movement for legal censorship in Virginia. Gunst requested that McGuire "rush special delivery all data" on the City Plan, which he intended to present to the Richmond City Council as an alternative to proposed censorship legislation. McGuire responded quickly; in addition to sending the literature, he offered to dispatch a representative who could explain why "local censorship is ineffective and unnecessary in view of work of National Board."[38] By 1918, both Richmond and Norfolk had adopted the NB's City Plan, owing in large part to the cooperation of the Wells Theatre circuit, one of the largest in the South, with theaters in Richmond, Norfolk, Atlanta, and New Orleans.

Richmond had emerged as a prominent industrial center and regional cultural capital in the late nineteenth century; by the turn of the twentieth century, it was the most densely populated southern city, with 85,050 residents concentrated in just five square miles.[39] In 1899, amusement entrepreneur Jake Wells opened the Bijou Family Theatre in the former Barton Opera House, home to a notoriously bawdy revue, and began the transformation of commercial amusements in Richmond. In 1907, Richmond's first nickelodeon, the Dixie Theater, opened on Broad Street; its success inspired many competitors to open nickelodeons nearby, and the area at Eighth and Broad streets came to be known as the Theatre District. By the 1910s, Wells was known locally as "Mr. Clean Entertainment" for bringing family-friendly, low-priced vaudeville and moving picture shows to Richmond. He and his half-brother, Otto Wells, operated theaters that showed special programs for children and families, guided by the NB's lists of selected films. Yet instead of being praised by city boosters, exhibitors had to continually defend themselves against ministers, legislators, and clubwomen, who blamed moving pictures for the city's imagined moral decline.[40]

During the long Progressive era, Virginia's social reformers shared many of their northern counterparts' concerns. In 1916, the Virginia General Assembly passed state prohibition, antigambling, anti–white slavery, and antiprostitution laws in what residents of the Commonwealth referred to as "The Great Moral Reform Session."[41] Clubwomen and other activist women became involved in campaigns to improve public education, health care, and city sanitation for Richmond's poor residents; others pushed for women's suffrage and a coeducational University of Virginia. A notable contingent of Virginia's Progressive women worked through the Ladies Memorial Association and the United Daughters of the Confederacy to commemorate the "Lost Cause" and promote white supremacy.[42] Taken together, these laws can be understood as the Progressive platform in Virginia, one that was increasingly interested in legislating moral issues.[43]

In July 1919, the NB received warning that State Senator G. Walter Mapp (D) planned to reintroduce a motion picture censorship bill when the legislative session opened in January 1920.[44] In anticipation of this, McGuire arranged to send Mary Gray Peck to Richmond to cultivate support for the NB's City Plan and Better Films Committee. McGuire assumed that Peck would share a worldview with Richmond's clubwomen that would allow her to change their minds, and she shared that assumption.[45] She noted that "most of the women interested in the subject" of censorship in Virginia were also "prominent suffragists," and, as it happened, she would be arriving "in Richmond on the same train with Mrs. [Carrie Chapman] Catt, who was due there for two speeches on the Ratification of the Federal Suffrage Amendment."[46]

Seemingly unbeknownst to Peck, however, many elite white Virginians—women and men—viewed federal women's suffrage with outright suspicion, regarding it as ill-suited to the South. Thomas Nelson Page, famous for his writings in the "Lost Cause" genre, spoke for many white Virginians when he wrote that the South had already "fought against . . . the question not only of the equality of the sexes, but the equality of the races."[47] Some southern women suffragists opposed the federal amendment and supported state amendments instead. As Adele Clark, the cofounder of the Equal Suffrage League (ESL) of Virginia, explained, one of the earliest and most ardent supporters of state suffrage amendments was a former Confederate soldier and member of the House of Delegates, a Mr. Young. He supported ratifying the Virginia state constitution to extend the franchise to women, but when the ESL tried to secure his support for the federal amendment, he replied: "Ladies, you cannot expect me to vote for anything federal. I still bear in my body a wound I received in Chancellorsville, and I would not vote for the federal government to do anything about the electorate."[48]

Arriving in Richmond under the banner of the National American Woman Suffrage Association may have harmed Peck's reputation before she even had the chance to talk about voluntary motion picture regulation and the movement for better films.[49] Peck soon learned that "the reform elements" in Virginia were among censorship's strongest supporters; she "could scarcely believe these [women] were reformers" as they stood in such "interesting contrast to the reformers of Boston."[50] Adele Clark, the ESL secretary, supported state censorship.[51] Mrs. Georgia May Jobson, president of the Social Service Federation of Richmond, also supported state censorship; she had worked tirelessly to unite several women's organizations in support of the Mapp Act for three successive legislative sessions. Nevertheless, Jobson took Peck to several meetings of local women's organizations to present the NB's point of view. State Senator G. Walter Mapp, author of the censorship bill, attended one of the talks, and Peck noted that he repeatedly tried to take the floor. She quickly cut him off, informing him that if he wished to learn about the NB's position, he needed to sit down and listen. "Being a Virginia Gentleman," she wrote, he complied. Peck proceeded, explaining that the NB opposed legal censorship "because it [was] non-representative and chaotic in essence." Instead, the NB supported "every sincere attempt to better conditions by means of co-operative censorship," mainly by "furnishing weekly lists of its pre-reviews" to established municipal government agencies, exhibitors, and local civic organizations, such as women's clubs.[52]

Following her tour of Richmond, Peck wrote to McGuire: "The censorship problem for the present is solved in the state of Virginia."[53] She noted that her meetings had been "informal and extremely friendly." However, she had seriously misjudged her audience. The Virginia clubwomen, although polite and receptive during the meetings, remained suspicious of the NB. They suspected that financial connections between the NB and the motion picture industry—and not a sincere interest in a cleaner screen—motivated the organization, and they were correct. After all, Peck was a paid employee of the NB, and a coalition of Virginia exhibitors had funded her lecture tour. Some Virginia clubwomen may have distrusted Peck's connections to the National American Woman Suffrage Association.[54] Moreover, the Virginia Federation of Women's Clubs (VFWC) had already been studying the "deleterious effect that moving pictures were having on the young people" since 1911, long before Peck arrived in Richmond, another fact McGuire and the NB overlooked.[55]

The Virginia Federation of Women's Club's Department of Civic Reform first passed a resolution on motion pictures in May 1911, during Richmond's theater-building boom, condemning "uncensored moving pictures and urg[ing] each club to take some action."[56] Mrs. J. Allison (Mary Gray) Hodges, who chaired the Virginia Federation's Department of Motion Pictures, presented the issue to the membership. A prominent Richmonder, Hodges had served as the president of the Richmond Woman's Club from 1916 to 1918, and she would go on to serve as president of the VFWC in 1923. She did not reveal to the clubwomen that she had been corresponding with the National Board and personally preferred its "selection not censorship" method. The assembled clubwomen voted to conduct a statewide survey of the movies before deciding on the best solution for Virginia.[57] In 1920, the Virginia Federation took up the motion picture problem anew, sending five hundred questionnaires to each club in the federation. Local clubs then appointed committees "to see every picture shown during that week" in 1920.[58]

The first section of the VFWC survey form, labeled "Concerning the Play and Plot," asked for the film's title and the name of the filmmaker. It also asked if the National Board had approved the film, as both Richmond and Norfolk used the City Plan. The form then asked nineteen additional questions about the film's content, including whether it portrayed "any obscenity, immorality or vulgarity," "infidelity or disregard of marriage vows," "objectionable drinking or barroom scenes," "prolonged objectionable love scenes," or "anything likely to contribute to the delinquency of the younger element." Finally, the form asked, "Does the play as a whole appeal to you as good or bad?"[59] The majority of the VFWC survey's questions targeted the moral character and content of the films, which allowed the clubwomen to stay, at least rhetorically, in what they considered their appropriate role as women, speaking on behalf of vulnerable viewers.

The VFWC questionnaire did not directly address racial themes or characters in the films, although this could have been due to the dearth of films featuring black characters at the time. Perhaps the clubwomen remained confident that "tradition" would continue to enforce racial segregation and, therefore, the issue did not need to be addressed directly. After all, the policies and practices surrounding southern moviegoing already strictly proscribed racial interactions. Segregation ensured that African Americans in Virginia had limited access to movie theaters; they typically had to attend separate shows or different theaters altogether. This pattern existed prior to passage of the Public Assemblages Act of 1926, which made the "mixing of audiences at public assemblages," including movie theaters, illegal.[60] In the period from 1910 to 1930, African Americans made up roughly 30 percent of Virginia's population—yet far fewer than 30 percent of Virginia's movie houses welcomed black audiences.[61]

When the VFWC compiled the data from its survey, it found that 90 percent of the pictures exhibited in Virginia were considered "satisfactory." The remaining 10 percent "were not really bad, they [just] were not suitable for young people." Based on this evidence, the clubwomen concluded that the moral condition of moving picture shows in Virginia was not so serious as to require legal censorship. Instead, they recommended that the VFWC and the exhibitors enter into a cooperative relationship through a Better Films Committee. But were the clubwomen really converted to the NB position, or did they arrive at this conclusion only after they realized how much political power they stood to gain from a voluntary regulation arrangement?[62]

Despite the professed willingness of the VFWC and the exhibitors to join forces with the NB and obviate the need for legal censorship, State Senator Mapp and his allies were not appeased. Mapp announced his intention to reintroduce his censorship bill in the 1922 legislative session.[63] The NB interpreted the reintroduction of the Mapp Act as an indication of Peck's failure, not of its own shortcomings. Were they truly unaware of the underlying issues that animated the censorship movement in Virginia?

G. Walter Mapp, representing the Accomac area on the Eastern Shore of Virginia, was widely acknowledged as "the leader of the moral reform element in the state senate" during the 1910s and 1920s. He headed the "dry" faction, winning passage of the state prohibition amendment in 1916, supported the bill against prostitution in 1916, and voted for women's suffrage in 1920. Throughout his career, he worked closely with many women's organizations, including the influential Women's Christian Temperance Union, which backed his censorship bill. Mapp was also an ardent white supremacist, supporting legislation to preserve "racial integrity" in Virginia. He believed that the "truest Anglo-Saxon strain of blood in the world, reverting to type in face and features . . . is to be found in the two Eastern Shore counties of Virginia."[64] Eugenics and the preservation of white supremacy motivated his efforts as well as those of many of Virginia's reformers.

Following the creation of the white nationalist Anglo-Saxon Club by eugenicist Earnest Sevier Cox and composer John Powell in Richmond in 1922, elite white Virginians increasingly supported legislation that dictated stricter race relations, which they understood as integral to maintaining moral and political order in the Commonwealth. Mapp was a great admirer of Powell's and a founding member of the Anglo-Saxon Club.[65] Taken together, the Mapp Act of 1922 on motion picture censorship, the Racial Integrity Act of 1924 banning interracial marriages, the Virginia Sterilization Statute of 1924, which permitted the sterilization of inmates at Virginia's mental hospitals, and the Massenburg Public Assemblages Act of 1926, prohibiting integrated groups in any public place, "even when that integration was fully voluntary," were all expressions of what historian J. Douglas Smith has termed "managed race relations."[66] By 1922, white Virginians were as openly concerned about racial management as they once were about protecting the vulnerable, and this influenced their opinion on motion picture censorship.

Virginians remained highly attuned to the perils of regulation from "carpetbaggers" into the twentieth century, and some observers regarded the anticensorship movement as an imposition of Republican Party politics on the South—and the NB as nothing more than a tool of the industry.[67] Progressive-era social activism succeeded when organizations cultivated local allies, built coalitions, and sustained that support over the long term. Although the NB's connections to northern reformers initially allowed it entrée to southern women's clubs, it continued to face obstacles because its members did not understand the fractious nature of women's political participation in Virginia and the role that the preservation of white supremacy played in the debate over censorship. This failure was compounded by the fact that the NB's board members had entered the debate in the midst of a political sea change, during which elite white southerners increasingly relied on the law to shore up the weakening traditions that had once enforced the racial hierarchy. McGuire decided that, in order to succeed in Virginia, he needed someone with "Southern connections" who knew "Southern people thoroughly" to deliver the anticensorship message.[68] After all, as Atlanta-based Paramount Pictures executive H. T. Jones observed, "things which originate and exist in New York seem to possess something of 'black magic' when brought to the South."[69]

6 / SOUTHERN ENTERPRISES:
BUILDING BETTER FILMS COMMITTEES
IN THE URBAN SOUTH, 1921–1924

WHEN THE PARAMOUNT PICTURES EXECUTIVE H. TURNER Jones first contacted the National Board in March 1921, he had inside information that censorship bills would be introduced in upcoming legislative sessions in seven southern states. Jones had identified the National Board's Better Films Committee as a viable alternative to legal censorship in the South—one that many members of women's clubs, who often supported censorship, also found acceptable. Southern Enterprises, a subsidiary of Paramount Pictures, was interested in suppressing support for state censorship and quashing itinerant exhibitors.

Paramount Pictures had been engaged in an active campaign to acquire exhibition spaces throughout the South in 1919 and 1920, "intimidating exhibitors" into selling theaters to Southern Enterprises, which was quickly becoming the exclusive Paramount distributor to eleven southern states.[1] Jones's job description included ensuring that Paramount exhibitors and distributors complied with local censorship organizations. In 1921, Jones and the NB executive secretary, W. D. McGuire, found common cause when "nearly one hundred measures relative to motion pictures were introduced in the legislatures of thirty-seven states."[2]

Like McGuire, Jones regarded the General Federation of Women's Clubs as a significant opponent in the campaign against legal motion picture censorship. Southern women's clubs had recently become "keenly alive to the harmful possibilities of motion pictures," Jones noted, and were "eager to initiate some movement for the betterment of the situation." "Due to ignorance and . . . unwise leadership," he alleged, clubwomen had "almost universally seized upon censorship as the only means leading to that betterment." However, Jones explained, "the Southern public is extremely ignorant of the activities and general nature of the National Board of Review." Therefore, he conceived of a partnership between Southern Enterprises and the NB to "di-

rect [clubwomen's] splendid efforts in wiser lines of endeavor"—namely, organizing NB-affiliated Better Films Committees. Executives at Southern Enterprises supported Jones's plan and committed to "supplying the Women's
Clubs of the seven Southeastern states with the Board's services and certain selected pieces of propaganda during a period of three months."[3] Jones
planned to equip southern clubwomen with "tools which can be used immediately" to improve motion pictures, "without the necessity for long delay and
Legislative fights." He inquired about a Speakers Bureau that "could be called
upon for propaganda work" among "the women's clubs."[4]

Although D. W. Griffith and Fox Films had donated to the NB in 1916–
1917 to support Mary Gray Peck's lectures, the Speakers Bureau never became an official department in the NB, or even a part of the regular operating
budget; rather, it depended entirely on donations. As the NB corresponding
secretary Alice B. Evans explained to Jones, "theoretically" the NB had a
Speakers Bureau, but "whenever we get a call for representation at a distance
the question of money comes up and we generally have to turn down the opportunity for that reason."[5] The NB was experiencing financial difficulties in
this period; the end-of-year Operating Statement in December 1921 reflected
a negative balance—and few concrete achievements.

NB records indicate that two months after his initial query, Jones traveled
to New York City to meet McGuire and other members of the executive board
in person. In meetings, they planned the details of their collaboration and so-
lidified their coalition and its goals—to eliminate the demand for state censorship throughout the South by organizing local clubwomen to form Better Films Committees. Upon returning to Atlanta, Jones wrote to McGuire to
tell him that "the home office" had approved the plan, and it was his "desire to
go forward with this work with the greatest possible speed." Southern Enterprises agreed to pay a salary and all expenses for the speaker.[6]

While Jones and McGuire were crafting their plan to co-opt the supporters
of censorship in the South, the New York State Senate was debating a motion
picture censorship bill. Governor Nathan R. Miller (R) had indicated that he
would sign the bill if it passed the Senate.[7] It was sponsored by Senator Clayton Lusk (R), a personal friend and political ally of Miller's. Lusk had made
a name for himself two years earlier as the chairman of the Joint Legislative
Committee to Investigate Seditious Activities, also known as the Lusk Committee. During the Lusk Committee's search for criminal anarchy in New
York State in 1919, its undercover agents had focused on Buffalo and New
York City, which both had substantial immigrant populations. It had raided
the offices of the Industrial Workers of the World (IWW), branches of the
Communist Party, and the socialist Rand School of Social Science. The Lusk
Committee had also blocked elected socialists from being seated in the New

York State Senate, and it had shared the names and addresses of alleged radicals with the FBI. Anxiety over immigrants and political radicalism informed the Lusk Committee's investigations and spilled over into the motion picture censorship bill under consideration.[8]

Lusk's motion picture censorship bill proposed the creation of a three-member censorship board with the "power to refuse a license to exhibition of films which in its opinion are 'obscene, indecent, immoral, inhuman, sacrilegious, or of such character that their exhibition would tend to corrupt morals or incite to crime.'"[9] Canon William Sheafe Chase had contributed to the content of the bill; the New York State Federation of Women's Clubs and the "drys," who supported the prohibition of alcohol, also backed the measure. To appeal to clubwomen upstate, Governor Miller even promised to appoint a "woman member of [the] regulatory board" if the pending legislation passed.[10]

Democrats from New York City decried the Lusk censorship bill as "un-American." State Senator John J. Boylan argued that such legislation took three men and "impose[d] upon them a task that would be beyond men with the wisdom of Solomon." Boylan noted that it would "be up to them, for instance, to standardize the screen kiss. How long should it last? Should it last a minute or only thirty seconds to pass muster?" Finally, he reasoned that if motion pictures were to be censored, then "the same rule should be applied, and with as good reason, to books, newspapers, and to stage performances." The New York State Senate's Democratic Minority Leader, James J. "Jimmy" Walker, a future mayor of New York City and the personification of a "wet," or anti-Prohibition, politician, attacked the censorship proposal, labeling it "the most un-American bill ever introduced into this Senate." Pointing at Senator Lusk, Walker bellowed, "You . . . are only a step behind the crackatoo who has written a pamphlet advocating a twentieth amendment to the United States Constitution abolishing religious liberty in this country." He proceeded to call the entire proposition "pure bunk." Walker concluded, "I don't know whether I will have to apologize for using hectic language, but it seems necessary to use strong American language to make gentlemen who are ever so much more cultured and refined than I am supposed to be understand."[11]

The bill passed the Senate in April 1921 in a party line vote, with all Democrats opposing it. According to *Motion Picture World*, the Republicans in the New York State Senate, "aware that this is a pet measure of Senator Lusk, right-hand man of Governor Miller," were "whipped into line like slaves of old."[12] Governor Miller signed the censorship bill into law shortly thereafter, on 14 May.[13] McGuire wrote to Jones that "Governor Miller decided to finally sign the New York State Censorship bill," but he did not think that it would "seriously affect" the NB.[14] After all, McGuire noted, the NB's "bulletin service [went] to the leading cities of 38 states" and "groups outside of New York State [had] been much more active in their cooperation with the National Board." "[A] prophet is not without honor save in his own country," he mused.[15]

CENSORSHIP AND WOMEN'S CLUBS IN SOUTHERN STATES

Despite the setback in New York, McGuire and Jones forged ahead with their plan to seed Better Films Committees across the South during the spring and summer. They organized a "rather intensive educational campaign in the six southern states (Georgia, Florida, Alabama, North and South Carolina, and Tennessee)," with Texas, Oklahoma, and Louisiana "to be included eventually." Jones provided McGuire with "an approved list of 54 cities, in these six states," including a "more comprehensive list of towns, and women's clubs in same."[16]

With the financial backing of Southern Enterprises, the National Board had established a significant foothold in the South by 1922, co-opting many of legal censorship's supporters and channeling them into "those citizen groups known as Better Film Committees, some of which are themselves cooperating with official amusement inspectors." Atlanta, Birmingham, Alabama, and dozens of other cities used the City Plan and became home to active Better Films Committees. Florida took an unusual path, ultimately passing a state law that required either the seal of the Board of Censors of the State of New York or the seal of the National Board.[17] All of this occurred through the deployment of members of the General Federation of Women's Clubs as traveling organizers on behalf of the Better Films Committee.

Florida

In late April 1921, shortly after New York passed Senator Lusk's censorship bill, Jones, from Paramount Pictures, contacted McGuire at the National Board about a "strenuous censorship fight" developing in Florida, with "the Women's Clubs . . . proving most active" in support of censorship legislation. Jones requested that a statement "against censorship" from "any prominent woman" be presented to the Florida legislature.[18] Three weeks later, Jones described the "fight" as "so hot as to necessitate a compromise." He had already proposed a solution to exhibitors and clubwomen: the "passage of a state law" in Florida "forbidding the showing of any pictures not passed by the National Board." He warned McGuire that "the time has come to advocate that law in every southern state." "Once on the books," Jones reasoned, the compromise measure would "automatically block" censorship for "several years"—or at least temporarily shift "the wrath of the public . . . from [the industry's] shoulders to yours."[19]

McGuire agreed to Jones's proposal for a compromise law in Florida; he believed that "all questions of state censorship" could have been avoided if members of the executive committee of the National Board had simply embraced "the legalization of the National Board's action on pictures" years earlier, but the executive committee's members remained "unwilling . . . to compromise themselves" on that point.[20] McGuire reminded Jones that, technically, the compromise law was "in direct contradiction to our principle of opposing legal censorship whether by the National Board or by anyone else."[21] He agreed to cooperate on the "Florida Compromise" plan anyway.

After New York's governor, Miller, signed the Lusk censorship bill into law in May, the situation in Florida took an unexpected turn. A "substitute bill" had been introduced, one proposing legal censorship that was "patterned" after the New York State law.[22] Within days, another compromise bill passed the Florida House of Representatives. This measure required all motion pictures exhibited in Florida to "carry the seal of either the National Board *or* the New York State Board." It also empowered the governor to appoint three members to the NB's National Advisory Committee. Jones reported that this expanded compromise bill was "practically assured" to pass the Senate, and he promised McGuire that he would "avoid the inclusion of the New York board" in the future.[23] However, "in this case it was necessary, or rather expedient, on account of the women's clubs," who remained distrustful of the NB.[24]

McGuire insisted that Jones include a proviso in the compromise bill in the future exempting "scenic, news, industrial and strictly educational pictures" from review, because "pictures of this type . . . by no stretch of the imagination raise any moral questions." McGuire emphasized that to require review of "the news pictures" would be "tantamount to a compulsory review of the motion picture press."[25] He included several NB pamphlets to guide Jones in writing the compromise bill, including "The Boston, Mass. Method of Motion Picture Regulation," a transcript of an address John M. Casey, Boston's license commissioner, had delivered in October 1919. McGuire recommended that Jones model the Florida compromise on the City Plan; Jones agreed and had his legal department draw up a revised copy of the bill, "exempting scenics, newsreels, industrial and strictly educational films."[26]

Opponents of censorship in Florida characterized the law—and the compromise—as paternalist politics. When state representative Truman G. Futch of Lake County, Florida, proposed using "taxes to pay for motion picture censorship laws," the *Ocala Evening News* asked, "What right has the state to tell the people what pictures they shall look at?" The short piece concluded, "This is paternalism sure enough. Mr. Futch should go and sit on himself."[27] The *Ocala Evening Star* wondered how effective a censorship board could be; after all, "we have a 'national board of censorship,' and its stamp of approval appears on the most rotten pictures thrown on the screen."[28]

Governor Cary Hardee of Florida signed the compromise bill into law in June 1921; in addition to requiring every film exhibited in Florida to bear the seal of either the New York State Board or the National Board of Review, it permitted the governor to appoint two members to the NB's National Advisory Committee.[29] McGuire balked at this point, but Jones emphasized that this "one phase of the bill" served as "the bait" that was "most attractive to our women opponents." Jones thought that, going forward, it would "be a good scheme" to include language stipulating that the governor must appoint at least one woman to the board. "This always appeals to the ladies and is apt to win their support. If it is clearly written into the bill they are apt to be for it without argument."[30]

Shortly after passage of the Florida compromise law, Jones hosted a conference for exchange managers and exhibitors to educate them on the finer points of compliance. He included Atlanta-based exchange managers, as they distributed products to Florida and now had to comply with the new law.[31] The exchange managers promised to contact their "home offices in New York" to explain "the importance of . . . attaching the approval of the Board" in the title sequence of any motion pictures intended for distribution to Florida. They "also agreed to put notations on their shipping instructions requesting operators not to cut the [seal of] approval of the Board from the films." Finally, the exchange managers "agreed to accept the official Bulletins of the Board."[32] Jones and McGuire were confident that the measure would appease censorship's supporters in the region, despite the fact that the region was home to many vocal opponents of the NB.

Georgia

Following the detour into Florida, Jones and McGuire continued with their original plan in Georgia, dispatching a speaker to organize clubwomen into local Better Films Committees that would oppose legal censorship. Jones insisted that he needed to "make a very careful personal choice of the speaker" for Georgia, emphasizing that "this speaker should be a woman and one intimately acquainted with the south if possible. I consider these two points of paramount importance."[33] McGuire recommended two women, Belle Clement and Louise Connolly, writing to Jones, "Both of these ladies are experienced public speakers of standing in the community, whose connections would unquestionably inspire confidence." For $350 plus expenses, Clement had agreed to "spend the month of June in Georgia meeting with the various women's clubs, parent-teacher associations and other groups, giving such public addresses as we could arrange and conferring informally with leaders in various communities." Connolly was "unwilling to undertake the work for less than $500 and her expenses," but McGuire described her as "a public speaker of rare ability," possessing "a keen sense of humor [and] a manner which wins confidence."[34]

Born in Washington, DC, in 1862, Connolly had earned bachelor's and master's degrees from Georgetown University. She had served as the supervisor of schools in Newark, and later Summit, New Jersey, before going to work as an "educational expert" at the Newark Free Public Library. Connolly had served in that position under the mentorship of John Cotton Dana, a Progressive librarian who pioneered the "open stacks" movement and helped to turn libraries into vibrant community centers rather than reliquaries.[35] Connolly supported women's suffrage and was a member of the Legislative Committee of the New Jersey State Suffrage Association; she was also a well-known religious educator, and she frequently spoke to parents' organizations about the place of motion pictures in religious education.[36] Finally, and perhaps most significantly, she was a member of the GFWC and had been a member of the club's original Committee on Motion Pictures in 1916.

Jones refused Connolly's salary request and expressed concern about whether she could be effective in the South, despite her impressive professional qualifications. She had recently appeared before a legislative committee in Florida, and Jones complained that she had exhibited "a lack of tact, was sarcastic, and failed to sense the situation which she had to meet." He believed that Connolly had "learned a lesson" in Florida, but if the plan failed in Georgia with her as the speaker, he feared the executives at Paramount's Southern Enterprises would "undoubtedly blame her and my poor judgment in selecting her." He requested information on two other speakers—Helen Duey and Mary Mason Speed, about whom he had heard "favorable" things from a colleague in Richmond. Jones implored McGuire to "not lose sight of the fact that personality and personal appearance are *almost* paramount to everything else."[37] Connolly may have had decades of professional experience, but she was sixty years old, unmarried, and did not have children.[38]

McGuire dismissed Duey, a former writer for *Woman's Home Companion*, as "a very expensive young woman" who "does not deliver the goods in proportion to the cost." He wrote that she had an "inclination to make anything with which she is identified a means of personal exploitation." Of Speed, McGuire explained, "We have known Mrs. Philip Speed for a good many years and think very well of her."[39] Speed had firsthand experience with film programs. In 1915 and 1916, she had designed and implemented Saturday morning entertainment programs for young people in New York City. During World War I, she had worked for the Community Motion Picture Bureau of the YMCA, selecting the films exhibited in army and navy encampments. In addition, she was a great-great-granddaughter of George Mason, one of America's Founding Fathers; of this connection, she wrote, "I sometimes feel that the Gods have decreed that [I] shall write a new Bill of Rights for this medium of expression that is understood by all the peoples of the earth."[40] McGuire noted that Speed had "the advantage of being a Southern woman," and her "appearance was good," but she was "not a deep thinker or remarkably logical."[41]

McGuire dismissed Jones's concerns about the traveling lecturer's appearance and continued to advocate for Connolly, arguing that her "standing and personal connections" would arouse "an unquestionably sympathetic response" among southern clubwomen.[42] McGuire either did not know or did not care that southerners had a long-standing suspicion of northern women with "causes," beginning with abolitionists and suffragists in the Antebellum period. During Reconstruction, white women had streamed into the South in the service of the Freedman's Bureau, often coming to work as teachers. During the late nineteenth and early twentieth centuries, particularly in southern newspapers and other literature, Yankee reform women were often held up as foils to the ideal southern woman.[43] Henry James's 1886 novel *The Bostonians* first introduced Americans to the concept of the "Boston marriage," in which independent, possibly lesbian, women lived together in same-sex partnerships. Prominent examples from the Progressive era included settlement-house worker Jane Addams and her partner Ellen Gates Starr; later, there was Mary Rozet Smith, as well as Bryn Mawr College's president, M. Carey Thomas, and her partner Mary Elizabeth Garrett. Southern society emphasized a woman's femininity and pleasing physical appearance; Boston's emphasized achievements. For example, Miss Ella Evans, the social representative for a theater company, told a crowd of society women in Atlanta that she found it a "pleasing relief" to be in a southern city, where the women "are really feminine both in dress and manners." During her travels, she had occasion to visit Boston, and found "the mannish women" there to be among the city's "most offensive" features. "Thank goodness Atlanta is free from these short-haired freaks," she proclaimed.[44]

Jones finally conceded to McGuire's judgment and confirmed Connolly's employment, agreeing to "$500 per month and expenses for the work in Georgia." He asked that Connolly arrive in Atlanta early so that, "in a couple of conversations," he could give her "local color [and the] history of local agitation," which would be "invaluable" in her organizing efforts. Jones also asked McGuire to issue "a polite warning . . . on the dislike of the South (more than other sections) for any form of criticism or sarcasm." He wrote, "She must understand that we are trying to reconcile people who are already committed to censorship—trying to lead them blindfolded from the path they are following and want to follow."[45] McGuire assured Jones that he would speak to Connolly before she boarded the train for Georgia; he knew her "well enough not only to discuss the Southern matter with her in terms of a polite warning but to lay considerable emphasis upon the necessity of utmost tact and diplomacy."[46] For her part, Connolly asked that Jones "elaborate" on his "point about inter-racial problems" when she arrived in Atlanta, but it remains unclear if that conversation ever happened.[47]

In advance of Connolly's lecture tour, the NB's Committee on Community Cooperation sent a circular letter to influential clubwomen across Georgia, offering to send her to address their organizations and to help seed local Better Films Committees. The letter claimed to "recognize the paramount importance of Southern women in establishing fine home standards for motion picture entertainment and . . . their power to influence the thought of their communities." Georgia's clubwomen were encouraged to book her as a speaker to "discuss 'better motion pictures and a definite community plan.'"[48] To sweeten the deal, Connolly traveled with a two-reel motion picture, *From Script to Screen*, which "show[ed] how motion pictures [were] made, which will prove illuminating to persons who have never visited a studio and are unfamiliar with the technique of motion picture construction." The motion picture, edited by McGuire himself, included scenes that represented the finest of the motion picture arts, such as *Les Misérables* (Fox, 1918) and *Tale of Two Cities* (Fox, 1917).[49] Connolly had her own strategies for working among southern women's organizations; she traveled with "objects illustrating the use of tangible and visible material in the teaching of religion," for example, and suggested a series of professional development talks for teachers "or an association of ministers or Sunday-school workers." Connolly argued that these "side shows on related subjects take away any impression of my being a spell-binder in the interests of the wicked producers, and give me professional power."[50]

Despite the circular letters sent out in advance of Connolly's arrival, she booked few meetings, and she struggled to obtain introductions once in Atlanta. After a few days, she wrote the first of several lengthy reports to McGuire and Rev. Orrin Cocks, head of the Better Films Committees, recounting her meetings and sharing her impressions of Georgia's clubwomen and clergy.[51] Her reports provide a glimpse into the regional differences and suspicions that divided northerners and southerners in the early twentieth century and the kaleidoscope of competing ideas that Progressives held simultaneously about race, gender, and authority.

During World War I, many white southern women engaged in war work for the Red Cross, the YMCA, and even the Commission on Training Camp Activities. After the war, they used the same skills to address the needs of their own communities. Younger clubwomen embraced the "volunteer" approach, and soon southern clubwomen were launching campaigns for improved public health and education, city beautification, and historic preservation.[52] Club work allowed them to engage in the public sphere in the midst of an increasingly constrained, patriarchal, and anti–women's suffrage environment.[53] This was certainly the case in Georgia, where the Atlanta Woman's Club had recently adopted "constructive" work on behalf of the community, successfully lobbying the city government for a dedicated space for the Municipal Curb Market. By the early 1920s, the Atlanta Woman's Club—which was described at the time in a book on Atlanta as "loving mother to the community"—had become concerned about a perceived rise in juvenile delinquency and disrespect for moral standards and the role that motion pictures were playing in these problems.[54]

Mrs. Basil Manly (Florence Barnard) Boykin, the president of the Atlanta Woman's Club and an active member of the Anti-Saloon League, was a gatekeeper to elite white society.[55] Under her leadership, the club's membership had grown to 1,200, "representing the most active, energetic, and patriotic women of Atlanta," according to the book on Atlanta written at the time.[56] Jones and "local people" had repeatedly warned Connolly not to approach Atlanta's clubwomen—especially Mrs. Boykin—without a formal introduction, as it would be a breach of social etiquette to do so.[57] Connolly expressed frustration with how long it was taking to gain access to Atlanta's clubwomen.

After five days in Georgia, Connolly finally arranged a few meetings and speeches in and around Atlanta, including a five-minute speech at a Mass Meeting of Mothers and a lunch at the Chamber of Commerce. She reported that the Fulton County Parent-Teachers Association "seem[ed] to be glad to get me on their program," but ministers frequently ignored her; those who did greet her did so with outright disapproval, despite her long experience in religious education. She was starting to feel dispirited, fearing there was "no hope for Little Lulie with her conservative use of movies." She wrote to Cocks, "I think I'll go to the movies, and I wish to see Charlie Chaplin and the Kid. Such is the effect of uplift on the uplifter."[58] Cocks replied, "I am sure that you are going to win a great many friends from the thoughtful sincere people, break the ranks of the hopelessly conservative, and compel a number of these sweet women who sympathize with their eyes and dream of their babies at homes, to wake up to the fact that things are really happening."

He assured her that Jones had spoken "enthusiastically" about her work and was "thoroughly impressed with the impression [she] made in Atlanta under adverse circumstances."[59]

Connolly did eventually secure an invitation to a luncheon at the Atlanta Woman's Club, where she was finally introduced to Mrs. Boykin. Connolly relayed to Cocks, "[She] received me cordially, calling me 'my dear,'" and "seated me beside her with no trace of embarrassment," even though, over the past several days—and with no explanation or apology—she "had broken three engagements and caused [me] to sit waiting on her for seven hours." Boykin proceeded to call the meeting of the Atlanta Woman's Club to order and, as Connolly described it, "conduct[ed] an enthusiastic and even violent mass meeting about late dances, joy rides, early morning suppers, and bootlegging at dances." As Boykin's address wore on, Connolly realized that "dozens of fluent speakers" were waiting for their turn to address the audience. She calculated that Boykin "would not hesitate to wind up her meeting without giving me a chance. . . . So I decided to introduce myself right in line with their orgy, and in the middle of it." Connolly stood and spoke for a few minutes on "their subject," sharing a tragic story that left "Mrs. Boykin with big tears running down her face."[60]

Despite her emotional reaction, Boykin was evidently not pleased about being interrupted. Connolly explained that, "in that accent," Boykin leaned over and whispered, "I guess I'll have to omit your talk, dear Lady." Connolly seized the moment: "'No, you won't,' says I. 'You introduce me right here and now. Do it quick!' And she did." Perhaps this was the kind of brusqueness that had worried Jones. According to Connolly, Boykin gave her just enough time to "get across" that the clubwomen "were to look out for any literature sent them, and even for my return among them, and be sure to read what they got, and to come hear me if I returned."[61]

By her own reckoning, Connolly's reception by prominent Atlantans had not been positive. The Atlanta Chamber of Commerce refused to permit her to speak at its meeting about the Better Films Committee. Ministers remained suspicious of her connections to the motion picture industry. Her inability to connect with fellow clubwomen, in particular, troubled her. In one report, she noted, "There is nothing wrong with the Southern mind. The trouble is that they are thinking of something else when they look at you with their sympathetic manner."[62] In another, she wrote, "I could go on the vaudeville stage with an account of the performances of Mrs. Boykin!"[63] Perhaps Connolly seemed abrasive to her audiences and dismissive of southern women—given these comments, that in fact seems likely—and this perception may well have hindered her efforts to organize Better Film Committees in Atlanta.

Connolly did discover that the Atlanta Board of Censors did "not function at all, except to back [Peacock] up, or down, occasionally." Connolly described Peacock, the secretary of the Atlanta censorship board, as "a special policeman to watch new productions to see whether the National Board cuts are made." The librarian of the local Carnegie Library opposed the National Board "because she thinks they are 'financed by the producers,'" Connolly wrote to Cocks. "She keeps scornfully clear of Mr. Peacock." Finally, Connolly noted that the penalties for violating the censorship law in Atlanta were "vicious, but not carried out."[64]

The *Atlanta Journal-Constitution* had a more positive assessment of Connolly's short talk before the Atlanta Woman's Club, quoting her as saying, "We do not want to take the fun and pleasure out of the films. . . . We want no blue laws which will curtail originality or emotional expression."[65] Writing to Cocks, Connolly said she acknowledged in the speech that "the particular angle" from which moving pictures would be censored in Atlanta would "be largely influenced . . . by the fact that negroes see the pictures in the theaters for their race"; she assured the audience that the NB "knock[ed] out anything inciting to riot."[66] Part of the purpose of her trip to Georgia, the *Atlanta Journal-Constitution* said, was "to secure the angles which must be considered in censoring pictures to be shown in other sections of the country than New York."[67] Connolly noted to Cocks that there was "a long story to tell . . . about the whole interracial situation," but if she later told that story to him, it does not appear to have been recorded or preserved.[68] Interestingly, by December 1923, the *Chicago Defender* had reported that the Atlanta Woman's Club had fully embraced the Better Films Committee concept, and had even started hosting "special programs," complete with chaperones, for the "colored" children of Atlanta.[69]

Following the conclusion of Connolly's lecture tour through Georgia in August 1921, Jones wrote to Cocks and McGuire with his assessment. He still expected the "introduction of one or more bills for the regulation of motion pictures" in the upcoming state legislative session, but he did not think they would "amount to much." He anticipated that the proposals "will be put to sleep in committee," and the compromise bill would not have to be introduced in Georgia at all. He reasserted that Southern Enterprises of Paramount Pictures saw "the compromise bill as a good policy only when the question of censorship is gaining the active interest of some appreciable portion of public opinion." It would "be poor policy to push the bill when our opponents are quiet," he noted.[70] When another censorship bill was introduced in the Georgia House of Representatives, Jones simply asked that Connolly forward the names of anyone she had met "during her tour of Georgia, of whose stand against censorship she is absolutely certain." He signed off: "Jones—who doesn't think the fight will be 'severe.'" He was already distracted by new "rumors of a special session in Alabama."[71]

Alabama

Birmingham had employed the NB's City Plan since 1915, but six years later, exchange managers and exhibitors were openly ignoring the NB's required edits. The Birmingham Department of Public Safety, eager to relieve its officers of the burden of screening motion pictures and the criticism that accompanied it, began to advocate for a state board of censors. McGuire warned Jones that unless he brought his exchange managers into line immediately, Birmingham officials would appear before the legislature "with proof that the exchange managers and producers cannot be depended upon to make the eliminations requested by the National Board." McGuire concluded sternly, "Do something."[72] Jones immediately sent instructions to his district supervisors and eleven exchanges, "calling for strict compliance with your recommendations." He claimed the lack of compliance was limited to "independent exchanges" and states' rights exhibitors, not the theater owners who were affiliated with Paramount.[73]

By the early 1920s, the motion pictures generating the most controversy in the South were no longer old "white slave traffic" films, exhibited by fly-by-night amusement entrepreneurs, but big studio releases from the most famous directors in the industry. Under Paramount's distribution structure, cities were classified according to population, and larger cities with "showcase theaters" received priority for new releases. Paramount limited new releases to one "showcase theater" in a city at a time, "where top ticket prices" could be charged. Less prestigious theaters only received access to new releases after the releases had completed their contractual first-run engagements at the showcase theaters. Theater owners in smaller towns received first-run films after they completed their major-city bookings, which could take a few months.[74]

In 1920, Birmingham's population was 178,806, whereas Atlanta's was 200,616, so Atlanta should have received Paramount's new releases first.[75] Yet Connolly had learned from a "special policewoman" in charge of amusements in Birmingham that some exchange managers in Atlanta, looking to capitalize on NB-excised material, had reversed their pattern of distribution, sending unedited films into theaters in smaller cities and towns in Alabama first, and then editing them for distribution to Atlanta and Florida later.[76] McGuire expressed concern that this practice would damage the NB's reputation, as these unedited pictures still bore the NB's seal.

One film in particular that generated pro-censorship sentiment in Alabama—and that was being distributed by Paramount—was Cecil B. De-Mille's *Affairs of Anatol* (Famous Players–Lasky, 1921). *Affairs* was a comedy-drama in the "eternal triangle" genre that exploited broken marriage vows, extramarital affairs, and romantic mishaps for laughs.[77] The all-star cast included heartthrob Wallace Reid, the "screen's most perfect lover," as Anatol de Witt Spencer, and Gloria Swanson, a rising Paramount star, as his "little bride," Vivian, together a fashionable and modern urban couple. The opening title card of the film presented this teaser: "This is the story of a romantic young man who has a passion for saving Ladies from real, or imaginary, difficulties—always like Don Quixote, with the most honorable of intent. But the wives of such chivalrous men are not so philanthropically interested in saving Other Women's Souls—however noble and sincere their husband's impulses."[78] The "first stern lesson" that Anatol and Vivian experience comes in the form of Emilie, portrayed by DeMille favorite Wanda Hawley, a young woman with whom Anatol had attended school. While at "a midnight café," Anatol spots Emilie in the company of Bronson, "a wealthy rake." He intervenes to save Emilie from Bronson, much to Vivian's fury. Later in the film, Anatol and Vivian come upon another troubled young woman, Annie Elliot, just as she is attempting to commit suicide. Anatol rescues Annie from drowning; she kisses him, seemingly out of gratitude, but picks his pockets in the process. As Vivian returns with a doctor, she catches the two in their embrace. Furious at finding her husband in the midst of yet another indiscretion, Vivian retaliates "at a society gathering," where she agrees to be hypnotized by Dr. Nazzer Singh, a "Hindu hypnotist." Anatol seeks revenge against his wife for this incident by having an affair with Satan Synne, the "wickedest woman in New York," played by Bebe Daniels. Synne, however, reveals to Anatol that she is not really a vamp; she is the devoted wife of "a disabled soldier in need of an operation." Anatol gives her the money for her husband's medical needs and returns "home to make peace with Vivian."[79]

Initially, the NB's Review Committee rejected *Affairs of Anatol*. During the prolonged review process, McGuire met with the producers, Jesse Lasky and DeMille (DeMille also directed). He told DeMille that if *Affairs* had been "generally released in the form in which it came before the National Board it would do more to make for motion picture censorship than could be offset in six months work." The movie undermined "the 'sanctity of the home,'" which was "the very thing that gets under the skin of people who are inclined to advocate censorship," McGuire explained. DeMille replied, "I agree that the picture ought to be cut for some parts of the country."[80] He complied with the NB's recommended edits, and the film was released in September 1921.

For McGuire, DeMille's remark reflected a distressing attitude emerging

FIGURE 6.1. Affairs of Anatol *lobby card*

among directors, "an exemplification of the foolish policy of not doing anything until matters reach the extreme of having to meet public demand."[81] If directors connected to legitimate studios continued to behave like DeMille and exploit marriage vows and sexuality for comedy and profit, censorship legislation was inevitable, in his estimation.[82] Ruth Rich, a newly appointed member of the National Advisory Board from Florida wrote to McGuire and confirmed that *Affairs of Anatol* had sparked "much discussion" about motion picture censorship "at the time of the hearing in Montgomery, Alabama," which she had attended on behalf of the NB.[83] McGuire was not surprised; he described the night he decided to travel past "a theater in a suburb of New York" where the revised *Affairs of Anatol* was being exhibited. The line was "three blocks long waiting to get into the last show," and the theater manager had already scheduled three evening performances to meet the demand "in a town of 2,000 people." McGuire bemoaned to Rich, "There is something the matter with the public as well as the pictures. Mr. DeMille and his sex pictures seem to be giving the public what they want. How is it going to be handled?"[84]

Then came *Midsummer Madness* (Paramount, 1921), directed by William C. de Mille (Cecil's older brother), produced by Famous Players–Lasky and distributed by Paramount.[85] This film stars matinee idol Conrad Nagle, playing Julian Osborne, and Lila Lee, playing Julian's wife, Daisy. While Daisy is away caring for her sick father, Julian falls "victim" to the allures of his best friend's "neglected wife," Margaret. Julian and Margaret resist the physical temptation, but when Daisy returns, she blames Margaret for putting her marriage in jeopardy. *Midsummer Madness* ends with Margaret's husband, Bob, portrayed by Jack Holt, acknowledging that "his neglect" had damaged his wife, and with "the truth thus revealed, both couples repent and are reunited in friendship."[86]

Several aspects of the movie may have offended religious or conservative audiences: it exploited the love triangle plot, asserted women's sexual agency, and featured a husband admitting his failure—as a lover and companion— to keep his wife at home. Indeed, the "special policewoman in charge of amusements" in Birmingham, Alabama, reported to Connolly that *Midsummer Madness* was so offensive that "everybody" in Alabama was becoming "committed" to the idea of state censorship, and "nothing [could] prevent Alabama from having state censorship next year."[87] The reason Alabamans became particularly incensed by the movie was not the love triangle or the portrayal of husbands and wives, however. The reason for their anger, in fact, is somewhat surprising.

Actress Lois Wilson played the neglected wife, Margaret Meredith, and she was an "Alabama girl," Connolly explained to Cocks. "Alabama, being

FIGURE 6.2. *Lois Wilson*, Midsummer Madness

proud of her, went *en masse*" to see *Midsummer Madness*. Although the picture was generally "good," according to Connolly, there was one scene "[at] which the whole state was appalled." The scene in question shows Margaret and Julian in a hunting lodge on the verge of submitting to desire. Wilson claimed she "cried and resisted" when de Mille asked her to do the love scene, Connolly reported, but he "forced her to play it as he ordered or lose her job. And Alabama's heart went out to her with chivalrous throbs." Connolly warned Cocks that Alabamans had become fond of "say[ing] the producers and the National Board are going to get what is coming to them in Alabama: the first is rotten, and the second is no good."[88] Ultimately, though, Alabama did not adopt state censorship legislation. Birmingham continued to use the City Plan and a special officer to monitor motion pictures until 1937.[89]

North Carolina

When Louise Connolly first met with the women of the North Carolina GFWC in November 1921, the clubwomen expressed interest in the work of the Better Films Committee. However, at that point they did not realize that Connolly represented the National Board; she downplayed her affiliation with it as part of her organizing strategy, just as she had done in Georgia. Once word of her NB affiliation got out, they refused to set up follow-up meetings with her or return correspondence.

Connolly wrote to Cocks from Raleigh, completely baffled and exhausted by the work in North Carolina. While she was waiting for the clubwomen to respond, she did some sightseeing: "I have seen the State Library, the State Historical Museum, the State Natural History Museum . . . and the back yard where Andrew Johnson was born," she wrote. "Then I telephoned Dr. Delia Dixon Carroll, and she came around and explained things to me." Carroll, the first woman physician in North Carolina, was also the sister of playwright Thomas Dixon; he opposed censorship, and Carroll supported it. Carroll explained to Connolly that North Carolina clubwomen had initially given her a warm reception because "they didn't catch on to the fact that [she] represented the National Board which was opposed to censorship." Connolly showed Carroll the NB's letterhead "and told her that [Cocks] undoubtedly writ to 'em all on that paper. That if they had been 'stung' it was because they couldn't read." Carroll replied, "Never mind; they will be mad all the same."[90] Although Connolly's report on North Carolina was likely an amusing read for the NB's executive board, it also provides evidence of the sarcasm and sense of humor that Jones had noticed.

After meeting with Mrs. T. Palmer Jerman, the president of the North Carolina Federation of Women's Clubs and an ardent supporter of state censorship, Connolly wrote to Cocks, "I have met the enemy, and while she is not yet mine, we have established a status quo, a modus vivendi, a truce, looking to a limitation of armaments." Jerman explained to Connolly that when she had recognized the names on the letterhead, she had realized that she "represent[ed] a society opposed to our campaign. So we would have none of you." Moreover, Jerman noted, "we see some dreadful things with [the NB's] sign of approval, and the fact that the picture men brag that they are with it sets us against it." Connolly countered, "I am affiliated with a society that preaches 'selection, rather than censorship.'" Jerman "looked at [Connolly] dubiously and said 'But how can I cooperate with a crowd opposed to censorship?'" Connolly replied, "When you've had your censors for a few years you'll want help in improving your movies. And we'll be just as glad to help you then as we would be now." Connolly noted that they "parted warmly," and she thought that their meeting had done "no harm," and "may have done much good."[91] North Carolina never adopted a state censorship board. Winston-Salem, Charlotte, Greensboro, and Raleigh all used the City Plan and Better Films Committees. Nevertheless, clubwomen in the South had become all too familiar with—and suspicious of—the NB's motives, and they continued to be suspicious as the campaign for better films—and censorship—developed.

Virginia

In early 1922, when State Senator Mapp reintroduced his motion picture censorship act in the Virginia legislature, local exhibitors once again contacted the National Board for assistance. Louise Connolly was already engaged, so the NB sent Mary Mason Speed for duty in her home state. When Speed arrived in Richmond in early February 1922, Virginians remained largely in favor of state censorship legislation. McGuire advised Speed to meet with exhibitor Jake Wells and the members of the GFWC in Virginia as soon as possible, to identify other possible allies, and to arrange meetings with them as well. Mary Mason Speed's status and connections as a native Virginian presented organizing opportunities that had not been available to her predecessor, Mary Gray Peck, or to Louise Connolly.

Shortly after arriving in Richmond, Speed secured an invitation to a private gathering at the home of John Stewart Bryan, the editor of the *Richmond News Leader*. She deemed his leadership key to defeating legal censorship, as she knew "the *News Leader* [was] read all over the State."[92] Bryan's wife, Anne Eliza (née Tennant) Bryan, was influential among Virginia's clubwomen. Also in attendance were Mrs. J. Allison Hodges, chairwoman of the Virginia Federation of Women's Club's Motion Picture Committee; Mrs. Randolph Maynard, who was active in the campaign for women's higher education in Vir-

FIGURE 6.3. *Betty Blythe as the queen of Sheba*

ginia; Miss Page Williams of the Association for the Preservation of Virginia
Antiquities; and Mrs. H. A. (Emma Speed) Sampson, who was a journalist, a
member of the VFWC, and Mary Mason Speed's sister-in-law. If Speed could
change the opinion of those in attendance, they, in turn, could influence their
peers to oppose legal censorship.

Shortly after the meeting began, Lieutenant Governor Junius Edgar
West informed Speed that "Virginia proposed to have a very superior Board
of Censors, both liberal and cultured." State censorship boards were often
openly criticized by their constituents and the motion picture industry—
whether it was for unduly harsh decisions or for lax ones; West's pronounce-
ment implied that he thought a Virginia censorship board could do better than
the ones that had stirred up such public conflict. Speed parried with the example of *The Queen of Sheba* (Fox, 1921). Written and directed by J. Gordon Edwards and released in 1921 by Fox Studios, this film dramatized the biblical
relationship between Solomon, king of Israel, and the queen of Sheba, depicting it as a love affair. Sheba, played by actress Betty Blythe, wore skimpy costumes that revealed her breasts. Speed reported that the mere mention of this
film "proved illuminating." Instead of consensus among the gathering of "liberal and cultured" Virginians, dissension ensued. One of the ministers asked

what the National Board could do about this "indecent, irreverent, inartistic and historically incorrect" film, whereas one of the women "exclaimed" that she thought *The Queen of Sheba* was "a lovely thing," and confessed that she "had enjoyed" the picture "from beginning to end."[93]

Speed knew that *The Queen of Sheba* would serve as an instructive example among those who assumed that they shared morals and standards. These Virginians, from the same social and cultural milieu, presumed they were also homogeneous in thought and taste. The minister seemed disturbed by this highly stylized and sexualized interpretation of a biblical story, which Fox was advertising as "the gigantic spectacle and story of the world's greatest love."[94] The clubwomen seemed taken with its artistry, its lavish sets, and its beautiful (if revealing) costumes. The assembled were surprised to learn that they disagreed with each other on this film, which suggested possible disagreement about others. Speed intended for the example to generate the kind of conversation that might happen on a state censorship board with so few members. She then proposed that they organize a local Better Films Com-

FIGURE 6.4. The Queen of Sheba *poster*

mittee to help exhibitors select motion pictures appropriate for exhibition in Richmond.

Despite Speed's initial—albeit limited—success in Virginia, the National Board directed her to leave Richmond and head to Tennessee, where pro-censorship forces were gaining converts. Speed communicated to McGuire that she thought this was a mistake. If he would permit her to stay in Richmond a bit longer, Speed explained, she could have "many conferences with individual Ministers"—especially since she had recently discovered that a coalition of clergy had sent out "an order to 1000 Ministers in the State for diligent effort in behalf of State Censorship."[95]

McGuire exhibited a tendency throughout these campaigns to distrust the women on whom he relied to accomplish his organization's goals. A letter from Mrs. Channing (Nadine) Ward, the film and arts reviewer for the *Richmond News Leader*, confirmed the gravity of the situation. The NB had grossly underestimated the power and influence of the clergy over elite white Virginians, she told McGuire, and the members of their congregations feared "social ostracism" if they strayed from majority opinion on "important issues" such as censorship.[96] McGuire replied that "advocacy of . . . measures by clergymen" should not be understood as "truly interpretive of the public view."[97] Ward thought that even if Virginians did not believe in censorship, they would likely support it if their clergy did. McGuire, however, did not seem to fully appreciate or understand her message.

After Speed left for Tennessee, exhibitor Jake Wells, by now known in some circles as "Mr. Clean Entertainment," took over as the spokesperson for the anticensorship campaign in Virginia. In an effort to win over the clergy, he sent free movie passes to a number of ministers. Wells hoped that the ministers would abandon their pro-censorship position after seeing that his theaters were clean, safe, and family-friendly. Most of those who had received the complimentary tickets, he told McGuire, responded with thank-you letters, which he interpreted as an embrace of the voluntary film review movement. When the ministers remained "all for censorship," Wells expressed surprise.[98] A small group of ministers in Richmond did oppose the Mapp Act: they thought only immoral films needed to be reviewed by the National Board, and that films that dealt with history, science, and religion should be treated "just as a book." Their position garnered little support, however, among their peers.[99] Wells (and Speed) were rightly concerned with the ministers' influence over state legislators and the public—a fact that NB executive board members in New York often discounted, to the detriment of their campaign.

This was the turning point for the National Board's campaign in Virginia. Speed's assessment of the situation had been accurate, but McGuire had dismissed it. When the General Laws Committee of the Virginia House of Delegates held a public hearing on the Mapp Act on 27 February 1922, the *Richmond Times-Dispatch* noted that "verbal clashes . . . marked the session, which closed without definite action being taken on the measure." The vote was still scheduled to take place later that same day.[100] Canon William Sheafe Chase traveled to Richmond to speak in favor of Virginia's proposed censorship legislation; Thomas Dixon, author of *The Clansman*, argued against it.

Virginians remained highly attuned to the perils of regulation from "carpetbaggers" into the twentieth century, and some observers regarded the anticensorship movement as an imposition of Republican Party politics on the South, and the NB as nothing more than a tool of the industry.[101] Even Canon Chase managed to offend Virginia's censorship supporters. When he suggested that if the General Assembly did not pass the Mapp Act, it was because they had been intimidated into silence by the motion picture industry, an editorial in the *Richmond Times-Dispatch* suggested that Chase's remark was akin to schoolboy "dares": "The General Assembly will approve censorship, or everyone will know what it is!" The editorial concluded that "Virginians whose desire for censorship is fully equal in warmth and honesty to that of Canon Chase have reported no trace of this blight on the courage of our legislature."[102]

In early March, when the NB realized that the situation in Virginia was unique (and dire), McGuire instructed Mary Mason Speed to return from Tennessee immediately. In an attempt to shore up the anticensorship position, she arranged to speak "at two gatherings of ministers, the Episcopal and the Baptist," upon her return to Richmond.[103] Much to her dismay, she found that the clergy's support for legal censorship remained strong. Rev. J. A. Crane of Norfolk persuasively argued that since the NB "had no power to enforce [any of its] decisions," it remained the weaker option when compared to a legal censorship board. He asserted, much like Mrs. Bulson from Michigan, that the only reason the NB even had "lecturers working in the states where Censorship was agitated" was because it was funded by the industry, to which his audience responded positively.[104]

After years of effort, the Virginia House of Delegates passed the Mapp Act on 9 March. According to the secretary of the Virginia Motion Picture Exhibitors League, "a crowd of Clergymen and Welfare workers walked into the Hall" after midnight and "had the clock set back and had the bill passed." This "well planned, prearranged affair" had been designed to exclude exhibitors, theater owners, and their allies from presenting their point of view to the legislators.[105] Despite being locked out of the discussion and process, the exhibitors still hoped the bill would die in the Senate.

By 10 March, the final day of the 1922 legislative session, the censorship bill had become hostage to political interests. Senator Robert F. Leedy, who opposed the Mapp Act and the concept of a political censorship board, proposed that Virginia adopt a hybrid law that empowered the National Board; he even threatened to filibuster the Mapp Act.[106] This would have prevented approximately 150 other bills from being heard and voted on before the end of the session, including a $12 million highway bond issue, the biennial state appropriations bill (which contained "many pet measures," such as a proposal for a new war memorial), and a compulsory education bill.[107]

Although Senator Mapp had sufficient votes to have his pet measure passed, his opponents continued to put up last-minute "parliamentary obstacles," including threatening to invoke cloture and change Senate rules, and these maneuvers forced Mapp to spend the last hours of the session making concessions and striking deals. Thus the censorship debate in Virginia came to its end with a powerful senator expending all of his political capital just to move the bill to the floor.[108] Censorship evolved into a political game in Virginia that no New Yorker could have entered, let alone influenced. On 15 March, the Senate passed the Mapp Act.[109] When it went into effect on 1 August, Virginia became the sixth and final state in the nation to create a censorship board.

When Virginia exhibitor Harry Bernstein wrote to the National Board to share the terrible news that the Mapp Act had been passed, he expressed the hope that at least the "right kind of men [might] be placed on this Board."[110] The new Virginia State Board of Censors was to have three members, who would be appointed by Governor E. Lee Trinkle. It was charged with "prevent[ing] the display of films that are 'obscene, indecent, immoral, or inhuman,'" or that "would tend to corrupt morals or incite to crime."[111] Nadine Ward contacted McGuire and reassured him that the first appointment to the state board, Evan Chesterman, was "a very excellent choice." Chesterman, a former writer for the *Richmond Dispatch* and a former member of the state board of education, had "been associated with newspaper and educational interests for many years," and Ward believed he could be "counted upon for a broad-minded constructive policy."[112]

Trinkle also appointed Emma Speed Sampson—Mary Mason Speed's sister-in-law—to the board. Emma Speed Sampson was a writer by profession and the chairwoman of the VFWC's Motion Pictures Committee. Ward described her as "a fine broad minded woman with a keen sense of humor."[113] In addition to movie reviews and home economics columns for the *Richmond Dispatch*, Sampson also wrote southern historical romances and novels that featured a "Negro" dialect, like *Mammy's White Folks* (1920) and the *Miss Minerva* series. Upon joining the board, she subscribed the Virginia State Board of Censors to the NB's publications list and agreed to send the Virginia board's reports to the NB.[114] The third appointee was Richard C. L. Moncure (D), a former state senator from the 13th District in northern Virginia.[115] The exhibitors initially thought they had little to fear from Governor Trinkle's appointments. Jake Wells wrote a letter of introduction to the National Board for Evan Chesterman, asking that the board teach him "the general way of reviewing pictures."[116] The NB also invited Emma Speed Sampson to New York for an orientation and training session, although it is not clear that she attended.

The Virginia bill empowered three censors to approve, make recommendations for cuts, or reject films. Films that "prove[d] so objectionable . . . as seemingly to defy improvement, even after undergoing numerous eliminations or deletions," would be rejected in toto. The law did not permit the board's members to "correct historical errors, or inaccuracies in literary form, however irritating such errors or inaccuracies may prove to sensitive souls." The standards that the Virginia State Board of Censors worked to uphold did not differ significantly from those used by the National Board. However, there was one key difference: the Virginia board's recommendations carried the weight of law. Any film that did not bear the Virginia license could not be exhibited in the Commonwealth. If a film was exhibited without a license, the board could slap fines on both the exhibitor and the filmmaker (typically $25 for the first offense). Moreover, the state board was controlled by white Virginians, and its decisions would prove to reflect white interests.[117]

The Virginia board began screening films in August 1922, and every two weeks, it published a bulletin that "contain[ed] a complete list of all the films licensed and of all of the eliminations made during the period covered by the report."[118] The board distributed its bulletin to theater managers and volunteer inspectors across the state, and many of the inspectors were members of the VFWC. The clubwomen had quickly reconciled themselves to the fact of legal film censorship in the state. Rather than abandoning the cause, they became directly involved—perhaps because Sampson continued her work as the VFWC's chairwoman on moving pictures.[119] She asked her fellow clubwomen to "see that all the films shown in their local theatres [bore] the Virginia State Seal and [had been] 'passed by the Virginia Board of Censors.'" She noted that the censorship board had "raise[d] the standard of the pictures shown in the state," but that there was "still room for improvement." The board "welcome[d] suggestions from the club women, as we know they have the interests of the youth of Virginia at heart."[120] Virginia's clubwomen embraced the opportunity to remain involved in, and central to, this political and cultural movement.

Virginia's pro-censorship forces not only had held their ground against the encroachment of the National Board and its alternative to legal censorship, but had achieved victory on their own terms, in the form of a state board. Moving pictures exhibited in Virginia would reflect the worldview of the elite white men (and occasionally women) who had been appointed to the board, which was preoccupied with racial management. Racial control was not explicitly written into the Mapp Act, and pro-censorship activists did not explicitly describe their work in the language of increased racial control. However, after the Virginia State Board of Censors began screening motion pictures, white supremacists easily deployed the Mapp Act in service of their vision. For example, the board declared in its first annual report (covering the years 1924 and 1925) that it had taken special care to censor films that contained scenes or subtitles "calculated to produce friction between the races." The report stressed that the board's members had "scrutinized with peculiar care all films which touch upon the relations existing between whites and blacks."[121]

Black filmmaker Oscar Micheaux repeatedly ran into difficulties with Virginia's censorship board because his films explored topics the censors found controversial, such as interracial relationships, lynching, and the complexities of racial "passing." His films do not appear on the National Board's lists of controversial films, but they were frequent targets of the Virginia board. After all, as historian J. Douglas Smith affirmed, most of those selected to serve on the screening committee "had gone on record as strict advocates of Virginia's Racial Integrity Act."[122] In 1925, the Virginia board screened Micheaux's *The House Behind the Cedars* (Micheaux Film Corporation, 1924), adapted from a book by African American novelist Charles Chesnutt dealing with interracial marriage. Although Micheaux agreed to the revisions and cuts first recommended by the board, the board decided that since the film was so controversial, it needed to be screened a second time to an audience of influential white citizens and state officeholders before a final decision could be made. After the second screening, the board rejected the film in toto, saying it would "cause friction between the races and might therefore incite to crime."[123] Micheaux responded with a strongly worded letter arguing that only "one picture incited the colored people to riot"—D. W. Griffith's *The Birth of a Nation*.[124]

Micheaux never enjoyed a good working relationship with the Virginia board—it did not improve over time. In 1932, he attempted to secure a license to exhibit his film *Veiled Aristocrats* (an adaptation of *The House Behind the Cedars*) at the Attucks, a black-owned movie theater in Norfolk.[125] *Veiled Aristocrats* follows the struggles of a light-skinned African American family in North Carolina. The son, John, is a lawyer successfully passing as white. When he learns that his sister, Rena, is engaged to a dark-skinned black man named Frank, he returns to his hometown. White residents have witnessed Rena and her betrothed together in public and assume they are an interracial couple. To protect her, John convinces Rena to move with him, and she, too, successfully passes as white; they even employ black servants. The film ends with Rena returning to Frank and marrying him. However, the state censors detected subversive content in *Veiled Aristocrats*: the main characters are African Americans successfully passing as white; they hold professional jobs and enjoy privileges usually available only to well-off white families, such as the ability to have household servants.[126] Perhaps the suggestion of white violence, targeting Rena and Frank, also concerned the censors. Rena's marriage to Frank moves her back into her place in the racial hierarchy, resolving one of the problems. What does not change is the perception of Rena and Frank as an interracial couple, and the still-looming threat of violence.

The Virginia State Board of Censors voted unanimously to reject the film in toto. Moncure, the director of the board, explained that *Veiled Aristocrats* would be "unsatisfactory to the Colored people of the State and . . . it is unfair to them." Moncure argued that if "Negroes would try to associate with the Whites in Virginia [it] would incite to crime."[127] Of course, the board had not consulted with African Americans to ask for representative opinions on the film; nor did it acknowledge that the movie was likely to be shown exclusively to black audiences. For the Virginia censorship board, the issue with *Veiled Aristocrats* in particular—and Micheaux's oeuvre in general—was that it depicted a version of the world in which the Racial Integrity Act and the Public Assemblages Act did not exist. Fearing that *Veiled Aristocrats* might inspire African Americans to cross boundaries of race and class, the board members moved to protect both white and black residents of the Commonwealth from those possibilities. Censorship had become part of the state's move toward increasingly managed race relations.

Through its censorship board, Virginians increased the power and reach of their state government into leisure activities in the name of racial control, sacrificing freedom of expression in the process. The lawyer Morris Ernst and the filmmaker Pare Lorentz, writing in their 1930 volume *Censored: The Private Life of the Movie*, posited that if Thomas Jefferson, "the loose-limbed figure of the Declaration of Independence," were to return to Virginia and learn of the motion picture censorship law, he would be forced to ask himself "whether, after all, it was worth it."[128] Despite the efforts of Mary Gray Peck, Mary Mason Speed, and other local allies, the National Board had fought a losing battle to protect motion pictures from government intervention in Virginia. From 1922 until 1966, when the Virginia General Assembly discontinued funding to the Division of Motion Picture Censorship and disbanded it, all motion pictures exhibited legally in Virginia were mediated and censored by political appointees who did not represent the needs or interests of black Virginians.

ALTHOUGH THE NATIONAL BOARD SYSTEM WAS DEFEATED in New York and Virginia, and supplanted by state departments of motion picture censorship, McGuire could be confident that it had thwarted legislation across the South. In a March 1922 letter to McGuire, Paramount's H. T. Jones reported on the concrete results of their educational campaigns to promote Better Films Committees. He noted that Paramount's Southern Enterprises had invested a "considerable sum of money in the speaking campaigns" of Louise Connolly and Mary Mason Speed, and that the "executives state openly that they have never spent a like sum in a better cause, nor have they received more satisfactory results." Jones was satisfied with the Florida hybrid law, and he declared that "Miss Connolly practically silenced censorship agitation in Georgia and broke its back-bone in North Carolina." He felt confident of "similar results" in Alabama, which, in fact, they achieved. As for Mary Mason Speed, she had "completely silenced the opposition" in South Carolina and Tennessee, where the major cities had adopted the City Plan and Better Films Committees.[129]

Together, Connolly and Speed were responsible for starting Better Films Committees in fourteen cities. These committees provided coverage for additional territory, given the patterns and practices of booking, distribution, and exhibition in the 1920s. Jones had nothing but praise for the Better Films Committees and believed their "full significance" had not been "recognized at first glance." These two women, he wrote, "organized our old opposition and are capitalizing their efforts and energies . . . to 'sell' our pictures for us." He noted that the industry benefited tremendously from this cooperation locally, citing the example of the Metropolitan Theatre in Atlanta, whose manager had seen an increase in receipts of $1,700 since the formation of the local Better Films Committee. In closing, Jones commended McGuire and the National Board, noting that "it is now the definite policy of this organization [Southern Enterprises] to show no pictures which fail to comply with the recommendations of the National Board."[130]

CONCLUSION: CENSORSHIP AND
THE AGE OF SELF-REGULATION, 1924–1968

WHILE EXHIBITORS AND GENERAL FEDERATION OF WOM-
en's Club members established fruitful partnerships through local Better
Films Committees, scandals continued to erode the motion picture industry's
public image. In July 1921, a corruption trial in Massachusetts generated startling revelations about the morals of motion picture industry members. Attorney General J. Weston Allen appeared in the State Supreme Court in Boston
to make a case for removing Middlesex County District Attorney Nathan A.
Tufts from office. Witnesses testified that, four years earlier, Tufts had solicited a $100,000 bribe out of a Paramount Pictures executive, Hiram Abrams,
in exchange for not prosecuting them for incidents "relative to certain midnight festivities at Mishawum Manor," a notoriously bawdy roadhouse. Allegedly, Abrams, Adolph Zukor, Jesse Lasky, and several other men left a dinner in honor of Roscoe "Fatty" Arbuckle at the Copley Plaza Hotel in Boston
and traveled a few miles to Woburn, the site of Mishawum Manor, a club operated by a woman named "Brownie" Kennedy. The men drank, danced, and
caroused with more than a dozen "professional" women into "the early hours
of the morning." Some spent the night, and Abrams was seen paying the entire bill the next morning.[1]

Two months later, on 10 September, Fatty Arbuckle, a popular comedian, was arrested and jailed for the murder of actress Virginia Rappe—and
women's club members, ministers, and moral reformers nationwide seized on
the scandal as evidence of the entire industry's irredeemable debauchery and
proof of the need for a federal censorship commission. Within days of Arbuckle's arrest, theater owners in California, Connecticut, Massachusetts,
Maine, Ohio, and New York canceled the exhibition of Arbuckle's films. The
head of the Memphis Board of Censors and the Rhode Island police commissioner exercised their local control options under the City Plan to stop exhi-

bition of his films in their respective jurisdictions until and "unless the actor cleared himself."[2]

In response to the Arbuckle scandal, major studio heads met immediately, creating a new trade association to replace the National Association of the Motion Picture Industry (NAMPI), which had been headquartered in New York. The new association was the Motion Picture Producers and Distributors of America (MPPDA), to be headquartered in Hollywood. In January 1922, the MPPDA announced that Will H. Hays, who was a Presbyterian elder, the chairman of the Republican National Committee, and the postmaster general of the United States, would head the organization and rehabilitate the industry's image. Hays's position was modeled on a recent innovation in the National Baseball Commission. After the 1919 World Series, which had been marred by accusations that several members of the Chicago White Sox had accepted bribes from the notorious gangster Arnold Rothstein to throw the game, baseball's public reputation was damaged. The National Baseball Commission had hired a federal judge, Kenesaw Landis, as the commissioner for baseball. Like Landis, Hays would serve as the arbiter of disputes in the motion picture industry, with a charge of acting in the best interests of motion pictures.[3]

The GFWC exerted tremendous influence on Hays to "temporarily" withdraw Fatty Arbuckle's films from the market during his prolonged trial. After Arbuckle's arrest in September 1921, Rose Wood Allen Chapman, who chaired the GFWC Committee on Motion Pictures, "wrote a letter of protest," and within a few days, Hays announced that Arbuckle's films had been "temporarily withdrawn . . . from circulation." Chapman then appealed to Hays to make the ban permanent.[4] Following Arbuckle's acquittal in April 1922, Hays asked exhibitors nationwide to cancel exhibition of the controversial comedian's films, and they complied. In late December 1922, just days before Christmas, Hays announced that Arbuckle's films would once again be available for public exhibition. Perhaps he hoped the announcement would go unnoticed during the holiday season, but a firestorm of opposition arose in response. "Mayors of the leading cities of the country . . . voiced their disapproval," along with "clergy and church organizations," women's clubs and other women's organizations, "associations of theater owners," the National Education Association, and the Catholic Welfare Council. The Los Angeles Woman's Club passed a resolution "opposing [Arbuckle's] reappearance in pictures." The Catholic Welfare Council noted that it was commendable that Hays wanted to give Arbuckle a second chance, but the "public was likely to suspect that the desire to recover the millions of dollars invested in unreleased Arbuckle films has outweighed the producers' announced purpose to serve the American public in a manner which would merit its respect." The

National Education Association pointed out that Arbuckle, as an actor, had an "influence on public ideals" that was "direct and powerful." Because screen stars were "idealized by tens of thousands of American youth," the NEA reasoned, Arbuckle's films should not be exhibited. The members of the association feared the films would corrupt America's children.[5]

After Hays's announcement, Boston Mayor James M. Curley, at the urging of Massachusetts clubwomen, banned the exhibition of Arbuckle's films in Boston. Clubwomen in Chicago, Philadelphia, St. Louis, Buffalo, and several smaller cities nationwide also protested Arbuckle's return to the screen, expressing disappointment in Hays and the MPPDA. Mrs. Charles (Elizabeth) Merriam of Chicago, chairwoman of the Better Films Department of the Parent-Teacher Association of Illinois, declared that it was "much more disastrous . . . for a motion picture star's private life to be tainted than for the star to have to play an evil character on the film. Arbuckle cannot come back to the Chicago screen, for the children will surely associate him with his recent sensational trial."[6] Clubwomen in Buffalo, New York, announced that Hays's decision to allow Arbuckle back on the screen broke their faith in the new MPPDA. Mrs. Charles Siegesmond, who chaired the moving picture commission of the Buffalo Women's Club, said, "We have been deceived by Will H. Hays."[7] Boston mayor Curley thought "all Arbuckle films should be barred, despite Mr. Hays's action," the *New York Times* said, paraphrasing him. The paper then quoted Curley as saying, "It is not only a matter of public morals but one involving the protection of the industry as well."[8]

In his "bid to improve the industry's public image," Hays adopted an "open-door policy" that, according to film historian Ruth Vasey, was "designed to recruit influential organizations in support of a publicly led program of motion picture reform." The MPPDA's Committee on Public Relations served as the "cornerstone" of that effort. Composed of "representatives of powerful community groups, which Hays hoped would serve to channel 'destructive' censorship energies into a constructive drive toward higher movie standards," Vasey wrote, the Committee on Public Relations would assume "a role similar to that of the National Board of Review; it would have been a source of information and advice without wielding any binding power."[9]

Rose Wood Allen Chapman, from the GFWC's Committee on Motion Pictures, asked clubwomen at the GFWC Sixteenth Biennial in Chautauqua, New York, during the summer of 1922 to accept that "if the motion picture can be made an influence for evil it can also be made an even greater power for good." They agreed to back Will Hays and the newly formed MPPDA. Chapman boasted that "among the first persons" Hays called "into consultation" upon arriving in Hollywood was Alice Ames Winter, the former president of the GFWC. Hays asked Winter to work in public relations for the

MPPDA, and Chapman interpreted the appointment as evidence of the power and influence of the GFWC. She announced that Hays and "practically the entire body of motion picture exhibitors" were finally "beginning to realize the power of the women and to appreciate their co-operative spirit." Chapman underscored that Hays's open-door policy ensured that "many helpful suggestions made by the women for the improvement of conditions will be accepted."[10]

Under Chapman's leadership, the GFWC also established its own "Reviewing Committee," which issued a list of recommended moving pictures directly to *Moving Picture Age*, a publication dedicated to the emerging field of visual instruction.[11] Chapman announced her intentions to strengthen the other committees within her department in order to meet the demand for lists of pictures suitable for children, families, religious instruction, and Americanization. Her committee had adapted the National Board's method, but rejected its authority, and backed the MPPDA.

After New York governor Miller signed the Lusk-Clayton Motion Picture Censorship Bill in 1921, establishing the New York State Department of Motion Picture Censorship, the National Board's executive secretary, McGuire, was unwilling to tolerate former allies who had now expressed support for a state board. When Dr. Francis Rowley, the president of the Massachusetts Society for the Prevention of Cruelty to Animals, contacted the National Board about *Trapping the Bobcat* (Pathé, 1921), McGuire responded with exasperation. *Trapping the Bobcat* was the second film in a popular Pathé series for children, *The Adventures of Bob and Bill* (Pathé, 1921). The one-reel shorts featured cute twin brothers "trailing the coyote," "outwitting the timber wolf," and investigating "mysterious tracks."[12] A member of the SPCA described *Trapping the Bobcat* as "a most disgustingly cruel picture" and said "its influence upon boys must be most demoralizing."[13] The NB Review Committee that screened *Trapping the Bobcat* on 1 November 1920 passed it subject to elimination. The NB asked Pathé to "shorten to flashes the scenes where the cat is on his back with the choking contrivance around his neck, while his feet are being tied."[14]

Because *Trapping the Bobcat* "could in a general way be termed a picture of outdoor life," McGuire felt that the NB had already tampered with it enough. McGuire believed that "the reducing of these scenes to short flashes carried the continuity and obviated the objectionable feature of the picture," but overall, he told Rowley in a letter, he "disagreed" that the "picture was a disgustingly cruel one." Moreover, he said, "I do not doubt that a great many of our members contribute to the SPCA." McGuire closed his letter by pointing out that the complaint about *Trapping the Bobcat* had come from Baltimore, Maryland. "You understand, of course, that there is a state censorship in Maryland." He advised Rowley to contact the secretary of the Maryland Board of Censors.[15]

McGuire exhibited a similar frustration when William O. Stillman of the American Humane Association contacted him about *Man vs. Beast* (Educational Film Company, 1922).[16] Stillman passed on a complaint from Rochester, New York, describing *Man vs. Beast* as "showing the struggles of . . . dying creatures," including giraffes and hippopotamuses. Stillman acknowledged that the movie was billed as "an educational picture," but he had nevertheless received multiple complaints against it "on the ground that it depicts cruelty and would tend to educate people, particularly children, to enjoy brutal and vicious scenes."[17] McGuire reviewed the ballots from the screening of *Man vs. Beast* and informed Stillman that "the people who reviewed the picture would unquestionably have recommended a change in it if the scene you referred to had impressed them as cruel or inhuman." He suggested that this complaint was "another case where . . . some oversensitive person who has happened to see the picture has made complaint upon it." He concluded by pointing out that the New York State Board of Censors had also passed *Man vs. Beast*. "As I recall the matter, you were quite active in the support of state censorship at the time the hearing was held in Albany and it is possible that you may wish to take the matter up with them."[18]

Animal rights activists subsequently turned to the MPPDA and their partner studios with complaints and concerns about animal cruelty. Two women, Fannie Thompson Kessler and Rosamond Rae Wright, who had been protesting "cruelties inflicted on animals in the movies and on the stage," successfully organized the American Animal Defense League (AADL) in 1923. The goal of the organization was to "combat cruelty to animals in motion pictures, vaudeville, and the circus." Like the MPPDA, it was headquartered in Los Angeles, which had emerged as the "center of the motion picture industry."[19] Fred Beetson, the MPPDA's secretary and treasurer, discovered that many studios were in the midst of battles over film content with the AADL. The Hal Roach Studios hired the Burns Detective Agency to investigate the AADL, but only uncovered "general information . . . more or less of a gossipy or hearsay nature." Beetson discovered that Wright's credentials from the Los Angeles SPCA and the Humane Society had lapsed, but she had somehow acquired a Los Angeles Police Department badge. Beetson noted to Hays that he was considering hiring the Pinkertons to investigate her further, and that Hal Roach was personally working on getting her LAPD badge revoked. "So far," Beetson wrote Hays, he had successfully kept Wright "off any of the important committees of the Federated Women's Clubs, of which of course she is a member."[20]

Ultimately, the National Board of Review and its animal welfare allies made significant and long-lasting contributions to the humane treatment of animal actors in motion picture and, later, television productions. The SPCA and the AHA pushed producers to adopt an industry-wide policy against harming animals in motion picture productions that was later adapted for TV and remains in effect to this day under the auspices of the AHA. Motion pictures are still required to carry a seal in the ending credits saying that "no animals were harmed" during the filming or production, and humane agents are on set to monitor the health and welfare of the animals being used.[21]

The NB also continued to monitor the treatment of newsreels by state censorship boards during the era of the MPPDA. The US Supreme Court issued several landmark rulings related to freedom of speech after the war; *Schenck v. United States* (1919), in particular, established the "clear and present danger" test to determine the limits of speech.[22] It was within this climate that McGuire and Samuel Gompers of the American Federation of Labor continued to push for policies exempting newsreels from the scrutiny of censors. Although the National Board ultimately failed to become the national arbiter of motion picture standards that it had set out to be, the organization bequeathed important legacies to the First Amendment history of motion pictures.

In November 1919, the Pennsylvania State Board of Censors censored a Pathé newsreel about the latest coal strike. The National Board had maintained, since its inception, that the censors' scissors should never touch newsreels; newsreels were organs of the press, and freedom of the press was sacrosanct. Even more alarming, the Pennsylvania censors had eliminated "statements of [the] miners' position regarding [the] coal strike" in the piece, as well as a "view of Mr. [John L.] Lewis directing [the] strike." McGuire wired Gompers: "Government's position is allowed to remain in picture, strikers' position has been ordered cut out."[23] From the NB's position, the Pennsylvania board's action against the Pathé newsreel was an entirely political, and therefore unconstitutional, censoring of the press. McGuire was more convinced than ever that "wherever state censorship of motion pictures is proposed it should be fought tooth and nail by the labor organizations of that state."[24]

In 1922, the Kansas Board of Censors cut scenes of a conflict known as "the Herrin Massacre" from Pathé and Selznick newsreels because they were exceedingly violent. In this event, unionized coal miners in southern Illinois had attacked and killed several strikebreakers. McGuire took an ideologically consistent position in this case, and the NB protested the Kansas board's action, even though the footage in question was not sympathetic to the union miners. The bottom line was that these were newsreels, and the Kansas board's action represented "the fastening of . . . designing, ignorant, irresponsible tyranny upon our free institutions," which, in the NB's pantheon, included "newsweeklies," that is, weekly newsreels covering current events.[25]

To the NB's dismay, the newly empaneled New York State Motion Picture Commission also ordered Pathé to cut out "certain scenes" from other newsreels. In February 1922, the Pathé Frères Company filed suit against the New York State commission, arguing that "newsreels are as much news of the day as articles or pictures printed in newspapers and are subject to the same freedom as is granted to the press by the State Constitution." Pathé's lawyers argued that the company's newsweeklies should not be considered in "the same category as fictional pictures" because they were "not reproductions or reenactments of the events depicted"; rather, they were "truthful pictures of actual events and actual things taken on the ground as they exist or occur with motion picture cameras and made by the usual processes of photographs." They should thus be exempted from New York State's requirement that the commission "examine and license all motion pictures."[26] McGuire contacted AFL president Samuel Gompers when the Appellate Division of the New York State Supreme Court issued its decision on newsweeklies. The court had sustained the lower court order granting the State Motion Picture Commission the right to censor newsreels. McGuire felt that this was "a serious matter from the standpoint of the AFL, because it gives control over the news weeklies to a political party." He suggested that the AFL join Pathé in its litigation against the New York law, warning that "the time may come when the Federation of Labor will have to present its own side of the labor question through a motion picture weekly." If newsreels were "subject to capitalistic censorship," he told Gompers, "you [would not be able to] get your case before the workers of the country."[27]

Although it is not evident from the correspondence, the Pathé newsreels in question featured "a picture of the beauty carnival held in Atlantic City," which included "pictures of several bathing girls in the carnival." The moving pictures were censored even though "similar pictures were printed in newspapers." Pathé's lawyers claimed that there was "no connection" between the beauty carnival newsreel and the timing of the lawsuit; rather, Pathé sought to address "the broad basis of constitutional rights granted the press," not just the right to publish pictures of bathing beauties.[28]

The AFL did not join the Pathé lawsuit, but it did unanimously adopt a resolution in 1922 at its annual convention, declaring that "censorship in any field of expression constitutes an insidious threat to freedom of expression through all mediums." Thus the AFL—and its newly affiliated craft unions within the motion picture industry—reaffirmed its opposition to "all forms of political and bureaucratic censorship boards and commissions as unwarranted and extremely dangerous infringement upon the freedom of expression and freedom of the press."[29] The AFL and the NB were in the vanguard of thinking about First Amendment protections and rights to speech and expression. The US Supreme Court did not fully recognize the freedom of the press, or reject any prior restraints on newspapers, until the *Near v. Minnesota* decision in 1931.

In December 1922, the People's Institute officially dissolved its relationship with the National Board of Review, in part because of the NB's failure to prevent the New York State censorship bill from passing, and in part because McGuire had been accused of compromising the integrity of the organization by allowing industry members to influence its agenda vis-à-vis the compromise laws.[30] The National Board continued its "critical" work as an independent organization, focusing on its annual prizes and supporting the work of the Better Films Committees, which many clubwomen supported and ran in their own communities.

In April 1923, the National Board had an unexpected change in leadership when McGuire suddenly died from complications related to surgery for appendicitis.[31] Wilton Barrett became the new executive secretary, with Dr. William B. Tower as chairman. By 1924, the board had retreated from its constructive work of voluntary regulation and its political work organizing against censorship and had redirected its efforts to three other areas: its Critique Committee, promotion of "exceptional photoplays," and publication of a magazine called *Films in Review*.

The National Committee for Better Films continued to grow in influence and in 1923 adopted a new "membership creed." The creed "emphasize[d] the necessity of improving pictures by selecting and patronizing the good photoplays," affirmed the need for "special family nights," and noted the need for active cooperation with exhibitors. Miriam Sutro Price and Birdie Stein Gans, who were both prominent in educational reform and in the Ethical Culture movement that arose in the late nineteenth century, remained active in the Better Films Committee, and their influence on the NB's way of thinking remains clear in the last section of the creed, which noted that "parents should . . . study their children and . . . regulate their attendance at motion picture theatres. If these rules are carried out all over the country then there won't be any need for a campaign to have better films."[32]

When the GFWC reconvened at its 1924 biennial, Mrs. Harry Lilly was chairwoman of the GFWC Committee on Motion Pictures, a position she had taken over after Rose Wood Allen Chapman's death. At the biennial, Lilly announced, "A moot question is that of censorship." The GFWC, as a body, now approved of the policy of "cooperating with the industry until it proves itself unworthy of our confidence in its efforts to improve its own standard."

She asked the clubwomen to "acquaint" themselves with the "provisions of the penal code of our respective states in its relation to public morals that we may learn the strength or weakness of our defense against the exhibition of objectionable pictures."[33]

In 1925, the Better Films Committee "denounced" government censorship of films. Censorship decisions, it said, too often were "political" judgments "representing a minority" opinion on given titles. The committee backed the efforts of Al Smith, the governor of New York, to repeal the state law, "and went on record as opposed to the Upshaw bill for a Federal censorship of the screen," according to the *New York Times*. The Better Films Committee favored the creation of "motion picture study clubs" nationwide. These would be "citizen groups" that would study different types of films in "a course developed by the National Committee [on Better Films]." The committee hoped that those who took the course might "become forces in their communities demanding, supporting and creating public support for good films of all types and especially for the unusual, artistic film which needs trained and appreciative audiences." These same study groups would be instructed to "ignore" films with obscene or objectionable content so as not to call attention to them, whether positive or negative. The National Board would provide the groups with lists of recommended films through its *Photoplay Guide*.[34] These curated lists of suggested films reinforced the concept of audience segmentation by age decades before the industry itself embraced the concept.

Among those who had devised the plan were Mrs. Harry Lilly, former chairwoman of the GFWC Motion Picture Committee; Ruth Rich, an editor of the journal of the National Association of Business and Professional Women, *The Independent Woman*, and a member of the National Advisory Board from Florida; Wilton A. Barrett, the executive secretary of the NB; Alice B. Evans, the secretary of the National Committee for Better Films (formerly of the NB); and Colonel Jason Joy, executive secretary of the MPPDA's Public Relations Committee.[35] Despite the MPPDA's open-door policy and its Public Relations Committee, motion picture producers had not fallen into line and joined in the effort to make more of the kinds of films that the boards and committees would welcome. As a result, Hays issued his "Thirteen Points" in 1922, followed by the "Don'ts and Be Carefuls" in 1927, and, ultimately, the Production Code in 1930. The NB conceded to Hays, the MPPDA, and the GFWC as soon as the threat of legal censorship had passed.

The six states with censorship boards, in addition to dozens of cities using the National Board's City Plan, continued monitoring the movies well into the era of the Production Code Administration, tailoring Hollywood's output to their local context. In Memphis, notoriously racist head censor Lloyd Binford continued to police the screens for miscegenation and any vision of "social equality" into the 1940s and 1950s, as historian Whitney Strub has detailed.[36] Atlanta's head censor in 1960, Christine Smith Gilliam, refused to issue a license for *Never on Sunday* (*Pote tin Kyriaki*, 1960). This film, a Greek romantic comedy, starred Melina Mercouri as Ilya, a vivacious prostitute, and Jules Dassin as Homer, an American classics scholar who falls in love with her. Of this Pygmalion tale, Gilliam thought that "no movie in which a prostitute's life is depicted as fun should be offered to the public."[37] Luther Alverson, a Superior Court judge in Fulton County, Georgia, reversed the ban, arguing that "parents, not censors, should be responsible for their children's moviegoing."[38] The Atlanta Board of Censors was relieved of its official censorship duties in 1963, but the city of Atlanta retained authority to "pass laws which make showing obscene movies a crime." This included the "authority to require the pre-screening of movies for the protection of youth."[39] After her retirement from public service in 1962, Gilliam reported seeing only one movie—the classic film adaptation of another Pygmalion story, *My Fair Lady* (1964).

By the time the Atlanta Board of Censors ceased operations in 1963, legal opinion on motion picture censorship was changing. For a few years, it had been moving toward a slow acceptance of the movies as more than a business, and as speech, art, and expression. In 1952, the US Supreme Court revised its own 1915 decision from *Mutual Film Corporation v. Industrial Commission of Ohio*. The new ruling, in *Burstyn v. Wilson*—often called the Miracle decision—concerned a short Italian film released in 1950 called *The Miracle*, written and directed by Roberto Rossellini and starring Italy's most famous actress, Anna Magnani, as Nanni, a naïve peasant girl suffering from mental illness. A man passing himself off as St. Joseph seduces Nanni and she becomes pregnant; she believes it is an immaculate conception. Catholics in New York City protested the film as sacrilegious, and they succeeded in pressuring the New York State Department of Education to revoke the license to exhibit the film on those grounds. When the US Supreme Court heard the case, it ruled that the New York State Censorship Board's act was a prior restraint on speech, and therefore unconstitutional. The justices noted that motion pictures had become "a significant medium for the communication of ideas" since 1915, and therefore, that they existed "within the free speech and free press guaranty of the First and Fourteenth Amendments."[40]

In 1962, a small act of defiance by one Baltimore exhibitor finally brought down the entire network of state censorship boards. The exhibitor, Ronald Freedman, decided to show *Revenge at Daybreak* (1952) without first submitting it to the Maryland State Board of Censors. In 1965 the US Supreme Court heard *Freedman v. Maryland* and ruled that state censorship boards were unconstitutional prior restraints. Henceforth, such boards could no longer ban films—they could merely rate them.[41] This decision brought an end to state censorship boards and to the era in which producers attempted to comply with the Production Code. In 1968, the Motion Picture Classification Board of the City of Dallas refused to issue a license to Interstate Circuit, the distributors of *Viva Maria!* (1965). *Viva Maria!* is a French comedy-adventure starring Jeanne Moreau and Brigitte Bardot, whose character performs a seductive striptease act. The Dallas board deemed Bardot's dance sexually promiscuous and "not suitable for young persons." Interstate Circuit challenged the Dallas classification system, and the case went to the US Supreme Court. In *Interstate Circuit Inc. v. Dallas*, the Court upheld the constitutionality of age-classification boards, so long as the systems employed were clearly defined.[42]

In 1968, Jack Valenti, the new head of the Motion Picture Association of America, quickly devised a response to the *Freedman* and *Interstate Circuit* decisions. He wrote that "the irresistible force of creators determined to make 'their' films (full of wild candor, groused some social critics) and the possible intrusion of government into the movie arena demanded my immediate action."[43] In November 1968, the MPAA announced its new voluntary film rating system, which would serve to "educate parents and families about the content of films and leave to them the choice of whether a particular movie is right for their family." To assure concerned parents, Valenti announced that there were "no experts on the [ratings] board," only "average American parents."[44] Despite the efforts of the social activists affiliated with the National Board to reject the logic that parents were best suited to monitor the movies, the MPAA enshrined that concept in its ratings system in an effort to pacify critics of the industry and forestall government intervention.

APPENDIX

A PARTIAL LIST OF CITIES COOPERATING WITH
THE NATIONAL BOARD OF REVIEW, 1918

The following information comes from a document entitled "Partial List of Cities Cooperating with National Board of Review" (1918), in the folder "Regional Correspondence, Oregon," box 68, National Board of Review of Motion Pictures Records, Manuscripts and Archives Division, New York Public Library, Astor, Lenox, and Tilden Foundations.

Alabama: Birmingham, Mobile
Arkansas: Little Rock
California: Oakland, Pasadena, San Francisco
Colorado: Denver, Pueblo
Connecticut: Bridgeport, Hartford, New Haven, Waterbury
District of Columbia: Washington
Georgia: Augusta, Atlanta
Idaho: Boise
Illinois: Evanston, Springfield
Indiana: Indianapolis, Elkhart, South Bend
Iowa: Davenport, Des Moines
Kentucky: Lexington, Louisville
Louisiana: New Orleans
Massachusetts: Boston, Brockton, Fitchburg, Haverhill, Lynn, Malden,
    Somerville, Worcester
Michigan: Detroit, Grand Rapids, Kalamazoo
Minnesota: Duluth, Minneapolis, St. Paul
Missouri: Joplin, St. Louis
Montana: Butte
Nebraska: Lincoln, Omaha
New Jersey: Elizabeth, Newark, Plainfield, Trenton

New York: Binghamton, Buffalo, Newburgh, Niagara Falls, Rochester,
     Syracuse
North Carolina: Charlotte, Greensboro, Raleigh
North Dakota: Grand Forks
Oklahoma: Guthrie
Rhode Island: Providence
South Carolina: Charlestown
Tennessee: Chattanooga, Memphis, Nashville
Texas: Dallas, San Antonio
Utah: Salt Lake City
Vermont: Montpelier
Virginia: Norfolk, Richmond
Washington: Seattle, Spokane
Wisconsin: Eau Claire, Beloit, Green Bay, La Crosse, Madison,
     Milwaukee, Superior

INTRODUCTION

1. *Enlighten Thy Daughter* (1917), American Film Institute (AFI) Catalog.

2. "Enlighten Thy Daughter," *The Charlotte (NC) News*, 30 May 1917, 9, www .newspapers.com/newspage/61378310.

3. "The Newest Film Crusade: 'Enlighten Thy Daughter' an Inept Movie Melodrama," *New York Times*, 29 January 1917; *New York Telegraph* quoted in "Selected Notes on the Meeting of the National Board in Wurlitzer Hall," 24 January 1917, folder "Controversial Films Correspondence: Driven—Eternal Grind," box 104, National Board of Review of Motion Pictures Records, Manuscripts and Archives Division, New York Public Library, Astor, Lenox, and Tilden Foundations. Hereafter NBRMP.

4. "Selected Notes on the Meeting of the National Board in Wurlitzer Hall."

5. Ibid.

6. Historian Rebecca Edwards proposed replacing the "standard Gilded Age/ Progressive era narrative" with a "long Progressive Era model," one that begins in the 1870s, during Reconstruction, and ends "in the 1920s or quite possibly with the New Deal." By continuing to separate the Gilded Age from the Progressive era, Edwards argued, historians obscure the "stories of political possibilities that were open before 1900 but closed off afterward." Likewise, by setting the 1920s off from the period that preceded it, as well as from the larger currents in US governance and statecraft, historians "marginalize several narratives of declension" that characterized the immigrant and African American experience, in particular. Rebecca Edwards, "Politics, Social Movements, and the Periodization of U.S. History," *Journal of the Gilded Age and Progressive Era* 8, no. 4 (2009): 465–466, www.jstor.org/stable/40542874.

7. Andrea Friedman devotes a chapter to the work of the National Board of Review and its inability to stop its home state, New York, from adopting a legal film censor board; she characterizes the board's method as one of "democratic moral authority." Andrea Friedman, *Prurient Interests: Gender, Democracy, and Obscenity in*

New York City, 1909–1945 (New York: Columbia University Press, 2000). Similarly, Alison M. Parker argued that reformers focused especially on the risks films posed to children, as they believed that the content of movies, which increasingly settled at the lowest common denominators of sex (vamps, nearly naked women) and violence, would turn "the potential for sexual arousal into the potential moral corruption of youths." Alison M. Parker, *Purifying America: Women, Cultural Reform, and Pro-Censorship Activism, 1873–1933* (Urbana: University of Illinois Press, 1997), 2. Historian Leigh Ann Wheeler analyzes how the GFWC's members staked out territory in the censorship debate by arguing that they were uniquely suited to protecting children and naïve young women from the dangers presented by moving pictures and the spaces in which they were shown, which they feared could become sites of physical attack and abduction. Leigh Ann Wheeler, *Against Obscenity: Reform and the Politics of Womanhood in America, 1873–1935* (Baltimore: Johns Hopkins University Press, 2004), 19. See also Daniel Czitrom, "The Politics of Performance: Theater Licensing and the Origins of Movie Censorship in New York," in *Movie Censorship and American Culture*, ed. Francis G. Couvares (Washington, DC: Smithsonian Institution Press, 1996), 16–43; Lary May, *Screening Out the Past: The Birth of Mass Culture and the Motion Picture Industry* (Chicago: University of Chicago Press, 1983), 56–57.

8. Mutual Film Corporation v. Industrial Commission of Ohio, 236 U.S. 230, 244–245 (1915).

9. Lee Grieveson, in *Policing Cinema: Movies and Censorship in Early-Twentieth-Century America* (Berkeley: University of California Press, 2004), explores the effects of early efforts to censor movies (up to the 1915 *Mutual* decision) and the impact of policing and regulation on the creative climate of motion pictures in the pre-classic Hollywood period. Grieveson defined the period from 1907 to 1915 as the "transitional period" in American cinema and found that it gave rise to the "classic Hollywood" genre, which was tailored to meet censors' expectations and demands. In short, Grieveson concludes that the regulatory response to early cinema shaped the medium. In *Freedom of the Screen: Legal Challenges to State Film Censorship, 1915–1981* (Lexington: University Press of Kentucky, 2008), Laura Wittern-Keller analyzes the effects of "prior restraint" on the motion picture industry (and, therefore, motion picture content). She presents an important distinction between state censorship boards and industry self-regulation in the guise of the Production Code of 1930. The former, "state agencies with broad [legal] power," reviewed completed motion pictures, whereas the latter "regulate[d] the content of its member studios' product" through negotiations that took place "before and during production." Industry self-regulation, designed to thwart federal censorship, ended up involving the censors (directly, or through the producers internalizing and deploying their standards) in the creation of the film. *Freedom of the Screen* is an indispensable and thorough study of legal film censorship; as such, Wittern-Keller is not as interested in the role of the National Board in the sea change she charts. She notes that the NB failed to make significant headway because "moral guardians, insistent on protecting children, were not mollified" by its efforts to create local review committees, and continued their calls for governmental censorship. Wittern-Keller, *Freedom of the Screen*, 6, 24–29.

10. Mutual Film Corporation v. Industrial Commission of Ohio, 236 U.S. 230, 244–245 (1915). *Mutual* remained good law until 1952, when the Supreme Court ruled in *Burstyn v. Wilson* that the New York State Board of Censors functioned as a "restraint on freedom of speech," and was therefore a violation of the First Amendment. Burstyn v. Wilson, 343 U.S. 495 (1952); Richard Randall, *Censorship of the Movies: The Social and Political Control of a Mass Medium* (Madison: University of Wisconsin Press, 1968), 28–32.

11. Samantha Barbas, "How the Movies Became Speech," *Rutgers Law Review* 64, no. 3 (2012): 665–745. On the history of the First Amendment and its relationship to obscenity, see Alexis J. Anderson, "The Formative Period of First Amendment Theory, 1870–1915," *American Journal of Legal History* 24, no. 1 (January 1980): 56–75; Amanda Frisken, "Obscenity, Free Speech, and 'Sporting News' in 1870s America," *Journal of American Studies* 42, no. 3 (December 2008): 537–577; Molly McGarry, "Spectral Sexualities: Nineteenth-Century Spiritualism, Moral Panics, and the Making of U.S. Obscenity Law," *Journal of Women's History* 12, no. 2 (Summer 2000), 8–29; John Wertheimer, "*Mutual Film* Reviewed: The Movies, Censorship, and Free Speech in Progressive America," *American Journal of Legal History* 37, no. 2 (April 1993): 158–189.

12. "Activities of the National Board of Review of Motion Pictures," 1 January 1921, folder "Pamphlets by the National Board," box 143, NBRMP.

13. Jennifer Fronc, *New York Undercover: Private Surveillance in the Progressive Era* (Chicago: University of Chicago Press, 2009), chap. 6.

14. "Activities of the National Board of Review of Motion Pictures."

15. Ibid.

16. The National Board of Review to the Editor of *The Richmond Virginian*, 10 May 1916, folder "Regional Correspondence—Virginia," box 79, NBRMP.

17. "Twenty States Have Censorship Bills," *Motion Picture World*, 10 February 1917, 861.

18. Advertisements, *Motion Picture News*, 3 February 1917, 29 September 1917, and March 1917.

19. Mrs. Albert Bulson, *GFWC Fourteenth Biennial Convention Official Report*, 1918, pp. 450–454, Bound Convention Programs, 1910–1927, General Federation of Women's Clubs Archives, Women's History and Resource Center, General Federation of Women's Clubs.

20. Theda Skocpol, *Protecting Soldiers and Mothers: The Political Origins of Social Policy in the United States* (Cambridge, MA: Belknap Press of Harvard University Press, 1992), 368 (emphasis in original).

21. Wheeler, *Against Obscenity*, 4.

22. Parker, *Purifying America*, 142–145.

23. On women's social activism during this period, see Kathleen M. Blee, *Women of the Klan: Racism and Gender in the 1920s* (Berkeley: University of California Press, 2009); Lisa Lindquist Dorr, *White Women, Rape, and the Power of Race in Virginia, 1900–1960* (Chapel Hill: University of North Carolina Press, 2004); Glenda Gilmore, *Gender and Jim Crow: Women and the Politics of White Supremacy in North Car-*

olina, 1896–1920 (Chapel Hill: University of North Carolina Press, 1996); Francesca Morgan, *Women and Patriotism in Jim Crow America* (Chapel Hill: University of North Carolina Press, 2005); Robyn Muncy, *Creating a Female Dominion in American Reform, 1890–1935* (New York: Oxford University Press, 1994); Lorraine Gates Schuyler, *The Weight of Their Votes: Southern Women and Political Leverage in the 1920s* (Chapel Hill: University of North Carolina Press, 2006); Marjorie Spruill Wheeler, *New Women of the New South: The Leaders of the Woman Suffrage Movement in the Southern States* (New York: Oxford University Press, 1993).

24. The GFWC traces its roots to 1868, during Charles Dickens's second and final tour of the United States. The exclusive, all-male New York Press Club hosted a dinner for journalists to meet Dickens, but it denied entry to Jennie June (née Jane Cunningham Croly) and other women journalists. In response, June organized Sorosis, a women's-only club for New York City professional women. The GFWC was founded in 1890 and emerged out of a nationwide conference of women's clubs; it was designed to serve as the umbrella organization. In 1892, State Federations began to form, applying for charters from the GFWC once they met membership quotas. Pre-existing women's clubs, often located in cities, were permitted to apply directly to the General Federation for membership. Mildred White Wells, *Unity in Diversity: The History of the General Federation of Women's Clubs*, Diamond Jubilee Edition (Washington, DC: General Federation of Women's Clubs, 1965), 4.

25. McGuire to D. W. Griffith, 14 February 1919, folder "Gray—Griffith," box 28, NBRMP.

26. Wheeler discusses a similar dynamic in chapter 4 of *Against Obscenity*, "Woman vs. Woman."

27. As of this writing in early 2017, the National Board of Review of Motion Pictures is still an active critical organization. See www.nationalboardofreview.org.

CHAPTER 1: THE LESSER OF TWO EVILS

1. Paula Uruburu, *American Eve: Evelyn Nesbit, Stanford White, the Birth of the "It" Girl and the Crime of the Century* (New York: Riverhead Books, 2009), 75–76.

2. "Thaw's Wife Adds to Her Sacrifice," *San Francisco Call*, 9 February 1907, California Digital Newspaper Collection, http://cdnc.ucr.edu/cgi-bin/cdnc?a=d&d=SFC19070209.2.6, accessed 29 October 2016.

3. "The Unwritten Law," *Variety*, March 1907, www.archive.org/stream/variety06-1907-03#page/n127/mode/2up/search/%22unwritten+law%22.

4. Anna Morra, "*The Unwritten Law*: Reel Life/Real Life," 10 October 2013, www.moma.org/explore/inside_out/2013/10/10/the-unwritten-law-reel-lifereal-life.

5. *Chicago Tribune* quoted in Richard Abel, *Red Rooster Scare: Making Cinema American, 1900–1910* (Berkeley: University of California Press, 1999), 98.

6. Lee Grieveson, *Policing Cinema: Movies and Censorship in Early-Twentieth-Century America* (Berkeley: University of California Press, 2004), 41–50.

7. "Public Opinion as Moral Censor," *Moving Picture World*, 11 May 1907, http://archive.org/stream/MPW01-1907-05#page/n18/mode/1up.

8. Douglas Gomery, *Shared Pleasures: A History of Movie Presentation in the United States* (Madison: University of Wisconsin Press, 1992), 21.

9. Abel, *Red Rooster Scare*, 98; *Moving Picture World* quoted in Grieveson, *Policing Cinema*, 38.

10. Gomery, *Shared Pleasures*, 21.

11. Robert C. Allen, *Horrible Prettiness: Burlesque and American Culture* (Chapel Hill: University of North Carolina Press, 1991), 244.

12. Kathryn Fuller, *At the Picture Show: Small-Town Audiences and the Creation of Movie Fan Culture* (Washington, DC: Smithsonian Institution Press, 1996), 24–25, 28.

13. Gomery, *Shared Pleasures*, 21.

14. Jessica R. Pliley, *Policing Sexuality: The Mann Act and the Making of the FBI* (Cambridge, MA: Harvard University Press, 2014), 157.

15. Grieveson, *Policing Cinema*, 38; Abel, *Red Rooster Scare*, 97. On moral panics, see Gayle Rubin, "Thinking Sex: Notes for a Radical Theory of the Politics of Sexuality," in *Pleasure and Danger: Exploring Female Sexuality*, ed. Carole S. Vance (Boston: Routledge, 1984), 3–44.

16. David Nasaw, *Children of the City at Work and at Play* (New York: Anchor Books, 1985), 134–140.

17. Abel, *Red Rooster Scare*, 61, 67, 101; "Picture Shows All Put Out of Business," *New York Times*, 25 December 1908. See also Daniel Czitrom, "The Politics of Performance: Theater Licensing and the Origins of Movie Censorship in New York," in *Movie Censorship and American Culture*, ed. Francis G. Couvares (Washington, DC: Smithsonian Institution Press, 1996); Garth Jowett, *Film: The Democratic Art* (Boston: Focal Press, 1976), 108–113.

18. Grievseon, *Policing Cinema*, 50; Czitrom, "Politics of Performance," 22–23. According to legal scholar Barak Y. Orbach, the first laws to address motion pictures date to the late 1890s, when several states enacted statutes prohibiting the exhibition of boxing and prizefighting films (to prevent racial conflict, they claimed). Barak Y. Orbach, "Prizefighting and the Birth of Movie Censorship," *Yale Journal of Law & the Humanities* 21, no. 2 (2009), http://digitalcommons.law.yale.edu/yjlh/vol21/iss2/3.

19. Jennifer Fronc, *New York Undercover: Private Surveillance in the Progressive Era* (Chicago: University of Chicago Press, 2009), 18–19; Timothy Gilfoyle, "The Moral Origins of Political Surveillance: The Preventive Society in New York City, 1867–1918," *American Quarterly* 38 (1986): 637–652.

20. On the history of antiobscenity activism in New York City, see Andrea Friedman, *Prurient Interests: Gender, Democracy, and Obscenity in New York City, 1909–1945* (New York: Columbia University Press, 2000). On the work of the Society for the Prevention of Crime, see Timothy Gilfoyle, *A Pickpocket's Tale: The Underworld of Nineteenth-Century New York* (New York: W. W. Norton, 2006).

21. Nan Enstad, *Ladies of Labor, Girls of Adventure: Working Women, Popular*

Culture, and Labor Politics at the Turn of the Twentieth Century (New York: Columbia University Press, 1999); Miriam Hansen, *Babel and Babylon: Spectatorship in American Silent Film* (Cambridge, MA: Harvard University Press, 1991); Lea Jacobs, *The Wages of Sin: Censorship and the Fallen Woman Film, 1928–1942* (Berkeley: University of California Press, 1995); Annette Kuhn, *Cinema, Censorship, and Sexuality, 1909–1925* (New York: Routledge, 1988); Kathy Peiss, *Cheap Amusements: Working Women and Leisure in Turn-of-the-Century New York* (Philadelphia: Temple University Press, 1986); Shelley Stamp, *Movie Struck Girls: Women and Motion Picture Culture After the Nickelodeon* (Princeton, NJ: Princeton University Press, 2000); Sharon Ullman, *Sex Scene: The Emergence of Modern Sexuality in America* (Berkeley: University of California Press, 1998).

22. In *The Rights of the Defenseless: Protecting Animals and Children in Gilded Age America* (Chicago: University of Chicago Press, 2011), Susan J. Pearson explored how anticruelty reformers "brought together the language of the heart with the power of the law in an ideology of sentimental liberalism" (p. 8).

23. Diane L. Beers, *For the Prevention of Cruelty: The History and Legacy of Animal Rights Activism in the United States* (Athens: Swallow / Ohio University Press, 2006), 60–89.

24. For more on Comstock and the early years of the SSV, see Donna Dennis, *Licentious Gotham: Erotic Publishing and Its Prosecution in Nineteenth-Century New York* (Cambridge, MA: Harvard University Press, 2009), 220–222.

25. Helen Lefkowitz Horowitz, *Rereading Sex: Battles over Sexual Knowledge and Suppression in Nineteenth-Century America* (New York: Vintage Press, 2002), 14, 358.

26. Ibid., 381, 394–395, 400–402.

27. Friedman, *Prurient Interests*, 16.

28. "Reports of Cases Argued and Determined in the Federal Courts," vol. 12, Ohio Federal Decisions, 12 O.F.D., (Norwalk, OH: Laning, 1902), 49.

29. Rosen v. United States, 161 U.S. 29 (1896).

30. Roth v. United States, 354 U.S. 476 (1957).

31. Historian Frank Couvares and sociologist Nicola Kay Beisel have described the intellectual foundations of antiobscenity reform. Couvares employed the term "vulnerable viewer" to describe the rhetorical foundation of early twentieth-century reform work, whereas Beisel analyzed the roots of Anthony Comstock's crusade on behalf of children. Nicola Beisel, *Imperiled Innocents: Anthony Comstock and Family Reproduction in Victorian America* (Princeton, NJ: Princeton University Press, 1998); Frank Couvares, "Introduction," in *Movie Censorship and American Culture* (Washington, DC: Smithsonian Institution Press, 1996). See also Rochelle Gurstein, *The Repeal of Reticence: America's Cultural and Legal Struggles over Free Speech, Obscenity, Sexual Liberation, and Modern Art* (New York: Hill and Wang, 1996).

32. Ida C. Craddock, *The Wedding Night* (1902), Paul Royster, ed., Zea E-Books in American Studies, book 14, http://digitalcommons.unl.edu/zeaamericanstudies /14, accessed 11 January 2016.

33. Ida C. Craddock, "Letter to the Public on the Day of Her Suicide," 16 October 1902, www.idacraddock.com/public.html, accessed 11 January 2016.

34. Grieveson, *Policing Cinema*, 43; Uruburu, *American Eve*, 260–261.

35. Neil Miller, *Banned in Boston: The Watch and Ward Society's Crusade Against Books, Burlesque, and the Social Evil* (Boston: Beacon Books, 2011), 3. See also Paul Boyer, *Purity in Print: Book Censorship in America from the Gilded Age to the Computer Age*, 2nd ed. (Madison: University of Wisconsin Press, 2002); Elisabeth Ladenson, *Dirt for Art's Sake: Books on Trial from "Madame Bovary" to "Lolita"* (Ithaca, NY: Cornell University Press, 2007).

36. New England Watch and Ward Society, "Forty-First Annual Report of the New England Watch and Ward Society, 1918–19," New England Watch and Ward Society Records, 1918–1957, Historical and Special Collections, Harvard Law School Library, http://nrs.harvard.edu/urn-3:HLS.Libr:4132950, accessed 8 December 2014.

37. New England Watch and Ward Society, *Quarter of a Century and 25th Annual Report: 1902/03* (Boston: Office of the Society, 1903), e-book, accessed 8 December 2014.

38. Miller, *Banned in Boston*, 13.

39. Thomas H. O'Connor, *The Boston Irish: A Political History* (Boston: Back Bay Books, 1995), 151–154.

40. Miller, *Banned in Boston*, 8.

41. Beisel, *Imperiled Innocents*, 129; Miller, *Banned in Boston*, 8. Miller asserted that 80 percent of Boston's elite lived within the city limits in the early twentieth century.

42. Sarah Deutsch, *Women and the City: Gender, Space, and Power in Boston, 1870–1940* (New York: Oxford University Press, 2002), 11.

43. Miller, *Banned in Boston*, 13, 7.

44. New England Watch and Ward Society, "Quarter of a Century and 25th Annual Report."

45. "Plays and Players," *Boston Daily Globe*, 18 December 1904.

46. "Display Ad 32," *Boston Daily Globe*, 31 January 1904.

47. Abel, *Red Rooster Scare*, 3.

48. Tom Gunning, "The Cinema of Attractions: Early Film, Its Spectator and the Avant-Garde," *Wide Angle* 8 (Fall 1986), 65, www.columbia.edu/itc/film/gaines/historiography/Gunning.pdf.

49. For more on early motion pictures and their sites of exhibition, see Fuller, *At the Picture Show*; Lary May, *Screening Out the Past: The Birth of Mass Culture and the Motion Picture Industry* (Chicago: University of Chicago Press, 1983); Charles Musser, *The Emergence of Cinema: The American Screen to 1907* (Berkeley: University of California Press, 1994).

50. "Memorial to Rev. Charles H. Parkhurst by the Society for the Prevention of Crime," 27 October 1933, folder "Miscellaneous, 1901–1950," box 50, Records of the Society for the Prevention of Crime, Rare Books and Manuscripts Library, Columbia University.

51. Society for the Prevention of Crime, "Executive Committee Meeting Minutes," 17 May 1909, folder "Administrative Minutes 1909," box 13, SPC.

52. "Miller to Approve Movie Censorship," *New York Times*, 4 March 1921.

53. Garth Jowett, Ian C. Jarvie, and Kathryn H. Fuller, *Children and the Movies: Media Influence and the Payne Fund Controversy* (Cambridge: Cambridge University Press, 1996), 28. According to the *New York Times*, Rev. Crafts was best known for "his attacks on popular amusements," including "screen vampires," "joy rides," and "close dancing." "Dr. Wilbur F. Crafts, Crusader, Dies at 73," *New York Times*, 28 December 1922.

54. Federal Motion Picture Commission, Hearings Before the Committee on Education, House of Representatives, 64th Cong., 1st sess., on H.R. 456, "A Bill to Create a New Division of the Bureau of Education, to Be Known as the Federal Motion Picture Commission" (Washington, DC: US Government Printing Office, 1916; repr., Breinigsville, PA: Kessinger Publishing Reprints, 2010), 19. See also Nancy Rosenbloom, "Between Reform and Regulation: The Struggle over Film Censorship in Progressive America, 1909–1922," *Film History* 1, no. 4 (1987): 307–325.

55. John E. Semonche, *Censoring Sex: A Historical Journey Through American Media* (Lanham, MD: Rowman and Littlefield, 2007), 100–101.

56. Abel, *Red Rooster Scare*, 98.

57. "Picture Shows All Put Out of Business," *New York Times*, 25 December 1908.

58. Ibid.; Abel, *Red Rooster Scare*, 100; Grieveson, *Policing Cinema*, 38–39.

59. "Picture Shows All Put Out of Business." See also Jowett, *Film*, 108–113.

60. According to Richard Abel, "the outcome of this famous confrontation" between McClellan and the nascent anticensorship movement in 1908—the industry, represented by the newly formed Motion Picture Exhibitors Association, and the People's Institute—was "that one middle-class notion of regulation, which favored 'rationalized discipline,' triumphed over another, which insisted on prohibition." *Red Rooster Scare*, 100–101.

61. Nancy Rosenbloom, "From Regulation to Censorship: Film and Political Culture in New York in the Early Twentieth Century," *Journal of the Gilded Age and Progressive Era*, 3, no. 4 (2004): 369; "The Saloon's Successor," *New York Times*, 16 February 1919, 47.

62. Jane Addams quoted in "Public Opinion as Moral Censor," *Motion Picture World*, 11 May 1907, http://archive.org/stream/MPW01-1907-05#page/n18/mode/1up, accessed 10 March 2014 (emphasis in original); Abel, *Red Rooster Scare*, 68–69.

63. Addams quoted in *MPW*, 11 May 1907.

64. Mrs. Josephine Redding, chairman of the Committee on Education and Publicity of the National Board of Censorship of Motion Pictures, "Statement of Facts About Some Questions Raised in the Letter from Mrs. Miller," February 1916, folder "Garland—General Federation of Women's Clubs," box 27, NBRMP.

65. Frederic C. Howe, *The City: The Hope of Democracy* (New York: Charles Scribner's Sons, 1913); Frederic C. Howe, *The Confessions of a Reformer* (New York: Charles Scribner's Sons, 1925); Charles Sprague Smith, *Working with the People* (New York: A. Wessels Company, 1908).

66. John Collier, "Charles Sprague Smith," *The Survey* 24 (April 1910), 80; Fronc, *New York Undercover*, 123–127, 209.

67. John Collier, "Cheap Amusements," *Charities and Commons* 20 (April 1908): 73.

68. S. Sara Monoson, "The Lady and the Tiger: Women's Electoral Activism in New York City Before Suffrage," *Journal of Women's History* 2, no 2 (Fall 1990): 100–135. On the Boston Women's Municipal League, see Deutsch, *Women and the City*.

69. Josephine Shaw Lowell, "Woman's Municipal League of the City of New York," *Municipal Affairs: A Quarterly Magazine Devoted to the Consideration of City Problems from the Standpoint of the Taxpayer and Citizen*, vol. 2 (New York: Reform Club on City Affairs, 1898), 465–466.

70. Redding, "Statement of Facts."

71. Friedman, *Prurient Interests*, 1–4; Michael M. Davis Jr., *The Exploitation of Pleasure: A Study of Commercial Recreations in New York City* (New York: Department of Child Hygiene of the Russell Sage Foundation, 1911), 23–24.

72. "John Collier," in *Encyclopedia of American Indian History*, ed. Bruce E. Johansen and Barry M. Pritzker (Santa Barbara, CA: ABC-CLIO, 2008).

73. Nancy J. Rosenbloom, "In Defense of the Moving Pictures: The People's Institute, The National Board of Censorship and the Problem of Leisure in Urban America," *American Studies* 33, no. 2 (1992) 47.

74. [John Collier], "Cheap Amusement Shows in Manhattan: Preliminary Report of Investigation," 31 January 1908, folder "Subjects Papers, 'Papers Relating to the Formation and Subsequent History up to 1925 of the National Board of Review of Motion Pictures,'" box 170, NBRMP; Redding, "Statement of Facts."

75. John Collier, "Cheap Amusements," 73.

76. Ibid.

77. Ibid.

78. Ibid.

79. Ibid.

80. Eileen Bowser, *The Transformation of Cinema, 1907–1915* (Berkeley: University of California Press, 1994), 49.

81. Charles Matthew Feldman, *The National Board of Censorship (Review) of Motion Pictures, 1909–1922* (New York: Arno Press, 1977), 23; Redding, "Statement of Facts."

82. Howe, *Confessions of a Reformer*. Both Collier and Howe later served in the administration of Franklin D. Roosevelt, Collier as the director of the Bureau of Indian Affairs (and author of the so-called "Indian New Deal)," and Howe in the Agricultural Adjustment Administration, as consumers counsel.

83. Rosenbloom, *In Defense of Motion Pictures*, 58.

84. Ibid., 57.

85. "Activities of the National Board of Review of Motion Pictures," 1 January 1921, folder "Pamphlets by the National Board," box 143, NBRMP; Federal Motion Picture Commission, *Hearings* (1916), 197–198.

86. McGuire to H. T. Jones, 7 June 1921, folder "Florida, Clearwater—Jacksonville, 1917–1926," box 51, NBRMP.

87. Linda Wagner-Martin, *Favored Strangers: Gertrude Stein and Her Family* (New Brunswick, NJ: Rutgers University Press, 1997), 103.

88. Marjorie Lehman, "Bird Stein Gans, 1868–1944," *Jewish Women's Archive Encyclopedia*, https://jwa.org/encyclopedia/article/gans-bird-stein.

89. Federation for Child Study, "Statement of Purpose," 1913, Child Study Association of America Records, University of Minnesota, Social Welfare History Archives, www.lib.umn.edu/swha.

90. "A Statement in Regard to the General Committee Meeting Held at the Liberty Theater on March 1st," folder "General Committee Minutes of Special Review Meetings, 1911–1914, 1915," box 121, NBRMP. The NB's executive committee members guarded the names of the reviewers from the public and all other inquirers in order to protect them from harassment and/or corruption. In addition, the NB did not reproduce minutes or extensive details from Review Committee meetings, just synopses in the *Bulletin*.

91. List of names included in "Partial List of Cities Cooperating with National Board of Review, 1918," folder "Regional Correspondence, Oregon," box 68, NBRMP. On Dr. V. O. Freeburg and the creation of a photoplay curriculum at Columbia University, see Dana Polan, *Scenes of Instruction: The Beginnings of the U.S. Study of Film* (Berkeley: University of California Press, 2007), 42–62.

92. *Bulletin*, 30 October 1914, folder "Rejections and Cutouts, 1914–1917, September," box 163, NBRMP.

93. "Censors Destroyed Evil Picture Films," *New York Times*, 14 May 1911.

94. "Activities of the National Board of Review of Motion Pictures," 1 January 1921, folder "Pamphlets by the National Board," box 143, NBRMP.

95. Richard Koszarksi, *An Evening's Entertainment: The Age of the Silent Feature Picture, 1915–1928* (Berkeley: University of California Press, 1994), 10–12.

96. Richard Abel, *Americanizing the Movies and "Movie Mad" Audiences, 1910–1914* (Berkeley: University of California Press, 2006), 245.

97. "Motion Picture Shows," *New York Times*, 17 March 1911.

98. There is an excellent historiography on the relationship between working-class women and cheap amusements. See, especially, Nan Enstad, *Ladies of Labor, Girls of Adventure: Working Women, Popular Culture, and Labor Politics at the Turn of the Twentieth Century* (New York: Columbia University Press, 1999); Miriam Hansen, *Babel and Babylon: Spectatorship in American Silent Film* (Cambridge, MA: Harvard University Press, 1991); Lea Jacobs, *The Wages of Sin: Censorship and the Fallen Woman Film, 1928–1942* (Berkeley: University of California Press, 1995); Annette Kuhn, *Cinema, Censorship, and Sexuality, 1909–1925* (New York: Routledge, 1988); Kathy Peiss, *Cheap Amusements: Working Women and Leisure in Turn-of-the-Century New York* (Philadelphia: Temple University Press, 1986); Shelley Stamp, *Movie Struck Girls: Women and Motion Picture Culture After the Nickelodeon* (Princeton, NJ: Princeton University Press, 2000); Sharon Ullman, *Sex Scene: The Emergence of Modern Sexuality in America* (Berkeley: University of California Press, 1998).

99. "Say Motion Picture Censorship Is Lax," *New York Times*, 8 November 1911; Rosenbloom, "From Regulation to Censorship," 369.

100. "Want a Censorship of Motion Pictures," *New York Times*, 2 December 1911.

101. Ibid.

102. "Motion Picture Law May Pass To-Day," *New York Times*, 14 May 1912.

103. William Sheafe Chase, "Bad Motion Pictures Should Be Officially Censored," *New York Times*, 14 December 1912.

104. "Plea for Folks Law to Govern 'Movies,'" *New York Times*, 17 December 1912.

105. Ibid.

106. "White Fights Folks Picture Ordinance," *New York Times*, 16 February 1913.

107. Chase, "Bad Motion Pictures."

108. "White Fights Folks Picture Ordinance."

CHAPTER 2: "CRITICAL AND CONSTRUCTIVE"

1. *Carmen* (1915), Fox Film Production, Director Raoul Walsh, American Film Institute (AFI) Catalog.

2. Farrer to National Board, 11 November 1915, folder "Blind Justice—Damaged Goods," box 103, NBRMP.

3. Wilton A. Barret to Farrer, 30 November 1915, folder "Blind Justice—Damaged Goods," box 103, NBRMP.

4. John Collier, "Statement of Standards," folder "Photographic *Parlantes*—Policies and Standards of the National Board of Censorship of Motion Pictures, 1912–1916," box 171, NBRMP.

5. "Report of Correspondent to National Board of Censorship of Motion Pictures," folder "4 Star Final—Inspector's Reports, 1916–1919," box 163, NBRMP.

6. Collier, "Statement of Standards."

7. Douglas Gomery, *Shared Pleasures: A History of Movie Presentation in the United States* (Madison: University of Wisconsin Press, 1992), 29.

8. Quoted in Richard Abel, *Americanizing the Movies and "Movie Mad" Audiences, 1910–1914* (Berkeley: University of California Press, 2006), 46.

9. Abel, *Americanizing the Movies*, 28–29; 40.

10. Collier, "Statement of Standards."

11. "How Motion Pictures Are Reviewed," Press Release, 14 July 1916, folder "Press Releases 1916–1917," box 140, NBRMP.

12. Collier, "Statement of Standards."

13. Ibid.

14. Ibid.

15. National Board of Censorship of Motion Pictures, "Annual Report for 1913," 10, folder "Pamphlets by the National Board," box 143, NBRMP.

16. Collier, "Statement of Standards."

17. *Bulletin*, 30 October 1914, folder "Rejections and Cutouts, 1914–1917, September," box 163, NBRMP.

18. *Bulletin*, 5 November 1914, folder "Rejections and Cutouts, 1914–1917, September," box 163, NBRMP.

19. Ibid.

20. M. Alison Kibler, *Censoring Racial Ridicule: Irish, Jewish, and African American Struggles over Race and Representation, 1890–1930* (Chapel Hill: University of North Carolina Press, 2015), 148–149.

21. *Bulletin*, 12 November 1914, folder "Rejections and Cutouts, 1914–1917, September," box 163, NBRMP; *Across the Continent* (1913), AFI Catalog.

22. Richard Abel, "Movies, Innovative Nostalgia, and Real-Life Threats," in *American Cinema of the 1910s: Themes and Variations*, ed. Charlie Keil and Ben Singer (New Brunswick, NJ: Rutgers University Press, 2009), 72. See also Dorin Gardner Schumacher, "Helen Gardner," in *Women Film Pioneers Project*, eds. Jane Gaines, Radha Vatsal, and Monica Dall'Asta, Center for Digital Research and Scholarship (New York: Columbia University Libraries, 2013), 27 September 2013, https://wfpp.cdrs.columbia.edu/pioneer/ccp-helen-gardner, accessed 8 August 2016.

23. Shumacher, "Helen Gardner."

24. *Pieces of Silver* (1914), AFI Catalog.

25. *Across the Continent* (1913), AFI Catalog.

26. *Bulletin*, 12 November 1914, folder "Rejections and Cutouts, 1914–1917, September," box 163, NBRMP. For more on temperance films as forces for education and reform, see Lee Grieveson, *Policing Cinema: Movies and Censorship in Early-Twentieth-Century America* (Berkeley: University of California Press, 2004), 80–81.

27. Frederic Howe, National Board of Censorship of Motion Pictures, "The Question of Motion Picture Censorship" (New York, 1914), 6–11, https://babel.hathitrust.org/cgi/pt?id=yul.11907740_000_00;view=1up;seq=3.

28. Letters from Humane Societies to NB, folder "Craig—Cruelty to Animals in the Movies," box 22, NBRMP. On the history of the Humane Movement, see Roswell C. McCrea, *The Humane Movement: A Descriptive Survey* (New York: Columbia University Press, 1910). See also Diane L. Beers, *For the Prevention of Cruelty: The History and Legacy of Animal Rights Activism in the United States* (Athens: Swallow / Ohio University Press, 2006).

29. Timothy Gilfoyle, "The Moral Origins of Political Surveillance: The Preventive Society in New York City, 1867–1918," *American Quarterly* 38 (1986): 637–652.

30. Lela B. Costin, Howard Jacob Karger, and David Stoesz, *The Politics of Child Abuse in America* (New York: Oxford University Press, 1996), 64.

31. Diana Belais to NBC, 7 July 1914, folder "Craig—Cruelty to Animals in the Movies," box 22, NBRMP.

32. Rev. Orrin G. Cocks to Motion Picture Exhibitors League, 27 June 1914, folder "Craig—Cruelty to Animals in the Movies," box 22, NBRMP.

33. Report on MPEL Meeting, *Motion Picture News*, July–October 1914, https://archive.org/stream/motionpicturenew101unse/motionpicturenew101unse_djvu.txt.

34. Collier, "Statement of Standards."

35. Rosen v. United States, 161 U.S. 29 (1896); Susan J. Pearson, *The Rights of the Defenseless: Protecting Animals and Children in Gilded Age America* (Chicago: University of Chicago Press, 2011), 16–17.

36. "Written on the Screen," *New York Times*, 14 May 1916.

37. *Hulda from Holland* (Famous Players, 1916), AFI Catalog; "Written on the Screen," *New York Times*, 14 May 1916.

38. Blanche MacDonald, "Films for Children," *American Club Woman Magazine*, October 1916, 55.

39. Mrs. A. C. Christianson to ASPCA, forwarded to NB, 7 August 1916, folder "Craig—Cruelty to Animals in the Movies," box 22, NBRMP.

40. Barrett to J. F. Freel, ASPCA superintendent, 11 August 1916, folder "Craig—Cruelty to Animals in the Movies," box 22, NBRMP.

41. Untitled document on animal cruelty, 12 June 1916, folder "Committee Papers, Review Committee, Memoranda; Reports and Miscellany," box 125, NBRMP.

42. On the use of animals in films, see Derek Bousé, *Wildlife Films* (Philadelphia: University of Pennsylvania Press, 2000); Jonathan Burt, *Animals in Film* (London: Reaktion Books, 2002); Gregg Mitman, *Reel Nature: America's Romance with Wildlife on Film* (Cambridge, MA: Harvard University Press, 1999).

43. *Bulletin*, 18 January 1915, folder "Rejections and Cutouts, 1914–1917, September," box 163, NBRMP. Richard Abel has argued of nonfiction films that the "variety program format characteristic of many moving picture theaters resembled that of monthly magazines or Sunday newspapers." Audience members "'read' nonfiction subjects much like short articles, the difference being that visual illustration dominated the verbal text, rather than vice versa, and the time of 'reading' was scheduled and condensed into a few minutes. . . . For both the industry and Progressive reformers, consequently, such films proved to be a critical means of defending moving pictures against those attacking their immorality or lack of worth." Abel, *Americanizing the Movies*, 180.

44. "A Badger Hunt," synopsis in *Motography* 12, no. 9 (1914), http://archive.org/stream/motography12elec/motography12elec_djvu.txt.

45. *Bulletin*, 18 January 1915, folder "Rejections and Cutouts, 1914–1917, September," box 163, NBRMP.

46. Coleman to NB, 21 July 1917; NB Membership Secretary to Coleman, 23 July 1917, folder "Craig—Cruelty to Animals in the Movies," box 22, NBRMP.

47. McGuire to Collier, n.d., folder "Reviews and Reports: 4 Star Final—Inspectors' Reports, 1916–1919," box 163, NBRMP; McGuire to AFL Secretary Frank Morrison, 14 February 1919, folder "AFL Correspondence," box 15, NBRMP.

48. East Youngstown 1916 Strike Photographs, Ohio Memory Collection, www.ohiomemory.org/cdm/ref/collection/p267401coll36/id/6005.

49. McGuire to Collier, n.d., folder "Reviews and Reports: 4 Star Final—Inspectors' Reports, 1916–1919," box 163, NBRMP; McGuire to AFL Secretary Frank Morrison, 14 February 1919, folder "AFL Correspondence," box 15, NBRMP.

50. "Against Government Censorship," November 1916, folder "Photographic

Parlantes—Policies and Standards of the National Board of Review of Motion Pictures," box 171, NBRMP.

51. Garth Jowett, "A Capacity for Evil: The 1915 Supreme Court *Mutual* Decision," in *Controlling Hollywood: Censorship and Regulation in the Studio Era*, ed. Matthew Bernstein (New Brunswick, NJ: Rutgers University Press, 1999), 16–17; Steven J. Ross, *Working-Class Hollywood: Silent Film and the Shaping of Class in America* (Princeton, NJ: Princeton University Press, 1999), 60–65.

52. "Membership in A.F. of L. Passes Two Million," *Buffalo News*, 13 November 1916.

53. Binder to McGuire, 29 January 1917, folder "AFL Correspondence," box 15, NBRMP; Dorward to Gompers, 21 January 1917, folder "AFL Correspondence," box 15, NBRMP.

54. Dorward to Gompers, 21 January 1917, folder "AFL Correspondence," box 15, NBRMP.

55. Kenneth C. Wolensky, "Freedom to Assemble and the Lattimer Massacre of 1897," *Pennsylvania Legacies* 8, no. 1 (May 2008): 24–27, 29–31, www.jstor.org /stable/27765129.

56. Fred J. Lauver, "A Walk Through the Rise and Fall of Anthracite Might," *Pennsylvania Heritage Magazine* 27, no. 1 (Winter 2001), accessed 12 January 2016, www.phmc.state.pa.us/portal/communities/pa-heritage/walk-through-rise-fall -anthracite-might.html.

57. Binder to McGuire, 29 January 1917, folder "AFL Correspondence," box 15, NBRMP.

58. McGuire to Dorward, February 1917, folder "AFL Correspondence," box 15, NBRMP.

59. Gompers quoted in Jacob Binder, Motion Picture Board of Trade, to McGuire, 29 January 1917, folder "AFL Correspondence," box 15, NBRMP.

60. McGuire to Gompers, 3 February 1917, folder "AFL Correspondence," box 15, NBRMP.

61. Gompers telegram to James L. Pauley, Secretary of the West Virginia State Federation of Labor, 4 February 1917, folder "AFL Correspondence," box 15, NBRMP.

62. McGuire to Frank Morrison, 18 February 1919; Morrison to McGuire, 6 February 1917; McGuire to Pauley, 6 February 1917, folder "AFL Correspondence," box 15, NBRMP.

63. McGuire to Morrison, 4 June 1919, folder "AFL Correspondence," box 15, NBRMP.

64. McGuire to Gompers, 3 February 1917, folder "AFL Correspondence," box 15, NBRMP.

65. See Section 22 of National Board of Censorship, "The Standards of the National Board of Censorship of Motion Pictures," pamphlet, revised in May 1914, folder "Photographic *Parlantes*—Policies and Standards of the National Board of Review of Motion Pictures," box 171, NBRMP.

66. "Suggestions to Producers of Motion Pictures," n.d., folder "Photographic

Parlantes—Policies and Standards of the NBMP, 1912–1916," box 171, NBRMP. This document refers readers to the board's "Standards" as updated in May 1914.

67. "The Standards of the National Board of Censorship of Motion Pictures," May 1914, folder "Photographic *Parlantes*—Policies and Standards of the NBMP, 1912–1916," box 171, NBRMP. See, especially, Section 22: "Sectional, National and Class Prejudices in Censorship."

68. "Hal Reid Melodrama Returns to People's," 14 September 1908, *Los Angeles Herald*, California Digital Newspaper Collection, http://cdnc.ucr.edu/cgi-bin/cdnc?a=d&d=LAH19080914.2.28.1, accessed 18 August 2015. "Its central figure is Parepa, a servant and supposed Octoroon, whose daughter has been educated as a white girl and in ignorance of her mother's Identity. The discovery is made to her under particularly harassing circumstances. In the end, however, Parepa is proved to be a Spaniard, not a part negro, and the story ends happily."

69. *At the Cross Roads* (1914), AFI Catalog.

70. *Bulletin*, 29 October 1914, folder "Rejections and Cutouts, 1914–17," box 163, NBRMP.

71. "Comparison: Ohio Board with National Board," folder "Reviews and Reports: 4 Star Final—Inspectors' Reports, 1916–1919," box 163, NBRMP.

72. "Author of Fox Play Discusses Its Basic Idea," *Motion Picture News*, 20 March 1915, 51. See also Cedric J. Robinson, *Forgeries of Memory and Meaning: Blacks and the Regimes of Race in American Theater and Film Before World War II* (Chapel Hill: University of North Carolina Press, 2007), 215–220.

73. McGuire to Casey, 18 March 1915, folder "Mass., Abingdon—Boston, 1914–1918," box 56, NBRMP.

74. "The Standards of the National Board of Censorship of Motion Pictures," pamphlet, revised May 1914, folder "Photographic *Parlantes*—Policies and Standards of the National Board of Review of Motion Pictures," box 171, NBRMP.

75. Kibler, *Censoring Racial Ridicule*, 135–137.

76. "Standards," revised May 1914, NBRMP.

77. "A City Ordinance for a Motion Picture Commission," as discussed in Collier's "Statement of Standards," folder "Photographic *Parlantes*—Policies and Standards of the National Board of Censorship of Motion Pictures, 1912–1916," box 171, NBRMP.

78. Ibid.

79. W. D. McGuire, "The Relation of the National Board of Censorship to Motion Picture Regulation," folder "Subjects Papers: State Censorship—Subject Indices of Articles in National Board of Review Magazine," box 172, NBRMP.

80. Collier, "Statement of Standards."

81. *A Square Deal* (World, 1917), AFI Catalog.

82. Covill to World Film Corporation, 16 March 1917, folder "Bridgeport—Hartford," box 49, NBR.

83. Ibid.

84. Assistant to Director-General to Covill, undated, folder "Bridgeport—Hartford," box 49, NBRMP.

85. "Activities of the National Board of Review of Motion Pictures," 1 January 1921, folder "Pamphlets by the National Board," box 143, NBRMP; McGuire, "Relation of the National Board."

86. McGuire, "Relation of the National Board."

87. Clarence A. Perry, "The Dissatisfaction with the Film and a Suggested Plan for Dealing with It," 22 June 1922, folder "Subjects Correspondence: Permanent Committee for the Prevention of Juvenile Delinquency—Perry," box 41, NBRMP.

88. Donald Ramsey Young, *Motion Pictures: A Study in Social Legislation* (Philadelphia: Westbrook, 1922), 49.

89. James J. Connolly, "Reconstituting Ethnic Politics: Boston, 1909–1925," *Social Science History* 19, no. 4 (Winter 1995): 479–509; Thomas H. O'Connor, *The Boston Irish: A Political History* (Boston: Back Bay Books, 1995), 177–200.

90. League of American Municipalities, *The Book of American Municipalities* (Chicago: Municipal Information Bureau, 1910), 30.

91. Neil Miller, *Banned in Boston: The Watch and Ward Society's Crusade Against Books, Burlesque, and the Social Evil* (Boston: Beacon Books, 2011), 13.

92. Casey's friends secured him the job as license commissioner after a tragic accident required the amputation of his arm, ending his two-decade career as a drummer with the Boston Symphony Orchestra. John Barry, "Casey—24 Years a Censor," *Boston Daily Globe*, 11 March 1928.

93. John M. Casey, chief of the Mayor's Bureau of Licenses, "The Boston, Mass. Method of Motion Picture Regulation," 1919, folder "Pamphlets by the National Board," box 143, NBRMP.

94. W. D. McGuire to James Bronson Reynolds, 15 October 1914, folder "Committee Papers, Local Conditions Committee—National Religious Advisory Committee," box 126, NBRMP.

CHAPTER 3: "AN HISTORICAL PRESENTATION"

1. "Birth of a Nation," *Boston Daily Globe*, 9 April 1915.

2. "Applause for Mr. Griffith," 10 April 1915, *Boston Daily Globe*.

3. Executive Secretary to Members of the National Board, 17 March 1915, folder "Birth of a Nation—Black Stork," box 103, NBRMP.

4. For a comprehensive discussion of Griffith's film and its reception, see Melvyn Stokes, *D. W. Griffith's* The Birth of a Nation: *A History of "The Most Controversial Motion Picture of All Time"* (New York: Oxford University Press, 2007), 17–21. See also Cara Caddoo, *Envisioning Freedom: Cinema and the Building of Modern Black Life* (Cambridge, MA: Harvard University Press, 2014), 140–181; Arthur Lennig, "Myth and Fact: The Reception of 'The Birth of a Nation,'" *Film History* 16, no. 2 (2004): 117–141; Paul McEwan, "Lawyers, Bibliographies, and the Klan: Griffith's Resources in the Censorship Battle over 'The Birth of a Nation' in Ohio," *Film History* 20, no. 3 (2008): 358.

5. Trotter quoted in Stephen R. Fox, *The Guardian of Boston: William Monroe Trotter* (New York: Atheneum, 1971), 193.

6. Executive Secretary W. D. McGuire to Members of the National Board, 17 March 1915, folder "Birth of a Nation—Black Stork," box 103, NBRMP.

7. Ibid.

8. McGuire to Casey, 8 April 1915, folder "Mass., Abingdon—Boston, 1914–1918," box 56, NBRMP.

9. Mary White Ovington, *The Walls Came Tumbling Down* (New York: Schocken Books, 1947), 128.

10. Stokes, *D. W. Griffith's* The Birth of a Nation, 21–22.

11. "Clansman Is Kicked Out of New York," *Chicago Defender*, 27 March 1915, ProQuest Historical Newspapers.

12. "Birth of a Nation Arouses Ire of Miss Jane Addams—Head of Hull House Views New Moving Picture in New York and Denounces Them in a Scathing Interview—They Excite Race Prejudice, Says Noted Woman," *Chicago Defender*, 20 March 1915.

13. "Birth of a Nation," *New York Times*, 2 April 1915.

14. "Mayor Mitchell [*sic*] Hears Protest: Prominent White and Colored New Yorkers Protest Against 'Birth of a Nation,'" *Baltimore Afro-American*, 3 April 1915.

15. Ibid.

16. McGuire to Casey, 8 April 1915, folder "Mass., Abingdon—Boston, 1914–1918," box 56, NBRMP.

17. John Collier, "Statement of Standards," folder "Photographic *Parlantes*—Policies and Standards of the National Board of Censorship of Motion Pictures, 1912–1916," box 171, NBRMP.

18. McGuire to Casey, 18 March 1915, folder "Mass., Abingdon—Boston, 1914–1918," box 56, NBRMP.

19. Casey to McGuire, 5 April 1915, folder "Mass., Abingdon—Boston, 1914–1918," box 56, NBRMP (parentheses in original); "The Boston, Mass. Method of Motion Picture Regulation," address by John M. Casey, chief of the Mayor's Bureau of Licenses, 1919, folder "Pamphlets by the National Board," box 143, NBRMP.

20. McGuire to Casey, 18 March 1915, folder "Mass., Abingdon—Boston, 1914–1918," box 56, NBRMP.

21. McGuire to Casey, 8 April 1915, folder "Mass., Abingdon-Boston, 1914–1918," box 56, NBRMP. See also Amy Louise Wood, *Lynching and Spectacle: Witnessing Racial Violence in America, 1890–1940* (Chapel Hill: University of North Carolina Press, 2009), 147–176.

22. McGuire also noted that the Chicago Municipal Board of Censorship, the San Francisco Board of Censors, and the Los Angeles Board of Censorship had all passed the film with minor changes. He cited a vote that was allegedly taken "at the Los Angeles theatre regarding the film, [and] there were 2500 votes favorable to it and 23 opposed." He also pointed out that *Birth of a Nation* had been screened for "members of the Supreme Court of the United States and the President's Cabinet, and letters of

recommendation regarding the film have been received from members of these bodies." McGuire to Executive Board, 17 March 1915, folder "Mass., Abingdon—Boston, 1914–1918," box 56, NBRMP.

23. McGuire to Casey, 8 April 1915, folder "Mass., Abingdon—Boston, 1914–1918," box 56, NBRMP.

24. Wilton A. Barrett, Review Secretary, to Mrs. H. W. Lung, Secretary of the Seattle Board of Theater Censors, 13 July 1921, folder "Washington, Seattle," box 79, NBRMP.

25. Michael C. Connolly, "The First Hurrah: James Michael Curley Versus the 'Goo-goos' in the Boston Mayoralty Election of 1914," *Historical Journal of Massachusetts* 30, no. 1 (2002): 50–74; Stephan Thernstrom, *The Other Bostonians: Poverty and Progress in the American Metropolis, 1880–1970* (Cambridge, MA: Harvard University Press, 1973; repr. 1999), 179.

26. "Censors to Pass on It," *Boston Globe*, 8 April 1915.

27. "Confers on Cuts in Photo Play Films," *Boston Globe*, 13 April 1915.

28. "'Birth of Nation' Causes Near-Riot," *Boston Sunday Globe*, 18 April 1915; "Negroes Mob Photo Play," *New York Times*, 18 April 1915.

29. By 23 April 1915, the *Globe* was reporting that the protesters had succeeded in getting the state to act on the "legally objectionable scene from the films of Birth of a Nation": "Judge Dowd's order to cut out the legally objectionable scene from the films of Birth of a Nation was carried out to the letter yesterday and the afternoon and evening performances of the photo-play were held without interruptions or disturbance of any kind." "Judge Dowd's Order Obeyed," *Boston Globe*, 23 April 1915. See also National Association for the Advancement of Colored People, "Report for the NAACP Chairman, ca. 1915," W. E. B. DuBois Papers (MS 312), Special Collections and University Archives, University of Massachusetts Amherst Libraries, http://credo.library.umass.edu/view/full/mums312-b009-i046.

30. Chapter 348, "An Act Relative to Revoking and Suspending Licenses for Theatrical and Like Exhibitions in the City of Boston," *Special Acts and Resolves Passed by the General Court of Massachusetts* (Boston: 1915), 316–317.

31. "A Fight for A Film: Struggles to Have 'The Birth of a Nation' Shown," *New York Sun*, 13 June 1915, *Chronicling America: Historic American Newspapers*, Library of Congress.

32. Photoplay Reviews, "Whom the Gods Destroy," *Motion Picture Magazine*, February–July 1917, accessed 20 August 2014.

33. "Say Irish Friends Start Movie Rows," *New York Times*, 25 January 1917.

34. McGuire to Casey, n.d., folder "Mass., Abingdon—Boston, 1914–1918," box 56, NBRMP.

35. M. Alison Kibler, *Censoring Racial Ridicule: Irish, Jewish, and African American Struggles over Race and Representation, 1890–1930* (Chapel Hill: University of North Carolina Press, 2015), 80.

36. McGuire to Casey, n.d., folder "Mass., Abingdon—Boston, 1914–1918," box 56, NBRMP.

37. Ovington to McGuire, 1 June 1916, folder "Birth of a Nation—Black Stork," box 103, NBRMP.

38. Clipping attached to Ovington's letter from the *Chicago American*, 23 April 1916.

39. John Collier, "The Real Meaning of the Proposed City Ordinance for Motion Picture Commissions," n.d. folder "Subjects Papers: State censorship—Subject Indices," box 172, NBRMP.

40. W. D. McGuire, "The Relation of the National Board of Censorship to Motion Picture Regulation," folder "Subjects Papers: State Censorship—Subject Indices of Articles in National Board of Review Magazine," box 172, NBRMP.

41. McGuire to Casey, 3 April 1916, folder "Mass., Abingdon—Boston, 1914–1918," box 56, NBRMP.

42. "To Fight Movie Censors," *New York Times*, 24 April 1916.

43. "May Veto Movie Bill," *New York Times*, 12 May 1916.

44. "Objections to State Censorship of Motion Pictures: State Censorship of Motion Pictures—An Invasion of Constitutional Rights," reissued March 1921, folder "Pamphlets by the National Board," box 143, NBRMP.

45. "Minutes of June 15, 1916 Meeting," folder "Minutes of Meetings and Reports," 1916–1935, box 95, NBRMP.

46. McGuire to Stillman, 16 January 1923, folder "Craig—Cruelty to Animals in the Movies," box 22, NBRMP.

47. "Activities of the National Board of Review of Motion Pictures," 1 January 1921, folder "Pamphlets by the National Board," box 143, NBRMP.

48. Hubert Parsons, "Ohio Clubwomen Assert Censorship Fails," *Moving Picture World*, August 1916, 1137. The meeting was held on 25 July 1916, when "representatives of fifty-four women's organizations and several motion picture exhibitors gathered at the Old Stone Church on the Public Square in downtown Cleveland, Ohio," to discuss "their plan to improve picture theater programs."

49. Blanche McDonald, "Better Motion Pictures," *American Club Woman Magazine*, vols. 11–14 (September 1916), 41.

50. McGuire to Griffith, 8 May 1916, folder "Gray-Griffith," box 28, NBRMP.

51. David Wark Griffith, "The Rise and Fall of Free Speech in America," 1916, available at Google Books, accessed 8 January 2015.

52. A 1916 memo from the NB's McGuire to an executive at Griffith's production company documents the donations made to support the Speakers Bureau: "The Speakers Bureau organized October 1, 1916 and its operations, are covered by the attached statement to December 31, 1916. . . . You will also note that there is a balance of $549.27 remaining in the fund of the Speakers Bureau, and that no future Budget for this Bureau is attached for the reason that the activities of the Bureau are entirely dependent on subscriptions received, which cannot be estimated in advance, with the exception of subscriptions already made, viz.: *Fox Film Company* $400.00 per month up to the first of June, and the *Epoch Producing Company*, and the *Wark Producing Company*, both of whom discontinue their monthly subscriptions of $200

at the completion of the work of Miss Peck on April 1, 1917." McGuire to J. C. Mc-Carthy of Griffith Productions, 21 December 1916, folder "Gray-Griffith," box 28, NBRMP. See also page 2 of the budget, under the heading "Speakers Bureau—Schedule of Receipts and Disbursements, October 1st to December 31st, 1916." William A. Milligan, CPA, to W. D. McGuire, 26 December 1916, "Suggestion for a Budget for 1917," folder "Financial Records, Financial Statements, 1909–1944," box 127, NBRMP.

Another document in the NB's records revealed the extent to which McGuire cultivated and solicited Griffith's donations: "In accordance with our understanding with Mr. Griffith I hand you herewith the statement covering the activities of Miss Peck during the month of October. The expense in this connection amounts to some $451.44. Of course, I appreciate that the Board must provide the balance over and above the $400, which Mr. Griffith agreed to provide and so I have made arrangements for this from our general fund. I would greatly appreciate you giving the matter your very early attention, and the National Board depends on the review of films to cover its current expenses and we have had difficulty even in advancing the $400 to Miss Peck in order to prevent having to call on you for an advance on her expenses, which I disliked doing. Therefore, if you could put this matter thru your treasury immediately, it will be a great favor." McGuire to J. C. McCarthy, Griffith Productions, 1 November 1916, folder "Gray-Griffith," box 28, NBRMP.

53. McGuire to Mitchell, 1 November 1916, folder "Gray-Griffith," box 28, NBRMP.

54. Mary Gray Peck, Committee on Motion Picture Survey, General Federation of Women's Clubs, "Where Does the Responsibility Lie?," *Social Service Review*, January 1917, 10.

55. Mary Gray Peck, "Children and Censorship," *American Club Woman Magazine*, January 1917, 9.

CHAPTER 4: "IS ANY GIRL SAFE?"

1. *Shackled Souls*, listed in the 21 February 1914 *Bulletin*. McGuire and Finley communicated about the motion picture in April 1914. McGuire to Mrs. Reed Finley, 25 April 1914, folder "Regional Correspondence, Texas—Abilene—Dallas, 1914–17," box 76, NBRMP.

2. McGuire to Mrs. Reed Finley, 25 April 1914, folder "Regional Correspondence, Texas—Abilene—Dallas, 1914–17," box 76, NBRMP.

3. Ibid.

4. Ibid.

5. *The Lure* (Blaché Features, 1914). See S. A. M. Harrison, "Censor Inconsistencies," *Moving Picture World*, 12 February 1916.

6. Finley to McGuire, 3 September 1914, folder "Regional Correspondence, Texas—Abilene—Dallas, 1914–17," box 76, NBRMP.

7. *Traffic in Souls*, Historic Films, www.historicfilms.com/tapes/38349, 2:43, accessed 6 November 2015.

8. Title card, *Traffic in Souls*, 5:34. See also Lee Grieveson, *Policing Cinema: Movies and Censorship in Early-Twentieth-Century America* (Berkeley: University of California Press, 2004), 151–153.

9. *Traffic in Souls*, 12:03.

10. Grieveson, *Policing Cinema*, 156–157.

11. Shelley Stamp, "Moral Coercion, or The National Board of Censorship Ponders the Vice Films," in *Controlling Hollywood: Censorship and Regulation in the Studio Era*, ed. Matthew Bernstein (New Brunswick, NJ: Rutgers University Press, 1999), 41. See also Grieveson, *Policing Cinema*, 158–165.

12. Quoted in Grieveson, *Policing Cinema*, 157.

13. Eric Schaefer, *"Bold! Daring! Shocking! True!" A History of Exploitation Films, 1919–1959* (Durham, NC: Duke University Press, 1999), 18, 38, 42–43. See also Jon Lewis, *Hollywood v. Hard Core: How the Struggle over Censorship Saved the Modern Film Industry* (New York: New York University Press, 2000), 198.

14. Richard Abel, *Americanizing the Movies and "Movie Mad" Audiences, 1910–1914* (Berkeley: University of California Press, 2006), 23.

15. Max Joseph Alvarez, "The Origins of the Film Exchange," *Film History: An International Journal* 17, no. 4 (2005): 457.

16. Abel, *Americanizing the Movies*, 24.

17. Schaefer, *"Bold! Daring! Shocking! True!,"* 38.

18. On the "vice trust," see Mara L. Keire, *For Business and Pleasure: Red-Light Districts and the Regulation of Vice in the United States, 1890–1933* (Baltimore: Johns Hopkins University Press, 2010).

19. John Collier, "Statement of Standards," folder "Photographic *Parlantes*— Policies and Standards of the National Board of Censorship of Motion Pictures, 1912–1916," box 171, NBRMP.

20. Stamp, "Moral Coercion," 42.

21. Schaefer, *"Bold! Daring! Shocking! True!,"* 38.

22. *Is Any Girl Safe?* (Universal, 1916), AFI Catalog.

23. Grieveson, *Policing Cinema*, 156.

24. "Vice Trust Leaders Use Movies as Lure; Botwin Confession Puts District Attorney on Trail of Old Offenders," *New York Times*, 14 August 1916.

25. McGuire to Casey, n.d., folder "Mass., Abingdon—Boston, 1914–1918," box 56, NBRMP.

26. "Court Bars 'Slave' Film," *New York Times*, 23 September 1916; Bell to W. M. Covill, 6 September 1916, box 32, NBRMP.

27. "Court Bars 'Slave' Film," *New York Times*, 23 September 1916.

28. "State Rights Productions," in "Complete Record of Current Films," *Motography* 12, no. 20 (17 November 1917): 1064.

29. "Attractions at the Theaters," *Boston Globe*, 1 October 1916.

30. "Exposes Great Moral Dangers," *Boston Globe*, 3 October 1916.

31. McGuire to Casey, n.d., folder: "Mass., Abingdon—Boston, 1914–1918," box 56, NBRMP.

32. "Censors Stop Majestic Film," *Boston Globe*, 4 October 1916.

33. Casey to McGuire, 11 October 1916, folder "Mass., Abingdon—Boston, 1914–1918," box 56, NBRMP.

34. MPEL to Hon. James M. Curley, Hon. Wilfred Bolster, and Hon. Stephen O'Meara, 30 October 1916, folder "Regional Correspondence—Massachusetts, Abingdon—Boston, 1914–1918," box 56, NBRMP.

35. Mary Gray Peck, "White Slave Films to Go," *American Club Woman Magazine*, January 1917, 13.

36. On exhibition in rural areas, see Kathryn Fuller, *At the Picture Show: Small-Town Audiences and the Creation of Movie Fan Culture* (Washington, DC: Smithsonian Institution Press, 1996). On the early history of distribution, see Alvarez, "The Origins of the Film Exchange," 431–465.

37. David F. Godshalk, *Veiled Visions: The 1906 Atlanta Race Riot and the Reshaping of American Race Relations* (Chapel Hill: University of North Carolina Press, 2005), 19; Tera Hunter, *To 'Joy My Freedom: Southern Black Women's Lives and Labors After the Civil War* (Cambridge, MA: Harvard University Press, 1998), 152, 19.

38. Godshalk, *Veiled Visions*, 21, 25, 14. See also Ted Ownby, *Subduing Satan: Religion, Recreation, and Manhood in the Rural South, 1865–1920* (Chapel Hill: University of North Carolina Press, 1990).

39. Godshalk, *Veiled Visions*, 36.

40. Walter White, *A Man Called White* (1948; repr., New York: Arno, 1969), 5–12.

41. "Deporting the Negroes," *New York Times*, 30 September 1906.

42. Clifford M. Kuhn, Harlon E. Joye, and E. Bernard West, *Living Atlanta: An Oral History of the City, 1914–1948* (Athens: University of Georgia Press, 1990), 9–10, 322.

43. "'Fear of the dark' at movie theaters was both literal and figurative," according to Siobhan B. Somerville, in *Queering the Color Line: Race and the Invention of Homosexuality in American Culture* (Durham, NC: Duke University Press, 2000), 68.

44. Lee S. Polansky, "I Certainly Hope That You Will Be Able to Train Her: Reformers and the Georgia Training School for Girls," in *Before the New Deal: Social Welfare in the South, 1830–1930*, ed. Elna C. Green (Athens: University of Georgia Press, 1999), 138–139.

45. Natalie J. Ring, *The Problem South: Region, Empire, and the New Liberal State, 1880–1930* (Athens: University of Georgia Press, 2012), 147.

46. Matthew H. Bernstein, *Screening a Lynching: The Leo Frank Case on Film and Television* (Athens: University of Georgia Press, 2009), 2–15.

47. Polanksy, "I Certainly Hope," 140.

48. Bernstein, *Screening a Lynching*, 28–29.

49. Ordinance by Councilman Boynton and Carnegie Library Trustees, City Council Minutes, 17 July 1913, line 31, page 183, box 5, section C, shelf 6, Atlanta History Research Center.

50. Atlanta Board of Censorship, Carnegie Library of Atlanta, W. M. Everett, President, Censorship Committee: Harrison Jones, Chairman; William L. Percy; Arthur Heyman, J. W. Peacock, Secretary, Letter to NB, 4 November 1914, folder "Regional Correspondence: Georgia, Connolly Correspondence: Albany—Atlanta, 1914–1919," box 53, NBRMP.

51. Godshalk, *Veiled Visions*, 22.

52. *Bulletin*, 22 January 1916, folder "Rejections and Cutouts, 1914–1917, September," box 163, NBRMP.

53. Peacock to McGuire, folder "Regional Correspondence: Georgia, Connolly Correspondence: Albany—Atlanta, 1914–1919," box 53, NBRMP.

54. McGuire to Peacock, 1 February 1916, folder "Regional Correspondence: Georgia, Connolly Correspondence: Albany—Atlanta, 1914–1919," box 53, NBRMP.

55. *He Fell in Love with His Wife* (Paramount, 1916), AFI Catalog.

56. McGuire to Oliver Morosco Company, 21 February 1916, folder "Regional Correspondence: Georgia, Connolly Correspondence: Albany—Atlanta, 1914–1919," box 53, NBRMP.

57. McGuire to World Film Corporation, 26 December 1916, folder "Regional Correspondence: Georgia, Connolly Correspondence: Albany—Atlanta, 1914–1919," box 53, NBRMP.

58. *The World Against Him* (Paragon, 1916), AFI Catalog.

59. McGuire to World Film Corporation, 26 December 1916, folder "Regional Correspondence: Georgia, Connolly Correspondence: Albany—Atlanta, 1914–1919," box 53, NBRMP.

60. Kelly to McGuire, 27 December 1916, in re: "CIRCULAR #164," sent to all branches, 8 December 1916, folder "Regional Correspondence: Georgia, Connolly Correspondence: Albany—Atlanta, 1914–1919," box 53, NBRMP.

61. "CIRCULAR #164," sent to all branches, 8 December 1916, folder "Regional Correspondence: Georgia, Connolly Correspondence: Albany—Atlanta, 1914–1919," box 53, NBRMP.

62. McGuire to Mr. W. L. Percy, 23 June 1916, folder "Regional Correspondence: Georgia, Connolly Correspondence: Albany—Atlanta, 1914–1919," box 53, NBRMP.

63. McGuire to Oliver Morosco Company, 21 February 1916; McGuire to Peacock, 21 February 1916, folder "Regional Correspondence: Georgia, Connolly Correspondence: Albany—Atlanta, 1914–1919," box 53, NBRMP.

64. McGuire to Mr. W. E. Atkinson, 5 December 1916, folder "Regional Correspondence: Georgia, Connolly Correspondence: Albany—Atlanta, 1914–1919," box 53, NBRMP.

65. Alvarez, "Origins of the Film Exchange," 454.

66. The ordinance also notes "the rendering of immoral, lewd or suggestive songs, dances, or like entertainment in electric or motion picture theaters and providing methods and means for regulating motion picture films and motion picture theaters." "Motion Picture Censorship (Immoral Pictures or Songs) 23/494," En-

tered by Councilman Ed. Mincey, Ordinance Book #11, City Council Minutes, 1915–1917—row 5, section C, shelf 6, Atlanta History Research Center. See also Peacock to McGuire, enclosure: "Ordinance Governing the Exhibit of Motion Pictures in Atlanta," folder "Regional Correspondence: Georgia, Connolly Correspondence: Albany—Atlanta, 1914–1919," box 53, NBRMP.

67. Ibid. See also Ira H. Carmen, *Movies, Censorship, and the Law* (Ann Arbor: University of Michigan Press, 1966), 212–224.

68. As McGuire suggested to William Percy of the Atlanta board: "The review of motion pictures in Atlanta is placed by city ordinance under the Board of Trustees of the Carnegie Library of Atlanta. A Committee of three constitutes the committee of review. Complete powers of motion picture regulation are delegated to this committee. The ordinance also provides for a secretary who acts as Executive officer of the Board. The Board of Review is the official correspondent in Atlanta of the NBR. The members are corresponding members of the NB and its chairman is a member of the National Advisory Committee of the central body. The weekly official bulletin of the NB forms the basis of advance information. It is therefore unnecessary that all pictures reaching Atlanta should be reviewed by the local committee. Complete information regarding their character is obtained as herein described and close cooperative relations are maintained between the Atlanta Board and the NB." McGuire to Percy, 22 January 1917, folder "Regional Correspondence: Georgia, Connolly Correspondence: Albany—Atlanta, 1914–1919," box 53, NBRMP.

69. Rev. Charles Parkhurst and Hal Reid, "Warning! The S.O.S. Call of Humanity," 1916, folder "Regional Correspondence: Georgia, Connolly Correspondence: Albany—Atlanta, 1914–1919," box 53, NBRMP.

70. "Warning!," folder "Tillers of the Soil—Warning," box 107, NBRMP.

71. McGuire to Correspondents, 23 March 1917, folder "Tillers of the Soil—Warning," box 107, NBRMP.

72. "Comments by Members of the General Committee on the Film 'The Warning,'" 8 December 1916, folder "Tillers of the Soil—Warning," box 107, NBRMP.

73. The *Bulletin* of 6 December 1916 classified Parkhurst's *Warning!* as rejected. McGuire to Correspondents, 23 March 1917, folder "Tillers of the Soil—Warning," box 107, NBRMP.

74. "Comments by Members of the General Committee on the Film 'The Warning,'" 8 December 1916, folder "Tillers of the Soil—Warning," box 107, NBRMP. Rev. Parkhurst was "present at the meeting of the General Committee" when the Photodrama Company returned with an edited version of *Warning!*, which the Ohio board passed in revised form. On 7 December 1916, McGuire invited Parkhurst to attend a screening of *Warning!* for the General Committee of the National Board of Review "on Friday, December 8th at three o'clock in the office of the Motion Picture Patents Company, 80 Fifth Avenue, corner of 14th Street, 16th floor."

On 24 January 1917, McGuire contacted his General Committee, alerting them to the fact that the Photodrama Company had "entirely revised" *Warning!* in order "to remove from the picture the element of white slavery." The Photodrama Company requested that the NB review *Warning!* again "in its revised form." A meeting of the board was held Friday, 26 January, 3 p.m., at the MPPC, 80 Fifth Avenue, sixteenth floor, in order to reconsider the picture. Folder "Tillers of the Soil—Warning," box 107, NBRMP.

75. McGuire to Percy, 8 February 1917, folder "Regional Correspondence: Georgia, Connolly Correspondence: Albany—Atlanta, 1914–1919," box 53, NBRMP.

76. McGuire to Peacock, 13 February 1917, folder "Regional Correspondence: Georgia, Connolly Correspondence: Albany—Atlanta, 1914–1919," box 53, NBRMP.

77. Percy to McGuire, 7 February 1917, and McGuire to Peacock, 13 February 1917, folder "Regional Correspondence: Georgia, Connolly Correspondence: Albany—Atlanta, 1914–1919," box 53, NBRMP (parentheses in original).

78. "This Week's Guide for Playgoers," *Washington Post*, 18 January 1920, 46.

79. Randy Astle, "Mormons and Cinema," in *Mormons and Popular Culture: The Global Influence of an American Phenomenon*, ed. James Michael Hunter (Santa Barbara: ABC-CLIO e-book, 2013), 6. A title card explains that "this costume, but with the cross substituted for the eye, was later adopted by the Ku Klux Klan." Richard Alan Nelson, "Commercial Propaganda in the Silent Film: A Case Study of 'A Mormon Maid' (1917)," *Film History* 1, no. 2 (1987): 152, www.jstor.org/stable/3815086.

80. Tom Rice, *White Robes, Silver Screens: Movies and the Making of the Ku Klux Klan* (Bloomington: Indiana University Press, 2015), 170.

81. Nelson, "Commercial Propaganda," 153.

82. *A Mormon Maid* (states' rights, 1917), AFI Catalog.

83. According to the American Film Institute catalog entry on *A Mormon Maid*, "a modern source claims that Paramount decided not to distribute the film due to pressure from the Mormon Church. Papers in the Cecil B. DeMille Collection at Brigham Young University indicate that Lasky did not feel that the film was up to company standards and the company wanted to release it as a state rights film. Existing prints of the film have retained the Lasky name, however." *A Mormon Maid*, AFI Catalog.

84. "Twenty States Have Censorship Bills," *Motion Picture World*, 10 February 1917, 861.

85. "Discuss Censorship with City Commission," *Salt Lake City News*, 14 February 1917, folder "Regional Correspondence, Utah—Vermont, Barnet—Montpelier," box 86, NBRMP; "Utah Censorship Discussion," *Motion Picture World*, 24 February 1917, 1237. City Commission records from Salt Lake City in this period are no longer extant.

86. Corresponding Secretary to Ferry, 1 March 1917, folder "Regional Correspondence, Utah—Vermont, Barnet—Montpelier," box 86, NBRMP.

87. Marcus to McGuire, 21 March 1917, folder "Regional Correspondence, Utah—Vermont, Barnet—Montpelier," box 86, NBRMP.

88. McGuire to Mr. L. Marcus, n.d. [March 1917], folder "Regional Correspondence, Utah—Vermont, Barnet—Montpelier," box 86, NBRMP.

89. "Pathe Plans Greater Program," *Motion Picture World*, 15 July 1916, 459.

90. "Little Mary Sunshine, 1916," *New York Times*, www.nytimes.com/movies /movie/99816/Little-Mary-Sunshine/overview; *Little Mary Sunshine* (Balboa Feature Films for Pathé Gold Rooster, 1916), AFI Catalog.

91. "Remarkable Character Interpretation," *American Club Woman Magazine*, September 1916, 42.

92. "Synopsis for *The Shine Girl*," *Moving Picture World*, 19 August 1916.

93. "The Shine Girl," *Moving Picture World*, 21 October 1916.

94. "Screen Vampire Brings Good Influence to Bear upon World; Professor of Photoplay Believes Theda Bara's Work of Uplifting Nature," *Winnipeg Tribune*, 18 November 1916, 21.

CHAPTER 5: "WHETHER YOU LIKE PICTURES OR NOT"

1. Mrs. Ambrose N. Diehl, "Committee on Motion Pictures," *GFWC Thirteenth Biennial Convention Official Report*, 1916, p. 167, in "Official Reports: 1914, 1916," Bound Convention Programs, 1910–1927, General Federation of Women's Clubs Archives, Women's History and Resource Center, General Federation of Women's Clubs.

2. *GFWC Thirteenth Biennial Convention Official Report*, 544–545.

3. Leigh Ann Wheeler, *Against Obscenity: Reform and the Politics of Womanhood in America, 1873–1935* (Baltimore: Johns Hopkins University Press, 2004), 4.

4. Cartwright quoted in *GFWC Thirteenth Biennial Convention Official Report*, 287.

5. "Report of Drama Committee," *GFWC Thirteenth Biennial Convention Official Report*, 283–287.

6. *GFWC Thirteenth Biennial Convention Official Report*, 220, 229–230.

7. Ibid., 167.

8. Sandra Gioia Treadway, *Women of Mark: A History of the Woman's Club of Richmond, Virginia, 1894–1994* (Richmond: Library of Virginia Press, 1995), 59–63.

9. Trumbull to McGuire, n.d., folder "Regional Correspondence, Oregon," box 68, NBRMP.

10. John R. Hornady, *Atlanta Yesterday, Today, and Tomorrow* (Atlanta: American Cities Book Company, 1922), 368–371.

11. Treadway, *Women of Mark*, 40–41.

12. Mrs. Josiah Evans Cowles, "President's Report," *GFWC Fifteenth Biennial Convention Official Report*, 1920, Bound Convention Programs, 1910–1927, General Federation of Women's Clubs Archives, Women's History and Resource Center, General Federation of Women's Clubs.

13. Elna C. Green, *Southern Strategies: Southern Women and the Woman Suffrage Question* (Chapel Hill: University of North Carolina Press, 1997); Marjorie Spruill Wheeler, *New Women of the New South: The Leaders of the Woman Suffrage Movement in the Southern States* (New York: Oxford University Press, 1993).

14. "President's Recommendations," *GFWC Thirteenth Biennial Convention Of-*

ficial Report, 247. According to "Women's Clubs Go on Record Against Censorship" in *Motion Picture News* no. 3923, 24 June 1916, the Motion Picture Committee included Mrs. Charles W. Cartwright (Minneapolis), Helen Varick Boswell (New York City), Mrs. George Zimmerman (Freeport, Ohio), Mrs. Dexter Thurber (Bristol, Rhode Island), and Louise Connolly (Newark, New Jersey); see https://archive .org/stream/motionpicturenew133unse/motionpicturenew133unse_djvu.txt.

15. "Women's Clubs Go on Record."

16. Wheeler, *Against Obscenity*, 77–78.

17. "Horace Mann School Survey," 4 January 1915, folder "Children and Motion Pictures, Related Papers," box 20, NBRMP.

18. Jennifer Fronc, *New York Undercover: Private Surveillance in the Progressive Era* (Chicago: University of Chicago Press, 2009), 126–140.

19. Barrows, "Report to the Executive Secretary of the National Board of Review Based on Investigation Made by Mr. Edward M. Barrows of the People's Institute," 22 March 1917, folder "Children and Motion Pictures, Related Papers," box 20, NBRMP.

20. Ibid.

21. NB to Clerk of the Children's Court, 12 June 1917, folder "Children and Motion Pictures, Related Papers," box 20, NBRMP; "Motion Pictures Not Guilty," 1917, folder "Subjects Papers: State censorship—subject indices of articles in Nat. Bd. of Rev. Mag.," box 172, NBRMP.

22. "Motion Pictures Not Guilty," NBRMP.

23. "Hang Boy 'Traitor' from Tenement Roof," *New York Times*, 22 August 1917.

24. Ibid.

25. Frances Benzecry, "Report of Investigations by Mrs. (Frances) Benzecry in Regard to Children Getting into Trouble Ascribed to the Influence of Particular Motion Pictures," 23–25 August 1917, folder "Children and Motion Pictures, Related Papers," box 20, NBRMP.

26. Ibid.

27. Ibid.

28. Ibid.

29. Linda Gordon, *Heroes of Their Own Lives: The Politics and History of Family Violence* (Urbana: University of Illinois Press, 2002); Mary E. Odem, *Delinquent Daughters: Protecting and Policing Adolescent Female Sexuality in the United States, 1885–1920* (Chapel Hill: University of North Carolina Press, 1995).

30. Peck quoted in McGuire to W. P. Capes, 11 November 1919, folder "New Mexico—New York, Adams—Bellmore," box 62, NBRMP (emphasis in original).

31. McGuire shared this insider information with W. P. Capes, director of the State Bureau of Municipal Information of the State Conference of Mayors and Other City Officials of the State of New York, located in Albany, and a member of the NB's National Advisory Committee. McGuire to W. P. Capes, 11 November 1919, folder "New Mexico—New York, Adams—Bellmore," box 62, NBRMP (emphasis in original).

32. Mrs. Albert Bulson quoted in *GFWC Fourteenth Biennial Convention Official*

Report, 1918, pp. 450–454, Bound Convention Programs, 1910–1927, General Federation of Women's Clubs Archives, Women's History and Resource Center, General Federation of Women's Clubs. Michigan passed a eugenics sterilization law in 1913. Harry Hamilton Laughlin, *Eugenical Sterilization in the United States* (Chicago: Psychopathic Laboratory of the Municipal Court of Chicago, 1922), 1–2, https:// repository.library.georgetown.edu/bitstream/handle/10822/556984/Eugenical SterilizationInTheUS.pdf.

33. "Motion Pictures at the Convention," *GFWC Fourteenth Biennial Convention Official Report*, 499. In *Against Obscenity*, Wheeler described Catheryne Cook Gilman's similar distrust of the NB. In Minneapolis, Gilman had helped defeat a censorship measure and initially supported the NB method; in 1924, however, she observed that "the motion picture situation has not improved." In large part, this was attributable to the fact that the NB was passing movies that women reformers regarded as "questionable" at best. By 1924, the NB's "credibility had slipped so low" that several prominent national women's organizations, including the WCTU and the National Congress of Parents and Teachers, had "sever[ed] their connection" with the NB, which had been serving as the "information clearinghouse of the alliance's better movie movement in Minneapolis." *Against Obscenity*, 76–77.

34. "Motion Pictures at the Convention," *GFWC Fourteenth Biennial Convention Official Report*, 499.

35. Ibid., 482–483.

36. McGuire to W. P. Capes, 11 November 1919, folder "New Mexico—New York, Adams—Bellmore," box 62, NBRMP.

37. *GFWC Fifteenth Biennial Convention Official Report*, 338. At the fifteenth biennial, 16–23 June 1920, in Des Moines, Iowa, one of the proposed and defeated resolutions was on the "Censoring of Motion Pictures." This resolution "request[ed] that the Congress of the United States provide for the proper censoring of all films before releasing them to be shown in any community for public entertainment." According to the report of the convention, "The motion LOST." Ibid.

38. NB to Gunst, 16 May 1916, folder "Regional Correspondence—Virginia, Petersburg—Winchester—Washington," box 79, NBRMP.

39. Richard L. Forstall, "Virginia Population of Counties by Decennial Census: 1900 to 1990," US Bureau of the Census, www.census.gov/population/cencounts /va190090.txt, accessed 14 March 2011.

40. Kathryn Fuller-Seeley, *Celebrate Richmond Theater* (Richmond, VA: Dietz, 2002), 20. For African Americans in North Carolina, theaters provided segregated seating areas, such as the balcony. See Charlene Regester, "From the Buzzard's Roost: Black Movie-going in Durham and Other North Carolina Cities During the Early Period of American Cinema," *Film History* 17 (2005): 113–124.

41. Ronald L. Heinemann, *Harry Byrd of Virginia* (Charlottesville: University Press of Virginia, 1996), 20–21.

42. Caroline Janney, *Burying the Dead But Not the Past: Ladies Memorial Associations and the Lost Cause* (Chapel Hill: University of North Carolina Press, 2008), 195.

43. "No Morals by Legislation," *Richmond Times-Dispatch*, 21 March 1922, 4.

44. C. F. Senning, Virginia branch of the First National Exhibitors' Circuit, to NBR, 26 July 1919, folder "Regional Correspondence—Virginia, Petersburg—Winchester—Washington," box 79, NBRMP.

45. Mary Gray Peck, "Report on State Censorship Situation in Virginia," n.d., folder "Executive Committee Minutes and Reports, 1919–1920," box 118, NBRMP.

46. Spruill Wheeler, *New Women of the New South*, 161–171.

47. Thomas Nelson Page quoted in ibid., 32.

48. Oral History Interview with Adele Clark, 28 February 1964, Interview G-0014-2, Collection #4007, Southern Oral History Program Collection, Southern Historical Collection, Wilson Library, University of North Carolina at Chapel Hill, published by Documenting the American South, http://docsouth.unc.edu/sohp /playback.html, accessed 19 March 2012. See also Spruill Wheeler, *New Women of the New South*, 38–71.

49. "Prepare for Women Vote," *Richmond Times-Dispatch*, 19 February 1920, 1.

50. Peck, "Report on State Censorship."

51. "New Movie Ordinance Creates Censor Board," *Richmond Times-Dispatch*, 9 May 1916, 1; "Censorship of Movies Killed by Committee," *Richmond Times-Dispatch*, 19 May 1916, 1.

52. Peck, "Report on State Censorship."

53. Ibid.

54. "Prepare for Women Vote," *Richmond Times-Dispatch*, 19 February 1920, 1.

55. Mrs. J. Allison Hodges, "Report on Motion Pictures," folder "Regional Papers—Vermont to Washington," box 153, NBRMP; Mrs. J. Allison (Mary Gray) Hodges, "Biographical Files, 1923–1925, Mrs. J. Allison (Mary Gray) Hodges," folder 11, box 1, Virginia Federation of Women's Clubs Records, 1907–1958, Accession #25115, Library of Virginia (hereafter VFWC).

56. Alice Ames Winter, president of the GFWC from 1920 to 1924, was deeply involved in motion picture issues. She became the director of the Department of Studio and Public Service for the Motion Picture Producers and Distributors of America in 1929. Following her term as president of the GFWC, the club created a permanent Motion Picture Commission. Headed by Mrs. Alfred T. Lee, this commission was housed in the "Education of the Adult Citizen Division" of the Applied Education Department. Virginia Federation of Women's Clubs, "1923–1925 *Yearbook*," folder "Biographical Files, 1923–1925, Mrs. J. Allison (Mary Gray) Hodges," box 1, VFWC.

57. "Projects: Resolutions," 11 May 1911, folder "Oversize, Research Cards, Administrations, 1907–1930," box 14, VFWC. Hodges was also the Virginia secretary for the National Civic Federation and vice regent of the North Carolina room of the Confederate Museum in Richmond. She was a member of the Society of Colonial Dames, the Daughters of the American Revolution, and the Association for the Preservation of Virginia Antiquities. She was married to Dr. J. Allison Addison Hodges of the Medical Society of Virginia, an influential scientific racist.

58. Hodges, "Report on Motion Pictures."

59. The other categories were "gambling made alluring or attractive," "religion

or law ridiculed or held in contempt," "irreverence," "grewsome [*sic*] subjects or death scenes," "suggestive or objectionable exposure of person," "any sex problem handled in an objectionable manner," "habit-forming drug using made attractive," "criminal methods in a way to give instructive ideas," "any obscenity, immorality or vulgarity," "objectionable bedroom scenes," "did moral of play (if it had one) outweigh scenes that might otherwise be considered improper," "did it have any educational feature," and "advertising matter O.K.?" Some version of this survey was employed by many of the GFWC's member clubs. Hodges, "Report on Motion Pictures."

60. J. Douglas Smith, "The Campaign for Racial Purity and the Erosion of Paternalism in Virginia, 1922–1930: 'Nominally White, Biologically Mixed, and Legally Negro,'" in *Other Souths: Diversity and Difference in the U.S. South, Reconstruction to the Present*, ed. Pippa Holloway (Athens: University of Georgia Press, 2008), 186.

61. By 1930, Richmond only had two black-owned theaters (out of fifteen theaters total) serving the 52,988 black people who made up approximately 38 percent of Richmond's population. According to US Census data, the white population in Virginia was 1,389,809 in 1910; 1,617,909 in 1920; and 1,770,441 in 1930. The black population was 671,096 in 1910; 690,017 in 1920; and 650,165 in 1930. The total population in Virginia in 1910 was 2,061,612; 2,309,187 in 1920; and 2,421,851 in 1930. Moreover, 32.55 percent of Virginia's population was black in 1910, and 67.41 percent of the population was classified as white. In 1920, 29.88 percent of the population was black and 70.06 percent was white. In 1930, 26.84 percent was black and 73.10 percent was white. Campbell Gibson and Kay Jung, "Historical Census Statistics on Population Totals by Race, 1790–1990, and by Race and Hispanic Origin, 1790–1990, for the United States, Regions, Divisions, and States," US Census Bureau, www.census.gov/population/www/documentation/twps0056/twps0056.html, accessed 24 May 2010. See also Douglas Gomery, *Shared Pleasures: A History of Movie Presentation in the United States* (Madison: University of Wisconsin Press, 1992).

62. By March 1923, the official publication of the VFWC, *Club Life in the Old Dominion* (vol. 1, no. 4), noted that Mrs. Allison Hodges of Richmond was still serving as the head of the Community Service and Motion Picture Division, housed in the Department of American Citizenship. In folder 10, "Biographical Files: 1921–1923, Mrs. Henry Lockwood," box 1, VFWC.

63. Heinemann, *Harry Byrd of Virginia*, 49–57; Pippa Holloway, *Sexuality, Politics, and Social Control in Virginia, 1920–1945* (Chapel Hill: University of North Carolina Press, 2006), 43–44.

64. G. Walter Mapp to John Powell, 26 December 1924, folder 37, box 39, Papers of John Powell, 1888–1978, Accession #7284, 7284-a, Special Collections, University of Virginia Library, Charlottesville, http://ead.lib.virginia.edu/vivaxtf/view?docId=uva-sc/viu03212.xml.

65. Ibid.

66. J. Douglas Smith, *Managing White Supremacy: Race, Politics, and Citizenship in Jim Crow Virginia* (Chapel Hill: University of North Carolina Press, 2002); see also Robert A. Hohner, *Prohibition and Politics: The Life of Bishop James Cannon,*

Jr. (Columbia: University of South Carolina Press, 1999), 72–90; Peter Wallenstein, *Blue Laws and Black Codes: Conflict, Courts, and Change in Twentieth-Century Virginia* (Charlottesville: University of Virginia Press, 2004), 5–9.

67. The op-ed "Autocracy of Censorship" asserts a relationship between state censorship, as a concept, and the New York State Republican Party. It noted that the New York State Department of Motion Picture Censorship was made up of Republican appointees, who he imagined censored films like *The Birth of a Nation* for partisan political reasons. *Richmond Times-Dispatch*, 26 February 1922, 4.

68. McGuire to Speed, 2 March 1922, folder "Regional Correspondence, Vermont, Morrisville—Wilmington—Virginia, Speed's Tour," box 78, NBRMP.

69. Jones to McGuire, 27 May 1921, folder "Regional Correspondence: Georgia," box 53, NBRMP.

CHAPTER 6: SOUTHERN ENTERPRISES

1. Richard Koszarski, *An Evening's Entertainment: The Age of the Silent Feature Picture, 1915–1928* (Berkeley: University of California Press, 1994), 75.

2. Garth Jowett, *Film: The Democratic Art* (Boston: Focal Press, 1976), 159.

3. Jones to Evans, 21 March 1921, folder "Regional Correspondence, Georgia, Atlanta, 1920–1922, March," box 53, NBRMP.

4. Jones to Evans, 11 March 1921, folder "Regional Correspondence, Georgia, Atlanta, 1920–1922, March," box 53, NBRMP; Jones to Evans, 21 March 1921, NBRMP. On 30 March, 1921, Jones wrote to Evans "re the letter of March 4th from Mr. McGuire asking for a contribution to the Board, I will take this matter up with our executives and feel confident that it can be arranged satisfactorily. I am in sympathy with all of your work and feel that it would further the interests of all to contribute as requested." Jones to Evans, 30 March 1921, folder "Regional Correspondence, Georgia, Atlanta, 1920–1922, March," box 53, NBRMP.

5. Evans to Jones, 16 March 1921, folder "Regional Correspondence, Georgia, Atlanta, 1920–1922, March," box 53, NBRMP.

6. Jones to McGuire, 14 May 1921, folder "Regional Correspondence, Georgia, Atlanta, 1920–1922, March," box 53, NBRMP.

7. "A Danger to the Arts," *New York Times*, 20 March 1921.

8. Angela M. Blake, *How New York Became American, 1890–1924* (Baltimore: Johns Hopkins University Press, 2009), 117–119; Todd J. Pfannestiel, *Rethinking the Red Scare: The Lusk Committee and New York's Crusade Against Radicalism, 1919–1923* (New York: Routledge, 2003), xii.

9. "Movie Censorship Bill Passes the Senate," *New York Times*, 12 April 1921. See Laura Wittern-Keller, *Freedom of the Screen: Legal Challenges to State Film Censorship, 1915–1981* (Lexington: University Press of Kentucky, 2008), 28.

10. "Miller to Approve Movie Censorship," *New York Times*, 4 March 1921; "Purity in the Pictures," *New York Times*, 13 March 1921; "More Censorship," *New York Times*, 2 April 1921.

11. "Movie Censorship Bill Passes the Senate," *New York Times*, 12 April 1921. On the contemporaneous political battle over Prohibition, see Michael Lerner, *Dry Manhattan: Prohibition in New York City* (Cambridge, MA: Harvard University Press, 2008), and Lisa McGirr, *The War on Alcohol: Prohibition and the Rise of the American State* (New York: Norton, 2015).

12. "Movie Censorship Bill Passes the Senate," *New York Times*, 12 April 1921.

13. "Movie Censor Law Signed by Miller," *New York Times*, 15 May 1921.

14. Jones to McGuire, 14 May 1921, folder "Regional Correspondence: Georgia, Atlanta, 1920–1922, March," box 53, NBRMP.

15. McGuire to Jones, 17 May 1921, folder "Regional Correspondence: Georgia, Atlanta, 1920–1922, March," box 53, NBRMP.

16. Jones to Evans, 26 April 1921, folder "Regional Correspondence, Georgia, Atlanta, 1920–1922, March," box 53, NBRMP (parentheses in original).

17. Barrett to George Fecke, 2 September 1925, folder "Educational Screen— Figved," box 3, NBRMP.

18. Jones to McGuire, 29 April 1921, folder "Regional Correspondence: Georgia, Atlanta, 1920–1922, March," box 53, NBRMP.

19. Jones to McGuire, 18 May 1921, folder "Regional Correspondence: Georgia, Atlanta, 1920–1922, March," box 53, NBRMP.

20. McGuire to Jones, 19 May 1921, folder "Regional Correspondence, Georgia, Atlanta, 1920–1922," box 53, NBRMP; McGuire to Jones, 20 May 1921, folder "Regional Correspondence, Georgia, Atlanta, 1920–1922," box 53, NBRMP.

21. McGuire to Jones, 20 May 1921, folder "Regional Correspondence, Georgia, Atlanta, 1920–1922," box 53, NBRMP.

22. Jones to McGuire, 27 May 1921, folder "Regional Correspondence, Georgia, Atlanta, 1920–1922," box 53, NBRMP.

23. Jones to McGuire, 1 June 1921, May 1921, folder "Regional Correspondence, Georgia, Atlanta, 1920–1922," box 53, NBRMP (emphasis in original).

24. Jones to McGuire, 4 June 1921, May 1921, folder "Regional Correspondence, Georgia, Atlanta, 1920–1922," box 53, NBRMP.

25. McGuire to Jones, 21 May 1921, folder "Regional Correspondence, Georgia, Atlanta, 1920–1922," box 53, NBRMP.

26. Jones to McGuire, 8 June 1921, folder "Regional Correspondence, Georgia, Atlanta, 1920–1922," box 53, NBRMP.

27. Editorial, *Ocala Evening Star*, 30 April 1921, *Chronicling America: Historic American Newspapers*, Library of Congress, http://chroniclingamerica.loc.gov/lccn /sn84027621/1921-04-30/ed-1/seq-4.

28. Editorial, *Ocala Evening Star*, 7 May 1921, *Chronicling America: Historic American Newspapers*, Library of Congress, http://chroniclingamerica.loc.gov/lccn /sn84027621/1921-05-07/ed-1/seq-2.

29. Ira H. Carmen referred to the Florida situation as "bizarre." Carmen, *Movies, Censorship, and the Law* (Ann Arbor: University of Michigan Press, 1966), 127.

30. Jones to McGuire, 8 June 1921, folder "Regional Correspondence, Georgia, Atlanta, 1920–1922," box 53, NBRMP.

31. Carmen, *Movies, Censorship, and the Law*, 127.

32. Jones to Cocks, 1 July 1921, folder "Regional Correspondence, Georgia, Atlanta, 1920–1922," box 53, NBRMP.

33. Jones to Evans, 26 April 1921, folder "Regional Correspondence, Georgia, Atlanta, 1920–1922," box 53, NBRMP.

34. McGuire to Jones, 10 May 1921, folder "Regional Correspondence, Georgia, Atlanta, 1920–1922," box 53, NBRMP.

35. On John Cotton Dana and Progressive librarianship, see Jeffrey Trask, *Things American: Art Museums and Civic Culture in the Progressive Era* (Philadelphia: University of Pennsylvania Press, 2013), 89, 98–105.

36. "Louise Connolly, Educator, Dies," *New York Times*, 18 July 1927.

37. Jones to McGuire, 14 May 1921, folder "Regional Correspondence, Georgia, Atlanta, 1920–1922," box 53, NBRMP (emphasis in original).

38. "Louise Connolly, Educator, Dies," *New York Times*, 18 July 1927, 17.

39. Jones to McGuire, 14 May 1921; McGuire to Jones, 16 May 1921, folder "Regional Correspondence, Georgia, Atlanta, 1920–1922," box 53, NBRMP.

40. Speed to Mrs. Randolph Maynard, 23 February 1922, folder "Regional Correspondence, Virginia, Petersburg—Winchester—Washington," box 79, NBRMP.

41. McGuire to Jones, 17 May 1921, folder "Regional Correspondence, Georgia, Atlanta, 1920–1922," box 53, NBRMP.

42. McGuire to Jones, 16 May 1921, folder "Regional Correspondence, Georgia, Atlanta, 1920–1922," box 53, NBRMP.

43. Gretchen A. Adams, *The Specter of Salem: Remembering the Witch Trials in Nineteenth-Century America* (Chicago: University of Chicago Press, 2008), 119–148; Peter Schmidt, *Sitting in Darkness: New South Fiction, Education, and the Rise of Jim Crow* (Oxford: University Press of Mississippi, 2008).

44. "Miss Evans Is Charmed," *Atlanta Journal-Constitution*, 8 October 1922, 4.

45. Jones to McGuire, 18 May 1921, folder "Regional Correspondence, Georgia, Atlanta, 1920–1922," box 53, NBRMP (parentheses in original).

46. McGuire to Jones, 20 May 1921; Jones to McGuire, 18 May 1921, folder "Regional Correspondence, Georgia, Atlanta, 1920–1922," box 53, NBRMP.

47. Cocks to Jones, 24 May 1921, folder "Regional Correspondence, Georgia, Atlanta, 1920–1922," box 53, NBRMP.

48. Circular letter, Committee on Community Cooperation, 26 May 1921, folder "Regional Correspondence, Georgia, Atlanta, 1920–1922," box 53, NBRMP.

49. McGuire to Jones, 20 May 1921, folder "Regional Correspondence, Georgia, Atlanta, 1920–1922," box 53, NBRMP. The circular letter was signed by the National Board Committee on Community Cooperation: Clarence A. Perry, Associate Director, Department of Recreation, Russell Sage Foundation; Miss Kate Oglebay, Vice President, New York Drama League; Mrs. Miriam Sutro Price, Chairman, Executive Committee of the Public Education Association; Mrs. Howard S. Gans, President, Federation for Child Study; George J. Zehrung, Industrial Department, International Committee of the YMCA; Orrin G. Cocks, Secretary of the Better Films Committee. Similar letters went out to clubwomen in North and South Carolina,

Tennessee, Georgia, Alabama, and Florida. Committee on Community Cooperation, form letter, 26 May 1921, folder "Regional Correspondence, Georgia, Atlanta, 1920–1922," box 53, NBRMP.

50. Cocks to Jones, 24 May 1921, folder "Regional Correspondence, Georgia, Atlanta, 1920–1922," box 53, NBRMP.

51. Connolly report, 3 June 1921, folder "Regional Correspondence, Georgia, Atlanta, 1920–1922," box 53, NBRMP.

52. Elna C. Green, *Southern Strategies: Southern Women and the Woman Suffrage Question* (Chapel Hill: University of North Carolina Press, 1997), 25.

53. The WCTU censorship advocates regarded themselves primarily as mothers acting on behalf of all children. Alison M. Parker, *Purifying America: Women, Cultural Reform, and Pro-Censorship Activism, 1873–1933* (Urbana: University of Illinois Press, 1997), 224.

54. John R. Hornady, *Atlanta Yesterday, Today, and Tomorrow* (Atlanta: American Cities Book Company, 1922), 369.

55. Florence Barnard married Basil Manly Boykin Jr. in 1893.

56. Hornady, *Atlanta Yesterday, Today, and Tomorrow*, 367–368.

57. Connolly, undated report (early June 1921), folder "Regional Correspondence, Georgia, Atlanta, 1920–1922," box 53, NBRMP.

58. Connolly to Cocks, 8 June 1921, folder "Regional Correspondence, Georgia, Atlanta, 1920–1922," box 53, NBRMP.

59. Cocks to Connolly, 13 June 1921, folder "Regional Correspondence, Georgia, Atlanta, 1920–1922," box 53, NBRMP.

60. Connolly to Cocks, 8 June 1921, folder "Regional Correspondence, Georgia, Atlanta, 1920–1922," box 53, NBRMP.

61. Ibid.

62. Connolly, undated report (early June 1921), folder "Regional Correspondence, Georgia, Atlanta, 1920–1922," box 53, NBRMP.

63. Connolly to Cocks, 8 June 1921, folder "Regional Correspondence, Georgia, Atlanta, 1920–1922," box 53, NBRMP.

64. Ibid.

65. "In and Around the Capitol," *Atlanta Constitution*, 28 June 1921.

66. Connolly to Cocks, 3 June 1921, folder "Regional Correspondence, Georgia, Atlanta, 1920–1922," box 53, NBRMP.

67. "In and Around the Capitol," *Atlanta Constitution*, 28 June 1921.

68. Connolly to Cocks, 3 June 1921, folder "Regional Correspondence, Georgia, Atlanta, 1920–1922," box 53, NBRMP.

69. "Better Movies for Atlanta Children," *Chicago Defender*, 1 December 1923.

70. Jones to Cocks and McGuire, 1 July 1921, folder "Regional Correspondence, Georgia, Atlanta, 1920–1922," box 53, NBRMP.

71. Jones to Cocks, 18 July 1921, folder "Regional Correspondence, Georgia, Atlanta, 1920–1922," box 53, NBRMP.

72. McGuire to Jones, 19 May 1921, folder "Regional Correspondence, Georgia, Atlanta, 1920–1922," box 53, NBRMP. Birmingham adopted the City Plan in 1915.

"Partial List of Cities Cooperating with NBR," 1918, folder "Regional Correspondence, Oregon," box 68, NBRMP. See also R. Bruce Brasell, "'A Dangerous Experiment to Try': Film Censorship During the Twentieth Century in Mobile, Alabama," *Film History* 15, no. 1 (2003): 81–102.

73. Jones to McGuire, 21 May 1921, folder "Regional Correspondence, Georgia, Atlanta, 1920–1922," box 53, NBRMP.

74. Max Joseph Alvarez, "The Origins of the Film Exchange," *Film History: An International Journal* 17, no. 4 (2005): 457.

75. "Birmingham's Population, 1880–2000," Birmingham Public Library website, www.bplonline.org/resources/government/BirminghamPopulation.aspx, accessed 19 November 2016.

76. Connolly to Cocks, 29 June 1921, folder "Regional Correspondence, Georgia, Atlanta, 1920–1922," box 53, NBRMP.

77. *The Affairs of Anatol* (Famous Players–Lasky, 1921), AFI Catalog.

78. *The Affairs of Anatol*, silent film, www.youtube.com/watch?v=vpgkhP1B VuM, accessed 11 December 2014.

79. *The Affairs of Anatol* (Famous Players–Lasky, 1921), AFI Catalog.

80. McGuire to Jones, 13 June 1921, folder "Regional Correspondence, Georgia, Atlanta, 1920–1922," box 53, NBRMP.

81. Ibid.

82. For an extended discussion of *Affairs of Anatol* and other contemporary films about marriage and modernity, see Lary May, *Screening Out the Past: The Birth of Mass Culture and the Motion Picture Industry* (Chicago: University of Chicago Press, 1983), 209–213.

83. Rich to McGuire, 21 October 1921, folder "Florida, Clearwater—Jacksonville, 1917–1926," box 51, NBRMP.

84. McGuire to Rich, 18 October 1921, folder "Florida, Clearwater—Jacksonville, 1917–1926," box 51, NBRMP.

85. Based on the novel by Cosmo Hamilton, *His Friend and His Wife: A Novel of the Quaker Hill Colony* (New York: Grosset and Dunlap, 1920).

86. *Midsummer Madness* (Paramount, 1921), AFI Catalog.

87. Connolly to Cocks, 29 June 1921, folder "Regional Correspondence, Georgia, Atlanta, 1920–1922," box 53, NBRMP.

88. Ibid.

89. "Movies Council Will 'Carry On,'" *Birmingham News*, 9 February 1937, folder "Birmingham—Movie Pictures File," Southern History Department, Birmingham Public Library, http://cdm16044.contentdm.oclc.org/cdm/singleitem /collection/p4017coll6/id/1064/rec/2.

90. Connolly to Cocks, 22 November 1921, folder "North Carolina, Durham—Raleigh," box 68, NBRMP.

91. Connolly to Cocks, 23 November 1921, folder "North Carolina, Durham—Raleigh," box 68, NBRMP.

92. Speed to McGuire, 19 February 1922, folder "Regional Correspondence, Vermont, Morrisville—Wilmington—Virginia, Speed's Tour," box 78, NBRMP.

93. Ibid.

94. Text from promotional poster for *The Queen of Sheba*, 1921, https://upload.wiki media.org/wikipedia/commons/6/6d/Queenofsheba-poster-1921-threepeople.jpg.

95. Speed to McGuire, 19 February 1922, folder "Regional Correspondence, Vermont, Morrisville—Wilmington—Virginia, Speed's Tour," box 78, NBRMP.

96. Ward to McGuire, 17 March 1922, folder "Regional Correspondence, Vermont, Morrisville—Wilmington—Virginia, Speed's Tour," box 78, NBRMP.

97. National Board of Review to the Editor of the *Harrisonburg News*, 14 June 1916, folder "Virginia, Alexandria—Norfolk," box 78, NBRMP.

98. Speed to McGuire, 16 March 1922, folder "Regional Correspondence, Vermont, Morrisville—Wilmington—Virginia, Speed's Tour," box 78, NBRMP.

99. "National Censorship of Films Proper Plan," *Richmond Times-Dispatch*, 13 March 1922, 3.

100. "Novelist Has Tilt with Dr. M'Daniel at House Hearing," *Richmond Times-Dispatch*, 28 February 1922, 1.

101. The op-ed "Autocracy of Censorship" asserted a relationship between state censorship as a concept and the New York State Republican Party. It noted that the New York State Department of Motion Picture Censorship was composed of Republican appointees, who he imagined censored films like *The Birth of a Nation* for partisan political reasons. *Richmond Times-Dispatch*, 26 February 1922, 4.

102. Canon Chase quoted in "Our Legislative Suspects," *Richmond Times-Dispatch*, 28 February 1922, 4.

103. Speed to McGuire, 16 March 1922, folder "Regional Correspondence, Vermont, Morrisville—Wilmington—Virginia, Speed's Tour," box 78, NBRMP.

104. "Chase Intimates Movie Men Hold Lash over Solons," *Richmond Times-Dispatch*, 27 February 1922, 1; Speed to McGuire, 16 March 1922, folder "Regional Correspondence, Vermont, Morrisville—Wilmington—Virginia, Speed's Tour," box 78, NBRMP.

105. Harry Bernstein to W. D. McGuire, 9 March 1922, folder "Regional Correspondence: Virginia, Petersburg—Winchester," box 79, NBRMP.

106. "Filibuster Threat Furnishes Scare to Bill's Backers," *Richmond Times-Dispatch*, 10 March 1922, 1.

107. "Discuss Measure at Public Hearing Before Delegates," *Richmond Times-Dispatch*, 27 February 1922, 1.

108. "Holds Premier Place in Public's Interest Last Day of Session," *Richmond Times-Dispatch*, 11 March 1922, 1. If Mapp's opponents had invoked cloture, parliamentary procedure requires the cloture petition to be read, then ignored for one full day while the Senate is in session. Because it was the last day of the legislative session, the bill, in theory, would not be taken up again until the second day of the new session.

109. Bernstein to McGuire, 15 March 1922, folder "Regional Correspondence, Vermont, Morrisville—Wilmington—Virginia, Speed's Tour," box 78, NBRMP. The Virginia State Board of Censors was established by H.B. 346 Chapter 257 of the Acts of Assembly, approved 15 March 1922, and went into effect on 1 August 1922.

110. Bernstein to McGuire, 15 March 1922, folder "Regional Correspondence, Vermont, Morrisville—Wilmington—Virginia, Speed's Tour," box 78, NBRMP.

111. *Report of the Virginia State Board of Censors for July 1, 1924, to June 30, 1925* (Richmond: Davis Bottom, Superintendent of Public Printing, 1925), 2, folder "Annual Reports, Bound and Printed, 1924–1965," box 48, Division of Motion Picture Censorship Records, Accession #26515, Library of Virginia (hereafter DMPC).

112. Ward to McGuire, 23 March 1922, folder "Regional Correspondence, Vermont, Morrisville—Wilmington—Virginia, Speed's Tour," box 78, NBRMP.

113. Ibid. See also Morris L. Ernst and Pare Lorentz, *Censored: The Private Life of the Movie* (New York: Jonathan Cape and Harrison Smith, 1930), 17–27.

114. Untitled memo, folder "Regional Correspondence Virginia, Petersburg—Winchester," box 79, NBRMP.

115. Ernst and Lorentz, *Censored*, 27.

116. Wells to McGuire, 15 May 1922, folder "Regional Correspondence Virginia, Petersburg—Winchester," box 79, NBRMP.

117. *Report of the Virginia State Board of Censors for July 1, 1924 to June 30, 1925* (Richmond: Davis Bottom, Superintendent of Public Printing, 1925), 2–3, folder "Annual Reports, Bound and Printed, 1924–1965," box 48, DMPC.

118. *Report of the Virginia State Board of Censors for July 1, 1925 to June 30, 1926* (Richmond: Davis Bottom, Superintendent of Public Printing, 1926), 3, folder "Annual Reports, Bound and Printed, 1924–1965," box 48, DMPC.

119. Untitled memo, folder "Regional Correspondence Virginia, Petersburg—Winchester," box 79, NBRMP.

120. "1923–1925 *Yearbook*," in Mrs. J. Allison (Mary Gray) Hodges, "Biographical Files, 1923–1925, Mrs. J. Allison (Mary Gray) Hodges," folder 11, box 1, VFWC.

121. *Report of the Virginia State Board of Censors for July 1, 1924 to June 30, 1925*, 2.

122. J. Douglas Smith, *Managing White Supremacy: Race, Politics, and Citizenship in Jim Crow Virginia* (Chapel Hill: University of North Carolina Press, 2002), 102.

123. Virginia State Board of Censors, memo on *The House Behind the Cedars*, folder 9, box 54, DMPC.

124. Oscar Micheaux to Virginia Motion Picture Censors, 13 March 1925, folder 9, box 54, DMPC. It is interesting to note that Micheaux's films do not appear on the National Board's list of controversial films.

125. R. C. L. Moncure to Oscar Micheaux, 22 April 1932, folder 5, box 56, DMPC. The Virginia board rejected several of Micheaux's earlier films, including *Son of Satan* (1924) and *The House Behind the Cedars* (1925). For a discussion of these films, see Charlene Regester, "Black Films, White Censors: Oscar Micheaux Confronts Censorship in New York, Virginia, and Chicago," in *Movie Censorship and American Culture*, ed. Francis G. Couvares (Washington, DC: Smithsonian Institution Press, 1996), 159–186; Smith, *Managing White Supremacy*, 100–103.

126. J. Hoberman, *The Magic Hour: Film at Fin de Siècle* (Philadelphia: Temple University Press, 2003), 138.

127. Moncure to Micheaux, 21 April 1932, folder 5, box 56, DMPC.

128. Ernst and Lorentz, *Censored*, 27.

129. H. T. Jones to W. D. McGuire, 16 March 1922, Record #66, Motion Picture Producers and Distributors of America Digital Archive, Digital Archive, http://mppda.flinders.edu.au/records/66, accessed 18 March 2016; Whitney Strub, "Black and White and Banned All Over: Race, Censorship and Obscenity in Postwar Memphis," *Journal of Social History* 40, no. 3 (2007): 685–715.

130. H. T. Jones to W. D. McGuire, 16 March 1922, Record #66, Motion Picture Producers and Distributors of America Digital Archive, http://mppda.flinders.edu.au/records/66, accessed 18 March 2016.

CONCLUSION

1. "Accused of Hushing Movie Men's Revels," *New York Times*, 12 July 1921; "Movie Men Feared Secret Indictment," *New York Times*, 13 July 1921.

2. "Many Theaters Ban Arbuckle Pictures," *New York Times*, 13 September 1921.

3. On the 1919 World Series scandal, see Charles Fountain, *The Betrayal: The 1919 World Series and the Birth of Modern Baseball* (New York: Oxford University Press, 2015).

4. Mrs. Wood Allen Chapman, "Report of Community Service Through Moving Pictures," *GFWC Sixteenth Biennial Convention Official Report*, 1922, p. 544, Bound Convention Programs, 1910–1927, General Federation of Women's Clubs Archives, Women's History and Resource Center, General Federation of Women's Clubs.

5. "Storm of Protest at Hays Restoring Arbuckle to Films," *New York Times*, 22 December 1922.

6. Ibid.

7. "Curley Against Arbuckle Films," *Boston Globe*, 22 December 1922, 12.

8. "Storm of Protest."

9. Ruth Vasey, *The World According to Hollywood, 1918–1939* (Madison: University of Wisconsin Press, 1997), 31.

10. Chapman, "Report of Community Service Through Moving Pictures," 542–543, 537–544.

11. Ibid., 543–454.

12. Buck Rainey, *Serials and Series: A World Filmography, 1912–1956* (Jefferson, NC: McFarland, 1999), 9.

13. MSPCA to McGuire, 24 March 1921, folder "Craig—Cruelty to Animals in the Movies," box 22, NBRMP.

14. McGuire to Rowley, 25 March 1921, folder "Craig—Cruelty to Animals in the Movies," box 22, NBRMP.

15. Ibid.

16. AHA to NBR, 9 November 1922, folder "Craig—Cruelty to Animals in the Movies," box 22, NBRMP.

17. Stillman, AHA, to NB, 9 November 1922, folder "Craig—Cruelty to Animals in the Movies," box 22, NBRMP.

18. McGuire to Stillman, 11 November 1922, folder "Craig—Cruelty to Animals in the Movies," box 22, NBRMP.

19. "American Animal Defense League," *National Humane Review* 11, no. 11 (November 1923), 204.

20. Beetson to Hays, 3 July 1924, Motion Picture Producers and Distributors of America, http://mppda.flinders.edu.au/records/152, accessed 16 September 2013.

21. American Humane Association, "No Animals Were Harmed," n.d., Humane Hollywood, http://humanehollywood.org, accessed 10 August 2016.

22. Schenck v. United States, 249 U.S. 47 (1919).

23. McGuire to Gompers, 28 November 1919, folder "AFL Correspondence," box 15, NBRMP.

24. McGuire to Frank Morrison, secretary of AFL, 14 February 1919, folder "AFL Correspondence," box 15, NBRMP.

25. "Censorship of News and Educational Films," 1922, folder "Pamphlets by the National Board," box 143, NBRMP.

26. "Pathé Suit Fights News Reel Censor," *New York Times*, 10 February 1922.

27. McGuire to Gompers, 12 July 1922, folder "AFL Correspondence," box 15, NBRMP.

28. "Pathé Suit Fights News Reel Censor," *New York Times*, 10 February 1922.

29. Gompers to McGuire, 17 July 1922, folder "AFL Correspondence," box 15, NBRMP.

30. Everett Dean Martin to William McGuire, 19 December 1922, folder "Subjects Correspondence," box 34, NBRMP.

31. "Obituary," *Daily Argus*, 17 April 1923.

32. "Movie Facts and Fancies," *Boston Daily Globe*, 3 February 1923, 14; "Mrs. Price Dead; Aided Education," *New York Times*, 4 March 1957.

33. "Mrs. Harry Lilly, 101 West 93rd St, NYC, Has Been Appointed Chairman of Motion Pictures in the GFWC, Succeeding Mrs. Wood Allen Chapman," *GFWC Seventeenth Biennial Convention Official Report*, 1924, p. 485, Bound Convention Programs, 1910–1927, General Federation of Women's Clubs Archives, Women's History and Resource Center, General Federation of Women's Clubs.

34. "Plan to Improve Movies Is Adopted," *New York Times*, 17 January 1925.

35. Ibid.

36. Whitney Strub, "Black and White and Banned All Over: Race, Censorship, and Obscenity in Postwar Memphis," *Journal of Social History* 42, no. 1 (Spring 2007): 688–689.

37. "Former Movie Censor Against Liberal Films," *Rome (Georgia) News-Tribune*, 15 February 1971.

38. Alverson quote from "Movies," *Life*, 23 February 1962, 102. See also Luther A. Alverson, interviewed by Anne Larcom, 22 October 1990, P1990-12, Series B, Public Figures, Georgia Government Documentation Project, Special Collections and Archives, Georgia State University Library, Atlanta.

39. Ira H. Carmen, *Movies, Censorship, and the Law* (Ann Arbor: University of Michigan Press, 1966), 219.

40. On the "Miracle" decision, see Garth Jowett, "'A Significant Medium for the Communication of Ideas': The *Miracle* Decision and the Decline of Motion Picture Censorship, 1952–1968," in *Movie Censorship and American Culture*, ed. Francis G. Couvares, (Washington, DC: Smithsonian Institution Press, 1996), 258–276. In another landmark case, *Jacobellis v. Ohio* (1964), the Supreme Court devised a test for determining whether a motion picture qualified as obscene, deferring to local community standards.

41. See Jeremy Geltzer, *Dirty Words & Filthy Pictures: Film and the First Amendment* (Austin: University of Texas Press, 2016), for further discussion of *Freedman v. Maryland* and the example of *Revenge at Daybreak*.

42. Interstate Circuit Inc. v. Dallas, 390 U.S. 676 (1968).

43. Jack Valenti, "The Movie Rating System," Appendix I, in Swope v. Lubbers, 560 F. Supp. 1328 (W.D. Mich. 1983).

44. Orit Michiel, "The Voluntary Rating System Promotes Free Speech," 24 December 2013, Policy Focus: Motion Picture Association of America, www.mpaa.org/the-voluntary-rating-system-promotes-free-speech, accessed 18 March 2016.

BIBLIOGRAPHY

ARCHIVAL COLLECTIONS

Atlanta City Council Records, James G. Kenan Research Center, Atlanta History Center, Atlanta.

W. E. B. Du Bois Papers, Special Collections and University Archives, University of Massachusetts Libraries, Amherst.

General Federation of Women's Clubs Archives, Women's History and Resource Center, General Federation of Women's Clubs, Washington, DC.

National Board of Review of Motion Pictures Records, Manuscripts and Archives Division, New York Public Library, Astor, Lenox, and Tilden Foundations, New York.

National Association for the Advancement of Colored People Papers, Microfilm, University of Massachusetts Libraries, Amherst.

New York State Department of Motion Picture Censorship, Manuscripts and Special Collections, New York State Library, Albany.

Papers of John Powell, 1888–1978, Accession #7284, 7284-a, Special Collections, University of Virginia Library, Charlottesville.

People's Institute Records, Manuscripts and Archives Division, New York Public Library, Astor, Lenox, and Tilden Foundations, New York.

Society for the Prevention of Crime Records, Rare Books and Manuscripts Library, Butler Library at Columbia University, New York.

William O. Stillman Papers, Manuscripts and Special Collections, New York State Library, Albany.

Virginia Federation of Women's Clubs Records, 1907–1958, Accession #25115, Library of Virginia, Richmond.

Virginia State Board of Censors, Division of Motion Picture Censorship Records, Accession #26515, Library of Virginia, Richmond.

NEWSPAPERS

Atlanta Journal, James G. Kenan Research Center, Atlanta History Center, Atlanta.

Atlanta Constitution, James G. Kenan Research Center, Atlanta History Center, Atlanta.

Baltimore Afro-American, ProQuest Historical Newspapers.

Boston Globe, ProQuest Historical Newspapers.

Chicago Defender, ProQuest Historical Newspapers.

New York Times, ProQuest Historical Newspapers.

Richmond Times-Dispatch, Library of Virginia, Richmond.

DATABASES

American Film Institute Catalog, ProQuest Online, www.proquest.com.

Chronicling America: Historic American Newspapers, Library of Congress Digital Collection, http://chroniclingamerica.loc.gov/newspapers.

Early Cinema Collection, 1855–1930, Media History Digital Library, http://media historyproject.org/earlycinema.

Motion Picture Producers and Distributors of America (MPPDA) Digital Archive, http://mppda.flinders.edu.au.

ProQuest Historical Newspapers Database, www.proquest.com.

ORAL HISTORIES

Luther A. Alverson, Oral History Interview with Anne Larcom, 22 October 1990, P1990-12, Series B, Public Figures, Georgia Government Documentation Project, Special Collections and Archives, Georgia State University Library, Atlanta.

Adele Clark, Oral History Interview with Winston Broadfoot, 28 February 1964, G-0014-2, Collection #4007, Southern Oral History Program Collection, Southern Historical Collection, Wilson Library, University of North Carolina, Chapel Hill, and Documenting the American South, http://docsouth.unc.edu/sohp /playback.html?base_file=G-0014-2.

SECONDARY SOURCES

Abel, Richard. *Americanizing the Movies and "Movie Mad" Audiences, 1910–1914.* Berkeley: University of California Press, 2006.

———. "Movies, Innovative Nostalgia, and Real-Life Threats." In *American Cinema of the 1910s: Themes and Variations*, edited by Charlie Keil and Ben Singer, 69–92. New Brunswick, NJ: Rutgers University Press, 2009.

—————. *Red Rooster Scare: Making Cinema American, 1900–1910*. Berkeley: University of California Press, 1999.

Adams, Gretchen A. *The Specter of Salem: Remembering the Witch Trials in Nineteenth-Century America*. Chicago: University of Chicago Press, 2008.

Allen, Robert C. *Horrible Prettiness: Burlesque and American Culture*. Chapel Hill: University of North Carolina Press, 1991.

Alvarez, Max Joseph. "The Origins of the Film Exchange." *Film History: An International Journal* 17, no. 4 (2005): 431–465.

Anderson, Alexis J. "The Formative Period of First Amendment Theory, 1870–1915." *American Journal of Legal History* 24, no. 1 (January 1980): 56–75.

Astle, Randy. "Mormons and Cinema." In *Mormons and Popular Culture: The Global Influence of an American Phenomenon*, edited by James Michael Hunter, 1–44. Santa Barbara: ABC-CLIO e-book, 2013.

Baldwin, Davarian. *Chicago's New Negroes: Modernity, the Great Migration, and Black Urban Life*. Chapel Hill: University of North Carolina Press, 2007.

Barbas, Samantha. "How the Movies Became Speech." *Rutgers Law Review* 64, no. 3 (2012): 665–745.

Beers, Diane L. *For the Prevention of Cruelty: The History and Legacy of Animal Rights Activism in the United States*. Athens: Swallow Press / Ohio University Press, 2006.

Beisel, Nicola. *Imperiled Innocents: Anthony Comstock and Family Reproduction in Victorian America*. Princeton, NJ: Princeton University Press, 1998.

Bernstein, Matthew. *Controlling Hollywood: Censorship and Regulation in the Studio Era*. New Brunswick, NJ: Rutgers University Press, 1999.

—————. *Screening a Lynching: The Leo Frank Case on Film and Television*. Athens: University of Georgia Press, 2009.

Black, Gregory D. *Hollywood Censored: Morality Codes, Catholics, and the Movies*. New York: Cambridge University Press, 1996.

Blake, Angela M. *How New York Became American, 1890–1924*. Baltimore: Johns Hopkins University Press, 2009.

Blee, Kathleen M. *Women of the Klan: Racism and Gender in the 1920s*. Berkeley: University of California Press, 2009.

Bousé, Derek. *Wildlife Films*. Philadelphia: University of Pennsylvania Press, 2000.

Bowser, Eileen. *The Transformation of Cinema, 1907–1915*. Berkeley: University of California Press, 1994.

Boyer, Paul. *Purity in Print: Book Censorship in America from the Gilded Age to the Computer Age*, 2nd ed. Madison: University of Wisconsin Press, 2002.

Brasell, R. Bruce. "'A Dangerous Experiment to Try': Film Censorship During the Twentieth Century in Mobile, Alabama." *Film History* 15, no. 1 (2003): 81–102.

Burt, Jonathan. *Animals in Film*. London: Reaktion Books, 2002.

Butters, Gerald R. *Banned in Kansas: Motion Picture Censorship, 1915–1966*. Columbia: University of Missouri Press, 2007.

Caddoo, Cara. *Envisioning Freedom: Cinema and the Building of Modern Black Life.* Cambridge, MA: Harvard University Press, 2014.

Carmen, Ira H. *Movies, Censorship, and the Law.* Ann Arbor: University of Michigan Press, 1966.

Collier, John. "Cheap Amusements." *Charities and Commons* 20 (April 1908): 73–76.

Connolly, James J. "Reconstituting Ethnic Politics: Boston, 1909–1925." *Social Science History* 19, no. 4 (Winter 1995): 479–509.

Connolly, Michael C. "The First Hurrah: James Michael Curley Versus the 'Googoos' in the Boston Mayoralty Election of 1914." *Historical Journal of Massachusetts* 30, no. 1 (2002): 50–74.

Costin, Lela B., Howard Jacob Karger, and David Stoesz. *The Politics of Child Abuse in America.* New York: Oxford University Press, 1996.

Couvares, Francis. *Movie Censorship and American Culture.* Washington, DC: Smithsonian Institution Press, 1996.

Czitrom, Dan. "The Politics of Performance: Theater Licensing and the Origins of Movie Censorship in New York." In *Movie Censorship and American Culture,* edited by Francis Couvares, 16–42. Washington, DC: Smithsonian Institution Press, 1996.

Davis, Michael M. *The Exploitation of Pleasure: A Study of Commercial Recreations in New York City.* New York: Department of Child Hygiene of the Russell Sage Foundation, 1911.

Dennis, Donna. *Licentious Gotham: Erotic Publishing and Its Prosecution in Nineteenth-Century New York.* Cambridge, MA: Harvard University Press, 2009.

Deutsch, Sarah. *Women and the City: Gender, Space, and Power in Boston, 1870–1940.* New York: Oxford University Press, 2002.

Doherty, Thomas. *Hollywood's Censor: Joseph I. Breen and the Production Code Administration.* New York: Columbia University Press, 2007.

———. *Pre-Code Hollywood: Sex, Immorality, and Insurrection in American Cinema, 1930–1934.* New York: Columbia University Press, 1999.

Donovan, Brian. *White Slave Crusades: Race, Gender, and Anti-Vice Activism, 1887–1917.* Urbana: University of Illinois Press, 2005.

Dorr, Lisa Lindquist. *White Women, Rape, and the Power of Race in Virginia, 1900–1960.* Chapel Hill: University of North Carolina Press, 2004.

Edwards, Rebecca. "Politics, Social Movements, and the Periodization of U.S. History." *Journal of the Gilded Age and Progressive Era* 8, no. 4 (2009): 463–473.

Enstad, Nan. *Ladies of Labor, Girls of Adventure: Working Women, Popular Culture, and Labor Politics at the Turn of the Twentieth Century.* New York: Columbia University Press, 1999.

Ernst, Morris L., and Pare Lorentz. *Censored: The Private Life of the Movie.* New York: Jonathan Cape and Harrison Smith, 1930.

Fairfield, John D. *The Public and Its Possibilities: Triumphs and Tragedies in the American City.* Philadelphia: Temple University Press, 2010.

Feldman, Charles Matthew. *The National Board of Censorship (Review) of Motion Pictures, 1909–1922.* New York: Arno Press, 1977.

Fountain, Charles. *The Betrayal: The 1919 World Series and the Birth of Modern Baseball*. New York: Oxford University Press, 2015.

Fox, Stephen R. *The Guardian of Boston: William Monroe Trotter*. New York: Atheneum, 1971.

Friedman, Andrea. *Prurient Interests: Gender, Democracy, and Obscenity in New York City, 1909–1945*. New York: Columbia University Press, 2000.

Frisken, Amanda. "Obscenity, Free Speech, and 'Sporting News' in 1870s America." *Journal of American Studies* 42, no. 3 (December 2008): 537–577.

Fronc, Jennifer. *New York Undercover: Private Surveillance in the Progressive Era*. Chicago: University of Chicago Press, 2009.

Fuller, Kathryn H. *At the Picture Show: Small-Town Audiences and the Creation of Movie Fan Culture*. Washington, DC: Smithsonian Institution Press, 1996.

Fuller-Seeley, Kathryn. *Celebrate Richmond Theater*. Richmond, VA: Dietz, 2002.

Gardner, Martha. *The Qualities of a Citizen: Women, Immigration, and Citizenship, 1870–1965*. Princeton, NJ: Princeton University Press, 2009.

Garland, Libby. *After They Closed the Gates: Jewish Illegal Immigration to the United States, 1921–1965*. Chicago: University of Chicago Press, 2014.

Geltzer, Jeremy. *Dirty Words & Filthy Pictures: Film and the First Amendment*. Austin: University of Texas Press, 2016.

Gilfoyle, Timothy. *City of Eros: New York City, Prostitution, and the Commercialization of Sex, 1790–1920*. New York: Norton, 1994.

———. "The Moral Origins of Political Surveillance: The Preventative Society in New York City, 1867–1918." *American Quarterly* 38 (1986): 637–652.

———. *A Pickpocket's Tale: The Underworld of Nineteenth-Century New York*. New York: Norton, 2006.

Gilmore, Glenda. *Gender and Jim Crow: Women and the Politics of White Supremacy in North Carolina, 1896–1920*. Chapel Hill: University of North Carolina Press, 1996.

Godshalk, David F. *Veiled Visions: The 1906 Atlanta Race Riot and the Reshaping of American Race Relations*. Chapel Hill: University of North Carolina Press, 2005.

Gomery, Douglas. *Shared Pleasures: A History of Movie Presentation in the United States*. Madison: University of Wisconsin Press, 1992.

Gordon, Linda. *Heroes of Their Own Lives: The Politics and History of Family Violence*. Urbana: University of Illinois Press, 2002.

Green, Elna C. *Southern Strategies: Southern Women and the Woman Suffrage Question*. Chapel Hill: University of North Carolina Press, 1997.

Grieveson, Lee. *Policing Cinema: Movies and Censorship in Early-Twentieth-Century America*. Berkeley: University of California Press, 2004.

Gurstein, Rochelle. *The Repeal of Reticence: America's Cultural and Legal Struggles over Free Speech, Obscenity, Sexual Liberation, and Modern Art*. New York: Hill and Wang, 1996.

Hansen, Miriam. *Babel and Babylon: Spectatorship in American Silent Film*. Cambridge, MA: Harvard University Press, 1991.

Heinemann, Ronald L. *Harry Byrd of Virginia*. Charlottesville: University Press of Virginia, 1996.

Hoberman, J. *The Magic Hour: Film at Fin de Siècle*. Philadelphia: Temple University Press, 2003.

Hohner, Robert A. *Prohibition and Politics: The Life of Bishop James Cannon, Jr.* Columbia: University of South Carolina Press, 1999.

Holloway, Pippa. *Other Souths: Diversity and Difference in the U.S. South, Reconstruction to the Present*. Athens: University of Georgia Press, 2008.

———. *Sexuality, Politics, and Social Control in Virginia, 1920–1945*. Chapel Hill: University of North Carolina Press, 2006.

Hornady, John R. *Atlanta Yesterday, Today, and Tomorrow*. Atlanta: American Cities Book Company, 1922.

Horowitz, Helen Lefkowitz. *Rereading Sex: Battles over Sexual Knowledge and Suppression in Nineteenth-Century America*. New York: Vintage, 2002.

Howe, Frederic C. *The City: The Hope of Democracy*. New York: Charles Scribner's Sons, 1913.

———. *The Confessions of a Reformer*. New York: Charles Scribner's Sons, 1925.

Hunter, Tera. *To 'Joy My Freedom: Southern Black Women's Lives and Labors After the Civil War*. Cambridge, MA: Harvard University Press, 1998.

Huyssen, David. *Progressive Inequality: Rich and Poor in New York, 1890–1920*. Cambridge, MA: Harvard University Press, 2014.

Jacobs, Lea. *The Wages of Sin: Censorship and the Fallen Woman Film, 1928–1942*. Berkeley: University of California Press, 1995.

Janney, Caroline. *Burying the Dead but Not the Past: Ladies Memorial Associations and the Lost Cause*. Chapel Hill: University of North Carolina Press, 2008.

Johnston, Robert D. *The Radical Middle Class: Populist Democracy and the Question of Capitalism in Progressive Era Portland, Oregon*. Princeton, NJ: Princeton University Press, 2006.

Jowett, Garth. "A Capacity for Evil: The 1915 Supreme Court *Mutual* Decision." In *Controlling Hollywood: Censorship and Regulation in the Studio Era*, edited by Matthew Bernstein, 16–40. New Brunswick, NJ: Rutgers University Press, 1999.

———. "'A Significant Medium for the Communication of Ideas': The *Miracle* Decision and the Decline of Motion Picture Censorship, 1952–1968." In *Movie Censorship and American Culture*, edited by Francis G. Couvares, 258–276. Washington, DC: Smithsonian Institution Press, 1996.

———. *Film: The Democratic Art*. Boston: Focal, 1976.

Jowett, Garth, Ian C. Jarvie, and Kathryn H. Fuller, *Children and the Movies: Media Influence and the Payne Fund Controversy*. Cambridge: Cambridge University Press, 1996.

Keil, Charlie, and Ben Singer, eds. *American Cinema of the 1910s: Themes and Variations*. New Brunswick, NJ: Rutgers University Press, 2009.

Keire, Mara L. *For Business and Pleasure: Red-Light Districts and the Regulation of Vice in the United States, 1890–1933*. Baltimore: Johns Hopkins University Press, 2010.

Kibler, M. Alison. *Censoring Racial Ridicule: Irish, Jewish, and African American Struggles over Race and Representation, 1890–1930.* Chapel Hill: University of North Carolina Press, 2015.

Koszarski, Richard. *An Evening's Entertainment: The Age of the Silent Feature Picture, 1915–1928.* Berkeley: University of California Press, 1994.

Kuhn, Annette. *Cinema, Censorship, and Sexuality, 1909–1925.* New York: Routledge, 1988.

Kuhn, Clifford M., Harlon E. Joye, and E. Bernard West. *Living Atlanta: An Oral History of the City, 1914–1948.* Athens: University of Georgia Press, 1990.

Ladenson, Elisabeth. *Dirt for Art's Sake: Books on Trial from "Madame Bovary" to "Lolita."* Ithaca, NY: Cornell University Press, 2007.

Laughlin, Harry Hamilton. *Eugenical Sterilization in the United States.* Chicago: Psychopathic Laboratory of the Municipal Court of Chicago, 1922.

Lauver, Fred J. "A Walk Through the Rise and Fall of Anthracite Might." *Pennsylvania Heritage Magazine* 27, no. 1 (Winter 2001), www.phmc.state.pa.us /portal/communities/pa-heritage/walk-through-rise-fall-anthracite-might .html, accessed 12 January 2016.

Lennig, Arthur. "Myth and Fact: The Reception of 'The Birth of a Nation.'" *Film History* 16, no. 2 (2004): 117–141.

Lerner, Michael. *Dry Manhattan: Prohibition in New York City.* Cambridge, MA: Harvard University Press, 2008.

Lewis, Jon. *Hollywood v. Hard Core: How the Struggle over Censorship Saved the Modern Film Industry.* New York: New York University Press, 2000.

Lowell, Josephine Shaw. "Woman's Municipal League of the City of New York." *Municipal Affairs: A Quarterly Magazine Devoted to the Consideration of City Problems from the Standpoint of the Taxpayer and Citizen* 2 (1898): 465–466.

Mathews, Nancy Mowll. *Moving Pictures: American Art and Early Film, 1880–1910.* Williamstown, MA: Williams College Museum of Art, 2005.

May, Lary. *Screening Out the Past: The Birth of Mass Culture and the Motion Picture Industry.* Chicago: University of Chicago Press, 1983.

McCrea, Roswell C. *The Humane Movement: A Descriptive Survey.* New York: Columbia University Press, 1910.

McEwan, Paul. "Lawyers, Bibliographies, and the Klan: Griffith's Resources in the Censorship Battle over 'The Birth of a Nation' in Ohio." *Film History* 20, no. 3 (2008): 357–366.

McGarry, Molly. "Spectral Sexualities: Nineteenth-Century Spiritualism, Moral Panics, and the Making of U.S. Obscenity Law." *Journal of Women's History* 12, no. 2 (Summer 2000): 8–29.

McGirr, Lisa. *The War on Alcohol: Prohibition and the Rise of the American State.* New York: Norton, 2015.

Miller, Neil. *Banned in Boston: The Watch and Ward Society's Crusade Against Books, Burlesque, and the Social Evil.* Boston: Beacon Books, 2011.

Mitman, Gregg. *Reel Nature: America's Romance with Wildlife on Film.* Cambridge, MA: Harvard University Press, 1999.

Monoson, S. Sara. "The Lady and the Tiger: Women's Electoral Activism in New York City Before Suffrage." *Journal of Women's History* 2, no. 2 (Fall 1990): 100–135.

Morgan, Francesca. *Women and Patriotism in Jim Crow America*. Chapel Hill: University of North Carolina Press, 2005.

Muncy, Robyn. *Creating a Female Dominion in American Reform, 1890–1935*. New York: Oxford University Press, 1994.

Musser, Charles. *The Emergence of Cinema: The American Screen to 1907*. Berkeley: University of California Press, 1994.

Nasaw, David. *Children of the City at Work and at Play*. New York: Anchor, 1985.

Nelson, Richard Alan. "Commercial Propaganda in the Silent Film: A Case Study of 'A Mormon Maid' (1917)." *Film History* 1, no. 2 (1987): 149–162.

O'Connor, Thomas H. *The Boston Irish: A Political History*. Boston: Back Bay Books, 1997.

Odem, Mary E. *Delinquent Daughters: Protecting and Policing Adolescent Female Sexuality in the United States, 1885–1920*. Chapel Hill: University of North Carolina Press, 1995.

Orbach, Barak Y. "Prizefighting and the Birth of Movie Censorship." *Yale Journal of Law & the Humanities* 21, no. 2 (2009), http://digitalcommons.law.yale.edu/yjlh/vol21/iss2/3.

Ownby, Ted. *Subduing Satan: Religion, Recreation, and Manhood in the Rural South, 1865–1920*. Chapel Hill: University of North Carolina Press, 1990.

Parker, Alison M. *Purifying America: Women, Cultural Reform, and Pro-Censorship Activism, 1873–1933*. Urbana: University of Illinois Press, 1997.

Pearson, Susan J. *The Rights of the Defenseless: Protecting Animals and Children in Gilded Age America*. Chicago: University of Chicago Press, 2011.

Peiss, Kathy. *Cheap Amusements: Working Women and Leisure in Turn-of-the-Century New York*. Philadelphia: Temple University Press, 1986.

Pfannestiel, Todd J. *Rethinking the Red Scare: The Lusk Committee and New York's Crusade Against Radicalism, 1919–1923*. New York: Routledge, 2003.

Pizzitola, Louis. *Hearst over Hollywood: Power, Passion, and Propaganda in the Movies*. New York: Columbia University Press, 2002.

Pliley, Jessica. *Policing Sexuality: The Mann Act and the Making of the FBI*. Cambridge, MA: Harvard University Press, 2014.

Polan, Dana. *Scenes of Instruction: The Beginnings of the U.S. Study of Film*. Berkeley: University of California Press, 2007.

Polansky, Lee S. "I Certainly Hope That You Will Be Able to Train Her: Reformers and the Georgia Training School for Girls." In *Before the New Deal: Social Welfare in the South, 1830–1930*, edited by Elna C. Green, 138–159. Athens: University of Georgia Press, 1999.

Rainey, Buck. *Serials and Series: A World Filmography, 1912–1956*. Jefferson, NC: McFarland, 1999.

Randall, Richard. *Censorship of the Movies: The Social and Political Control of a Mass Medium*. Madison: University of Wisconsin Press, 1968.

Regester, Charlene. "Black Films, White Censors: Oscar Micheaux Confronts Censorship in New York, Virginia, and Chicago." In *Movie Censorship and American Culture*, edited by Francis G. Couvares, 159–186. Washington, DC: Smithsonian Institution Press, 1996.

———. "From the Buzzard's Roost: Black Movie-going in Durham and Other North Carolina Cities During the Early Period of American Cinema." *Film History* 17 (2005): 113–124.

Rice, Tom. *White Robes, Silver Screens: Movies and the Making of the Ku Klux Klan*. Bloomington: Indiana University Press, 2015.

Ring, Natalie J. *The Problem South: Region, Empire, and the New Liberal State, 1880–1930*. Athens: University of Georgia Press, 2012.

Robinson, Cedric J. *Forgeries of Memory and Meaning: Blacks and the Regimes of Race in American Theater and Film Before World War II*. Chapel Hill: University of North Carolina Press, 2007.

Rosenbloom, Nancy. "Between Reform and Regulation: The Struggle over Film Censorship in Progressive America, 1909–1922." *Film History* 1, no. 4 (1987): 307–325.

———. "From Regulation to Censorship: Film and Political Culture in New York in the Early Twentieth Century." *Journal of the Gilded Age and Progressive Era* 3, no. 4 (2004): 307–325.

———. "In Defense of the Moving Pictures: The People's Institute, The National Board of Censorship and the Problem of Leisure in Urban America." *American Studies* 33, no. 2 (1992): 41–61.

Ross, Steven J. *Working-Class Hollywood: Silent Film and the Making of Class in America*. Princeton, NJ: Princeton University Press, 1999.

Rubin, Gayle. "Thinking Sex: Notes for a Radical Theory of the Politics of Sexuality." In *Pleasure and Danger: Exploring Female Sexuality*, edited by Carole S. Vance, 267–319. Boston: Routledge and Kegan Paul, 1984.

Saylor, Richard C. "Dr. Ellis Paxson Oberholtzer and the Early Years of the Pennsylvania State Board of Censors (Motion Picture)." *Film History* 16, no. 2 (2004): 142–162.

Schaefer, Eric. *"Bold! Daring! Shocking! True!" A History of Exploitation Films, 1919–1959*. Durham, NC: Duke University Press, 1999.

Schmidt, Peter. *Sitting in Darkness: New South Fiction, Education, and the Rise of Jim Crow*. Oxford: University Press of Mississippi, 2008.

Schneider, Mark R. *Boston Confronts Jim Crow, 1890–1920*. Boston: Northeastern University Press, 1997.

Schuyler, Lorraine Gates. *The Weight of Their Votes: Southern Women and Political Leverage in the 1920s*. Chapel Hill: University of North Carolina Press, 2006.

Scott, Ellen C. "Black 'Censor,' White Liberties: Civil Rights and Illinois's 1917 Film Law." *American Quarterly* 64, no. 2 (June 2012): 219–247.

Semonche, John E. *Censoring Sex: A Historical Journey Through American Media*. Lanham, MD: Rowman and Littlefield, 2007.

Skocpol, Theda. *Protecting Soldiers and Mothers: The Political Origins of Social Pol-*

icy in the United States. Cambridge, MA: Belknap Press of Harvard University Press, 1992.

Smith, Charles Sprague. Working with the People. New York: A. Wessels, 1908.

Smith, J. Douglas. "The Campaign for Racial Purity and the Erosion of Paternalism in Virginia, 1922–1930: 'Nominally White, Biologically Mixed, and Legally Negro.'" In Other Souths: Diversity and Difference in the U.S. South, Reconstruction to the Present, edited by Pippa Holloway, 167–207. Athens: University of Georgia Press, 2008.

————. Managing White Supremacy: Race, Politics, and Citizenship in Jim Crow Virginia. Chapel Hill: University of North Carolina Press, 2002.

Somerville, Siobhan B. Queering the Color Line: Race and the Invention of Homosexuality in American Culture. Durham, NC: Duke University Press, 2000.

Stamp, Shelley. "Moral Coercion, or The National Board of Censorship Ponders the Vice Films." In Controlling Hollywood: Censorship and Regulation in the Studio Era, edited by Matthew Bernstein, 41–59. New Brunswick, NJ: Rutgers University Press, 1999.

————. Movie Struck Girls: Women and Motion Picture Culture After the Nickelodeon. Princeton, NJ: Princeton University Press, 2000.

Stewart, Jacqueline Najuma. Migrating to the Movies: Cinema and Black Urban Modernity. Berkeley: University of California Press, 2005.

Stivers, Camilla. Bureau Men, Settlement Women: Constructing Public Administration in the Progressive Era. Lawrence: University Press of Kansas, 2000.

Stokes, Melvyn. D. W. Griffith's The Birth of a Nation: A History of "The Most Controversial Motion Picture of All Time." New York: Oxford University Press, 2007.

Stromquist, Shelton. Re-inventing "The People": The Progressive Movement, the Class Problem, and the Origins of Modern Liberalism. Urbana: University of Illinois Press, 2006.

Strub, Whitney. "Black and White and Banned All Over: Race, Censorship and Obscenity in Postwar Memphis." Journal of Social History (2007): 685–715.

Thernstrom, Stephan. The Other Bostonians: Poverty and Progress in the American Metropolis, 1880–1970. Cambridge, MA: Harvard University Press, 1973; repr., 1999.

Trask, Jeffrey. Things American: Art Museums and Civic Culture in the Progressive Era. Philadelphia: University of Pennsylvania Press, 2013.

Treadway, Sandra Gioia. Women of Mark: A History of the Woman's Club of Richmond, Virginia, 1894–1994. Richmond: Library of Virginia Press, 1995.

Ullman, Sharon. Sex Scene: The Emergence of Modern Sexuality in America. Berkeley: University of California Press, 1998.

Uruburu, Paula. American Eve: Evelyn Nesbit, Stanford White, the Birth of the "It" Girl, and the Crime of the Century. New York: Riverhead, 2009.

Vasey, Ruth. The World According to Hollywood, 1918–1939. Madison: University of Wisconsin Press, 1997.

Wagner-Martin, Linda. Favored Strangers: Gertrude Stein and Her Family. New Brunswick, NJ: Rutgers University Press, 1997.

Wallenstein, Peter. *Blue Laws and Black Codes: Conflict, Courts, and Change in Twentieth-Century Virginia*. Charlottesville: University of Virginia Press, 2004.

Wells, Mildred White. *Unity in Diversity: The History of the General Federation of Women's Clubs*. Diamond Jubilee ed. Washington, DC: General Federation of Women's Clubs, 1965.

Wertheimer, John. "Mutual Film Reviewed: The Movies, Censorship, and Free Speech in Progressive America." *American Journal of Legal History* 37, no. 2 (April 1993): 158–189.

Wheeler, Leigh Ann. *Against Obscenity: Reform and the Politics of Womanhood in America, 1873–1933*. Baltimore: Johns Hopkins University Press, 2004.

Wheeler, Marjorie Spruill. *New Women of the New South: The Leaders of the Woman Suffrage Movement in the Southern States*. New York: Oxford University Press, 1993.

White, Walter. *A Man Called White*. New York: Arno, 1969 [1948].

Wittern-Keller, Laura. "Controlling Content: Governmental Censorship, the Production Code, and the Ratings System." In *Hollywood and the Law*, edited by Paul McDonald, Emily Carman, Eric Hoyt, and Philip Drake, 130–153. London: Palgrave on behalf of the British Film Institute, 2015.

———. *Freedom of the Screen: Legal Challenges to State Film Censorship, 1915–1981*. Lexington: University Press of Kentucky, 2008.

Wolensky, Kenneth C. "Freedom to Assemble and the Lattimer Massacre of 1897." *Pennsylvania Legacies* 8, no. 1 (May 2008): 24–27, 29–31, www.jstor.org/stable /27765129.

Wood, Amy Louise. *Lynching and Spectacle: Witnessing Racial Violence in America, 1890–1940*. Chapel Hill: University of North Carolina Press, 2009.

Young, Donald Ramsey. *Motion Pictures: A Study in Social Legislation*. Philadelphia: Westbrook, 1922.

White, Stanford, 8, 14

white slavery, 64, 68–70, 72, 76, 79, 95, 164n74

white slave traffic films, 64

white supremacy, 71–72, 95, 98–99, 125

Whitman, Charles Seymour, 60–61, 85

Whom the Gods Destroy (Vitagraph, 1916), 57–58

Wilson, Lois, 115

Wilson, Woodrow, 42

Winter, Alice Ames, 129, 169n56

Wise, Rabbi Stephen, 55

women activists, 6–7, 20, 23, 30, 44, 54, 61–63, 80–81, 84–137; as audience members, 5, 9–10, 25, 32, 57, 72, 82–83; onscreen, 16, 33, 83; as vulnerable viewers, 11, 15, 17, 66–69, 142n7; working-class women as, 66, 70–72

Women's Christian Temperance Union (WCTU), 6, 61, 65, 84, 98, 168n37, 174n53

Women's Municipal League (WML), 20, 25–26

women's suffrage. *See* Equal Suffrage League; General Federation of Women's Clubs; National American Woman Suffrage Association; Nineteenth Amendment

Woodward, J. G., 76

World Against Him, The (Paragon, 1916), 74–76

World Film Corporation, 48, 74–75

World War I, 41, 107, 109

Wright, Rosamond Rae, 131

Wurlitzer Hall (New York City), 2

Young Men's Christian Association (YMCA), 13, 37, 65, 107, 109

Zukor, Adolph, 127

The Truth About Day Trading Stocks

Founded in 1807, John Wiley & Sons is the oldest independent publishing company in the United States. With offices in North America, Europe, Australia, and Asia, Wiley is globally committed to developing and marketing print and electronic products and services for our customers' professional and personal knowledge and understanding.

The Wiley Trading series features books by traders who have survived the market's ever changing temperament and have prospered—some by reinventing systems, others by getting back to basics. Whether a novice trader, professional, or somewhere in-between, these books will provide the advice and strategies needed to prosper today and well into the future.

For a list of available titles, visit our Web site at www.WileyFinance.com.

The Truth About Day Trading Stocks

A Cautionary Tale About Hard Challenges and What It Takes to Succeed

JOSH DIPIETRO

WILEY

John Wiley & Sons, Inc.

Published by John Wiley & Sons, Inc., Hoboken, New Jersey.
Published simultaneously in Canada.

For general information on our other products and services or for technical support, please contact our Customer Care Department within the United States at (800) 762-2974, outside the United States at (317) 572-3993 or fax (317) 572-4002.

Wiley also publishes its books in a variety of electronic formats. Some content that appears in print may not be available in electronic books. For more information about Wiley products, visit our web site at www.wiley.com.

Library of Congress Cataloging-in-Publication Data:

DiPietro, Josh, 1976–
   The truth about day trading stocks : a cautionary tale about hard challenges and what it takes to succeed / Josh DiPietro.
      p.   cm. – (Wiley trading series)
   Includes index.
   ISBN 978-0-470-44848-9 (cloth)
1. Day trading (Securities)   2. Electronic trading of securities.   I. Title.
   HG4515.95.D57 2009
   332.63′228–dc22

                                        2008054930

Printed in the United States of America

10 9 8 7 6 5 4 3 2 1

*I would like to dedicate this book to all day-traders,
amateur and professional, who have learned the hard way.
To the traders who understand that becoming a successful
day-trader is a process that cannot be fast-tracked.*

Contents

Preface

The most successful turtle was apparently Curtis Faith. Trading records show that Mr. Faith, who was only 19 when he started the program, made about $31.5 million in profits for Mr. Dennis.
—Stanley W. Angrist, The *Wall Street Journal*

The above is a dangerous citation. No one should use it as assurance. Not every amateur day-trader succeeds like Curtis Faith. Many beginners lose all of their start-up capital—sometimes more than once. The purpose of *The Truth About Day Trading Stocks* is to caution, and to some degree reprogram, the naïve, heedless amateur day-trader. I want to prevent beginners from watching their money disappear.

In this book, I offer the amateur day-trader, a candid account of the challenges I've encountered while developing in the profession. By candid I mean brutally truthful, mostly about myself, mostly with the side-splitting laughter that the distance of hindsight provides!

This is my personal story, and I tell it like it is, just as if we were kicking back and having ourselves some brews, letting it all hang out at times—that is, confessing all my mistakes. My personal day-trading horror stories are a constant, vivid motif. Laced through that saga is my identification of key psychological factors that destroy wise day-trading performance, interspersed with my cache of antidotes, all self-disciplinary, that I've developed in the contemplative aftermath of my most harmful mistakes.

My tone is both comical and compassionate, with a practical and generous infusion of informative techno-speak. My approach to instruction is an emphatic departure from "golden goose" strategies, and my overall intention is twofold: to slow down the hazardous fervor of the average amateur, and to demonstrate the ways he can become a professional and not lose his shirt in the process. Throughout the book, you'll notice the word "**hold**" highlighted when I discuss disastrous situations involving "**holding**" stocks without any real plan of exit. If you're reading this you're probably a beginner in day-trading. Or maybe you're somewhat experienced, but not yet a confident pro. You're highly motivated and eager to learn how to day-trade with success. You're probably a risk-taker by nature, with a high tolerance for stress.

You're willing to stop at nothing to achieve the status of a professional trader who's thriving—a badge of honor. In the beginning, the process may seem thrilling. The opportunity to trade for a living looks wonderful. This is gonna be an adventure! You've found there are scads of outfits to train you (for a hefty fee, of course). And you could line a mansion's mantel with how-to books. You sign yourself up for a training program. You're greeted with head-swelling optimism and hope by the truckload, and you start harboring dreams of grandeur. The prospect of succeeding as a trader is making you almost giddy. Now you have a vision of perfection: you see wealth, freedom and leisure!

Who wouldn't want to make $5000 a week from home, sitting in his or her underwear?

I'll be the first to admit it: I'm guilty of indulging in euphoric expectation without the self-disciplined expertise to make it all come true. I started down my path to day-trading glory late in the 1990's. I moved to San Diego from Buffalo, New York. When I got to the West Coast I immediately learned of this potentially lucrative career.

Well, it's 2009—a whole decade has passed and I'm here to warn you about something that nobody wants to hear: You'll probably never master the profession without losing money first. Many beginner traders are brought to their knees by despair and lose their will to deal with the market. Even the more fortunate protégés, those who got into trading with almost unlimited wealth, learn that the pain of losing can take a big toll on their egos.

I realize that my focus on losing sounds annoying and counterproductive. Well, you can trust me on this one: I have reasons for emphasizing loss. Taming the loss monster is paramount to creating your long-term, *consistent* success. In day-trading, consistency rules.

The Truth About Day Trading Stocks shows how trading decisions are bent and shaped by emotions. Day-trading is a psychological process. Day-trading is emotional. Anyone can learn how to research and scrutinize fundamental business data. Anyone can master chart pattern analysis. But in the end the execution of an *actual real-time order* is all that really matters. That's why feelings take over. I show what can happen when feelings are heightened—especially by the powerful factors of inevitable fear and greed. The outcome can be very dismal.

Again, I'm *not* here to show you the "golden goose" of ultimate strategizing, while neglecting to reveal the grim hazards involved in keyboarding for money all day. I feel that it's crucial to emphasize the downside, in order to shed light on the maddening fact that most new day-traders are pickled and stewed in the positive view of this career—encouraged to inflate with ambition and adrenaline—all at their neophyte peril.

I designed this book not only as an escape from dry tedious texts, a ramble down Easy Read Lane, but also as a reference tool for serious day-trading careerists. If you approach this tome as a tool, you may be inclined to pick only the passages that address your most pressing questions. I feel that I should warn you not to do that. You should read the chapters in order. Later chapters build on ideas presented in earlier chapters, and if you skip around, the ideas may not gel.

When it comes to pure technical know-how, I've made sure that my advisories take off and expound in ways that five-day seminars don't. I reveal some harsh truths about day-trading stocks; my intention is to burst the greenhorn's bubble. Then, with the illusions dispensed with, I proceed to realistically useful advising. I compare pay-per-trade with pay-per-share brokers, determining which works best, and when; I define how day-trading isn't gambling; I repeatedly stress the wisdom of maintaining low exposure; and that's just a sampling of my arsenal of disaster-averting discussions.

Although I conclude with a chapter that exemplifies a great trading day, I did not write this book to spotlight and boast the performance of perfect trades. I wrote it to offer suggestions on how to avoid the prospect of perfect trades turning ugly. Throughout the book, I describe my development of acute self-awareness while figuring out how to succeed. My goal, in that blunt self-portrayal, is to help you create a disciplined mindset, and apply it to your own trading style.

In the back of the book, you'll find a section called "Rules to Remember," a list of over eighty rules, simply stated and easy to grasp, to benefit amateurs' performance.

I close with an offer of mentorship, designed to equip you with the tools to succeed. I believe that the best way to learn is direct experience under the supervision of a well-seasoned guide. Through my mentorship program, I will day-trade with you live, one-on-one, for an entire week or month. For more information, go to: www.DayTraderJosh.com.

In response to my ominous precautions, maybe you're thinking: *"If I want to make money, don't I just buy low and sell high?"*

Well, take that simplistic outlook and throw it right out the window. Why? Because it will hurt you. I sure wish someone had told me that when I started out.

Acknowledgments

I want to first give special thanks to Serene Sao. She is the person, very close to me, who initially supported my decision to become a professional day-trader.

I wish to thank Georgianna Groen, a fabulous author and mentor, for her tireless editorship. She has aided and encouraged me throughout my work on this book.

Many thanks to my father and his friend Lee McCormick for accommodating me in their beautiful cabin style home, in its mountainous New England setting. The atmosphere has been perfect for my clarity of mind, for both day-trading and my work on this book.

The Wholehearted Amateur

The year was 1999. I was in my car, on a mission.

I was driving to Irvine from my home in San Diego. Every mile glowed with deep indigo skies and the kiss of a warm, mellow sun; these were the everyday blessings I enjoyed in Southern California . . . even in the middle of winter. This climate made me hopeful and encouraged. It felt like a good luck charm. I had moved here from the cold, gloomy Rust Belt.

I was headed for a three-day program of training that focused on day-trading strategies. One week before this, while talking on the phone, I had become convinced I should go. The sales rep I spoke to from the sponsoring firm had performed his job admirably; he had made me charged up to attend.

Up to this point in my business career, I'd been trading stocks for six months. I hadn't yet done any day trading, however, and I was gung-ho to learn how. As I narrowed the distance between myself and Irvine, my expectations were high. I never took in any scenery; I was so deep in thought that I was driving by reflex.

I kept thinking of the things that I was going to buy soon after I got back from the training program, when the big bucks were going to flow. You see, I was brimming with confidence. In my short time in the profession of dealing with stocks, I had made a few really good trades.

It had never yet occurred to me that they were just dumb good luck.

Well, I got to the designated luxury hotel and let it gouge my credit card, and then I settled in for three mind-blowing days of comprehensive, motivating coaching.

When it was over and I was driving home, I was so pumped up to start day trading that my eagerness ran amok. I had to unload it on someone. I pulled up to my fiancée's workplace with my tires screeching a bit. I couldn't wait to tell her in person about what I'd just learned.

It came out of me allegorically: "Honey, I've been given a golden goose! Things are going to change like lightning!"

I couldn't have been more right about the "change" part. I was pitifully wrong, however, in my belief that it would be change for the better.

The next morning, as soon as I rolled out of bed, I made calls to all the online resource companie—the ones that were required by my newly learned "bullet-proof" system for day trading. Mostly it was access to real-time data feeds and proprietary stock analysis.

In a heartbeat, I had it set up.

So there I sat in my shorts, with my bare back feeling winged. I was magically launching into professional day trading, all in the comfort of my home! Because now I possessed all the big-time tools that the big boys on Wall Street had . . . right?

The California sunshine streamed through my den window and smiled on my new life. My fiancée and I had recently bought the house I sat in. The location was the lovely but costly enclave of Oceanside, North San Diego. She and I were currently splitting all the bills. I was determined to start paying for everything, as soon as the money poured in. My girl was proud and happy for me, supportive and full of encouragement.

And so it all began. Armed with the training and the sunshine and support, and with all my online access and resources, every morning I stretched, scratched, stepped into my shorts, and went to work with bare feet and shoulders.

At first I was not trading live; in other words, I was "paper trading." That means I was doing everything I'd been trained to do when executing a real-time order; but this was only practice. I was simply noting the entry price in a log, on paper. Paper trading is designed to teach methodology without real losses or gains. Well . . . just like the handful of good stocks trades that I'd lucked into in the past, it gave me a false sense of confidence.

Oh, yeah. That first month I developed a lot of self-assurance, because of the paper trading. In that short time, I made over $100,000 in fake money. I was buying 10,000-share blocks at a time, on paper. My confidence levels were off the charts, literally. . . .

And then came the months after that, the months when I lost everything.

But during those first few weeks paper-trading, fresh from that three-day seminar, with over 20 books on the subject read to shreds, I felt just like a pro. I had subscriptions to several money-market magazines, like the

Wall Street Journal and *Stocks & Commodities*. I had all the tools, all the resources.

I had very little *real* experience.

I was using a prominent pay-per-trade online broker. Back then I was paying $15 per trade.

I'll never forget my very first day of *real* day trading. That means with my own real money. I was online in front of my 36″ Gateway computer monitor, and also my separate laptop, and I felt as though both could talk! The successful-but-fake paper trading was all behind me now.

Today I was going *live*.

I clearly remember how nervous I felt when placing my first real monetary trade. My feelings were overwhelming. They were 10 times more powerful than when I made successful small trades in stock, those lucky ones I've mentioned, the ones before my day trading training. None of them had been on this scale!

And all trades thereafter were scary. Every trade I got into now made me extremely anxious. There's something about taking your hard-earned money and putting it on the line, like when you bet at casinos. Your heart rate doubles instantly, and your mind begins to race.

It's hard to think clearly like that. I think every trader has felt that, even those who can fall back on a healthy cushion of cash. Nobody likes to lose money!

A wise man once said, "It's smart to learn from your own mistakes, but it's wiser to learn from others.'" I ended up learning from only myself. For you it will be somewhat easier . . . here you have my blunders to study.

PART I

Psychological Truths and What to Do about Them

I 'm amazed at how seldom the day-trading training programs address the vital subject of beginners' emotional response. Anyone offering instruction in this work should know that day traders *will not* have consistent success until they've learned to control their emotions.

Therefore, my first goal is to explore the psychology of day trading, and to offer my hard-learned advice. I've placed this part first so you'll study it first. My hope is to dissuade you from thumbing to the technical-strategy chapters—not until you've thoroughly internalized what's here.

Why is this so important? It's absolutely critical to understand yourself before you get deeper into this high-stress career.

CHAPTER 1

Truths about Yourself to Know First

Y ou'd be totally realistic to ask this: *What is day trading, exactly? How does it differ from other types of stock trading?* And last but most definitely not least: *What's my skill level in day trading? Where do I fit in?*

Before you get into the profession full time, you should know all the answers to those questions.

You may find, however, that the answers don't come easily. Confusion about just what day trading involves is common in the stock brokerage industry, and gauging just how adept you are at it can feel a bit nebulous, too.

Consider the *Investopedia* definition of day trading:

Day trading is defined as the buying and selling of a security within a single trading day.

Does that description define much?

As a beginner, you should start with an awareness of the distinct separation of day trading from investing. Be clear about which one you're interested in, and just how well-honed your skills are. You may find that sorting out these questions requires some headwork, because day trading has come to be associated with a variety of workplace scenarios.

Prior to the Internet takeover, a decade or more ago, for the most part day traders worked at bank or investment firms and were known as equity investment specialists, or else fund management pros. But now, in the midst of both changing legislation and proliferating prospects online, day trading has emerged as a popular calling for thousands hooked up at home. *Private equity trader* has become their official job title.

Approach two strangers on the street, ask them what they think a day trader is, and they'll probably mention either Wall Street or a person online in his den. One of them might talk about a brow-sweating guy with his tie loose and shirtsleeves rolled up, barking market orders across the pit to a just-as-harried colleague on the floor. The other one might talk about a barefoot guy in his shorts, glued to his PC all day.

Both of the people surveyed would be right. There's no single definition of a day trader anymore. Day trading has vastly diversified. And as if the expansions I've mentioned aren't enough, there are also, within those assorted scenarios, traders with assorted approaches. This is where things get even murkier. You've probably heard of the handles that express styles and strategies: momentum trader, scalp trader, equity trader ... whew.

If you find yourself getting a little bit flustered by all that stuff to take in, remember that the main point to focus on is this: Professional day traders close out all positions at the end of the day; day traders don't **hold** overnight.

The best way to further get the gist of day trading is to recognize what it is not: It is not investing. With regard to stocks, investing differs from day trading because of four primary factors:

1. Investing in a stock requires substantial research and knowledge of the company.
2. Usually a large portion of your capital is used in a single position.
3. The general plan, when investing, is to **hold** a position longer to get a bigger return. How long you **hold** the security is a major indicator of your expected return on investment (ROI).
4. Investing requires forecasting the future.

Stock investments are classified as short term or long term. A short-term investment is usually a position **held** for one business quarter or less—that's up to three months, never longer. A long-term investment is usually **held** for longer than one business quarter, with an expectation of receiving dividends and future earnings growth in the company.

When the term *invest* is very loosely applied, you can actually call day trading investing. It's true that you're taking your funds, for the moment, and investing them in a stock. But you don't have to know the stock's company like you know the back of your hand, you're not (well, I hope you're not) putting up most of your money, you almost never **hold** overnight, and you don't need to forecast the future. That's why you're referred to as a *trader* as opposed to an *investor*.

When the term *investor* is aptly applied, we're usually talking about hedge fund managers and portfolio investment pros. Those brokers usually work in large firms, like Goldman Sachs or Merrill Lynch. They handle investment capital that numbers into the millions, and that money belongs to their clients. Because it's not their own capital, their licensure is a must. Their time is spent researching companies, forecasting earnings, seeking out new clients, and retaining existing clients.

Those managers, or licensed brokers, however you want to call them, decide on what companies to add to investment portfolios and how to manage the risks. Once they know how much of their clients' money they want to invest in a stock, they alert their firm's trading desk. A hired day trader then purchases the shares on the order form given to him.

That sort of day trader is not an independent. Like the broker, he has to be licensed. His job is to fill all the execution orders he receives throughout the day. Most likely he's paid a base salary and some sort of a commission.

The independent day trader (or independent equity trader) goes by the same name, but his job is decidedly different. He uses only his own funds. He doesn't have to get himself licensed. He either works alone from home or at a private-equity trading desk, usually at a pay-per-share firm.

The role that all types of day traders share is that they spend their time immersed in the business of placing intraday trades. Their attention is riveted to the volatile price swings that are so characteristic of stocks.

Day traders care mostly about how volume and price movement are being affected by those swings. They don't get caught up in the huge panorama of forecasts and company analysis. That would be like viewing the forest, not the trees. Day traders squint, up close, all day long, at the endless flitting motion in the trees.

Since day traders don't plan to **hold** overnight, news about stocks and any earning announcements aren't likely to affect their day's trading. Though company information and other fundamentals are somewhat important to traders, they aren't critical. Remember, they're not investors. They're not betting their lives on a company. They're trading on the volume created by intraday investor interest in a chosen company's stock price.

Well, at this point you may be thinking I'm making it sound as though day traders don't care about the companies they're trading. You'd be half right to assume that. Chapter 14, "Stock Picking: Simplifying the Process," and also Chapter 15, "Why News Can Be Just Noise," further drive that point home.

In response, you might pose the question: *Just what does a day trader do that's beneficial to the market?*

For starters, day traders are crucial to a stock's price movements, called market liquidity. The more liquidity there is in a stock, the better the stock will trade. Liquidity means that there are many buyers and sellers interested in the stock. Without day traders, investors wouldn't be able to buy large volumes of any given stock without driving up the price as they were buying up their positions. Conversely, and just as importantly, when investors begin to sell off, day trading liquidity helps keep the stock from dropping precipitously.

Now that you're clearer on what a day trader is and does, and also what a day trader isn't and doesn't do, your immediate priority should be to ascertain your *skill level*. If you were discussing that subject with me, I'd have several questions for you. Going from most to least important, they'd be:

- How *often* do you trade, and how profitably?
- How *much* are you trading in capital and leverage?
- How *long* have you been trading?
- *What* are you trading (your financial instruments)?
- Are you trading *other people's money*, or only your personal capital?
- Are you a *licensed* trader, or trading independently?
- *How* were you trained?

And then we'd elaborate on all of them.

HOW OFTEN DO YOU TRADE, AND HOW PROFITABLY?

More than any other factor, your skill level is based on how many trades you place per day and the consistency of the profits. If you do well with one trade per day, that's great, but the same intraday performance with a hundred trades is much more desirable. Your *frequency* of trades is the quintessential signpost that indicates your level of skill. Frequent trades, frequently profitable, are the visible proof of a pro.

HOW MUCH ARE YOU TRADING IN CAPITAL AND LEVERAGE?

An affluent beginner might trade with a million dollars. With a 50-to-1 leverage, he can capitalize on his margin mightily. Does this mean his skill level is higher than that of a guy with just five thousand bucks? The answer is clearly *no*.

In order to buy ten times the shares, of course, you always need ten times the capital. If you have that kind of capital, that's great. But that won't ensure you more profits. It just means you'll make more or lose more.

You don't want to increase the share size just because your funds make it possible. *Your share size should only increase with your skill.* I recommend a very slowly graduating climb from 100-share blocks to 200, onward and upward in increments that small, in careful correlation with your growing expertise. Whenever you find that increasing your share size is causing your profits to crash, you need to back down to something smaller. No matter how much capital you play with, there's no sense in losing big chunks of it just because your skill level is low.

I always use 100-share blocks as a starting point. Why? If you consistently trade at a profit by executing 100 trades per day and sticking with 100-share blocks, then what you've developed is a *high* level of skill when trading with the amount of capital required for purchasing 100 shares at time.

Here's the flip side. Take any average stock, let's say a $50 stock. All you need is $5,000 to purchase 100 shares. If you have $1 million in capital you can purchase 20,000 share blocks, or four similar stocks each in 5,000 share blocks, and so on. Can you see where I'm going with this? The more funds you have, the more likely you'll get in trouble if your skill level isn't sufficient.

Here's an unpleasant scenario I've lived through.

Part of being an amateur, for me, was learning to properly handle my leverage. With my initial, traditional pay-per-trade broker, it was usually 4 to 1. This increased my buying power (my capital), so I felt as if I was four times as rich. I immediately began to purchase larger share blocks, sometimes 10,000 share blocks at a time. What followed was a nightmare of loss.

As I take you through my confessions, which essentially make up this book, I reiterate that nightmare, and others, from different angles in different chapters, to help you see where I went wrong. In this chapter, what I want to make clear is that I lacked the skills that the increase in capital made me think I had.

I eventually discovered that a highly skilled trader profits, no matter how great or how little his funds. Even if he's playing with as much as $1 million, he'll wisely purchase only 100-share blocks, and he'll utilize his skill and decrease his risk by trading multiple stocks.

That guy could buy 20 stocks in 100-share blocks in a heartbeat. Maybe you're thinking, if he were to do that, then he'd be spread way too thin.

Watching 20 stocks is scary, that much is very true. But it's still better than putting all of your capital into one stock and one trade. You certainly don't want to start out as a day trader nervously eyeballing multiple stocks, but later on, after some practice, the wise thing to do is just that: to diversify your daily portfolio. Literally speaking, that's your stock list, and by making it longer and having a lot to watch, you minimize your risk by about 80 percent.

Though having more capital does not in itself increase your skill level at all, it does make you gradually smarter, because you have money for practice. But fear not, comrades with average funds: whether or not you have a truckload of capital, this is the thing to remember: learn how to manage your risk. The higher your skill level, the better you'll do that.

Risk management is knowing when to use your capital—just how much, and when. Chapter 6, "The Importance of Risk Management," illuminates that mastery, applied to intraday trading.

HOW LONG HAVE YOU BEEN TRADING?

This question implies some tough answers. I've heard of amateur traders who have gone to a mentorship program, read a couple of books, practiced for a couple months, and then began trading with a great degree of consistency and profit. In less than a year, all of a sudden they're exemplary professional day traders.

And then there are the traders, myself included, who must struggle for years to find their niche. It's difficult, if not downright impossible, to approximate how much time it takes for individual traders to build and improve their skills.

The longer you're in this industry, of course, the more skill you'll acquire. And here's something I'll assert with conviction to any and all day traders, no matter how quickly or slowly they profit, because time always proves this truth: The key to increasing your skill level is to remain very active in trading.

The question of how long you've been day trading does not just address the time spent; the underlying query—the important thing to know—is what have you been doing with that time? Have you been using it wisely?

Here's a list of suggestions that can help speed up your process of attaining trading skills.

- Be active. Stay with it—full time.
- Budget, borrow, or plan what you have to in order to be able to take some time off to focus *only* on day trading.
- Get involved in a mentorship program with someone you can watch.
- Get your New York Stock Exchange Series 7 (General Securities) license and go to work for a salary-based position at a brokerage firm like Merrill Lynch (optional).
- During your free time, inundate yourself with market information, especially day-trading tactics and strategies.

WHAT FINANCIAL INSTRUMENTS ARE YOU TRADING?

Are you trading stocks, commodities, treasuries, option contracts, future contracts, penny stocks, or some other financial instrument?

A professional day trader can trade virtually any medium of exchange. Most beginners, however, only trade in equities (stocks). That, in my opinion, is the safest place to start. Stock exchanges have the most transparency and market data available; what that means is that for the beginner, they're the simplest instruments to learn from.

That doesn't necessarily mean that if you never trade options or future contracts, you'll never reach professional status. It really boils down to what you're comfortable with and what interests you the most.

The key is to find your niche, and stick with it. For instance, if you choose to trade only stocks, then over time you'll become a master at trading in equities. Most likely you'll find that you only trade one type, such as tech stocks or energy stocks. The more you fine-tune your trading style—as a "scalp trader" or whatever—the more skill you'll acquire for that financial instrument.

ARE YOU TRADING OTHER PEOPLES' MONEY OR YOUR PERSONAL CAPITAL?

In order to invest clients' money, you have to be a licensed broker. And no one, of course, is going to trust you unless you're extremely experienced. But just the same, always remember: Just because you're an unlicensed, independent trader doesn't mean you're not a professional.

ARE YOU A LICENSED TRADER, OR TRADING INDEPENDENTLY?

If you're trading from home, you're most likely an independent. If you opt to trade at a professional trading desk, you have a couple of choices: You can remain independent and trade from the floor of a pay-per-share firm, or you can obtain a license (Series 7) and apply to work for a large investment firm like Goldman Sachs.

I've learned to never judge traders by where they're trading from or whether they're licensed. I've known some licensed day traders who can't be consistently profitable. And I've known some home-based, unlicensed traders who've had sterling track records for years.

In day trading, a license doesn't make you a professional. If you study for your Series 7 license, as I have, the first thing you'll notice is the manuals' remarkable thickness. They're loaded with virtually everything to know about corporations and all the information you could ever cram in about how the stock market functions. You'll learn all the federal Securities and Exchange Commission (SEC) regulations, and the entire process of how corporations disclose their earnings statements. Basically, you'll get an entire overview of the stock market universe.

Most large investment firms require the license as part of their application process. You don't actually learn how to day trade until they show you how. That's why the license means nothing—It's really just your pass for admission. Having one proves you've been checked out for things like a criminal record.

But you still have to learn how to day trade.

HOW WERE YOU TRAINED?

Training is everything. If you've only been to a seminar or read a book or two, you're like a lamb being led to the slaughter. You can't possibly learn how to day trade from reading manuals and getting tested or licensed. The most effective form of training is by far the mentorship programs, sometimes called in-house training. Most of those programs have you and a professional trader working one-on-one.

Stay tuned for a lot more on mentoring.

Well I hope that I've helped you be clearer, at this point, on whether you're meant for day trading or investing. And I also hope that I've helped you get a fix on your current skill level.

That way you're more likely to know just exactly what you're getting yourself into!

 RULES TO REMEMBER

- Increasing your skill level is a gradual process; never rush it without the help of professional mentorship or in-house training.
- A Series 7 license doesn't mean you're a professional day trader. You still need to be trained.
- When day trading, always remain active. That's the key to increasing skill.

CHAPTER 2

How Emotions Can Destroy a Trade

I n day trading it's immediately obvious: Your emotions can be your worst enemy. They're usually counterproductive to all your day-trading efforts. As an amateur trader you learn right away that emotions are the bane of your strategies.

The control or even the elimination of feelings should be the Holy Grail of day trading. If you're out there high-strung, acting like a loose canon, you're not day trading, you're gambling. You're not in control of your trade.

You know when your feelings are wrecking a trade. You're in one and it goes against you. You **hold**, and then you **hold** it for longer, and then you get mad at the stock.

If you're like me when I was a greenhorn, you might start to viciously mutter: "You better go back up, or I'll throw this monitor out the window!"

At one time or another, all day traders feel that way, and it leads to big trading mistakes. Though few of us ever smash up the equipment, when we feel that frustration we *do* have a tendency to actually break trading rules. We also tend to invent new rules that make no sense at all.

To err is human . . .

We know, we know.

Emotions are like frenzied little voices in your head. They get riled when things don't go as planned. They're the part of you that freaks at uncertainty. Well, uncertainty in day trading is a given, a fixture, so . . . what can you do about that?!

I've been struggling with that irony for my entire day-trading career. I can never make my feelings disappear. I've tried to rid myself of them, but they're part of me, they're permanent residents: They're just as attached as my hands and my feet, and just when things start to get rough in a trade, just when I need to rely on my wits and not my proliferating angst, that's when they make the most noise.

I've learned that this problem must be dealt with proactively. The issue is just as threatening as hurricanes are to buildings. We have to construct strong defenses against our own primal reactions. In trading, as in any other worthwhile endeavor, both anxiety and acquisitiveness are instinctive and neither can be removed, but lessening their damage is crucial. We must learn to corral them and manage them, just like a highly skilled animal trainer who effectively reins in his beasts.

I've identified the worst of the monsters. They are, as you'd probably guess, *fear* and *greed*. When I'm angry, depressed, desperate, or scared, those are the underlying factors.

THE FEAR FACTOR

Let's begin with the fear factor. Our minds are hardwired with fear. This is the vital, indispensable reflex that keeps us alive and strong. Fear serves us well when we're running from lions, or clobbering each other in wars. But when fear overpowers the detached, calm analysis that's always required in day trading, the mechanism meant to secure our survival turns into the cause of our downfall.

Amateur traders, of course, get beat up the most by fear. Their lack of experience creates overconfidence, and that, as we'll later observe, creates recklessness, which causes nosedives to big losses. The result is someone who's completely lost his nerve—now he's completely scared and discouraged. From the quagmire of defeat he must now learn to rise and wield the great tool of true confidence.

True confidence is all about learning the virtue of old-fashioned, joyless-sounding prudence. Prudence is an extremely underrated state of mind. Prudence helps traders discover the path to losing a much less, and successfully taming the fear. I'll return to that virtue in a bit.

When I was a beginner, the fear factor undid me. It messed with my need to make quick and wise decisions. It came down to two main scenarios.

First, and most often, the fear would take over just before I entered a trade. I'd look at my charts and see a perfect setup, and just when it was time to get in it. . . . I'd stop. My emotions were suddenly churning. I was questioning my system of trading. I was suddenly thinking, *The trade is too risky*. My jam-up might take just 10 seconds, but in day trading, 10 seconds can be way too long.

I eventually learned that the way to quell fear is to find a comfort zone. To find it, know it, and stick to it, always, as a mandatory self-imposed recourse.

Here's a simple rule to remember: When you feel the fear, lower your risk. Don't think about it, just do it. Do it right then and there. It's the obvious way out, but in that kind of pinch, you might hesitate. So learn to *automatically* do it. If you're about to make a trade with a 1,000-share block and the fear factor kicks in, immediately lower your exposure to 500 or 100, whichever amount feels okay. I can almost guarantee that your anxiety will vanish if you're *programmed* to *immediately* decrease your exposure.

The second scenario happens when you're already into the trade. Your fear can make you sell miserably short of a decent, attainable profit.

Suppose you've just entered a trade. You got in at $49.75 with a 100-share block. You expect to sell once it hits $50 (Limit) or sell at $49.65 (Stop/Loss). You want to make $25 on the trade (25¢ × 100), or you risk losing $10 (10¢ × 100).

In rare cases the stock will shoot up to your exit point, allowing you to quickly and painlessly sell at (All *right!*) a planned profit. But most likely the stock price will exhibit volatility and bounce on a one-minute chart. It will soar to $49.90, just shy of your $50 exit point, and then all the way back down to your $49.75 entry price. It might actually test below it. Figure 2.1 illustrates this scenario.

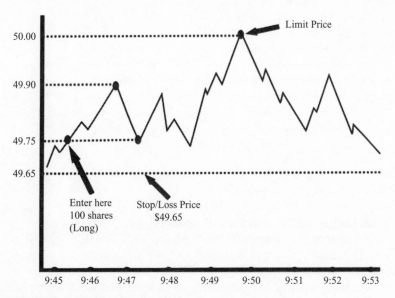

FIGURE 2.1 Intraday 1-Minute Chart

The volatility on the up-trend direction toward $50 can cause you to get emotional during the five minutes of trading. The price very seldom shoots straight down or straight up.

The hard part is dealing with this several times over, all in the space of one minute. Amateur traders get nerve-wracked, and tend to sell short of their predetermined exit points. They'll either sell at a loss before they hit those points, or they'll sell when the price, though ascending, is shy of the upper limits.

The fear factor urges them to sell *right now*, before the predetermined $50 exit point, especially if the price doesn't zoom straight up.

For example, take me when I was a beginner. I sold at $49.80, because the suspense was too grating. Then I only made 5¢ on the trade. Or I sold at a loss when it dipped just short of $49.75, bailing out too soon. Either way I had messed up the trade, because the fear factor froze me. I was overexposed when trading a 1,000-share block. I was afraid to continue.

So there it was again, like the moment before the trade, when I was too scared to jump in. Anxiety was causing me to lose bigger profits. My emotions were getting the best of me.

Those intraminute oscillations can cross your eyes, tense you up, and make you want to run. They can make you reconsider the wage-slave life—broke, living paycheck to paycheck, and bored right out of your mind, but at least you're not tearing your hair out.

Eventually, I discovered some inner solutions. Along with the prudence I've mentioned, I found out how right my mom had always been about the power of patience. Add those two virtues to much less exposure, and now you've got it together.

I'll return to those virtues again.

The less your exposure, the less your fear factor; anyone can see that on his own; but a beginner might not see quite soon enough that he needs to establish a powerful *reflex of instant exposure reduction*. That way, when he's caught in that intraminute bouncing, he doesn't have to freeze up and wonder what to do; instead, he decisively acts.

GREED IS NOT GOOD

Now let's move on to the *greed factor*. Greed, just like fear, is inherent in humans, and it can't be avoided, only tamed.

In day trading, we actually need a little greed. That's the fuel that keeps us going. Acquisitive goals, the motives and the reasons to take higher risks, distinguish us from plodders and wage slaves.

But greed can create overconfidence. Greed can make a day trader reckless. Diametrically opposed to the fear factor, the greed factor causes the amateur to jump into numerous trades without enough hesitation. Uncontrolled greed can push him to break his sensible system, hazard trades he normally wouldn't, and get himself in all kinds of trouble.

Greed is by far the most dangerous emotion. Fear, though detrimental, won't make you lose big. The greed factor, however, can destroy you. Greed can lead to excessiveness, and in the end, inconsistency. Your greed can land you in a devastating number of ruinous trading situations.

The greed factor causes two downfalls.

The first can occur when you're in a good trade, and you exit with a small well-planned profit. "Good" and "well-planned" are important terms here; they suggest that you've been prudent and patient.

But now you've just noticed that the stock price keeps shooting on upward. So you eagerly opt to get back in, and follow the run-up even farther.

And that's when your avarice kicks in. You're avidly re-entering at a much higher level than you did in your *good* trade, and of course you're expecting, with beginners' foolish courage, to see the price trade to the upside.

Unfortunately, it does not. The price turns against you, and now you're losing money, and you regretfully, belatedly recognize that you entered these straits on emotions.

And there's more. The greed factor isn't yet through with you; here comes downfall number two. With the trade gone against you, now you **hold**. You **hold** with the hope (and isn't hope an emotion?) that the price will go back up.

You're now at the mercy of the market, with all your good planning shot, and all I can say is, *Good luck.* Are you getting a sense of the proverbial snowball, getting larger as it rolls down a slope? That's the greed factor at work in you, doing its dubious magic.

One day I was trading Amazon.com (AMZN)—and I stuck with it all day. I was trading smart. I was entering only when I knew my exit points. I was only buying 100-share blocks. It was a good day to trade—there was little volatility. The stock price kept trending up. Virtually every trade I entered went up to my limit price quickly. Easy trading!!

It was 3:00 P.M., the final hour, and after commissions I was up about $650 for the day. I'd been trading consistently all day, in and out, with $15, $25, and $40 profits. I had a few stop/losses of $20 to $40, but that's normal and expected.

In this very last hour of trading, I was watching the charts and lo and behold, I noticed a big spike in volume. Then the price shot up about a dollar—*in just under five minutes.* It hadn't spiked that much, that quickly, all day. There was no particular news about AMZN, and the indexes were relatively steady.

It annoyed me to miss out on that spike. I wanted to make more money. I wanted to make a nice round $1,000 profit for the day; I wanted a few hundred more.

I wanted . . . I wanted . . . I wanted. That's greed. And then it turned to smoldering envy. I felt as though everyone was getting rich but me. All day I'd been making chump change, and now that the stock was running strong to the upside, I coveted a piece of that pie.

I began to psyche myself up. I convinced myself that the stock was going to keep ascending gloriously. I let my greed morph to that dangerous headiness that makes you or breaks you—and breaks you more often. I abandoned my prudent consistency. I purchased 1,000 shares.

And soon after I bought that huge block, the stock dropped 20¢.

No problem; I was used to 20¢ moves. That's how things went, all day. The hundred-share blocks meant a 20¢ move would gain or lose me $20. But this time, remember, I was strapped to a thousand shares. So this time, I was down $200.

I lost control. I could feel the greed completely take over. I didn't care; it was just like a gambling compulsion. I began to average down. I purchased another 1,000 shares, then another, and another. By the time I realized how screwed I was, I was trading 5,000 shares.

The stock price dropped an average of 35¢ on my 5,000 shares, accumulated while averaging down. Within 20 minutes, I was down $1,750 (5,000 × 35¢).

My greed then collapsed into panic. I knew that if the price continued to drop, I was going to lose much more money. So I surrendered and sold all 5,000 shares at a $1,750 loss.

This horrible scenario is illustrated in Figure 2.2.

Up till three o'clock I traded consistently in 100-share blocks. The very first 1,000-share block just happened to be near the top of the late-day spike. If I had purchased only a 100-share block I would not have gotten into so much trouble.

On the bright side, the stock did retrace down, all the way to the closing bell. If I had **held** any longer, I would have lost another $5,000. After I exited, it dropped a full dollar.

But what if it had gone back up? Would I have made a bad decision to sell at a loss? Those are the questions that can scrape on your brain, and make you lose sleep at night. Either way, I was fatally greedy to purchase the first thousand-share block. I vowed to never do that again. But I did. . ...

As I mentioned at the start of this confession, fear and greed are unavoidable. The traits are psychological fixtures; they're a part of us, and can only be tamed, not destroyed. Trading in 1,000-share blocks is greed that hasn't been tamed. The 100-share blocks are small increments, quite manageable even if you lose. Every time you enter a new trade, 100-share

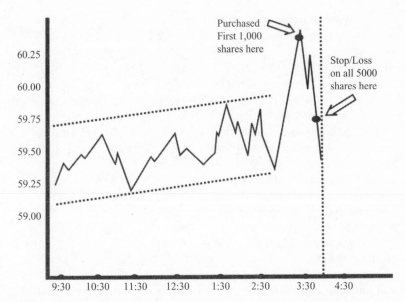

FIGURE 2.2 Intraday 30-Minute Chart

blocks fuel your want, your desire, to make more money all day—and yes, that's greed too—but it's tamed.

Greed is a vital but lethal beast, licking its chops inside you. Greed should be locked behind bars. It should only be freed in the vigilant presence of leashes, restraints, and charged stun guns. In other words, when you're consistent—when you're sticking to a strict risk-management system, like trading in hundred-share blocks—your greed is still there, but not loose.

Understand the powers of fear and greed; understand the dangers and advantages. Know that self-discipline is key. In day trading, your primal emotions must be caught and confined, yet masterfully drawn upon also. Lock them down, scrutinize them, and train them. I'm talking about *you against you*, here: the quintessential human condition. Making great money in day trading is all about beating the human condition.

 RULES TO REMEMBER

- If you feel yourself being controlled by your emotions—reduce your market exposure immediately.
- Stay consistent *all day* while trading—stick with 100-share blocks.
- Set realistic profit goals, and create a realistic budget.

CHAPTER 3

Preventing Overconfidence

With remorse I think back to my excessive confidence, back when I was fresh from my first training program. I was using what I'd been taught to believe was a wonderful, "bullet-proof" system. I actually had so much faith in myself that my initial losses didn't bug me.

But I got over that fast. My losses were so consistent that I had to. And then I desperately needed to know just *why* I was losing so much. The first thing I started to realize is that I was too sure of myself.

Confidence in trading styles is similar to the way a busy cook relates to his pot mitt. The wise cook, no matter how harried, always takes the time to put on his mitt before he grabs a pot off his stove.

So it's not the inanimate mitt that protects him; the bottom line is that it's the cook himself. Knowing when it's necessary to put that glove on and having the good sense to do it is what he's really relying on. Accordingly, the day trader must fully understand that it's his judgment, much more than any system he's learned, that affects his trading the most.

Confidence, just like the cook's pot mitt, is a tool. If the trader's confidence wildly balloons and he becomes zealous, stubborn, or careless, then he's just like the heedless, inexperienced cook who thinks he'll get by without his mitt. In both of those scenarios, overconfidence burns.

I'm aware of no chart pattern or stock analysis methodology that shows you a confidence factor. No system will tell you to buy or sell with 100 percent certainty—because there simply is no such certainty!

But we traders need confidence—lots of it—in spite of the uncertainty. Without that mental asset, there would be no trading career. Too much of it, however, can destroy us. Confidence it is a tool that must be utilized, but always judiciously. Otherwise, it gets in the way. It tosses good judgment in the trash. To literally understand this, you need only to think of the hurry-up cook who doesn't use his mitt when he should. You know what will happen to his hand, and then his ability to work.

For the day trader, overconfidence is that detrimental. Mastering confidence as a tool, not an obstacle, is a lifelong, ongoing process. I am still growing in that process, and at this point I've learned some reliable skills in it.

But during my first weeks of day trading, my confidence levels were overzealous: They were hardly a powerful tool. Soon I began to understand that overconfidence led me astray into two classic trading mistakes.

Those mistakes are ignoring your predetermined stop/loss price and **holding** too long.

IGNORING YOUR PREDETERMINED STOP/LOSS PRICE

I enter into a trade, it immediately goes against me, and I **hold**. This is *after* the triggering of my predetermined stop/loss price—and I don't give a damn.

To **hold** is an act of stubbornness. It's a lethally wishful kind of thinking. This is where I'm allowing my confidence to become, not a tool, but something irrational. Now I'm just being a daredevil, like a bungee-jumper. I'm bouncing in midair, and risking a deadly collision.

And then I make things worse for myself. I buy more—I average down.

At this point I've blundered into the minefield of way-too-confident trading. To buy more at a lower level, after the initial trade has gone against me? What was I thinking? Now my emotions control me. I got into a trade and it down-slid, and now I'm irritated and worried, and I'm kicking myself for failing to wait for it to decline before buying in the first place.

So basically, I've now bucked the system. Now all I'm doing is gambling. I'm betting that the price will go back up, with the faith of the fools at casinos.

HOLDING TOO LONG

I'm in a trade and the price goes up, but in my opinion, not enough. So my overconfidence tells me to **hold** for just a while longer. Then (of course!) the stock price retreats to break-even, so I've lost out on a good trade. That same trade might even continue to retrace into the red.

It doesn't get any more ugly than that. I feel like an idiot for failing to sell when I had a profit and I should have had a clear plan of exit.

So now I could see that it was getting imperative to harness my confidence, somehow. To grab it and throw it onto a table, deep inside my head, and strap it down and hone it into a tool that would fit my needs.

After a day of that self-search, I understood what to do. My confidence, if made precise with prudence, would help me pick my own realistic entry and exit price levels. Overconfidence amounted to a careless lack of that precision.

I needed to *trust and never abandon* a system of reliable stop/loss and limits. Then I'd be halfway to Mecca.

I've never regretted those insights.

The key is to stick to your plan. If your chart analysis indicates you should stop/loss when the price hits $50, then *do it!* Sell at a loss, then move on. You'll feel even worse if you **hold** past your exit point. Whenever you put yourself in that situation, you're at the mercy of the market.

When structured right, your confidence serves you, just like a trusty wrench. If I enter a trade and I feel pretty sure that I'd sell it at two price levels—the stop/loss price and the limit price—then I'm using my confidence correctly. I'm making that trait a useful component in my mental system of trading.

Yes, I found that my predetermined price level is where that tool does me good. For instance, if I lose on the trade, at least I can feel sure I was right to get out. The price may continue to fall further against me, but now I'm safe on the sidelines and free to get back in at even lower levels, pending further stock price analysis.

If a price movement shows a clear pattern and my current trading system is indicating an entry price, then my confidence gets high, but not foolishly so. I can never know for sure, but I can fairly approximate how much I'll make or lose, because of my stop/loss and limit exit points.

To conclude, overconfidence is your confidence tool broken apart and malfunctioning. It compels you to try to pick bottoms or tops. It's crucial to be cautious instead, and to know your stock very well. You must know it just like you know the lyrics of your favorite song.

You must know your stock's rhythm like the back of your hand. If you don't, and you're trading it anyway, that's another sign of overconfidence.

Analyze the average daily price ranges and minute ranges, take note of how fast or how slowly they move, and how they retrace during trends, and when. You should mentally trade your stock first. Once you feel sure enough to dance with it, then and only then should you begin your careful planning of entry and exit points.

Trading with confidence is all about being familiar with your stock, and prudently sticking to your plans. Trading with overconfidence is neglecting to know your stock and haphazardly changing the exit points while already in the trade. If you're an amateur trader, that's a very perilous stratagem. Only the experienced trader can handle it, and even he might regret it.

If you think you can trade like a pro, then most likely you're overconfident, and most likely, you'll lose your shirt. Stick to the program, every time! Be reasonably certain, not reckless! If you're a born risk-taker or daredevil, it will take force of will to achieve that.

 RULES TO REMEMBER

- Confidence is an emotional tool, and you must harness it and control it.
- Never enter a trade without knowing your exit points.
- Once you've predetermined your exit points, always stick to them.

CHAPTER 4

From Impatient to Cool, Calm, and Collected

Your-day trading performance is the result of your patience, or your sorry lack thereof. No matter how well-schooled you've made yourself in the technical applications, if you're short on that virtue, you're in big trouble.

Impatience is a threat, and it's constant. As an amateur you'll sometimes feel edgy, no matter how determined you are to stay cool. You'll have to chase down your impetuousness, and catch it and totally stun it, and lock it up tight with the greed.

No matter whether you've traded for a dozen years or mere days, your level of self-discipline is crucial. In pondering that fact I've come to understand that patience, when seen as an emotional tool, actually divides into two: the tool of amateur patience and the tool of professional patience.

The beginner's need for patience is simple, yet challenging. For him or her, it's all about staying power. He's a lot like a determined new dieter, trying to stick to a stringent way to eat.

Impatience, in amateur day traders, reminds me of the foolishness of dieters taking the easy way out. They might get tummy tucks, or have their stomachs stapled. Are they doing anything, or learning anything, that will consistently keep the weight off?

And the ones with the tummy tucks? If they haven't learned to successfully diet, then they just keep on overeating—and all that surgically tightened-up flesh begins, once again, to swell and bulge and droop.

In the effort to conquer obesity, what matters the most is to comprehend the underlying personal factors. What causes the overeating in the first place? How can it be overcome? A lot of self-searching is required for that, and self-searching requires patience. The commitment to study and renovate oneself isn't easy for fat people, or anyone. It amounts to the acceptance that there is no easy way, and that only the long haul works.

In day trading, if you want to *consistently* profit, then you need the intensive, nonstop self-vigilance that accompanies victorious dieters' weight loss. You have to grow that much patience.

As I've established in Chapter 3, first you must develop a prudent trading style, and the discipline to always stick to it. Patience is the in-the-thick-of-it glue that keeps it all together. Strengthening that virtue can't be done overnight; you won't walk away from a seminar with it. It's a process that you, the beginner, must gradually, painstakingly master, while executing multiple intraday trades.

It's all about baby steps ... and who wants to move that slowly? I'm sorry, but that's what it takes. Keep your shirt on. Take a deep breath. Slowly count to ten. *Patience.*

Most beginners sit there for hours, waiting for a price to hit. Sometimes they even wait for days. That isn't patience, that's obsession, the confusing of a virtue with the grave mistake of **holding**. That certainly isn't day trading. Neither is the flipside, impatience, the hurry-up quest for quick results.

Patience, especially for the young or inexperienced, is all about learning to control one's annoyance. It's about a high endurance for tough day-trading situations. To achieve that takes dedication to active trading days.

To help yourself develop your patience, it's crucial to find your niche. You might change your strategy at least 20 times before you see what works best. Some find that day trading several stocks, daily, results in a relatively peaceful state of mind. Others feel best when they trade just one stock. The point is that you, the beginner, must find yourself a method that bolsters your tolerance while you're caught in the gyrations of a trade.

Yet after you find your most comfortable trading style, you'll still have to struggle with yourself. I can't think of one trade I've ever been in that didn't demand a great focus. Whenever I've enjoyed a good trade, it's usually because I made myself wait for the hit of the entry and exit points. A lot of my bad trades have been all about the flipside: I failed to wait for the proper setup, or I exited too soon or too late.

I may have a superior chart-reading system, and an arsenal of proven techniques. All of it increases my chances of successfully selecting intraday bottoms and tops. But what matters the most, as I've stated before, is my confidence in my system. Once I decide on which price I need to enter and exit a trade, the key is to stick to the plan, and that's where the virtue of patience comes in. I know I'm getting redundant here, but sticking to the plan can be so hard to do that I don't mind repeating that point.

It could take several minutes for the price targets to hit. Waiting that out is critical to the success of the trade. If boredom makes me sway from my predetermined price levels, then I'm regressing, I'm committing the beginner's mistake. Just as with the fear and greed factors, now I'm trading just on emotion. It's been said that the essence of patience is all about clear thinking, unencumbered by any emotion. Who but a sociopath can do that!

A day trader has to learn how.

THE WAITING IS THE HARDEST PART

Tom Petty and the Heartbreakers have a classic-rock hit: "The Waiting Is the Hardest Part." Oh, yeah. The chords and the beats and Petty's wail of that tune are the sound of your knuckles clenched up. They're the sound of you holding your breath in pure angst, so tense that your stomach feels squeezed. You listen to it knowing that somebody understands and has spun the tedium into a song.

Waiting for your price level to hit can be boring beyond words. It's especially hard on the days when the market is trading sideways. But there are some ways around it. For instance, if you're waiting for more then 10 minutes for your entry or exit point, then most likely, on that day you've picked the wrong stock to trade. Chapter 14, "Stock Picking: Simplifying the Process," advises on that problem.

Here I want to reiterate rule number one: only trade 100-share blocks at a time. And when you get fed up with the monotony of it, always remember this: trading in 100-share blocks does *not* mean you're *not* trading like a professional.

Impatience is what often causes amateurs to place large and risky trades. Impatience makes you go for unrealistic profits, when you should be thinking much smaller. Your *only* objective should be a keen focus on keeping your profits consistent.

When you're trading in 100-share blocks, you're not going to make any more than $50 on each trade, but you *will* build consistency and skill. Most stocks, with $45 to $85 price ranges trade in 25¢ cent ranges within five minutes. During these intraday swings, you can easily grab 25¢ to 50¢. Those moves usually take anywhere from 10 seconds to 10 minutes, depending on the stock.

Let's say you have a $50 stock. It has an average daily volume of five million shares traded. It also has a proven track record of moving 25¢ within five minutes, and it does this all day long. That's a good stock to trade. That's a potential profit of $25 every five minutes throughout the entire day, when trading in 100-share blocks (see Figure 4.1).

At 9:45 the price was $58.75, and at 10:25 it retraces back to $58.75. On the surface it appears the stock is trading sideways, but take a closer look at the intraday swings. You can make 25¢ trading long or short. That's a stock you'll stay relatively patient with, and consistently profit from.

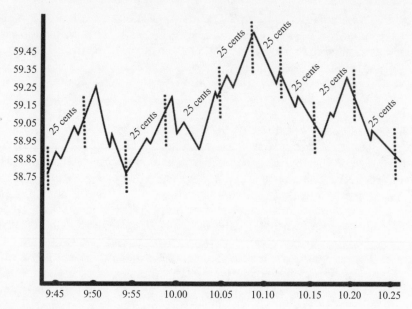

FIGURE 4.1 Intraday 5-Minute Chart

If the stock can fluctuate 25¢ within every five-minute rolling period, all throughout the day, then you can make a lot of trades. There are 78 five-minute periods in a trading day, excluding premarket and after-market trading. Therefore, you have a chance to make 78 trades, producing an average profit of $1,950 per day (78 × $25 profit per trade).

Not a bad take for the day!

(If you're trading with a pay-per-trade broker, as opposed to pay-per-share, then it's just as true that you should trade in 100-share blocks. The difference is you should *intraday* **hold** the stock for longer periods. That way you can afford the outrageous commissions you're made to pay on each trade. I know that sounds contradictory, because I usually say never **hold**. (Chapter 17, "Picking the Right Online Broker," explains that incongruity.)

Whenever you get tired of the fluctuations or waiting, think of the nerves of steel it takes to be a long-term investor. You're waiting for months, not minutes! The point is whichever you are—hedge fund manager or day trader—impatience is extremely detrimental, and must be controlled and outgrown.

Imagine yourself a college freshman, demanding a diploma in your very first semester. That's pretty much what you're doing if, as a beginner day trader, you're expecting to immediately make a huge profit.

Patience, patience, patience. That trading seminar or infomercial may have strongly implied that you can, but the truth is you're not going to consistently make $5,000 a week. What's closer to the truth is that things won't take off until you've lost so many times that you're humbled. At that point you'll learn to respect the market. You'll learn to understand every trade that's gone against you. You'll learn to take the time to understand exactly where you went wrong.

When I was a beginner, I had great difficulty. I had no consistency, no confidence in my schemes, and my emotions ran wild on each trade. I was constantly changing my stock-picking methods and trying new chart-reading strategies. I had no committed system. I was a mess.

I was wildly impatient and intolerant.

I began to search for penny stocks that were going to "pop" (yeah, right!) I also made some big trades, overexposing myself to more risk and uncertainty—the bigger the trade, the bigger the loss. What little staying power I had was running so thin that I felt I couldn't breathe. I felt suffocated by my wrought nerves and failures. I needed to slow down. I was completely desperate to know how to trade consistently and profitably, but far too impetuous to learn.

According to my talks with seasoned pros, it seems that many day traders go through that phase, at first. If you're losing on trades, losing confidence, and losing your keen interest in the market, then you're being controlled by impatience.

DECIDING TO LEARN MORE

One day I accepted that I was bad at day trading, but I also knew I wanted to learn more. This was the true beginning for me. Wall Street had beaten the tar out of me, but I got up and wiped off the dust and blood, and I realized I wasn't as good as I thought I was. I realized that all of my training and education had not been nearly enough. Something was missing, and I knew it was my fault.

As a beginner I began to understand that I had to learn to strategize against my flaw of impatience. For instance, I noticed that every time I placed a stop/loss, the darn price would go back up, after I was out. *Ouch!* That felt like a slap in the face. I thought that the market was stealing from me. I could swear there was a guy who was watching my trades, and then he would trade against me, just to tool with me. (Note: This can actually happen if you're trading certain stocks; refer to Chapter 14, "Stock Picking: Simplifying the Process.")

I eventually got over the conspiracy theories. Except for the situations parenthesized above, I stopped placing blame on others. I started to try out new things. Instead of attempting a whole new method of stock picking or chart reading, I tried an approach of risk management. I simply began purchasing smaller share blocks. Though I did make less on each trade, my newfound willingness to take baby steps was slowly but surely propelling me forward.

Most beginners who refuse to blame themselves certainly do blame the stock market. They grumble, "Its one big scam." Have they taken the time to study their bad habits, and to learn from their mistakes? I think not.

They probably just need to slow down, like I did, and stop being so impatient. The money will come: You have to earn it. The stock market isn't a slot machine. You can't just keep pulling the handle and hoping for the best.

After you've been day trading and profiting consistently for at least three months nonstop, you're past the amateur phase. If you're making at least 10 round-trip trades per day and never **holding** overnight, then you're approaching professional day trader status.

Professional patience evolves when you're so busy placing trades that you haven't any time to get annoyed. Indeed. I've found that the more trades I make, the less time I wait. This minimizes my risk of becoming impatient.

But when I was an amateur, I sometimes sat there all day, trying to purchase 5,000 shares of one particular stock. I had to make sure the entry price was right, and that was far too much pressure.

So why do most amateurs do that? Maybe because they're trading on emotion created by botched trades, and now they're desperately trying to get back what they've lost. The point is, they're no longer trading. Now they're just gambling.

If you're trading that way, take a time-out.

Try to find the patience to read this book.

Learn from my mistakes.

The execution of a 100-plus trades per day requires professional patience. To sit with back aching and shoulders tensed, pumping out multiple trades while making multiple decisions, requires the precision and focus of a dedicated, competitive skeet shooter. The shooter makes split-second decisions on which flying clay target to hit, and he does this over and over, sometimes for hours at a time.

If he misses a few, he doesn't get riled. He keeps himself focused and confident. He takes aim and almost always fires with accuracy, with less than a moment to think, and he ends the day with a respectably high percentage of hits, even if he started off lagging.

Such skill isn't learned overnight, by either skeet shooters or day traders.

Most of the trades we place don't exceed 100 shares at a time. So we tend to place many trades all day long, usually exceeding 100.

To monitor such small profits, incrementing all day, requires tremendous self-discipline. The average professional day trader makes only about $15 to $25 on a trade. But here's the thing to consider: $15 to $25 multiplied by a 100. That's totally worth the tedium.

When do you know that you're trading with a professional level of patience? The virtue is admirably evident when you're completely in rhythm with your stock. You're like the skeet shooter smashing flying clay targets with barely a second to aim. Stocks prices, like the movements of rapidly flung discs, move up and down all day. Your charts indicate when to enter and exit. Your patience is the intangible tool that enables you to wait for the perfect moment to execute an order. You're almost preternaturally focused.

In the amateur day trader, patience is all about never giving up. It's the process of changing bad habits into productive habits, and finally earning consistently, as surely as true dieters finally begin to slim down.

In the professional day trader, patience has become a deep skill. It's been growing right along with trust in his system. As with the habitual skeet shooter, his aim has been perfected with practice.

 RULES TO REMEMBER

- Never pick entry or exits point when feeling out of control and impatient.
- Find stocks that move at least 25¢ every five-minute period.
- Do not trade more than 100-share blocks per trade until you become more advanced.
- Don't expect to make a lot of money in the beginning.
- Finish reading this book before you begin or go back to day trading.

CHAPTER 5

Taking Breaks

I f I had a dollar for every time I've taken a break from day trading, I could buy you and me a lot of drinks. In my early days in the profession, I timed-out when I ran out of money. I needed time off to save up more money for starting all over, reinvesting.

That pattern is typical.

That pattern is pathetic.

Depending on the state of my finances, my breaks were for differing segments of time. The result of those time-outs, however, was always exactly the same: I kept going back into the arena and getting beaten up again.

I wasn't yet aware that taking a break is supposed to be for attitude adjustment. It's also for improvement of strategies. It's *not* supposed to be about sadly attempting to find more funds to throw in.

I felt like a compulsive gambler, and in many ways, I was. But gradually, during the course of each time-out, I learned something new. Those downtimes were causing some soul searching. I was slowly recognizing my shortcomings.

That was when I actually wrote my first book. It was one year after my first day of trading. It was after I sold my first house. Some major losses I'd suffered, which occurred in the 2000 recession, had forced me to relinquish my beautiful California home. That house, you'll recall, was the property my fiancée and I purchased just prior to my first day trading seminar in Irvine.

That sacrifice, as you can imagine, was one of the roughest points in the saga of my day trading journey.

That first writing project was self-therapy, a way to reaffirm some good strategies. In the end, however, I could see that it was basic to a fault. It was typical, just a step-by-step manual of all the essential rudiments: how to set up accounts with online brokers, how to read basic chart patterns, and how to scrutinize fundamentals. It was nothing I wanted to publish.

What I left out was the hard truth. At the time I hadn't yet faced it. I only knew how to buy and sell stocks. I wasn't yet aware that buying and selling is only 1 percent of day trading.

Eventually I came to see that almost anyone can go online and learn how to buy and sell, within a few measly hours. And that making *consistent* profits is something else entirely.

I was zealous to learn to successfully day trade, and as I've described before, I saw that my zeal was my problem. My eagerness and overexuberance were blinding me from the truth. The truth is that the stock market is like a merciless shark, digesting its dinner and not caring about *me*.

Day trading is a little like car racing. Both are intense and hair-raising, and both require much rest. You the day trader are like the NASCAR driver who learns how to speed to a 500-victory and not wreck his car or himself. Both of you must be deeply prepared, before every race or each trade, because what you've done during your downtime will directly impact your performance, whenever you dare to return.

After my first time off, which followed the loss of my first house, I began to understand that day trading is more than watching chart patterns and forecasting fundamentals. After all, if it were that easy, college campuses around the world would have day-trading courses and majors.

Please don't get me wrong about this: By taking a break I never mean that you're moving in the direction of quitting. I'm actually suggesting the opposite: During your time-outs, you should remain very acutely involved.

I didn't trade during my downtimes, but I continued to monitor the market. I studied the stocks' movement in conjunction with news and economic announcements. I got even more involved than before, in spite of my backseat position.

My time-outs grew into sabbaticals. My breaks became my chance for regrouping. They were also my times to heal. They were sojourns when I went deeply inward, to examine my day-trading faults, and to discover the ways I could strengthen my skills.

So many times in the past, I'd blamed the market for my misjudgments. Take, for example, the Enron debacle, my largest loss to date. Back in early 2001 I purchased 80,000 shares of Enron. I remember buying when it hit low at $1.00; a lot of Wall Street brokers did the same. The big bad news (you remember that nightmare!) came out the very next day. The stock eventually crashed down to less then 30¢ per share.

So I lost over $55,000 in no time, because I was an amateur.

In that case, that landmark, infamous case, it was easy to fault the market. But in truth, it was I who had screwed up. Here's why.

During my time off I did a little research. I found out that most of the people who lost on Enron were independent investors, along with the unfortunate Enron employees who had company stock in their 401(k) retirement packages.

The reason that the stock dove so sharply is that the Wall Street day traders, who purchased the stock at $1.00 when I did, knew enough to sell it when it dropped to 90¢ with incredible volume to the downside.

What happened over the next few days was disastrous for me, of course. But for the savvy Wall Street day traders, it was business as usual. I had thought I was smarter than Wall Street. When Wall Street began selling, I **held** my shares, overconfident. I believed that the price would go back up.

Well, I know better now. Basically, there is no conspiracy. If you lose on a trade it's simply because you didn't see the signs.

Those Wall Street day traders saw the signs. They bought Enron at $1.00, sold at 90¢ cents, and only lost 10 percent. I, on the other hand, **held**, all the way down to almost nothing.

My fault, my fault.

During the break I took afterward, I agonized over how Wall Street knew to sell at 90¢, at a loss. I discovered the basic strategies that Wall Street day traders live by. I'll state it here very simply: they're masters of risk management. I elaborate on that mastery in Chapter 6, "The Importance of Risk Management." Also, they have billions of dollars to invest, intraday. This is why you see huge swings on an intraday chart.

The challenge for the independent day trader is to learn how to ride on Wall Street's coattails. I can't stress that point enough. Whenever you take time off from day trading, you must stay in touch with your stocks. You can learn so much from simply watching how the stock prices fluctuate, intraday.

This doesn't mean that when you return to active trading, you'll be ready to roll with the big boys; but staying involved is a start.

If you think you can totally disconnect, totally ignore the market, and return when your pain of losing has passed, and if you haven't learned a thing while you've been gone, then you're setting yourself up for another big fall, caused by repetition of mistakes.

Let's get some basics together with regard to this "taking a break" thing. Like, just *when* and *why* should you walk? And most importantly, *what*, exactly, should you do on that time off?

I'll begin with the *when*.

BREAK WHEN YOUR CONFIDENCE IS LOW

The time to take a break is when you've lost all your confidence. Because of your sagging self-assurance, your system of trading has been demolished, and you find yourself way too emotional.

If you're slapping the side of your computer monitor, then by all means get out of there. If you're so stressed out that you're taking it out on people, even the people you love, then you obviously need some downtime.

But even if you're a whole lot calmer than that, there may be other indicators of how badly you need to walk. If you find yourself constantly changing your strategies, especially intraday, then you need to immediately recognize that you're getting confused and scared, and it's time to cease and desist.

Accordingly, if you're only trading in order to regain yesterday's losses, then you're fueled by sheer desperation, and again, you should get away.

Here's some good news, however: Most of the problems you're having are psychological, and they can be repaired.

Now I'll go into *why* you should walk.

BREAK BECAUSE IT'S JUST NOT WORKING

The main reason to take a break is that your current system's not working. You need to back off, and regroup. In day trading, taking a break is never the act of a loser or a slouch. It's not any sign of incompetence. On the contrary, it's part of the day-trading process. Everyone takes a time-out at least once—it's absolutely crucial to do so. How can you handle the pressures and pitfalls of learning to day trade consistently, without taking breaks to gauge your performance?

Everyone makes mistakes day trading, even the Wall Street experts. Their errors can cost millions, and so, just like the amateurs, they walk sometimes, too.

Time-outs are much like when you were a kid, and your parents told you not to hit. "You should walk away and calm down," they wisely admonished.

Taking a break takes off pressure. Your emotions begin to subside. You can bask, for a while, in a sense of relief. Once all those panicky emotions are no longer controlling your thoughts, only then can you recuperate, and intelligently work out your kinks.

Okay, so let's move on to the *what*.

BREAK AND THEN WHAT?

What do you do on your time off? For one thing, you rebuild your self-confidence. *Overconfidence* most likely got you into this trouble, and now you've completely one-eightied: Now you've lost so much money that you're shut down and afraid.

What you need to do, first, is brush off your mistakes. View them as surmountable obstacles, and never as signs to quit.

But wait a minute, you might want to say to me. While reading this chapter on taking a break—on stopping, desisting, and resting—maybe you're thinking: *This is crazy. I can't just seize up, fall down all defunct, and shuffle off to some mental rehab.*

Who does this guy think I am, you want to know. *One of those trust fund babies? I've got bills to pay!*

Believe me, I understand. I would be blowing steam in your face if I didn't consider the need to pay bills, not to mention eat. We day trade with money in order to make more money, because we really need more money! So I know how tough a decision it can be to just *stop* trying to earn.

But here's the thing. After each episode of taking a break (usually a week or two), I returned with a much better mindset, and my trading performance improved. That's when I realized that having no income, for just a short, purposeful time, is better than continuing to trade at a loss. I realized that I should internalize time-outs as part of the process of becoming successful.

Here's what to do to get through it:

First you should remind yourself that you're a beginner, and admit that you have much to learn. How fast you progress past amateur status depends on your trading frequency. If you're only executing one trade per day, then you're not day trading like pros. You should execute at least ten round-trip trades per day. Then you'll have enough samples for statistical significance when you gauge your performance, during breaks.

Frequency of trading is the key to success. If you've been making just one trade per day and winning every trade, that's great, but how much are you making long-term? That you made a lot on that one trade means either of two things: you purchased a lot of shares in one trade, or you got extremely lucky because the stock shot up in one day, and you **held** all day, then sold before the close.

Good luck keeping that up.

Another risky system is habitual overexposure. That, as addressed in Chapter 7, "How Overexposure to the Market Can Hurt," is day trading stocks with huge share blocks of 1,000 or more at a time. A word to the wise: Most day traders on Wall Street usually purchase only 100-share blocks at a time. Just watch any Level 2 table and you'll witness the actual trades in real time. In case you were not sure, a Level-2 table displays streaming and real-time bid and ask quotations on any given stock. This allows for transparency in market prices: You can watch the trades being executed right in front of you.

In Figure 5.1 I show an actual Level 2 quote chart.

The quantity column in Figure 5.1 shows real-time orders. Most of them are in 100-share blocks (as indicated by the arrow). You don't usually see any orders over 500 shares. Most execution orders are based on the most current bid and ask price.

When you're trading consistently and frequently, you're likely to do very well. But once you become routinely inconsistent, that's when it's time for a break. Take that break, and tell yourself it's normal. Don't allow your ego to dictate that it's not. Nobody gets rich overnight in this career that requires so much skill.

Second, have a good budget or even another job. The advice offered in Chapter 8, "Budgeting: Knowing Your Financial Limitations," will get you through the time-offs.

Bank of America CP					
Enter Symbol **BAC**					
HI	**32.80**	CHG			−2,28
LOW	**30.50**	CHG%			**6.91%**
LAST	**30.68**	VOL	**69,911,280**		

Qty	MM	Price	Qty	MM	Price
100	ISLD	30.67	100	ISLD	30.68
200	ISLD	30.66	100	ISLD	30.69
100	ARCA	30.65	100	ARCA	30.70
100	ARCA	30.64	200	ARCA	30.71
400	ISLD	30.63	400	ISLD	30.72
100	EDGX	30.62	100	EDGX	30.73
200	BATS	30.61	300	BATS	30.74
100	ISLD	30.60	200	ISLD	30.75
100	BTRD	30.59	400	BTRD	30.76
200	ARCA	30.58	100	ARCA	30.77

FIGURE 5.1   Level 2 Quote Chart

Such planning and budgeting require the trait that encapsulates this book's major theme, that personal tool called self-discipline. Build it, own it, and use it. It's you making yourself work. It's you getting the most of your on-the-job training, and also your time-outs. It's you holding down that day or night job if you have to, while you learn and grow as a day trader, taking the necessary breaks.

Even if you're wealthy, and you don't have to work, and you simply add cash to your trading account whenever you lose big, you need to take a break when your gains go south. Affluent friends of mine have lost insane amounts of money simply because they let their egos get the best of them, and they never took off to seriously ponder where they went wrong and how they could improve.

Rich or poor, seasoned or amateur, make sure that you take those breaks!

Use them for stock research. Go back to every trade you've done and scrutinize each one. Find your strength and weakness points. Ascertain your primary issues.

For instance, are you only losing on trades that you average down on? Or are your biggest losses the ones that you **held** overnight? Whatever you discover, focus on it. Then you'll see, as clear as the daylight, that you should *just stop doing it.*

Yeah, right.

I'm chuckling right now. I know it's not quite that simple. In my early trading years, I knew that I had to stop **holding** overnight, but I kept on doing it anyway. I did it because the stock price had not gone up by the end of the day, so I figured I had another day—another chance—if I just **held** that long.

That's a very common amateur blunder, not to mention poor strategy. At one time or another, most of us have been guilty of it. And if you, the reader, are a very new trader, then I suspect that no matter how much I warn you not to do certain things, sometimes you just might anyway, and learn the hard way like us all.

And that's why we all must withdraw, and reflect. Any time we recognize a pattern of trading mistakes, that's when we should take off.

I define the time frame for "pattern of mistakes" as one full trading week. If you're trading all day long for five days straight and you're in the red every day, then you definitely need to regroup. Don't go thinking your luck will simply turn around next week. That kind of mindset might influence you to start gauging your performance on only a monthly basis, and that's not often enough.

Technically, your "break time" is every single evening, after the market closes. That's your time to recap your daily trades, and plan for the next day. Accordingly, you should determine your performance levels *daily.*

Yes! We do need to do homework.

I'm not suggesting, however, that you should take a time-out after just one bad day. But if by the end of the week you're persistently unsuccessful, then you should take the *whole* next week off. Sit on the sidelines, think it all over, and transform your trading style and behavior.

Day trading is a never-ending learning process. Don't be discouraged when, after you return to your trading, something *else* stops you from profiting!

Not everyone is cut out for this high-stress profession. You may like the stock market and enjoy buying and selling equities, but that doesn't make you a day trader. You'll know that you're a true day trader if you keep coming back and keep on improving because day trading is a process, and that process requires you to continually evolve.

 RULES TO REMEMBER

- Don't take time off just to get more cash.
- Gauge your performance at the end of each trading day.
- Log in the reasons why a trade went wrong.
- When things get consistently inconsistent, stop and take time off.
- During your time off, actively research your mistakes. Mentally prepare yourself for the return.
- Plan a budget for the inevitable—the time offs.

PART II

The Truth about Your Risk

I n terms of the potential for heavy financial losses, day trading is a high-
risk profession. No one should contemplate day trading without giving
thought to the ways he can lose, and all the ways to lessen or avoid
them.

I've elaborated on the primary areas of risk. This part offers some vital
techniques that can greatly minimize losses. Risk management and budgeting are deterrents to gambling, which day trading must never become. My
goal in this part is to have you come away understanding how to budget for
training, and also how to decrease your risk.

CHAPTER 6

The Importance of Risk Management

T he higher your skill level, the better you are at protecting your capital from taking huge hits. Along with that key capability, you typically trade in the green. So the big question is, the only question is, how in the world do you get there?

In day trading, it usually boils down to how well you manage your risk. This amounts to some educated guesswork. You figure—you try to very nimbly figure—just exactly when you should use your funds, and how much to risk at a time.

The subject of minimizing risk is so hot that it could fill several books on its own. It could dominate the five-day live training programs—and I've been shocked to find out that it doesn't. Though all of the programs and seminars I've attended have somewhat conveyed the hazards, I feel that they've failed to teach amateurs precisely how to avoid them.

To be frank, I'm disgusted by the inadequacies I've witnessed. At those vital hubs of instruction, risk often isn't even mentioned until the very last hour of the very last day.

I've been bored by advisements on the obvious, like: "You should never trade money you need."

Duh!

Here's one so brief and deficient that it really gets under my skin: "Know your limitations and stick to them."

That's like telling a toddler to stay in, and not bothering to explain to him why, and then leaving the front door wide open while you nap and he's wide awake.

Likewise, instructors warn of day-trading dangers, but they neglect to present any practical guidelines for building trainees' skill in risk reduction. They toss their enrollees some vague platitudes, and then they send them into the real trading world sorely lacking in any real knowledge of how to use vital precautions.

I actually think that's criminal. I intend to right that wrong. For starters, this is the main point, and I urge you to keep it in mind: the potential to lose big in day trading is an ever-present threat, and strategies for decreasing that potential must be part of your trading style. They must bolster your trading psychology.

The following are predominant factors of risk:

- The amount of trading capital allocated to each trade
- The timing for allocating capital to trade
- Overexposure to risk
- The stock or company you're trading
- The time of day you're trading
- Gambling

Now I'll elaborate on each factor and on ways to reduce or totally avoid the losses that can result.

THE AMOUNT OF TRADING CAPITAL ALLOCATED TO EACH TRADE

The question of just how much money to use, combined with the myriad options regarding just why and when, is the core of all investment strategizing. We're expected to have this stuff down like the pros.

Well, do we? *Can* we? Let's address those qualms first.

When it comes to stock market professionals, you have investment managers with doctorates in finance, and hedge fund managers who handle multibillion-dollar portfolios. All of them struggle with the perils of risk, and all of them astutely maneuver.

How can we, the independent traders, possibly know what they know?

Good news! Our challenge isn't nearly as formidable as the one that the Ph.D.s face. We have a few major advantages.

We only have to focus on money that's *our own*, and we can choose to deal with only one, diminutive trade at a time. Our money is usually in just one account, and it's comparatively easy to calculate the balance on an intraday (not long-term) basis. We almost never **hold** a position overnight, and we usually trade small positions (under 1,000 shares).

Those conditions, which amount to only having to watch out for ourselves, mercifully set us apart from pro investors.

So now you might ask, how much of my trading capital should I allocate to a trade?

It depends. In response, I'd ask you this: *What's your skill level? How long have you been trading that particular stock? What's your threshold for stop/loss amount, per trade?*

If your answer indicated to me that you're a beginner at day trading, I'd dictate a rule of thumb I've enshrined, torn straight from my tale of hard knocks:

The amount of shares you trade in one particular stock should equal your sustainable risk.

Your reaction to that rule might go something like this:

If my stock price fluctuates 50¢ every five minutes or so, and I can afford to take a $500 loss on each trade, then it's okay to trade in 1,000-share blocks, right?

My reply to that would be instantaneous! The volume of my voice would get louder! I'd tell you *that may be true in theory, but don't put it into practice!!* I'd say that you, as an amateur, do *not* possess the skill level needed to deftly handle such losses, especially when they can happen every five minutes, all day!!

I would urge you to take this advice: *only trade in 100-share blocks.*

I've stated that before, in the previous chapters, and I feel I can't stress it enough. Once you establish that maxim, your risk will be minimized, and besides that you'll find that it's always a breeze to come up with a capital value. For instance: if your stock is priced at $50 per share, then in order to invest in the trade, you'll only need $5,000. You won't have to worry about ratios and percentages, as in what amount of your investment money to allocate to which stock, because lowering your exposure to the risk by trading in 100-share blocks has made such calculations unnecessary. If you don't have $5,000, all you have to do is find a lower-priced stock.

Your next question might be: *When* do I allocate capital to a trade?

THE TIMING FOR ALLOCATING CAPITAL TO A TRADE

The issue of when is a bit more complex. Suppose you have enough capital to purchase 20 trades at a time, when trading in 100-share blocks. With $100,000 in buying power (trading capital), this would be easy to do. But what does that mean? Should you purchase 20 stocks all the time? Certainly not! You need to know your personal limitations. Every trader has different thresholds and tolerances to risk. For instance, some traders only trade one stock all day, placing over a 100 trades. Other traders like to deal with several stocks all day, and place only a handful of trades on each one. It's all about what you feel comfortable doing.

Once you get a feel for the stock you've been trading—a real sense of knowing how it moves—you can eventually start trading it in 200-share blocks, and gradually increase to 500. Everything depends on your skill level, and how quickly or slowly you grow there—and that's where I urge cautious treading. Chapter 1, "Truths About Yourself to Know First," is placed at the beginning for that very reason. Knowing your skill level *before* you increase your risk is the biggest point I'll ever make; I make it emphatically there, and I don't mind repeating it here.

The average independent day trader, trading for primary income, is aware of the amount he needs to make daily, and of what he can afford to lose. Though no exact science exists out there for negotiating the hazards, especially for independents, I'd bet that limiting exposure to each and every trade eliminates nine-tenths of risk.

Hence my clear directive to trade in 100-share blocks: When you doggedly (if with boredom) stick to that rule, you may not make as much as you want to in a day, but you certainly won't lose a lot, either. As an amateur, that's all you should venture. You're also not likely to lose very much if the amount of your risk taking parallels the rate of your gradual skill.

OVEREXPOSURE TO RISK

For *all* the lowdown on disasters that can happen when you're overexposed, make sure you tune in to Chapter 7, "How Overexposure to the Market Can Hurt." For now I'll just offer a word or two about it—but notice my urgent tone!

As I've shown in the section on emotion, it's easy to know when you're overexposed because you become stressed. Maybe you're safely trading in prudent 100-share blocks, but just the same, your nerves feel shot.

Well, I'd bet the farm that the reason for your angst is that you've let the price drop past your exit point (stop/loss), and now you're sitting there **holding**. You're sitting there praying it will go back up. That's a typical beginners' fiasco.

My advice here is simple: don't do it again! Whenever your stop/loss price hits, you should exit. Just take the loss and move on. It should only be a small loss of $25 to $50, and you can get that right back. Remember, you have all day.

That's only one cause of overexposure. The other causes are: choosing to trade in more than 100-share blocks without first trading in 100-share blocks; trading several new stocks at once (and by "new" I mean unfamiliar); and attempting to trade in premarket and after-market hours.

Anytime you feel as though you're losing control, most likely you're overexposed. To minimize your risk, you should minimize your exposure, always, in every trade.

THE STOCK OR COMPANY YOU'RE TRADING

Most would assume that the greatest risk of all is the chosen company itself. Well, we day traders don't have to go there. We don't have to get ourselves bogged down in company analysis and earnings forecasts. We only need to know what's transpiring on *that* day.

With that said, however, there's another point to make, and this is essential in day trading. Each stock *does* come with different risk levels, depending on the company you're trading intraday. For instance, if a stock is affected by government regulations, then it might just drastically drop in price, right when you're sitting there trading it. For example, an announcement might go out, right then, intraday, that Congress has just passed a strict new law that devalues the company's product.

So when you consider that kind of risk, it becomes obvious that your chosen companies should be able to boast the following:

- Little chance of regulatory processes that might affect the product, as in antitrust laws (for example, Microsoft), and FDA rulings on biotech products.
- No chance of filing bankruptcy soon (as with Enron and WorldCom).
- No chance of an employee strike taking place, as in the airline industry.

See Chapter 14, "Stock Picking: Simplifying the Process," for details on the process of choosing the stocks best tailored for intraday trading.

THE TIME OF DAY YOU'RE TRADING

This risk factor is pretty straightforward, and so is its management.

Premarket and after-market trading are too chancy. A lot of volatility occurs at those times, and besides, when it's too early, you haven't yet viewed the development of the current intraday trend.

Have you noticed how, in the first 15 minutes, from 9:30 to 9:45 A.M., the market trades fast and crazy? The rule here is *don't trade until after 9:45*. Not until you're very highly skilled.

Also, right around 3:00 P.M., when the Futures and Treasury markets stop trading in Chicago, the stock/equities market picks up volume. This part of the day can be very unpredictable. You may have been in rhythm with your stock all day, and then, at the hour of 3:00—, whoa! Suddenly your stock movements become completely erratic!

This is a great time to simply stop trading, or at the very least, to limit your exposure.

During certain times of the day, most stocks react the same way, especially the frequently traded. The key to decreasing the time-of-day risk is to know your stock very well, particularly how it trades daily. The longer you trade your stock, the more you will know its price movements and rhythm, and the better you will be at perceiving exactly when to bail.

GAMBLING

In Chapter 11, "Gambling versus Day Trading," I elaborate on the big differences between casino-hopping and day trading. Here, I'll be brief but emphatic.

If you have a strict risk management system and then you abandon it, I can assume that essentially, you're gambling. When you go that route you're *failing to use* some vital strategic options. They are:

- Subtracting money (lowering your exposure) if the price goes against you
- Predetermining your stop/loss and limit prices
- Adding more money as the stock price goes up
- Changing stocks
- Intraday **holding** until it retraces (note: this is only for experts)
- Averaging-down your position (also only for experts)

Whenever you gamble as a day trader, you've put yourself at the mercy of the market. You're praying that the price action will favor what amounts to your roll of the dice. Your plan, if you can call it that, is to **hold** until the price retraces, and if it doesn't, you're in trouble.

If you're willing to take that kind of risk, then you're not *managing* risk. You're trading like a crazy person! You're trading just like a degenerate gambler who's placing wild bets at casinos.

In a nutshell, risk management boils down to your skill level. The more you experience risk, the more you master your tolerance for it. This is why the low-risk (low exposure) trades are crucial: you learn without getting killed.

It takes time and patience to acquire expertise. As an amateur, the key to minimizing risk is to think small and trade small at first. Eventually you'll understand the nature of your risk, and you'll deal with it expediently.

The ultimate goal of a professional day trader is to wheel and deal in a high-risk environment without *ever* losing his shirt. This is when the real money flows to you. But for now . . . patience! Take tentative baby steps. . . .

 RULES TO REMEMBER

- Trade only the amount of shares, in one particular stock, that won't exceed the risk you can handle.
- If you're an amateur, always trade in 100-share blocks.
- If you're feeling stressed, get out of the trade.
- Until you're highly skilled, don't trade until after 9:45 A.M.
- Practice learning your tolerance levels in low-risk (low-exposure) trades.
- Never overexpose yourself in any of the ways we've discussed.

CHAPTER 7

Why Overexposure to the Market Can Hurt

E xposure to the market usually refers to how much you can afford to lose. Overexposure occurs when you're not prepared for the losses, and in some cases, even the gains. Overexposure can indicate that you've purchased too many shares at one time, and you're not yet used to the swings and the rhythm of the stock. Overexposure can also mean that you've purchased a stock at the wrong time, as in premarket or after-market, and uncertainty is dangerously high.

In the rare circumstance of the trader who enjoys unlimited wealth, it doesn't matter much to him if his stock price plummets. Because he has no pressing financial concerns, he's never overexposed.

If you're reading this, however, I can bet my life you're not him; neither you nor I will ever indulge in his carefree, cash-burning capers. We and the other struggling hopefuls on this planet are consumed by the quest for more money, and the fostering of a personal tolerance level to the losses that hit us like bricks. Some of us would rather deal with our losses at the end of the trading day, and some of us prefer to recognize them after every trade. Either way, overexposure is an intraday threat that we have to learn to manage.

Suppose you've been trading a particular stock all day, and you've gotten into its rhythm. You've been trading 100-share blocks the whole time, in and out. Overexposure happens as soon as you choose to purchase more than 100 shares at a time, or if you begin averaging down.

There may be something more than simple financial exposure going on. You may be creating a sort of mental overexposure when you give in to your temptation to hazardously stray from a tried-and-true, "bulletproof" strategy. To swerve like that from your system, especially mid-day, is a risk you shouldn't be taking. Your system is based on the exposure you're used to, and that's where you should stay.

If you've been trading 100-share blocks all day, then you're comfortable with the price swings, and how those swings affect the margins for profit and loss. As soon as you add exposure, however—by way of more shares or more highly priced stock—then you've just become overexposed.

I mentioned in the first paragraph of this chapter that overexposure can happen when you buy stock at the wrong time. I believe that bad timing is the worst of the pitfalls that torture amateur day traders. Eventually, however, time teaches.

TIME VERSUS TIMING

Time is a term with several different applications.

Time, when understood as amount of experience, can conquer overexposure, because after you've gained familiarity with the share blocks you're trying to handle, what was once a scary minefield is now your norm, your safe haven.

But in the market there's another meaning of time. It's simply the time of day. During different points in the day, you can expose yourself to more risk.

I'll never forget the times I lost big while trading in premarket and after-market. And also when big news was developing, and I was in a trade just before. Trading premarket and after-market has benefits, of course; like when you get in before the big move. That's a very tempting situation, and hence, very hard to resist. But that's also when you can lose so much that you still cringe from the memory, years and years down the road.

I'm not necessarily saying that you should *never* trade premarket or after-market, or that you should *never* trade in tandem with relevant news and announcements. Right then you can trawl for a lot of easy money. But watch out: You're overexposed. You're diving into treacherous seas. You might as well be gambling.

If you're going to jump in over your head, then at the very least you should lessen the danger by limiting how many shares you buy, as in 100-share, not 1,000-share, blocks. That avoids overexposure, because when you trade prudently, then you're only exposed to the market risk that you've proved is tolerable for you.

For instance, if you know that you're going to sell at a loss when the price hits a certain level, then all the risk you're exposed to is an amount that you've prepared yourself for, in the event that the price goes against you.

You should *always* have a plan of exit in place, *before* you enter any trade. This point is obvious yet hard to apply, and so I've thought up a rule. Commit this rule to your memory. But no, do better than that. Write it in rainbow magic-marker colors on a big chunk of white posterboard, and tack it right over your desk.

Yeah, write it up just like that. Then patent it and sell it, because every trader needs it, and you could get rich just selling that proverb.

It doesn't matter whether the price spirals up or down: You should always know when to sell. All you need to know are two specific price points: the one to sell at a profit and the one to sell at a loss (see Figure 7.1).

The price levels of $49.50 and $50 are example levels that you should buy or sell when the price reaches that level (it varies depending on if your position is short or long). The gray areas of Figure 7.1 represent the overexposure zones. If you **hold** past your predetermined exit price, then you're trading without a plan of exit. This exercise separates gamblers from day traders.

Never forget that those price points *are* your exposure levels. As soon as you slide past them, you're overexposed and gambling with your money.

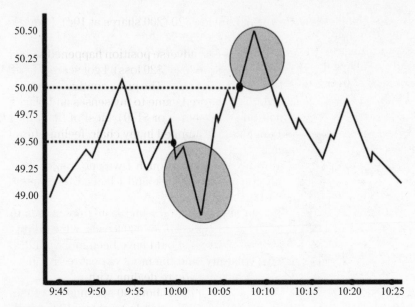

FIGURE 7.1 Intraday 5-Minute Chart

Even when you **hold** past your exit price for profit, you're overexposing yourself. This means that if you become used to **holding** past your price point when it goes into the green, you're slathering yourself in that deep mental quagmire we've identified as the greed factor.

As soon as greed loosens your exit points, you're no longer trading with a plan.

You need to get accustomed to making or losing a certain amount of money on each trade. I can't stress that point enough. I know that selling your profits short sounds rather counterproductive, but all it takes is a few episodes of breaking your protocol and losing, and then you'll understand what I'm saying.

Self-discipline means avoiding the consequence of overexposure to market uncertainty. Here's an example of the need for that avoidance from my own regretful experience:

I was successfully trading all day with Pepsi Inc. (PEP). I'd been trading 100-share blocks (with a pay-per-share firm) and making an average of $12 per trade (loss and profit). I had about 30 trades so far; 25 were in the green and 5 were in the red. I was up about $240 for the day ($25 \times 12 =$ $300 and 5 \times 12 = 60).

It was around 1:30 P.M., just after lunch, when I decided to change my system. I began to purchase 200-share blocks. My first trade went smoothly.

The price quickly went up 10¢, so I made $20 (200 shares at 10¢). I continued trading with 200-share blocks.

Then everything went south. My first adverse position happened so fast that I didn't have time to sell at a 10¢ stop/loss ($20 loss). I got scared, froze up, and waited for it to retrace, but it never did. The price continued against me. The price dropped another 50¢ before I came to my senses and placed a stop/loss. I lost 70¢ on the trade (200 shares or $140). Most of my profits for the day were gone, and I dejectedly slumped in my chair, feeling stupid for switching up after lunch.

I had much to learn from my mistake. Though I was no longer a beginner, I still struggled with consistency issues, and I lacked a complete understanding of the effect of overexposure.

With chagrin I recall my dumb rationale for increasing my shares to 200. I figured I was up over $200 and I could afford $20 losses. What I didn't anticipate was the increase in *volatility*. I should have been more mindful of the fact that there's always volatility, and the more exposure and more shares you have, then the more volatility you're dealing with.

Earlier that day I had been in a trade for about 30 seconds at a time. That particular stock, PEP, took about 30 seconds to move 10¢, which meant that my 100 shares would become a $10 loss or profit in about 30 seconds. I was accustomed to that intraday timing, I was comfortable with its price swings and rhythm, and I didn't think that doubling the shares would make much difference at all.

But two things went terribly wrong. First, I was unprepared for the volatility boost when changing from 100- to 200-share blocks. Second, I was still at a point in my know-how where I allowed my emotions to control me. I **held** the fallen stock, which was falling with twice the impact I was used to all day long. I broke down completely, and was totally at the mercy of the market.

Please understand that I'm *not* advising you to *never* go ahead and buy 200-share blocks; not at all. I'm establishing the importance of being consistent when dealing with the issue of exposure. I'm showing how consistency, or the lack of it, directly affects your ability to master your performance, when exposed to market uncertainty. As soon as you change your familiar routine, if you don't give yourself time to adjust, you're overexposing yourself.

Whether you choose to trade in 100- or 200-share blocks, it only makes a difference when you *increase* the share volume, or trade a more expensive stock. This means that you can choose to start off trading 200-share blocks, and you'll get used to trading in that volume. But when you decide to increase the share size to 300 or more, you should start it fresh in the morning, and you should have paper-traded it for at least a few trades to get a feel for the swings and the rhythm.

If you want to trade larger share blocks, then I suggest that you begin with stocks of half the value. For instance, if your goal is to trade a $50 stock in 100-share blocks, then first trade a $25 stock in 200-share blocks.

The point is that the day trader should never try anything new—not share sizes, stock prices, or a different time of day—until he has practiced his strategy in low-exposure trades first.

In conclusion, the key to avoiding overexposure is to first take the *time* to create consistency in low-exposure environments, and then gradually work your way up. For more on this strategy, see Chapter 19, "Trading for Skill versus Trading for Income."

 RULES TO REMEMBER

- Always trade stocks that are new to you in amounts no larger than 100-share blocks.
- Until you're consistently profiting during regular hours, avoid premarket and after-market hours.
- When you're feeling completely lost and are most likely overexposed, apply stop/loss immediately.

CHAPTER 8

Budgeting: Knowing Your Financial Limitations

In day trading, there's the ever-present potential to make a fantastic income. But you could also lose everything, fast. Avoiding big losses takes frugality and patience. I know my tone might crash and burn your dreams of professional grandeur, but there's really no way around it. I feel that my job is to tactically slow you, to help you stay financially safe.

For the beginner in day trading, the management of finances is two-phased. The first phase is all about floating your boat during your full-time training. The second is all about later on, when you're actively trading for income and you need a reliable cash flow.

I'll assume that before you started reading this book, you already had some knowledge of day trading. Most likely you looked at the subject online, and you purchased several good reads. So far, maybe that's all you've spent on it. Most likely you've still got your day job. You haven't yet taken the plunge.

I'll also assume that at this point, you're ready for some serious training. Well, before you do that, you need a budget. I'm talking about a budget that keeps you afloat during *live* trading, while training. Because even when you get to where you can safely trade with real money, you're basically still a cadet. Even if you've done more than buy a few books—even if you've dished out thousands of bucks for a week-long day trading program—you're still a rookie, deep in training, and you need a trainee's budget. (Refer to Chapter 16, "About Training Programs," for more thorough revelations about that.)

Remember this distinction about training: when you go live for the first time, you should view yourself as someone who's still a trainee, *not yet* an amateur day trader. Because if you think you're going to earn much during your first few months, you're in for a rude awakening.

And now make another distinction. Ask yourself this question: which kind of trainee am I? A rich one or a poor one? If you're not in the wealthy category, then you're definitely feeling the crunch. Accounts with traditional online brokers require at least $1,000 dollars to start. And later, it will get a lot worse. When you're ready to bravely go to bat with any of the pay-per-share firms, these days they usually require a minimum of $25,000.

Maybe you're feeling the bite even more, because you've paid for a training program. Did that endeavor clean you out? Did it gouge away your life savings? If so, then you've got to prepare yourself for all the new hurdles to come. You need a carefully tailored budget.

To the well-off guy or lady with a huge hefty cushion who doesn't have to be a wage slave or a tip-chaser and can easily shrug off a job, I'd still offer frugal advice. I'd say try not to lose gory chunks of your wealth. I'd advise you to train in small share blocks. You might scoff at that; devastating losses don't scare you. But can you afford the mental anguish and embarrassment when you're trading too often in the red? Your main source of pain is your ego. To offset that pain you should train just as if you're on a very tight budget, like the rest of us.

To the rookie, rich or poor, my advice is the usual: Don't trade in more than 100-share blocks.

DON'T QUIT YOUR DAY JOB: CATCH-22

Now I'll get back to the financially deficient, a category that includes many more people than the other categories. I'll begin with the obvious. Make sure you don't quit your day job!

I know I sound just like your skeptical friends, or else your nagging mother. Wasn't it somebody just like that who immortalized that insult?

Most of you are holding down day or night jobs, and you do have to watch your wallets. And you don't need me to tell you. What you might need me to tell you is this: being monetarily average doesn't necessarily mean that you can't get your feet wet in day trading. You just have to be creative and careful.

But creative and careful may not be enough. There's a major Catch-22. You need to pay bills, but you also need time for active day-trading training. So right about now you'd ask the obvious question: If I have to traipse off to a job every day, and working nights isn't an option, then how can I train as a day trader? Argh!

My answer returns us to the main point: budgeting. You have to plan for time off from work. That means you have to have enough money saved to pay your bills during that period. A three-month leave is about what you need, if you're going to train all alone. But if you take advantage of my mentoring, then the time it takes for you to gain expertise will be cut by about two-thirds. Over the course of about a month's time, you'll learn to trade safely and profitably. (Refer to my website, www.DayTraderJosh.com, for more information on my mentorship program.)

The amount you'd have to budget would be gauged by your training time frame. In order to train by yourself, you'd need to free up about three months. If $5,000 dollars a month is what you require to feed the relentless bill monster, then you'd have to have $15,000 saved up. If you trained under my mentorship, then you'd only have to budget for one month off from work, and you'd need only $5,000 saved.

If you couldn't get an authorized leave from your job, and you didn't know whether the job would still be there if you decided to return, then you'd have to have another job firmly lined up. Otherwise you'd have to be certain that day trading is it, that there would be no turning back, and you'd have to be determined to learn how to keep yourself firmly financially safe there.

Don't expect to make much money during your training time, whether you're alone or training with me. If you have nothing saved then you'll likely find out that some of your bills won't get paid—certainly not from your trading! If you need $5,000 per month, then you need to *consistently* make about $225 per day trading, and that's *after* you deduct taxes. As a trainee you'll be trading in very small amounts, only 100-share blocks, so realistically you won't make any more than $150 per day, and you can bet your life it won't be consistent. Your time spent as a rookie is for learning, not earning. You should view it as a full-time college semester.

During my first three years of day trading, I went through a miserable cycle. I would trade for a few months and either break even, or I'd lose a lot. As soon as things got too crazy, I would go back to my job.

Upon reflection I realized that I repeatedly failed because I didn't see my comebacks as training and progress. I saw them as last-ditch chances to get back the money I'd lost. I was focused on making money, not on learning from my mistakes. I was desperate!

That's why your prior training period is crucial. I can't stress that enough. It will prevent you from edging too close to the holes that sucked me down into hell.

You'll recall from Chapter 1, "Truths about Yourself to Know First," my point that it's essential to be totally committed, in other words, to trade full time. In order to be a full-timer, you need to trade five days a week. Otherwise, your skill level will fail to grow as it should. You *won't* become successful at day trading by placing a few weekly trades from your current work place computer. You *won't* get the in-depth experience required to make you professional.

I'm not saying you shouldn't be placing trades ever, in your free time, at work. That can be a great way to start out, and if you get lucky and make a little money, you can allocate the proceeds to a carefully planned budget for training full time.

Okay, let's say now you've finished with my one-month mentorship program, or you've finished that three-month stint by yourself, and things have gone really well. You're ready to evolve from active live training to active live amateur day trading. You're just like a newly certified teacher, fresh from the halls of academia. You're ready to become a professional, but you're green as leaves on a tree. You're ready to use day trading as your primary source of income, but your lack of experience in the real world is sure to make your path rocky.

Along with this, your debut in professional day trading, your budgeting now must change. Chapter 1, "Truths about Yourself to Know First," and Chapter 13, "Trading Consistently All Day," nail home the importance of learning to be consistent before you try trading for income. During your training period, you should have mastered strategic consistency. You can now put together the second budget phase, which amounts to another type of consistency, the very strict management of income.

CRUNCHING THE NUMBERS

If you've been profiting an average of $250 each day and limiting yourself to $100 losses for each day, then you can start depending on that. This is performance-based income, after all. You're in charge.

I like to gauge my performance on a monthly basis. If I have a bad day, I don't get too stressed about it, though I do have a daily limit for both profit and loss. What matters the most is that I meet my monthly quota. If I fall below my monthly budget, then I step up my efforts. Determining my monthly profit/loss is simple. I always have a minimum amount in my account. Whatever exceeds that amount is my profit.

On every first of the month, I complete my monthly budget. I simply take the base amount (the minimum requirement or more) and subtract the total account value. So if I have $25,000 in my account at the beginning of the month, and at the end of the month I have $30,000, then my gross profit is $5,000 that month.

Here's how I do my taxes. I allocate 30 percent of my gross profit for the month toward taxes. I keep that 30 percent in a separate, interest-bearing account. Example: with a $3,500 (.7 × $5,000) net profit for the month, I set aside $1,500 (.3 × $5,000) for taxes.

So at the end of the year, the money I need to pay taxes is there. Once I prepare my taxes, I can immediately recognize my tax returns. Let's say that in that fiscal year, I've made $60,000. I've already taken out the 30 percent; therefore I have $18,000 (plus the annual interest accrued) to allocate to my owed taxes.

Note: If you have a good tax attorney, one who specializes in trading equities, then you'll most likely get to keep a healthy portion of the saved $18,000. The amount you don't have to send to the IRS is considered your tax return.

Well, all of the above is an idyllic scenario, a world made controllable by budgeting. I'd be grievously remiss to give that impression and ignore my obligation to modify it somewhat.

CUSHION CASH

Never forget this truth: In day trading, nothing is guaranteed.

You always have to have a Plan B. You need to have funds set aside for the bills, just like when you were training. You could have a very bad month; you could end up in the red. You might not have enough in your trading account to withdraw for all your expenses.

You'll never have to worry about any of that if you've socked away enough. And if you decide to take a break from trading in order to reflect and learn, then you've got that reserve to fall back on.

Can you imagine trying to trade every day, with absolutely no safety net, knowing that if you lose you'll be living on the streets? Don't do that to yourself, *ever!*

Before you decide to start trading for income, you should set aside enough money for at least three months (cushion cash), and you should keep backup money on the sidelines in excess of your account minimum. For instance, if you're required to have $25,000 in your account (most pay-per-share firms enforce this), then you should have at least an additional $10,000 sitting in a separate account, serving only as a cushion. In other words, *to begin trading, you should have at least $35,000.*

I hate to be the bearer of bad news, but there's a strong chance that a couple of times, you'll fall well below your minimum balance. The $10,000 backup fund is your savior. It's your safeguard against going crazy when you get an equity call to add more cash to your account, in order to maintain the minimum. If you don't have backup cash, then you won't be able to day trade on your account until you find more money. That stinks! Trust me, I've been there, and the aim of my mentorship program is to minimize your chances of having to go through that nightmare.

Don't make the mistake of being overconfident, thinking that you're one of the lucky ones. Here I'm coughing up very hard-wrought advice. Trust me, it's better to be safe then sorry. Do not start trading for income until you have cushion cash. Furthermore, don't keep that cushion in your trading account. Trust me again on this one—not using it will be very difficult, especially if you're trading on emotion.

Knowing your financial limitations, and wisely planning and budgeting, can greatly increase your chances of survival in this high-risk, low-certainty environment. Prepare an Excel spreadsheet for your budget. Use it every day that you trade. Keep all your accounting up to date. If you don't know how to use Excel, then use a software program like QuickBooks to keep your finances in order.

In day trading, you need to be organized and diligent, not to mention good at saving cash.

 RULES TO REMEMBER

- If you're planning to train on your own, save up to prepare for three months of unemployment. If you're planning to be professionally mentored, save up for one month of unemployment.
- Don't try to trade for income until you're consistently profitable, after three months of training on your own or one month of mentoring.
- If you quit your day job, make sure you can get it back. Or, as an alternative safety net, bolster your day trading training with mentoring.
- Always have cushion money set aside for both your training and your active trading.
- Never keep your cushion money in your trading account.
- Use budgeting software to keep your accounting up-to-date and available.

CHAPTER 9

Minimizing Your Risk with Stop/Loss

A s it goes with every investment system, the fundamental risk for a day trader is trades that run into the red. From the viewpoint of accounting, that red might as well be spilled blood. The good news is that as a day trader, you can control the amount of spillage. With a proper stop/loss system in place, you're in charge of how much you can lose.

Just what is stop/loss, exactly? The answer to that question is a little complicated, because day traders have different definitions and strategies. In general, stop/loss is the choosing of a predetermined price at which you immediately sell your positions, if they nosedive or skyrocket *to* that price. The point is that you sell at a loss, a small loss you've determined you can handle—so it's never a devastating loss.

MAKING STOP/LOSS AUTOMATIC

By *consistently* applying strict stop/loss procedures, you minimize your *unplanned* risk. As soon as you meander from that method, you invite unpleasant surprises. Therefore, the application of stop/loss should be engrained in you, automatic.

That sounds like a no-brainer, doesn't it? Well, it's not quite as easy as it seems. You have to be on the lookout for your own capricious temptation. It's so easy to stray from your system, especially when you're an amateur.

Take me, for example. I remember first learning how to stop/loss. It was back in 1999, at my very first training program. They made it all sound so simple. If your trade goes against you, they told us, all you have to do is sell your position at a small, very tolerable loss. Then you just move on.

Well, I certainly can't say they were wrong about that; the procedure really is that straightforward. The trouble with the whole thing, I found, lies within me. It's just not that easy, psychologically speaking, to dump something I'm fixated on.

And then there was the other psychological pitfall that affected me when I stop/lossed. After I consecutively did it, my losses were more than my profits. That's when I began to get peeved. The stop/loss system was working, all right! I kept selling at a loss!

I had learned how to minimize my risk, but now I had to also learn how to minimize my stop/losses. After all, I complained to myself, if you want to make money in day trading, you have to log more green trades than red!

The training program had neglected to prepare me well for that problem. I hadn't been drilled on how to avoid excessive stop/loss maneuvers. My instructors had only showed me the general importance of integrating that routine. I'd been taught, for example, to try to make 10 points on a trade, and then sell at a loss when it moved 2 points against me.

Again, that all sounds so simple.

A few things were missing from that training program. There are issues that should have been dealt with, such as the fact that not every trading situation is the same. Some stocks are highly volatile, and you need to allow yourself more distance for the price to run against you, before it retraces back up to your profitable exit price. And in other situations, you may actually want to average-down before you impose a stop/loss (this strategy, however, is only for advanced traders).

Because of these reasons, learning how to use stop/loss involves some trial and error. And that's another reason for my continual exhortation that until you increase your skill level, you should only trade in 100-share blocks.

Here are some basic guidelines and strategies to help you along your way to mastering stop/loss.

First of all, before you even try to gauge the price level you want to sell at, you need to know your financial limitations. For instance, if you figure you can handle a $200 loss for the day, then you can afford to stop/loss when you're down $200 on the trade. If you plan on placing multiple trades, then you may want to limit your loss on each trade in terms of your daily loss limit. For example, if you plan to place 20 trades per day and your daily financial limitation is a $200 loss, then you should limit each trade to a $10 loss ($200 per 20 trades).

That's a plan any training program will show you. Now I'll expand on it.

You're a human being, so you know this: you may have a daily budget, but there's no guarantee that you'll stick to it. Trust me when I say that in day trading, it's especially hard to do that. I can't tell you how many times I've exceeded my daily budget—by a lot. It's happened whenever I've found myself losing on most trades, on that day. I've abandoned my stop/loss system midday, and started trading like a chest-banging ape.

The problem didn't come from the stock I was trading, or even from the market itself. The issue was that during my intraday action, I failed to tailor my system. So I set about learning how. I learned that throughout the day, a day trader's stop/loss exit points should change on each trade.

Though it's true that once you enter a trade you should stick to your predetermined stop/loss exit point, the intraday stop/loss levels need constant reevaluation. For example, during your first trade, you may have decided to stop/loss once the price hits $44.00 (if in a short position) or $42.75 (if in long position). On your next trade, however, in same stock, the stop/loss exit price may need to be changed to $44.50 and $42.50, respectively.

How do you predetermine all those stop/loss exit points? What you do is keep your eye on the charts. You continuously reevaluate the intraday support levels and resistance levels. You stay cognizant of how the prices react when they approach and/or break through. You take note of how far the prices move, once they exceed those levels.

The stop/loss points should be placed just outside the new resistance and new support levels. Notice in Figure 9.1 how after the new resistance and new support levels are formed, the price retraces.

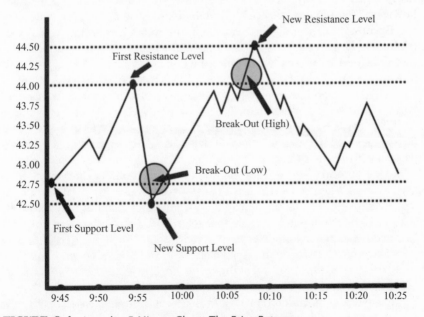

FIGURE 9.1 Intraday 5-Minute Chart: The Price Retraces

The intraday reversals are perfect opportunities to make a quick 15¢ to 30¢, or more. The breakout zones (as indicated in Figure 9.1) are great areas to enter a trade.

And that's where things can get tricky. To master the strategy of stop/loss takes a lot of experimentation.

I came to understand that intra-day stop/loss exit points are flexible and changeable. I realized I needed to grow competent at intraday stock price analysis. Each trade has different stop/loss thresholds. Here, in a nutshell, is what I found out: your exit points should never be static. Both they and you should be *dynamic*. You're learning to mentally juggle a number of variables. When you're gauging the right stop/loss exit price, you should focus on more than just how much you can afford to lose on the trade. From one trade to another, your exit points must never be set to the same dollar amount or price level.

Some stocks take an hour to move 10¢. Others move 10¢ in 10 seconds. Suppose you're just trading one stock. I'll assume you've been trading it long enough to be well aware of its rhythm, meaning you know how the price moves intraday. You also know how fast and how much the price breaks through support and resistance levels. With all that lined up you can dynamically gauge what the proper stop/loss point should be, on any given trade.

Here's an example of how changeable things get. I like to trade stocks that move about $1 every 20 minutes. I like them highly volatile during their $1 moves. That means the stock price fluctuates 10¢ to 20¢, one way and then the other, but ultimately it moves a full dollar in one direction, over 20 minutes. By knowing the rhythm of my stock that well, I can effectively tailor my stop/loss points, throughout the entire day.

Suppose the stock Amazon.com (AMZN) is trading at $70 today. Before I can gauge the stop/loss points, I need to know a few things. I scrutinize the charts. I'm looking for the major intraday support and resistance levels. I take the previous day's *high*, and I make that today's resistance level. Then I take yesterday's *low*, and make that today's support level. I use these levels to start trading AMZN.

Now I can prepare to trade lightly, meaning (you guessed it) in 100-share blocks. When the stock price begins to approach my predetermined intraday support or resistance levels, I usually start planning my entry. If the price breaks through a resistance level (top), I may choose to *sell short*. If it breaks through a support level (bottom), then I may chose to *go long*.

Wait, you might respond. You'd say, *Shouldn't you have done just the opposite? Why would you* sell short *if the stock price is shooting up and breaking though a major resistance level?*

My answer to you would be this: Wall Street brokers have to take profits on their trades. When they sell their positions, the prices retrace, and that's when you should make your move. It's much harder to predict how much the stock price will continue on any trend up or down, but it's almost guaranteed it will retrace. The price is most likely going to retrace at major levels. Our job as day traders is to capitalize on those quick (and fairly certain) reversals.

I've found that at those levels, they almost always retrace. And if they don't retrace, I quickly stop/loss. Having a predetermined exit price (a stop/loss plan of exit) means there's virtually nothing to worry about.

Suppose a major intraday resistance level for AMZN is at $70.50. I will wait for the price to reach $70.50. It may take only minutes. Once it hits that level, that means it's way overbought, and ready to retrace, just a bit. Or so you think.

If you're in good rhythm with your stock, you know at this point what direction it will most likely continue, and how fast. The key is to patiently wait for the intraday support or resistance levels to hit. Once the price hits those levels, you should be looking to enter. Before you enter you should already know your predetermined exit points: the profit price (limit) and stop/loss price.

If I enter the trade at $70.75 (short sell), I will most likely have a $71.05 stop/loss price in mind. If the price hits $71.05 I'm going to lose $30 on the trade ($70.75 − $71.05 = $.30 × 100 shares). If the price continues down I will cover my short position at a profit when it hits $70.25. In Figure 9.2, I was forced to stop/loss at $71.05.

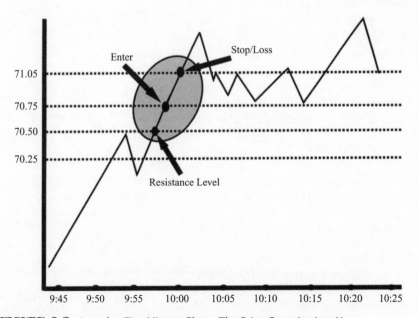

FIGURE 9.2 Intraday Five-Minute Chart: The Price Goes Against You

The gray area in Figure 9.2 represents the trading range. The price never retraces, so I quickly stop/loss at $71.05.

The time it takes from entry to exit is only about four minutes.

When the price breaks through a major support or resistance level, in most cases it retraces by about 25¢ or more. This happens before it continues to new and higher levels, so I tend to allow my stop/loss points to be about 25¢ past where I enter trade. I usually enter trade once the price shoots past the original intraday support and resistance levels by about 25¢. Therefore, I am allowing the price to travel a full 50¢ past the original intraday resistance level before I stop/loss. There is a much higher chance that the price will retrace once it shoots past the resistance level than continuing to shoot straight up to higher levels.

In the AMZN case in Figure 9.3, I would like to show what happens when things go right, using the previous situation from Figure 9.2.

Suppose the price breaks the $70.50 original intraday resistance level and then shoots up 25¢ past it (extremely overbought). I entered the trade (short sold) at $70.75, and then it quickly retraced to $70.50 before it hit $71.05, so I made a quick $25 on the trade. (Translation: *shorted* stock at $70.75 with 100 shares, *covered* at $70.50.)

I entered trade around 9:58 A.M. and exited about three minutes later. Notice how the price retraced after I got out. It shots back up. Once it

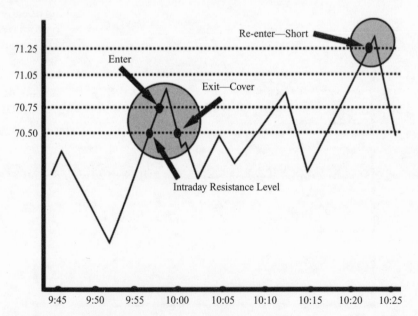

FIGURE 9.3 Intraday 5-Minute Chart: Things Go Right

hit $71.25 I would most likely have reentered a short-sell position. The stop/loss and profit exit points will be different on the next trade. I would probably cover at $71.00 this time, or stop/loss at $71.50 (this is what I mean by *dynamic* exit points).

That seems like a lot of planning and waiting for a measly $25 profit and a possible $50 loss. Well, keep these things in mind:

- Your initial setups, done properly, have 10 times the chance of retracing when they hit the major intraday support and resistance levels, before they continue to new levels.
- As your skill level increases, you'll be watching more and more setups. I usually watch 10 stocks at a time. Most of the time, every one to five minutes, at least one of them hits a major level. It might only take one minute to get in or out of the trade.

The point is that it's okay to stop/loss, because I've lined up other trades, so I can get back my money. For instance, I may stop/loss on 5 or 10 trades, but I'm going to profit on 50 or more, all throughout the day.

Accordingly, I've learned to resist **holding** a losing position past my stop/loss exit point. Not only am I placing myself in treacherous waters, but my capital is getting tied up. In the time that I'm **holding** my losing positions, I could be placing other quick trades, and profiting from them.

Here, as in every other chapter, I stress patience and the taking of baby steps while you trade as an amateur. While you're learning how to properly stop/loss, there's unavoidable guesswork. You'll certainly make some mistake. This, however, I can promise: The more you trade a particular stock, the more you'll get to know it, especially with regard to how it approaches the entry and exit levels. Eventually you'll get much better at gauging which prices are best to enter, and which prices are best to exit, all on an intraday basis.

 RULES TO REMEMBER

- Learning how to properly stop/loss is a process of trial and error. So again: trade in small (100-share) blocks.
- Never try gauging a stop/loss price until you've determined the support and resistance levels for that day.
- Before you even try to gauge what price level you want to sell at a stop/loss, know your financial limitations for that day.
- On every trade you enter, always stick to your predetermined stop/loss exit price.

CHAPTER 10

Averaging-Down: A Skilled Strategy

A veraging-down is a strategy to lower your average cost in a stock that has dropped in price.

Question: Is this a truly good maneuver, or are you just chasing a botched trade?

The answer depends on your skill level.

Here's how it works. In a typical averaging-down situation, you buy 100 shares at $50 per share, then the stock drops to $49 per share. So you buy another 100 shares at $49 per share, which lowers your average price to $49.50 per share.

On the surface that sounds like a good plan, but now you're trading a 200-share block. Overexposure just became a real issue, and that's especially true for amateurs. Beginners aren't ready to *keep on* averaging down, which means 300 shares, and then 400 shares, and so on and so on.

The key to successfully averaging-down is to have a shrewd, careful plan. Amateurs might start with smart strategies, but things can get ugly fast, because when they add more shares to a trade, they may forget their overexposure. I'll address that issue right here and now with a loud and clear proclamation:

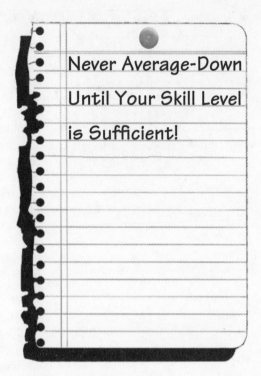

Go ahead and make another sign for your wall out of that.

An amateur must struggle to consistently profit when only trading lightly. That means 100-share blocks. He doesn't possess the expertise to execute complex maneuvers. Averaging-down is a *professional* device. A beginner might try it and get lucky a few times, but all it takes is one trade gone south and he's likely to **hold** until the cows come home.

And he'll probably lose really big.

TO AVERAGE-DOWN SUCCESSFULLY TAKES MASTERY

So how do you know when your skill level's sufficient? If you're trading a stock often and profiting consistently, then maybe you're ready to try something advanced. In order to gauge your readiness, refresh yourself with Chapter 1 on evaluating your skill, "Truths about Yourself to Know First."

I've averaged-down as an amateur, and then again as an experienced trader. As an amateur I've suffered bad consequences. As a seasoned trader, I've done much better. As usual I'll now share the dark gory details of how badly I bombed as a beginner, and then how, when I'd garnered a lot more skill, I made the maneuver work.

My heaviest *unplanned* losses to date have been caused by *incorrectly averaging-down*. As a beginner I had basic know-how—you know, buy low and sell high (yeah right). I would enter knowing what price to sell at, if the price happened to shoot up to my limit price (profit), and I also had a planned stop/loss price. But if the price dropped very quickly or I was having a bad trading day, I would get too emotional. I would get angry at the stock. I wouldn't apply my stop/loss; instead, I would watch it continue to drop. I would then buy more stock at lower price levels.

I would completely abandon my original plan. If the stock continued to drop, I would buy even more without hesitation. I did try to find new support levels, but once I started *incorrectly* averaging-down, I was dangling, and I had no smart stratagem. This would go on until I used up all my capital.

Sometimes, if I were lucky, the stock would rebound just enough for me to break even. You might ask why I didn't allow it to run up into the green. Usually I never let it ride any higher because I was so drained from being in over my head that I just wanted out, and quickly.

In some cases I was down over $1,000 on one single intraday trade, and then it would finally retrace, at the end of the day. Once it got back to break-even, I was so stressed that I sold all my positions and bailed out. I was relieved, but also I felt lucky, because, after all, I was gambling.

Most trades where I averaged-down unfortunately never rebounded, so I had to sell at a very large loss, or else I **held** overnight. When I **held** it was because I was hoping, of course, that tomorrow it would go back up.

And most often, of course, it did not.

Averaging-down as an amateur, I broke every trading rule. I wasn't emotionally disciplined, and I lacked the experience to execute complex technical tricks. I felt like a starving puppy, lost and alone in the woods, trying to outfox my prey, and ending up more lost and hungry than ever.

Later on, when I'd gained more experience, I began to average-down with success. Eventually I was able to include the device as part of my overall strategy.

KNOW-HOW DOESN'T GROW OVERNIGHT

For over a year I'd been trading a few select, reliable stocks. I was totally in rhythm with them. I was very familiar with their price swings. I knew their reactions to support levels and resistance levels. I had confidence in every trade I made. But I hadn't yet reached the sufficient skill level to master averaging-down.

In Chapter 18, "Paper-Trading Strategy, I stress the importance of trading on paper or demo before going live with what's new. That's true of both stocks and your strategies. I also point out the importance of never trading in large share blocks until you're consistently profitable when trading in 100-share blocks.

After I learned to *just stick to that*, I soon became very successful in trading those 100-share blocks. Then I promoted myself to 200-share blocks. But I had learned to be very careful. I only traded the very familiar, very predictable stocks that way.

The point is that before you try averaging-down, first you must master your ability to trade in 200-share blocks. In other words, don't bother trying to hit the ball until you know you're in shape to run the bases.

For me, a normal averaging-down scenario is 200 shares as my maximum. I start off the trade with 100 shares, and then, assuming the price falls, I purchase an additional 100 shares at a lower level.

Before I enter the trade, I *always* devise a plan, and this takes me seconds to do in my head. I quickly ask myself *why* I want to average-down this trade. Usually it's because, on that particular day, the stock I normally trade in 200-share blocks is being a little unpredictable. So I lower my exposure to it, allowing myself to enter at half the normal risk (100 shares versus 200 shares).

What exactly is the risk I'm avoiding? When I trade the same stock in 200-share blocks I normally allow myself a $50 loss. So I'm willing to risk $50 on the trade (200 shares $\times .25 = 50). This means if the stock price drops 25¢ I have to stop/loss at $49.75, assuming I entered the trade at $50.00.

Now that I know my threshold for risk ($50 on 200 hundred shares) I can devise an order execution plan. I'll enter the trade when the stock price hits $50, and at first I'll purchase only 100 shares. When the price drops to $49.90 (a $10 loss so far), then I'll buy an additional 100.

Now that I have a 200-share block trade, again I've got to stick to my plan. And I have to do some more quick calculations. When I purchased the second 100-share block, I averaged-down my cost of the position. I paid $50.00 for the first hundred shares and $49.90 for the second, so my *average* per/share cost is now $49.95. I'm used to taking *only* a $50 loss on my trades, when trading 200-share blocks, so I can allow the price to run down to $49.70 ($49.95 – $49.70 = 25¢$).

I'll stop/loss on the 200-share block, if it reaches that low point.

At this point you might ask why I put myself through all that when I simply could have purchased 200 shares to begin with.

Remember, it's all about overexposure. If I feel that the stock is trading unpredictably, I elect to initially trade only half of what I'm accustomed to, in order to cut down the risk. And there's another factor at play there. When a stock is being unpredictable, it's harder to pick support and resistance levels on the charts. Therefore it's wise to allow some extra margins for error.

Using my previous example, for instance, it's easy to see how that works. If you purchase all 200 shares at $50.00, you can only afford the price to drop to $49.75 (not $49.70). This 5¢ difference may not seem like much, but it could be exactly the cushion you need in order to stay in the trade, and that's helpful on volatile days.

I've been stopped out of trades where the price then retraced within pennies of my stop/loss price. If I had skillfully averaged-down, I could have stayed in the trade a bit longer, without losing more than I'm used to (my $50 threshold).

The method I've described is risky, especially when it's hard to have a clear plan of entry and exit. Again, it takes a high skill level to perform this strategy effectively. That's why I urge that you paper-trade this, until you feel ready to go live.

 RULES TO REMEMBER

- Never attempt to average-down until you're sufficiently skilled.
- Never average-down beyond your threshold for risk.
- Only average-down on your consistently profitable stocks.

CHAPTER 11

Gambling versus Day Trading

G ambling is the act of placing a bet. What's involved is a system of win-or-lose odds. *Odds* is the mathematical likelihood that an event will or won't occur. Odds are the key to the gambling process. On the contrary, day trading, or intraday investing, involves maneuvers in a much more controllable system. The system itself influences results—and this does *not* mirror the gambler's dependence on hazardous numerical odds.

A casino gambler who decides to try day trading might construe the profession as betting. That assumption could actually be horribly true, if he doesn't know what he's doing. Ask any professional day trader whether he sees himself as a gambler, and most likely he'll respond with this question, *Are we talking about when I was an amateur, or now that I'm much more experienced?*

I will return to that question later in the chapter.

When players stride through a casino, they all have the same chance of winning or losing at any machine or table. They all want to beat the odds. Sure, some players are seasoned, and their skills at prediction are keen; they win somewhat more than the rookies. But even so, they're just betting, they're just casting their fates to the wind, because in gambling, the risk is uncontrollable, it's unswervingly 50-50. With every single hand or roll of the dice or pull on a slot machine, the fulcrum is pure, simple chance. The payouts may vary, but what it boils down to is they walk away either beaming, or trying hard not to cry.

In day trading the chances are apparently the same, but a closer look shows that's not true. The trader does not simply attempt to press his luck in the gambler's inflexible circumstances. He's concerned about how to best minimize his risk. That risk is considerably more complex, and also more malleable, than the win-or-lose stakes at casinos. The professional trader makes it work for him.

Here's the main reason why day trading isn't gambling: The price swings are always evolving. There's no fixed probability. That's the condition that establishes the leeway for consistent, not hit-or-miss, profits.

As soon as you place a casino bet, you're done. All you can do is just stand there and wait to see where the dice stop. But in day trading—even hunch trading—right in the middle of the trade, you have choices. Your advantage is planning, not odds. Therefore the challenge in day trading is to have an accurate as possible system of accurate intraday forecasts.

Day trading pros are a little bit like the psychics at the casinos. When psychics play roulette, they can foresee the outcome. Before the dealer calls out final bets, they're aware of where the ball will stop. They're sure of which number the ball is going to land on, so they bet everything on that number.

Behind the scenes human watchdogs are stationed, on the lookout for those gifted seers. Whenever they zero in on one, they oust him and black-ball him!

The day trader isn't a psychic, but he commands some similar choices. He can see the price action moving. It's like watching roulette balls spinning. Though he doesn't have mystical powers, and can never be totally certain of where the price will end up, he can modify the dangers while the trade is in play, while the ball is still rolling.

Let's say that you blindly buy a stock on a hunch. You buy it because you *feel confident* that it will keep rising in price. What you're doing, right then, is like placing a bet. You might as well be at a casino.

But here's what's unique about trading: even when you capriciously hazard a hunch, you have options that are absent in gambling. This is where things get interesting. This is where risk management sets day traders apart.

As I mentioned in Chapter 6, "The Importance of Risk Management," there are several strategic options:

- You can add more money as the price goes up.
- If you find the price going against you, you can take some money off the table.
- You can predetermine your stop/loss and limit price.
- You can change stocks.
- You can **hold** (intraday) until it retraces (note: only experts should try this).
- You can average-down your position (again, only experts should try this).

When asked about gambling versus day trading, the professional day trader will probably tell you that most amateurs basically gamble. He's assuming that they haven't yet mastered the safety-net-strategy options, and they haven't yet profited consistently. He knows their ineptitude regarding risk management is a lot like rolling the dice.

I'm aware that a professional gambler would say something pretty similar. He'd tell you that you need to be focused, working only within a strict budget. He'd be right to say that, but he'd also be revealing the brutal simplicity of odds. He'd have little to say about managing risk, because in gambling, you can't change the odds.

On the contrary, every professional trader has an individualized, strict risk management system. Pros for the most part maintain some consistency in how they evaluate their exposure to risk. Chapter 13, "Trading Consistently All Day," and Chapter 7, "How Overexposure to the Market Can Hurt," both emphasize how important it is to stick to a plan that works.

Now I want you to never forget this: Every time I've lost big in trading, it's because I've been gambling.

And I want to make a confession. I admit that even as a pro, in the past I've occasionally abandoned my own risk management system, and virtually gone for broke.

I'd be trading, as usual, in 100-share blocks, and consistently profiting. Then something would come over me. Be it boredom, or a pressure to make more money, or just a random attack of greed, whatever the cause, it was compulsive. Suddenly I'd opt, against all my rules, to start trading in 1,000-share blocks.

I'd be highly aware that I was overexposing myself to 10 times the risk I was used to. I'd know that I was breaking my tried-and-true, safe and consistent routine—that I was throwing my own advice right out the door with the trash!

But I was hungry for money—much more money. And just then, I didn't care. I didn't care that now I was gambling. And now, just like at casinos, I could lose everything I was betting.

I had sacrificed the strategies listed above, such as averaging down or intraday **holding,** because I'd already gotten in over my head by initially purchasing such a large block of shares. So each time I entered the trade, I hoped and prayed the stock would go up in my direction, before it went against me and destroyed me.

This was pure gambling! A 50-50 chance!

If it went against me I was *in big trouble.* If it went up I was *lucky.*

More times than not, it went against me. I did make a few quick profits, but if the price dropped fast and I had 1,000 shares, then we're talking a $1,000 loss for every $1 drop in price.

I was used to trading stocks that fluctuate $1 every 10 minutes.

Now I might have to stomach a $1,000 loss in 10 minutes.

On the bright side, there is one good thing I learned, even though it isn't worth much: even when I've day traded in that crazy manner, it's still a little better than gambling, because at least I've lost a little bit slower. Think about it: if you place a $1,000 bet on a blackjack table, your money will be gone in less then 10 minutes. It might disappear in the mere 30 seconds it takes for the dealer to deal the cards.

Talk about feeling powerless, the hapless victim of chance! Talk about instant disaster!

That's gambling.

Whenever I've broken my consistency, I've fallen from day trader to gambler. It doesn't matter how many seconds or minutes it took to lose everything; the point is, I slipped into gambling. Never forget this: Luck is a gambler's best friend. *Not needing luck* is the day trader's distinction.

 RULES TO REMEMBER

- Learn risk management before you start day trading, or else you're just rolling the dice.
- Hone the skills of risk management during initial live-trading experiences. Always take advantage of the strategic options that day trading offers you—options you don't get in gambling.
- Never, ever ask yourself whether you're feeling lucky today.

PART III

Intraday Trading Truths

This part is a collection of advisories and warnings that can increase your intraday success rate. In order to benefit the most from this part, you must first be familiar with all of the previous chapters.

This part includes chapters that will cover typical intraday trading mistakes. I cover technical issues that revolve around the most basic requirement in day-trading consistency. I also offer a systematic way of acquiring stocks to trade. I end the part by explaining how to deal with news.

CHAPTER 12

Why Some Traders Make More Mistakes

Y ou can hold an M.B.A. in business, and you can go through the intensive and pricey routine of day trading seminar trainings. Do any of those drills make you a day trader?

No.

As I've stated before, your learning internalizes only when your trading becomes very personal, meaning trading with your own money. Your valuable lessons only evolve from your disastrous, though enlightening, mistakes and the disaster-free assistance of a mentor.

It's not just by chance that in the first section, I emphasize emotional pitfalls. I highlight them first because they make you or break you. Mistakes made in day trading almost always involve some self-destructive psychology. Self-discipline is the powerful antidote.

While trading, we all face emotional issues. We all have to calm the interior storms that cause most of our costly missteps, and then we must resolve to continue—even after devastating losses. Our comfort lies in knowing almost every loss is preventable, if only we'd stick to our safeguards. The successful professional trader is resilient. His confidence evolves from his ability to recover fast from his blunders, and his resolve to never repeat them. That force of will hones his victories.

Such professionals, however, do sometimes make mistakes. Some make more mistakes than others, and here we can witness a dramatic example of natural selection. There are two sides to every trade. For every profiteer, there's a loser, and as a matter of vicious Darwinian fact, the market depends on one side to perpetually take heavy hits. Whenever somebody loses, somebody else makes a big profit. Every time you profit from a trade, it's because you just made money from another day trader's error. You picked the just-right price level, but the other guy miscalculated or lagged. His misstep or balk made your profit.

Every time the price moves in one direction fast, the reason is that many buyers or sellers are trading that way, in high volume, and it's up to you to know when this is likely to reverse. So if you buy into selling momentum to the downside, then you'd better pick the bottom correctly.

If you fail to pick the bottom correctly, the money you lose on the trade becomes profit to those who are short-selling past your stop/loss, or those who chose to exit at a minimal loss.

Conversely, if you do pick the bottom correctly, then you actually profit from the short-sellers, because they failed to cover when the price began to go back up.

What does all this have to do with learning from your mistakes? Well, if you find yourself on the losing end you should know what you did wrong, and you should also know what the winners did right. In order to move on and not repeat your errors, you need that two-sided view.

To achieve that, you probe and analyze every one of your losing trades. You ask yourself why you sold or bought at that level, and you determine why others did not. Remember: There are no day-trading conspiracies. There's no little troll in your computer who personally trades against you. The troll is at his monitor, trading the same stock as you. When he trades in the opposite direction from you, only one of you is right.

All day traders are fighting for the best price level to enter and exit a trade. It's your job to make some good judgment calls when competing for the right price. To help you diminish bad calls, here's a list to ponder. These are the areas where traders are most likely to mess up:

- Picking stocks to trade
- Lacking concentration
- Not watching market-moving news

PICK YOUR STOCKS CAREFULLY

When it comes to stock picking, most beginner day traders are pretty much all over the place. Their foundation for determining what makes stocks good to trade is weak and shaky at best. As yet they have no solid trading system. They don't realize that *first* you develop that system, and *then* you select the stocks, because it's all about working with the right stocks for your personal trading style.

Accordingly, if you're accustomed to the rhythm and swings of a stock, and you've traded that stock with success, then you should pick stocks that are similar. (Chapter 14, "Stock Picking," elaborates on this concept.)

Most botched trades are due to beginners who are trying out unfamiliar stocks. I realize those mistakes are hard to avoid. You have to start somewhere, right?

Yes, but that doesn't mean you should be betting the farm without prior monitoring and qualifying. Several times, as an amateur, I learned that the hard way. Most of the stocks I lost money on were stocks I found the night before. Like a fool I went and traded them the very next day. First I should have researched them, and by that I mean for *days or weeks*!

Eventually I learned to carefully limit my exposure to new stocks. Until I felt confident with them, I knew I should take that precaution. Then I *gradually* traded them more actively. Indeed, I now successfully trade many of the stocks that originally broke me. It's been much like learning how to deal with the playground bully. I beat him with my brains.

These days, if I find a new stock with the qualities of my core stocks, I take it slow for awhile. I'm always on full alert, watching it closely but not yet interacting. It's like making sure that the bully is not behind me when I'm standing in the water fountain line. I always keep the danger in sight.

When I finally choose to trade that new stock, I may wait all day for just one trade of just 100 shares, and only make $20. (Of course, I'm simultaneously trading my proven stocks, and doing so much more actively.)

It's critical to be patient with your less familiar stocks. Don't ever capriciously use them to replace your losing stocks. First you must scrutinize them closely. You should treat all new stocks like the bully, or a newly assigned work partner, or even like a first date.

The new stock you're carefully studying might turn out to be a bad stock to day trade. That's why, initially, you should drastically limit your exposure. Stock picking is the arena of many day traders' blunders. Tread very lightly there, comrades.

FOCUS, FOCUS, FOCUS

Lack of concentration is another beginner's weakness. After burning himself a few times, the need to develop great focusing skill gets seared into a day trader. A classic example is when the trader walks away for only a few minutes, maybe to make a quick sandwich, or else to use the bathroom. He returns to his trading station, and finds that in his short absence, his stock has plummeted.

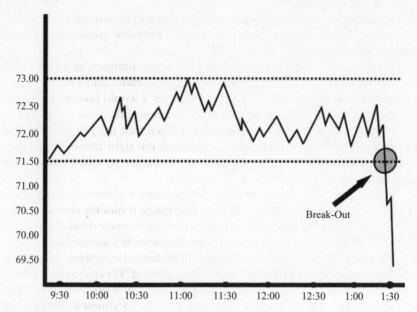

FIGURE 12.1   Intraday 30-Minute Chart: Breakout

In Figure 12.1, the stock was trading in a tight range up till 1:30 P.M., then it quickly breaks out of range to the downside. If you are not watching this quick breakout you will lose very fast. It drops two dollars in under a few minutes.

He should have had a stop/loss in place, right? This is true, but many of the best trades happen when you sit there totally glued, patiently watching for exit points. Not all trades should have automatic stops and limits. Sometimes it's better when you manually place your exits, because you don't have any time to place limit orders. You're only in the trade a few minutes. Plus, sometimes your limit prices never hits at all, so you have to just be there, watching, in order to make adjustments.

Either way you slice it, you should never take your eyes off a trade! Innumerable mental culprits can break your concentration, and all of them try to sneak up. Talking to your significant other, checking emails on another screen, or simply dozing off . . . all of those distractions are concentration destroyers.

While trading, you should be virtually meditating. That is no exaggeration. I really do mean you should be entranced. That state of mind will maintain you in an intimate rhythm with your trades. Every single second, your Level 2 quotes and 1-, 5-, and 15-minute charts are displaying real-time data. That data is speaking to you, and you should be attentively listening. You can't miss one note of that conversation between you and your monitors.

I used to break my concentration for a few minutes at a time. That turned out to be costly. I'd be in a tight-range trade, and I'd find myself getting bored. My mind would begin to wander. I would take a five-minute break. I'd go to the kitchen, or else make a phone call.

And when I returned to my screens, I'd see that the price had instantaneously jumped, and then retraced back to the tight range. So because I hadn't focused on the trade, I'd missed my chance to make money—the easy kind that gets offered on a silver platter.

In Figure 12.2, the stock price trades between $70 and $71.50 all morning. When it breaks out of the tight trading range it quickly shoots up two dollars. It only takes five minutes before it retraces back down.

Lack of concentration will punish a day trader. It's almost as detrimental as being a soldier who's shot because he failed to be vigilant. You should view the problem as a pitfall of being self-employed. There's no boss prowling around you, making you afraid to relax and slack off. You have to remember you're working. Your challenge is to keep yourself focused. No one but you is there to make you concentrate.

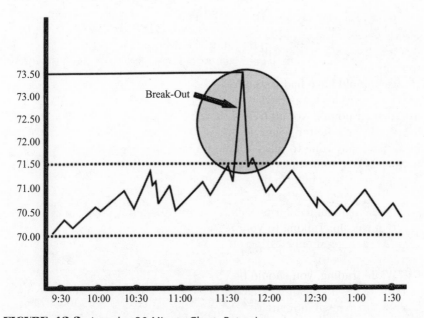

FIGURE 12.2 Intraday 30-Minute Chart: Retracing

PAY ATTENTION TO MARKET-MOVING NEWS

Not watching market-moving news can also impact your trade badly. You can be trading a stock all day, and it will be moving consistently. But all it takes is some company news, or another major market announcement, for your stock to start moving very quickly in one direction, hopefully not against you.

You've got to be prepared for that development.

When the Federal Reserve Board (Fed) announces interest rate drops or hikes, that's when you've got to look out. As a beginner, I had no idea how much the Fed influences the market. Even with a B.S. in business, I was clueless. I'd be in a trade and the Fed would announce its intentions, and immediately the whole market would go haywire. This would last for about an hour. Whatever stock I was in would move too, and it would almost always stop/loss me out of my trade.

Earnings is another kind of stock news that can dramatically influence your trade. If the stock you're trading is coming out with an after-market earnings announcement or the next morning's premarket earnings, either way you'll see a volatility increase. The price direction will be very hard to read. Also, industry leader stocks that have earnings can directly influence your stock. For instance, say you're trading a software company that is mid-cap (mid-range in terms of capitalization), and Microsoft has its earnings released while you're in the trade. Your company will most likely feel Microsoft's earnings effects, and accordingly, your stock's price may jump up or shoot down.

But some news is best left alone and ignored. You should never be trading when news is the major factor in the stock price movements. You should wait to see where the stock settles after the volatility subsides. By waiting, you won't get burned.

How many times have you seen this: Great news comes out and the stock price shoots up 10 percent in the first five minutes? For example, a $50 stock shoots up $5, to $55. Then, in the next five minutes, you watch the stock retrace about $4. You can easily get whiplashed out of those trades. They can instantly turn your hair grey. Why do that to yourself?

For elaboration on all the news issues that a day trader has to deal with, see Chapter 15, "Why News Can Be Just Noise."

Remember: the most valuable lessons you'll ever learn will come from your own blunders. In this chapter I've mentioned some common mistakes. Be aware of which ones you're making: It's up to you to address them. Your missteps are very expensive lessons, so learn from them. Don't shrug them off. If you do, you'll be one of those misfortunate day traders who makes the most mistakes, and makes them the most often.

RULES TO REMEMBER

- Never take your eyes off a trade!
- Log every one of your mistakes.
- Your mistake is another trader's profit, so understand what he did right.
- Focus on eliminating your chronic mistakes.
- Instead of shrugging them off, learn and grow from your errors.

CHAPTER 13

Trading Consistently All Day

There's nothing worse than having a great trading day—all day—and then losing every dime in the last 10 minutes! If there's anything good to be salvaged from that nightmare, it's the easiness of figuring out the *cause* of such a big loss. The probable reason is incredibly simple: You disrupted your consistency.

I know that's been true for me.

Back in the beginning, it took several losses—end-of-day, so cruelly timed—to jerk me awake and make me face my missteps and learn the importance of constancy. Now go and get a magic marker and poster board. Make a sign, a really big sign:

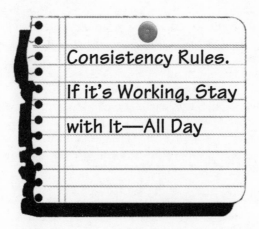

Consistency Rules.

If it's Working, Stay

with It—All Day

Put this sign on the wall above your monitor.

When I was beginning to trade like a professional, I routinely purchased 100-share blocks of a few select stocks, like Met Life (MET), Pep-
siCo (PEP), and Amazon.com (AMZN). I only watched the one-minute
chart on each. When they reached a support or resistance level, I would
either buy or short. I would only try to get $10 to $20 swings—that's 10¢ to
20¢ moves.

For the most part the stocks would always retrace at major sup-
port/resistance levels, and I would sell/cover at a $10 to $20 profit. I would
do this all day long. I would not buy 200 or 500 shares; I stuck with 100
at a time. If the price went against me for more then $20, I would always
sell/cover at a stop/loss. The system seemed virtually bulletproof. It really
was bulletproof.

But you see, I strayed from it sometimes—and wandered right onto a
minefield.

All it takes is *1 mistake* out of 40 perfect trades to lose *all* your profits
for the day. I should know. I know more about that than I would like.

When I was trading in 100-share blocks, I would sometimes get anxious
and (you guessed it) overconfident, and I'd purchase 200 or even 500 share
blocks of the same stock I'd traded all day. I was pumped up, you see, from
making perfect trades, while staying with the 100-share blocks.

Almost every time I did this the stock price went against me, and then
(you guessed it) I'd **hold.** There seemed to be no way around it—I was
quickly exceeding my $20 stop/loss—and then the fear factor kicked in. I
figured I'd **hold** until it came back down to at least my break-even point,
but it almost never did. I would continue to **hold**, even if it went $1 against
me; that's $200 for every 200-share block.

So basically, I'd start the day running uphill, and end the day dead, in a
gorge. Starting with 100-share blocks, with an average of 40 good trades, I'd
make $10 to $20 profitable trades. I'd be up about $500, but then I'd waste
it. All it took to create this disaster was *1* trade of a 500-share block that I
allowed to run against me by a full dollar!

The only way I could rectify that pathetic state of affairs was to sell *all*
500 shares at a loss, and get to break even for the day!

Well, in spite of all I was losing, one good thing was emerging: I was
slowly but surely developing a *consistent* pattern of sorts. I was constantly
fixing my mistakes, and that in itself was a step in the right direction; I
had learned very early to stop **holding** overnight, and then I learned to
use stop/loss at the end of the trading day. In the process I was gradually
becoming an authentic—if battered—day-trading professional.

Now I want you to stop in your tracks right here and read this
point, and remember: most amateurs will make almost any excuse to
hold a losing position, especially overnight. Learning to never do that

again is the first and foremost horrible lesson a beginner will stagger away from.

So here's another colorful sign to make and hang somewhere close to your desk; make it big and dead-level with your eyes:

Don't take that sign down until you know you've outgrown it. Then pass it along to your cousin down the street, the one who started day trading last week. But don't give it to your cousin until after you've learned that rule must be unswervingly followed. The tremendous uncertainty of **holding** is why. Instead of overnight **holding**, you've learned to take your losses and move on.

You should *always* sell by day's end. If you're consistent with that rule, you'll be one step closer to becoming a successful day trader.

That sounds pretty easy, doesn't it? Yeah, right. Look out. Beware. Staying consistent with a day-trading method is extremely difficult to master—and the issue here, as usual, is really about mastering *yourself*. Sticking to your system ... never straying ... well, for some people that's simple, I guess. The totally one-track minded or people severely inclined against risk might suffer minimal losses. But you're probably a typical random-willed human with an instinct to experiment and gamble. Temptation and greed may start gnawing at you just like hunger pangs, or lust.

I learned it was a two-sided challenge. I had to control myself, and I had to understand the market. Soon one fact became clear: besides finding out that I can profit all day with either 100- or 200-share blocks, I also learned that what's crucial is not the amount of the shares; what matters is the market exposure. The 200-share blocks would expose me twice as much as 100. That means that if I was used to taking $20 losses when trading in 100-share blocks, then I'd now have to get used to taking $40 losses when trading in 200-share blocks.

Every trader has different tolerance levels to stop/loss points, and I don't mean to insist that my personal amount of $20 for 100-share blocks and $40 for 200-share blocks is the level that's right for everyone. What I do mean to emphasize is the importance of consistency, of sticking to a pattern that works.

For example, if you have a percentage system for stop/loss, that can be applied here, as well. Let's say you have a stop/loss and a 10 percent profit system in place. If you purchase a $10 stock in 100 share blocks ($1,000 in security), then you sell once the stock price reaches either $9.50 (a loss of $50), or $11 (a gain of $100).

The thing to do is to get used to your tolerance levels for losses or profits, and then stick to them like glue. In the previous scenario, you have a 5 percent stop/loss in place. If your trade goes against you when you own 100 shares of a $10 stock, it causes a $50 loss. When it goes up, however, your 10 percent profit on the 100 shares of the $10 stock will grant you a $100 profit.

Make sure that you don't change a thing. For example, if you're accustomed to trading a $10 stock, then *always* trade stocks that are near $10 and only trade in 100-share blocks, and you'll never slip into a situation that tests your tolerance levels. You want to avoid that nerve-wracking ordeal—especially in the middle of the trading day.

Here's an example of how day trading can give you gray hair: You're up $300 after about seven successful trades and eight stop/losses (in a consistent pattern, that's $700 in profit and $400 in stop/losses). You then decide to change your stock picks. During the middle of the day, you purchase some $30 stocks. That's three times the value of the $10 stocks that you've been consistently trading. It's mid-afternoon. You're allowing those stocks to move $150 against you before you stop/loss. That's 5 percent of $30 in 100 shares. You're trying to make a $300 profit—that's 10 percent of $30 in 100 shares.

At this point everything seems consistent, but no, take a closer look. What's changed is the amount you'll have to adjust your tolerance levels. When trading a $10 stock, you're used to the $50 stop/losses and the $100 profits. Now, while trading a $30 stock, you're going to subject yourself to three times that amount.

I can guarantee one thing: it will be much harder to wait for those levels to hit, and you'll be very tempted to alter your exit points. Any detour from your system is an inconsistency, and once you lose your consistency, you and your trades will suffer.

Consistency is more than just force of habit, or the principle of sticking to a pattern. It's also about realistic confidence levels, all throughout the day. If you're consistent you're less likely to get yourself into situations where you're anxious, agitated, and dangerously tempted to take dire risks. You can pick any stock price you want. You can have any good system of stop/loss in place. You can trade any amount of share blocks, as long as you're not overexposed. The key to success is: Whatever pattern you choose, keep it consistent throughout the entire day.

 RULES TO REMEMBER

- Find your tolerance levels, and adjust your stop/loss and profit system accordingly.
- Discipline yourself to trade the same way, *all day long*.
- Never **hold** a losing position overnight!

CHAPTER 14

Stock Picking: Simplifying the Process

C *aution!* Do not read this chapter thinking this is all you need. This chapter is about how to *choose* stocks, *not* about how to *trade* stocks. Just the same, amateurs may think stock selection is the "golden goose" of good strategies. Beginners might read my Contents and flip right to this page.

That would be a huge mistake.

Trust me, you need to read the whole book. Stock picking is just a small aspect of the process of day-trading mastery. I'd want you to know, for instance, before you got to this chapter, that your choice of a promising stock doesn't mean you can safely trade in larger than 100-share blocks.

The good news is that the selection of stocks is one of your easiest hurdles. With clearly defined indicators and preconditions, finding good stocks to day trade is a breeze. Dependable analysis brings good results, and to help that process along, I've compiled a list of vital criteria:

- The average daily volume (calculated over the past three months) must be at least one million shares traded daily.
- The stock price must be between $10 and $100.
- The average intraday price swings must be sufficient to trade (as evidenced by chart analysis).
- There must be no stocks affected by government regulations and/or approvals.
- There must be no current news headlines that directly affect the stock.
- There must be no chance, in the near future, that the company will file bankruptcy.

If you apply all those rules, you'll find worthy stocks for your Watch List. You'll be armed with awareness of requirements that enable you to choose your stocks wisely and easily.

Adherence to the rule list results in two benefits. First, the criteria help filter out the high-risk, don't-chance-it stocks and stocks that don't perform well when day traded. Second, and most important, when you stick to such cautious selecting, you're ensuring your continued *consistency* in your current trading system. Think about it. If you constantly change your system of stock picking, then your trading style changes also, and I've previously established why change is not good.

After you look at the list, you might think to yourself, is that it? Where are the earnings per share (EPS), the growth rate, and other fundamentals?

Remember you're not an investor, you're a day trader, and that means you don't **hold** positions overnight. There's no need for you to embroil yourself in the concerns of long-term investors. All that you need to be focused on is what can affect the intraday price movement of your chosen stock.

Let's scrutinize all the criteria.

YOUR STOCK SHOULD HAVE AN AVERAGE DAILY VOLUME OF ONE MILLION SHARES OR MORE

The average daily volume (calculated over the past three months) must be at least 1 million shares traded daily. This is by far the most critical factor. *Make sure* that you study the past three months' average. If you only look at the daily volume, you're just getting a snapshot. The volume may have spiked for *only* that day.

You need to find stocks that have been consistently trading, meaning an average of a million or more shares in volume per day. You can simply look at a three-month chart, and make sure that the volume bars have consistently stayed above 1 million shares, for the entire course of that time span.

If they haven't, then forget it. Just put that stock out of your mind.

I don't care what cool new product the company has coming out, or what is being said about it in the *Wall Street Journal*. Forget about all that until the stock measures up to the requirements on the list. Consider this: if the company is so good, then why is the volume trading so low? Low volume means low interest. You want to be trading a stock that has high interest. Your stock should have at least 1 million shares trading *daily*, and this is because of *liquidity*. Liquidity is an indicator of trading activity, or trading interest. The more liquidity there is, the less are the chances that Market Makers will manipulate your trading activity.

Market Makers (MMs) are traders who buy and sell the majority of the shares on any given stock, on any given day. The best example of their price manipulations can be found in penny stocks. I can't begin to stress how risky things get when you expose yourself to penny-stock trading activity. Just think of the little bit of capital it takes to purchase penny-stock shares. A penny stock may have over a million shares traded, but if each share is only 20¢ then it takes just one MM $200,000 to control a million shares in volume for that day. This means there is very little liquidity. If you come in with your $5,000 capital trade, I can guarantee the MMs will counter your activity, and profit from your losses. This is why you see low-priced stocks (penny stocks and/or stocks priced under $10) fluctuating in intraday value from 25 percent to 100 percent, which is absolutely insane! This is the MMs muscling in and manipulating the price swings to their advantage.

So don't ever day trade penny stocks.

If you have a cartload of money to burn, then sure, by all means go crazy. Maybe 1 out of every 20 penny stocks pops. Then you'll certainly profit. But do you really want such slim chances? Do you want to virtually gamble?

In a nutshell I'd say just avoid low-volume stocks, and/or low-priced stocks with high volume. There's very little interest in the company. If Wall Street isn't trading those stocks in high volume, then you shouldn't be trading them, either—unless you're sure you know something that Wall Street hasn't caught wind of; in that case, all I can say to that is, good luck!

CHOOSE STOCKS BETWEEN $10 AND $100

The stock price must be between $10 and $100. A stock price above $10 usually indicates a company's good health, and tends to indicate healthy/high liquidity.

Most stocks that trade above $10 have a consistently proven track record. Unlike the lower-priced stocks, their price movement history is good; it shows they won't dramatically fluctuate. For example, you rarely have to worry that the stock might lose over 25 percent of its value in one day.

On the other hand, however, stocks priced over $100 tend to be highly volatile, and have more of a chance of retracing. Even when trading in 100-share blocks you can still be overexposed. I suggest that you don't day trade stocks priced over $100—not as an amateur.

Stocks in the $10 to $100 range tend to have consistent intraday patterns. You'll find that stocks priced at $10 to $30 will usually trade in a 50¢ range all day, and may fluctuate by 10¢ every 10 to 30 minutes. If you want a faster moving stock, try those priced at $50 to $100. Such higher-priced stocks usually trade in a $3 range all day, and intraday they tend to fluctuate by 50¢ in under a minute.

See Chapter 19, "Trading for Skill versus Trading for Income," for a more in-depth discussion on how to treat differently priced stocks. For now, just remember this: Don't add stocks to your Watch List that are priced under $10 or over $100.

PICK STOCKS THAT DISPLAY TRADABLE INTRADAY PRICE SWINGS

The average intraday price swings must be sufficient to trade (as evidenced by chart analysis). You have to make sure that you spend enough time studying the intraday chart patterns. You need data feeds that access historical data, for example, the view of a five-minute chart dating back at least three days.

With regard to a stock in question, your goal is to determine whether the intraday price swings are consistently fluctuating. You want the price to be bouncing off the intraday support levels and resistance levels. You want your stock to have lots of intraday price movement. A bad stock will exhibit an intraday pattern of barely discernible activity. A bad chart pattern will exhibit sideways price action all day.

You don't want to get yourself too bogged down by this single criterion, however, so keep it all simple and short: just stay away from stocks that show intraday patterns that resemble a heart patient flat-lining. Always keep in mind that you can't make any money if the stock doesn't bounce intraday.

The stock price in Figure 14.1 stays within a tight three-dollar range over a three-day period. The price is constantly fluctuating, and bouncing off support and resistance levels.

DON'T TRADE STOCKS AFFECTED BY STRICT FEDERAL REGULATIONS

You do not want to trade stocks that can be directly affected by government regulations.

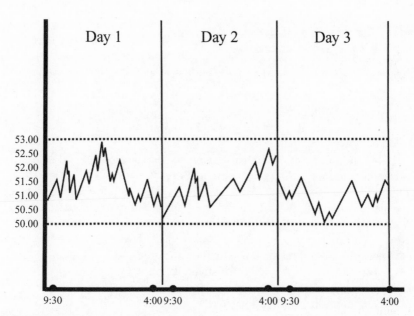

FIGURE 14.1 Intraday 5-Minute Chart

Biotech stocks and pharmaceutical stocks exemplify this bad category. You don't want to be trading a stock when the company is subject to strict regulations that drastically affect their sales. A perfect example is the drawback of U.S. Food and Drug Administration (FDA) approval requirements. Biotech companies must secure that consent before they can launch a new product.

If you're trading a stock and, on that same day the FDA decides more testing is needed and postpones a product's approval, then I guarantee the stock price will plummet so fast that your eyes will instantly cross.

You want to search for companies that sell stable consumer products, such as:

- Retailers like Wall-Mart (WMT) and Amazon.com (AMZN)
- Beverages stocks like Pepsi (PEP) and Budweiser (BUD)
- Tech stocks like Qualcomm (QCOM) and Microsoft (MSFT)

Another situation to dodge is the mergers. Companies that are merging are difficult to day trade. During the merging process, there's choppy volatility and/or sideways price action. Mergers usually have to jump through several political regulatory hoops before they can close the final deal. You don't want to get caught up in that.

BEWARE OF STOCKS DIRECTLY AFFECTED BY CURRENT NEWS HEADLINES

There must be no current news headlines that directly affect the stock.

How do you find out about this? You do good, old-fashioned research. You can learn a lot about your stocks by reading through the news headlines. The less news, the better, trust me.

In the next chapter, "Why News Can Be Just Noise," you will see how distracting and misleading news can be. I'm not saying all news is bad; I'm making the point that too much news can create a cloud of uncertainty.

Uncertainty usually leads to the foggy straits of choppy volatility.

So how do you decipher the news? You read through each headline, if any, on a stock you're thinking of choosing. If you notice that several headlines discuss relevant dates to the stock that aren't earnings dates, then avoid that stock for now. Most likely, until crucial news dates are reached, that stock will be unpredictable. You eliminate that headache by *not*, for the moment, adding it to your Watch List.

If you have a stock that you've been comfortable with trading but it gets into the headlines because of upcoming events, then beware. If you feel you must trade that stock—if you simply can't resist the temptation—then at least be restrained from trading that stock on the day of the announcement and the day just before it. You *do not* want to be in a trade just before the anticipated news hits the wire. You're gambling, not day trading, if you think you can predict how the stock price will react to the news.

There must be no chance, in the near future, that the company will file bankruptcy.

Duh!

Who would invest in a company that has filed or is going to file bankruptcy? The answer may surprise you.

Some daredevil day traders (gamblers) only trade companies under reconstruction. Those same traders usually seek companies that have stock values less then $1 per share. They're trading penny stocks, and I've shown how that's crazy-risky.

Their reasoning isn't quite crazy, but I would call it naïve: they figure they can buy those stocks cheaply and then **hold**. They're anticipating, with extreme optimism, that the reconstruction period will turn out positive. Here we go again. Always remember we're day traders, and we *never **hold** overnight*. Do you really want to be trading a stock that's likely to lose 50 percent or more of its stock value overnight or intraday? Of course not!

Stay away from any stock you've found that is even considering bankruptcy.

Now that you have a reliable stock selection system, you can begin the initial day-trading process. I suggest that you try to find 15 stocks in three different price ranges: 5 from $10 to $30, 5 from $30 to $50, and 5 from $50 to $100. Once you have that Watch List, you can begin to monitor everything on it, and eventually to trade each stock.

Reminder: Do *not* start trading the stocks you've found until you've read this whole book.

 RULES TO REMEMBER

- Even with a good stock to trade, never lower your guard and/or trade in larger share blocks.
- Find stocks that have been trading consistently, over a three-month period, above 1 million shares in volume per day, on average.
- Never trade penny stocks.
- Only add stocks to your Watch List that are priced in the $10 to $100 range.
- Stay away from charts that exhibit intraday flat patterns.
- Don't trade stocks whose companies are dependent on regulations that can drastically affect their product sales.
- Don't be in a trade just before anticipated news hits the wire about it.
- Stay away from any stock that is even considering bankruptcy.
- Read this whole book before you trade stocks you've found.

CHAPTER 15

Why News Can Be Just Noise

As day traders, we *only* need information that *directly* affects the stock that we're trading *intraday*. Here's something else that should go on a big sign:

If Intraday News Is Directly Affecting a Stock ... Stop Trading It!

It's easy to keep an anxious ear on the news that impacts your stock. The tricky part is to know when to listen, and also when *not* to listen. Certain types of news can drastically interfere with the intraday price action, including premarket and after-market action. That's news worth hearing.

The following news items, if related to your stocks, are broadcasts you must keep abreast of:

- Earnings announcements
- Fed interest rate cuts/hikes
- Core product issues
- Merger talks
- Class action lawsuits
- Bankruptcy announcements
- Employee strike threats
- CEO resignations
- Governmental interventions
- Chief competitor advancements

If you fail to get the initial scoop on events like those listed above, then you won't be prepared for the rollercoaster ride that's likely to immediately follow. *Beware!* Most of those items will hit the news wire without any prior warning. If you don't know that they've just transpired, you'll likely get hit with the worst kind volatility, the unexpected kind, right in the middle of a trading session.

Conversely, however, you should totally ignore certain buzzing. Too much buzz about your stock can seriously mar your daily rhythm, and can negatively influence your decision-making process. When it comes to intraday price movement, most of the talking you hear about your stock will not directly affect it.

Maybe you'll be caught up in trading a stock, and a discussion on the relevant company comes at you over the airwaves. It turns out it's a couple of opinionated analysts, debating the firm's future growth.

Depending on what you absorb from their talk, you may feel persuaded to trade either more, or less. Well, because of this buzz that has nothing to do with the intraday price swings, you've just broken your intraday consistency and rhythm.

The skill of news filtering is hard to master. As an amateur you're very impressionable, and you may lack focus. You need to learn which news will hurt you in a trading situation, and which news is dispensable, just noise.

I almost never listen to analysts' recommendations. Remember, we're not investing. It's not for us day traders to care what price the stock may or not be worth, three months down the road.

On the other hand, you should memorize the list I provided at the beginning of this chapter. These are critical news announcements that directly and immediately affect your stock. Most likely the stocks you're trading won't get rocked around by those issues, at least not on a daily basis. (If they do, then you've chosen some bad stocks. Stocks that are constantly affected by the news should not be on your Watch List. Refer to Chapter 14, "Stock Picking," if you need to refresher on that concept.)

A great example of a stock that should not have been day traded was Washington Mutual (WM), during the months leading up to its liquidation buyout by JPMorgan in late 2008. Almost every day there was news debating the bank's fate. The stock exhibited extreme volatility every time analyst predictions hit the wire, especially when Merrill Lynch and JPMorgan analysts spoke.

If you were trying to predict how the stock would trade in such a noisy and uncertain environment, then you most likely were going crazy trying to trade this stock intraday.

Why do that to yourself? Why are you so attached to one particular stock?

There are thousands of stocks you can choose to intraday trade. All I am expressing here is the importance of not trading a stock if it is reacting to news and announcements on an intraday basis.

Simply trade stocks that have low news-related profiles.

TRADING ON NEWS VERSUS MONITORING NEWS

Even if you've chosen some great stocks to day trade, you should not try to trade on the news; rather you should remain aware of any new and relevant news that hits the wire. You don't want to be in a trade when bad news is released.

There are a couple of ways you can do this. I'm always tuned in to CNBC Business News Channel, which is always broadcasting on a nearby TV as I trade. I have to warn you, however, that CNBC announces important news a few minutes after Wall Street gets it, so it's a good idea to gain access to what Wall Street uses for news wires. I've found that most real-time news feeds, like Market Wire, are as fast and efficient as it gets.

Unless you have chummy relations with relevant company public relations directors, then you need to subscribe to direct access news. Once you gain access you can customize the feed so you only get information that's germane to your stock.

While most of the news on the list I've provided involves items you don't often hear of, the one that you need to be constantly on the watch for is earnings announcement dates. Those dates are always preannounced. You need to have them logged and noted. Since company earnings are released each business quarter, you can easily find out when they are. Simply go to Yahoo Finance. Click "News," then click the "U.S Earnings" tab, and type in your stock symbols. You can only get an exact date once each business quarter. You should know this date like your own birth date. Mark it on your calendar, plan around it, and make another sign to tack up:

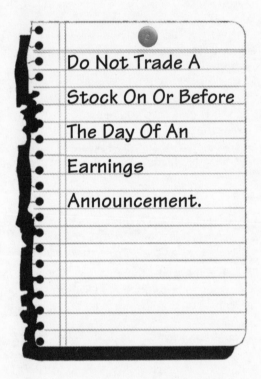

Do Not Trade A Stock On Or Before The Day Of An Earnings Announcement.

Those are the two dates that I can guarantee will be extremely difficult days to trade that stock. You'll see unusual volume and price movement. You can expect the unexpected as well as high volatility. You should not attempt to ride this roller-coaster. Take a break from that stock for a couple of days. You should have other stocks to trade, on or before that date. Besides, when you're on the sidelines, you have a better opportunity to wait for a major gap-up or gap-down.

Now let's return to those other announcements on the list. They're rare, but when they do happen, you won't be able to plan for them. If the news hits the wire midday and it's immediately affecting the stock price, you should just stop trading that stock. Get out of your position quickly; take a loss if you have to. The price could drop 10 times faster then you're used to, and it could do that in seconds. As you would with the earnings announcements, avoid that ugly scene by trading other stocks for the remainder of the day.

Trading on news is very risky and unpredictable. But it's dangerously easy for an amateur to perceive the news as a leading indicator for stock price predictions. If an analyst announces, quite officially and with pomp, that he thinks the price target will reach X amount of dollars, then the amateur might be persuaded to trade in that direction.

Don't.

You should perceive the news as a tool, not an indicator. Then you'll understand that it's a mistake to trade on news. Your stock charts are indicators of where the stock is heading, and the news should only be heeded when it's the type of information that will *clearly* interfere, *intraday*.

Having access to the news is a very useful tool, but remember that it is only a tool. When an earnings announcement gets released by the wire, you should know that within seconds, the charts will go crazy. Other than that and the other items listed, you should ignore all the buzzing and spinning that's part of the endless, cacophonous babble.

 RULES TO REMEMBER

- Know which news will hurt your trade, and which news is just noise.
- Always know your stock's earnings announcement dates.
- Do not trade a stock on or before the day of an earnings announcement.
- If the news hits the wire midday and it's immediately affecting the price of your stock, stop trading that stock for that day.

PART IV

The Truth about Training and Preparation

One purpose of Part Four is to help the beginner choose a training program commensurate with his skill level. I discuss both the benefits and the shortcomings of those programs.

My ultimate goal is to have you understand that after you attend a training seminar, you have a lot more to learn. I emphasize the importance of not expecting a lot. But this part is not only for the beginner: I also advise the more experienced amateur on the helpful paths he can take that won't be redundant, and will build expertise.

Furthermore, in Part Four you will find eye-opening information regarding the differences between pay-per-trade firms and pay-per-share firms. You will also find that Chapter 18, "Paper-Trading Strategies," and Chapter 19, "Trading for Skill versus Trading for Income," offer great learning techniques.

CHAPTER 16

About Those Training Programs

D uring my amateur day-trading years, I was finishing my education at San Diego State. I left, both relieved and exhausted, in possession of a Bachelor of Science degree in Business Marketing. Right next to my collection of textbooks from school, I was building a personal library on day trading. When asked what I wanted for my birthday or Christmas, I requested more titles on the subject.

During that time I also attended several day-trading training seminars.

Everywhere I went, I sought day-trading knowledge. The subject soon came up with anyone I talked to.

I noticed that professional mentors were scarce. I did have a couple of contacts who worked in the stock brokerage industry. Though they themselves didn't day trade, their advice armed and inspired me with a greater understanding of the stock market.

As I struggled past the hazardous amateur phase, I came to see that I learned the most from my actual experience in day trading, and also from those advisors. The day-trading programs and college business courses did teach me good strategies and trading styles, but it was clear that the *real* education was hands-on, when I performed with real money.

Now, please don't get me wrong here. I'm not suggesting that you shouldn't attend any training programs, courses, or seminars—especially if you're a beginner. Amateurs need structured guidance, and that's what such tutoring offers. I feel I must warn you, however, that *consistent* gains come *only* with *experience*.

With that said, I'll now express my opinions of those training programs. There are basically two kinds. There are seminars out there for the greenhorns, and there are quasi-mentorships for the in-between guys, the traders with somewhat more experience, who aren't yet in the major league. I'll start with some thoughts on the outfits designed to instruct and equip the beginners.

SEMINARS FOR THE GREENHORNS

The first thing to consider is the eyebrow-raising tuition, and then what you're going to get for it. Day-trading seminars want your money upfront. After they take it and train you, you're totally on your own. They don't hire you after the program. They don't offer you a position on their trading floor; they don't even have a real trading floor. They also don't have their own trading platforms (proprietary software). For a profit they pump you with strategies and trading knowledge, and then they throw you to the wolves.

If afterward, you fail miserably, that's no sweat for them. They will lose nothing if you do, and they could care less how you end up. Show me a program that will reimburse your fees if you subsequently lose everything, and I'll take my shirt off and eat it.

But you, the beginner, need guidance from somewhere, so that's where you'll likely have to start. The lucky alternative is having a friend who's also a professional day trader, patient as a saint with your greenness, and happy to show you the ropes for a song.

You're probably bereft of that blessing. Many newcomers are. So you'll be forced to seek programs-for-profit.

The key to reaping rewards from those outfits is to hold back your money and ask cautious questions, like whether they teach during market hours. That way, if you decide to sign up, you'll witness their trading system truly put to the test, working in market time. Also: you want to pick programs with coaches who are active day traders themselves. You don't want to be taking instruction from someone who doesn't day trade. Never sign up unless you can prove that they definitely are, and do. At the end of this discussion you'll find a detailed list of helpful questions to ask.

When I was getting started, I took part in a few of those training programs. Soon the pros and cons of it all were starkly evident. Here are some essentials to consider:

Pros

- You're introduced to proprietary trading methods, in a compellingly structured environment.

- A trained staff answers all your questions.
- You get a little hands-on experience, usually some actual trading, during market hours.

Cons

- This is usually very expensive, ranging from $1,000 to $7,000, with absolutely no guarantees.
- The training is usually limited to just one week or less.
- These programs *do not* teach you how to trade with *pay-per-share* brokers.

On the surface, the pros look really good. You're getting some practical training. They teach you how to trade with their system. They show you how to read chart patterns. They cram your brain with information that only Wall Street uses. And yes, you're exposed to several *professional* trading strategies.

Also: most programs limit their class size. They usually have at least two instructors (though not always professional day traders) working with groups of ten to twenty. You feel like you're getting some personalized attention, and to a certain extent, you are; that's one of their selling points.

As I mentioned, most of those programs incorporate some actual trading in their class time. During the first couple of days, they show you how to use their system. After you've learned it, you apply it. Usually they have you pick a stock in accordance with their system, and then you paper-trade the market, or trade on their demo software, using monopoly money.

They look over your shoulder, and they guide you. They effectively ensure that you, their protégé, are applying their system correctly.

So far, that all sounds great!

But now let's discuss the cons.

Well, first there's the obvious negative: those fees. If the cost of those programs is overwhelming, you should hold off until you can handle it. The value you'll get for your sacrifice isn't worth going into hock over.

When you do reach a point where you can throw them some money, or wallop a credit card, then check things out, tread very carefully, and understand all the limits. This is an investment, like college, and it's crucial to choose the right one. The cost is very comparable to state university fees.

You might think, the fee's really worth it, because what you'll learn will make you *big* profits really *soon*. Didn't the sales rep imply that? Didn't he practically *promise?*

But he didn't offer a guarantee, did he?

Now take a look at that time frame. You're supposed to pay through the nose, stay for just a few classes, and walk out of there a pro. You're going to make back the thousands you paid in days, or just a few weeks.

Yeah, right.

You have to become an *experienced* trader to make that much that fast. Remember Chapter 4, "From Impatience to Cool, Calm, and Collected." If you're a beginner, reread it. Revisit my tales of the blunders that keep new guys' gains very small (and that's if they gain at all).

It might take you an entire year to make back the training fee. Or else you just might lose so much, it's like the fee got quadrupled. So here's the most urgent of all my advice: after you walk out of that seminar, keep expectations *low*. That's a reminder of everything I warn about, back there in the first section.

And now for the last con I listed, which is by far not the least: Most training programs completely leave out instruction on pay-per-share trading. I have a problem with that.

In the following chapter you're going to learn that it's much better for a day trader to be charged a commission based on pay-per-share, *not* pay-per-trade. That's because a pro day trader places several executions per day, and he needs to avoid falling into the quagmire of the much, much higher commissions he's charged when he's doing pay-per-trade.

I suspect there's an ulterior motive behind the omission by most training programs of instructions on trading pay-per-share. I suspect it has something to do with the fact that a lot of the training programs have made special deals with the prominent pay-per-trade brokers.

Here's an example. One of the programs I attended is featured in a well-known trading academy with satellites all over the world. A steady flow of new day traders completes their program everywhere, daily.

During our class instruction, we were required to use a prominent on-line broker with a pay-per-trade commission structure. At the end of the program we were offered this seemingly awesome deal: if we day traded through this broker, then for our first 1,000 trades, we would only have to pay $5 on every $10 trade. That was a discount of $5 per trade, a savings of $5,000 after 1,000 trades.

That would virtually pay for the training! Sounds like a great offer, right?

I never took them up on it. I knew about the better alternative, pay-per-share. I knew about the high commissions imposed in pay-per-trade situations, and I knew that those commissions are much, much less when working with brokers who offer pay-per-share. I knew pay-per-share is the way to go when trading several times daily.

I thought about the newly-trained amateurs who are easily impressed by that so-called discount. I began to get a fix on what *shady practice* means. I realized the seminars are businesses, out for profit like everyone else, but when they deliberately omit information—like the pay-per-share option that saves day traders big money—that made my blood start to boil. The boil started rolling when I considered the fact that day traders are never required to have any certification or proof of high skills, yet pay-per-trade brokers will take all our money without any questions asked.

That alone made me skeptical, especially when I also considered the fact that pay-per-share brokers require some experience in the day traders they take on.

To be fair, some training programs skip pay-per-share info *not* to net beginners into pay-per-trade commissions, but simply because the pay-per-share brokers don't want to deal with the amateurs. Just the same, however, I feel seminar coaches should inform clueless greenhorns about the drastically lower commission fees in pay-per-share day trading.

Then I'll be less suspicious.

So pick your training program, by all means, sign yourself up ... but go there with your eyes wide open. Don't become just a cracked, muddied cog in the wheel of those corporate deals that just use you.

And now I'll turn my attention to the day trader getting past the neophyte stage.

TRAINING PROGRAMS FOR THE MORE EXPERIENCED TRADER

If you've been day trading long enough to have an advanced trading style, then no one will call you a beginner. It may be just as true, however, that you're not yet professional. You may need additional training, and that's where things can get tricky. You've got to make sure that the program you pick is one that exceeds your knowledge. You've got to take care to match what it offers to precisely your *current* needs.

I can illustrate just how important that is by admitting to a costly mistake I once made. About five years into my trading career, I attended my second training program. It turned out to be a total waste of time. It was $5,000 down the drain! Why? I was much more advanced than I thought I was. The program lasted five days. Every day I heard info and strategies that I already knew.

Imagine how cheated I felt. Imagine how cheated I *was*.

What can *you* do to avoid that?

You can circumvent a disaster like that by gauging the depth of your skill. To review that critical subject, reread Chapter 1, "Truths about Yourself to Know First."

And if you do, then what? You're actively trading every day, you've been doing so for some time, your knowledge exceeds the trainers', yet you feel that you still need some coaching.

What you're ready for is a mentorship program. Such learning is for day traders who would never get a headache while trying to keep up with a pro, and wouldn't be wasting the time of that pro with the questions of a beginner.

A mentor is a professional day trader, who trades actively every day. You could benefit greatly from working with that person—while he trades with his real money.

For you, the experienced day trader, anything else is just fluff.

Mentoring is where pay-per-share brokerage firms shine. Most of those firms have their own trading floor. You can trade on their floor for free, provided you pay per-share. While there, you're exposed to veteran traders, and many of them are natural mentors.

And many of the pay-per-share firms actually offer an in-house classroom. They usually charge nothing for it, and you're learning some valuable info. They want to make you savvy and sharp, a profiting team member that *they* profit from. The better you trade, the more money they make. You're their investment, so they educate you, and at absolutely no cost to you. It's a win-win situation.

If you think that you're ready to day trade like a pro and talk to a pay-per-share brokerage, and if they agree with your opinion that you're no longer green, they'll offer you a probationary training period. This usually involves trading for one or two weeks on their demo software. They'll evaluate your performance and natural trading style. They'll expect you to be consistent and lucrative. If you're not, they'll let you go. They'll pat you on the back and advise you to return after you've gained more experience.

That's why, in spite of the flaws and the scams, I wouldn't advise the beginner to avoid pricey training programs. Again, you have to start somewhere.

Are you getting a sense of a hit-or-miss minefield, in this risky business of training? The potential to lose money or waste it, or else waste your precious time, is tremendous. You should be feeling very wary.

TIPS FOR SELECTING THE RIGHT PROGRAM

In an attempt to help you circumvent those scary possibilities, I've put together a list of questions to ask the purveyors of trainings, before you commit to go. Whether you're a beginner or experienced, getting answers to these queries should help you decide where you fit.

First of all: When researching training programs, make sure that you speak with an actual instructor—not just the sales rep who wants to gouge your card. If you can't get through to a teacher, forget it. If you can, then explain your trading experience, and expect him to patiently listen to every minute detail. Ask how the program can advance your trading style, or how the program *cannot*. Drill him as if you know more than he does. You might just find out that you do.

The Before Questions

- Will I learn about pay-per-share brokers?
- Do the coaches have active day trading experience? If they do, then how much experience?
- What's the coach-trainee ratio?
- What trading software is used?
- Describe the trading stations. How many screens at each station?
- Will there be real-time trading during classes?
- What percentage of the training is live trading?
- Does the program have a large emphasis on risk management? If so, how is it applied?
- How much hands-on mentorship is included in program?
- Why is this program so expensive? (Mention cheaper ones, if you know of any.)
- If I bring a list of questions, how much time will I have to get and discuss the answers?
- Are there any reimbursements or guarantees? (Ask this just to watch their response.)
- Can I use my tuition money to trade your system with? If I lose I don't pay? (Again, ask this just to watch their response.)

I also have a list of "after" questions—concerns you should demand to get answers to after they've taken your money. It's your hard-earned cash or credit that you just dished out to them, so maximize your learning experience with an arsenal of queries like these:

The After Questions

- If it hasn't yet been volunteered, ask for information about pay-per-share brokers.
- Ask the instructor to elaborate on his or her experience.
- Ask how much the instructor is losing that day by teaching instead of trading.
- Ask to be shown how he or she personally trades.

And don't stop with my questions. Make up a list of your own. Bring up the concerns that have been teasing your mind throughout your day trading experience. You should have a ton of questions related to trading scenarios. The more questions the better.

At some point during the program they'll have you apply their system. You'll hunch over a trade station, probably a computer with only one small, flat screen, and that's when you should get a taste of mentorship. Someone should be monitoring your trading activity and giving you structured guidance. This is when you're closest to getting your money's worth.

Whenever I've attended a training seminar, I've been seated at a computer and trading with their demo software, which is basically paper trading. It's always been my habit to grab an instructor and practically force him to stay with me for just as long as I need him. I've noticed how most of the other participants just silently sit at their computer stations all day, trying to trade the new system on their own.

I was just as able to use the new system. It's just that I had a lot of questions prepared, and I wanted them answered while I was actually trading. I suggest that you do the same. Don't feel like you're hogging the coach. If you sense that you're taking too much of his time, then stop right there and go to the administration office or sales rep, and frankly explain your concerns. You just paid a lot of money for this, and you have every right to ask questions, even if it's eating up class time. Make the point that understaffing is certainly not your fault.

Finally, don't view the training program as a place to go and be shown how to day trade from scratch. Even if you're an amateur, you should already know the basics. Don't go there just to take notes. Know enough to get involved in class discussions. Get your money's worth.

Once you leave the program you're completely on your own. You may have befriended a few students in the class, but you're basically just a lone wolf.

In this chapter on training and preparation, there's one last issue to address. Many pay-per-share firms require their day traders to obtain a Series 7 license. These firms are aware that the Securities and Exchange Commission (SEC) may soon enforce the licensure in all new pay-per-share traders.

Your standard day trading academy or seminar won't instruct you in how to pass the licensure test. I strongly suggest that you instruct yourself in it. It's important to recognize that day trading is a profession, and the higher up the chain you go, the more rigorous are the requirements.

It costs about $300 for the Series 7 license study materials. I suggest that when you budget for an expensive day trading course, you also put some money aside for that.

RULES TO REMEMBER

- If you're a beginner day trader, go for some form of structured training.
- Go to training programs armed with questions.
- Don't expect to be a pro upon completion of any short-term program.
- Insist upon information about pay-per-per share brokers.
- If you're an advanced beginner, seek out mentorship programs.

CHAPTER 17

Picking the Right Online Broker

Pay-per-Share versus Pay-per-Trade

There are two types of day-trading options: pay-per-trade and pay-per-share. The one that's right for you depends on how often you trade, and also on your level of experience, and the amount of your trading capital.

If you plan to be a professional day trader, meaning you want to do multiple round-trip daily trades and you'll never **hold** overnight—then sooner or later you'll want to escape the high pay-per-trade commissions. For serious day traders who are in for the long haul, the way to go is pay-per-share brokers.

I have to confess, however, that along with the alternative, I do keep a pay-per-trade account. I've found that the pay-per-trade brokerages are useful for certain things, even for a pro. Traditional online brokers offer crucial stock research tools. They can boast great platforms to trade on, and they impress with slews of incentives, like ATM cards, free checks, and free data feeds. For all of those reasons the pay-per-trade brokers are the place where a greenhorn should start. They facilitate a beginner's transactions. They provide great customer service. They offer the market data that's needed to build a newcomer's skills.

STARTING OUT WITH PAY-PER-TRADE

Here's the most important reason to get your feet wet with pay-per-trade: when you're beginning they'll only let you trade with your actual capital amount. The minimum capital required is usually only $500. That policy effectively diminishes your exposure to perilous market risk.

Think about it. At a pay-per-share firm, usually you're required to open an account with at least $25,000. The leverage you're given may be as much as a whopping 20 to 1. In buying power, that equates to $500,000.

As an amateur, imagine how much trouble you could get into!

Pay-per-trade brokers don't let that happen, and that's all well and good, but remember: I mentioned high commissions. With pay-per-trade brokers you're paying roughly $8 to $10 per trade. That's $16 to $20 per round-trip trade. That's prohibitive!

And it gets worse.

As a beginner I exclusively used a traditional pay-per-trade broker. Everything was fine until I established myself. When I traded more than four round-trip trades in a five-day rolling period (any string of five days in a row), I got sprung from normal trader status to "pattern day trader."

At first I felt good, as if I'd gotten promoted. Then I discovered the baggage. I'd gotten strapped with a bunch of new rules. To maintain my "pattern trader" standing, my account became required *at all times* to have at least $25,000. The good news was the 4-to-1 margin I'd earned, meaning now my buying power was four times more than my balance. That was cool, but then came the kicker: whenever I fell below the $25,000 minimum, my account went into an "equity call." My trading privileges got severely curtailed. I had lost the 4-to-1 margin, and that was painful enough, but here's where things got outrageous: before I could purchase another trade, I had to wait three days for each trade to clear!

Meaning, until I could deposit more money, I was basically unemployed. And if I had nothing to deposit, well, suddenly life really sucked.

I've just gotten started and already you can see that there are mind-boggling advantages and disadvantages to both of the day trading options. I look back and realize how careful I must be in advising a beginner on which type of broker to start with, and especially for *how long*.

Put succinctly, new traders should start with pay-per-trade, and stay there until they get busy, and then they should move to pay-per-share once they decide to start trading full time.

TRANSITIONING TO PAY-PER-SHARE

Pay-per-share brokers have drastically lower commissions, and that will make you want to jump in—but whoa. Take a closer look at this water. It's swirling with hungry sharks. Pay-per-share brokers are generous with your leverage to an extremely dangerous degree. As I've mentioned, they'll leverage your $25,000 minimum to as much as 20-to-1. They'll provide you with a training-probation period, but it's likely to be only a month, and right away they'll probably offer you a leverage of at least 10-to-1. That means they'll be letting you have $250,000 buying power against your $25,000. That's pretty scary stuff.

And then, when you prove to be consistent and profitable, they'll bump your leverage higher. I've seen 20-to-1. For instance, a $25,000 minimum can result in a 20-to-1 leverage maximum. If you add more to your account, the leverage will increase. Usually a $100,000 balance will allot you $2 million in buying power, or a 20-to-1 leverage. Each pay-per-share firm has different policies on leverage allocation.

One good thing about those hazardous straits is that if you have a bad day, you're not made to walk the plank. Well, at least not all the way. If you fall below your minimum requirement, you're not in a bind like it goes with pay-per-trade. With the pay-per-share brokers, there's wiggle room. You can lessen your leverage a tad. Depending on your skill level and your rapport with the risk managers, your minimum account value will vary. For example, suppose you start your account with $25,000, and you're given the normal trial leverage, 10-to-1. If you lose, let's say $5,000, then unlike with pay-per-trade-brokers, you can still trade with what remains. Your leverage will be lowered; you can expect to lose half of your leverage until you've returned to the $25,000 minimum; but at least you're still day trading, there's no immediate equity-call.

And now I'll get on to the hassles of the pay-per-share trading scenario. I'll start with the minor ones.

Pay-per-share brokers tend to be independently owned firms with limited customer service and banking capabilities. Most likely you'll *not* be provided with an ATM card or personal checks. In order to make withdrawals, you'll have to request wire transfers or certified checks. It's a bit of a pain, but the people you work for are likely to make it worthwhile. If you need cash today, they'll probably cover you, even though the pay structure is usually biweekly. These firms aren't big banks with fancy bells and whistles, but they will cover your needs.

After a day of trading, I used to walk around the corner with the principle owner of my pay-per-share brokerage, heading for a bank near Wall Street. We chatted in line while we waited for him to withdraw some cash for me.

I think such rapport, with a real human being, with the New York Stock Exchange (NYSE) in the background, is considerably more inspiring than the impersonal perks of the pay-per-trade giants online.

But now I'll describe the *big* hassle. I didn't start using a pay-per-share broker until after eight years with a pay-per-trade Goliath. For two of those years I was a "pattern day trader," putting up with the terrible penalties. I hadn't yet learned about pay-per-share brokerages that give you those 20-to-1 leverages; most of those firms are in major northern cities.

I, of course, lived in paradise.

Why would I even consider looking over the fence at those winters?

Well, one day I did about 36 round-trip trades. My fees, of course, were insane: $9.99 per trade, with 36 to buy and 36 to sell. By the closing bell I had $540 in profit, which should have been an okay day, but when I included my cost to trade—$720—my profit of $540 became a loss of $180!

I decided that from that day forward, I'd search for pay-per-trade brokers with lower fees per trade.

Then I found out there's no such thing.

Things began to feel pretty dismal. I desperately needed to find a cheaper way to trade, or else I'd be forced to limit myself to only a few trades a day.

Only a few trades a day?

Yeah, right. Ask a Wall Street day trader to do that, and he'll tell you to go take your meds. So I searched for another kind of broker. I went online and found scads of such companies in New York City (of course). That's where I discovered pay-per-share. And that's when I was forced to acknowledge that a switch to pay-per-share might cost me *miles*. About 3,000 miles.

I might have to move to New York.

Most pay-per-share brokers are called proprietary equity trading firms. They have their own trading floors, complete with trading desks, and if you're a beginner at pay-per-share, then they want you right there, at those desks.

I got interested in a firm near Wall Street. I assumed that they wouldn't consider me until I'd traded with their demo software for a probationary period. I figured they'd probably require me to have a Series 7 brokers license, which I did not yet have.

It turned out I was wrong. They were willing to allow me to download their software and trade with them from home, but only with a painfully limited leverage, designed for remote beginners. What they really wanted to do with me was literally watch over my shoulders. I quickly realized that what I needed to do was pack myself up and just *go*.

I won't belabor the inevitable miseries that happened to me next: the anguish of tearing away from the gorgeous, sunny West Coast, leaving lots of people I loved, and also a lot of my belongings. But log this and note it, because you might move, too—if you're serious about day trading, you may have to.

I got to Manhattan and went through the rigors of finding a cubbyhole to live in. Then overnight, I became a New Yorker. God, that process is fast.

Each morning at dawn I showered, shaved, pulled on some warm winter clothes, and joined the subway-crushed rush-hour masses to get to the firm's trading floor. I had sacrificed working at home in my shorts, but I had also ditched the high pay-per-trade commissions, and I soon found myself enjoying the privilege of notably high leverages to work with.

Pay-per-share brokers do charge you a monthly fee, and, depending on what data feeds you require, it comes to $150 to $250. That plus their daily pay-per-share fees may sound like quite a lot, but compare it to the pay-per-trade commissions, and it starts to look like nickels and dimes.

The average per-share cost is between $.0035 and $.0065. That means that if you buy 100 shares of any given stock, you pay only 35¢ to 65¢ cents for that 100-block execution, not $9.99 like with online pay-per-trade fees.

So you can imagine how happy I was with the dramatic fee decrease. If I traded 30 round-trip trades (60 executions) with 100 share-blocks, then my commissions for that day were roughly $30 to $35 (30 round-trip trades of a hundred shares: 60 × 100 = 6,000 shares—6,000 × $.0055 = $33). That same trading day with a pay-per-trade broker would have cost me $600 (60 trades × $9.99)!

So okay, now maybe you're wondering: *What if I wanted to purchase 20,000 shares in one trade?*

That's an excellent question, and the answer is frightening.

With a pay-per-trade broker that would cost you only $9.99, but with a per-share broker it would cost you $110 (20,000 × $.0055 per share). Yeah, that's not a misprint.

The point here is that you should *never* purchase more than 500-share blocks at a time, unless you're a whale trader (professional day trader). To refresh on this critical issue, reread Chapter 7, "Why Overexposure to the Market Can Hurt." That's where I elaborate the danger of purchasing huge share blocks.

As I write this, I remain in New York. Eventually I'll move back to California. I plan on creating my own trading group, back in my beloved San Diego.

Regardless of where I want to live, however, or for that matter where you want to live, I believe that any new trader should come to New York for a while. You should stay for at least a month or two, to thoroughly learn a pay-per-share system, as well as its trading platforms. Later on, when the firm feels you're ready and will give you high leverages remotely, then you can move anywhere in the world and trade with that firm from a distance. The fees and direct access will remain the same, no matter where you are.

But now let's get back to the risks. It's very important to *not* take full advantage of the insanely generous leverage opportunities that pay-per-share brokers offer. Make no mistake here, be certain they will, and it's up to you to decline them.

As it goes with any business, their priority is profit, and it's all off your trading volume (in shares). So when you've moved past beginner status, they'll offer you tons of buying power. The more leverage you have, the more you will trade. They need you to trade a lot.

HIGH LEVERAGE PROS AND CONS

When I first started day trading at my Manhattan firm, they offered me a 20-to-1 leverage. I was naïve, and I took it. I had opened an account with the required minimum of $25,000, so that meant I had $500,000 of intraday buying power.

Going for that much was a huge mistake. I wasn't accustomed to that much buying power, and let's emphasize the word *power*. It was very hard for me to resist using all that leverage, so I placed some really large trades.

My first week of trading with a 20-to-1 leverage was a roller-coaster ride. One day I would make $3,800 and the next I would lose $4200. In some cases the profits and/or losses were only from one trade. It didn't take me long to see that I had to limit my exposure.

I was purchasing 100-share blocks just like always, but then I would also string-trade. That means I would buy 100, then 100 more, then 100 more, and so on. I would do this until I reached my buying power limit. Then, when the trade went against me ... *ouch!* I had accumulated 5000 shares of a $100 per/share stock ($500,000 worth of equities). I knew I was much too overexposed to the uncertainty of the stock swings.

Don't ever end up there. Avoid being unsure of where things are headed, and at the same time, having too many shares. The way to go is self-limitation. Take only a 10-to-1 leverage until you can handle more. Eventually I figured out what I could handle. When 100 shares moves $1.00 in stock price, I gain or lose only $100. I can take that kind of pressure because the risk isn't bad.

Accordingly, you should know your comfort zone, and never deviate from it. See Chapter 13, "Trading Consistently All Day."

If you're given a lot of leverage, and throughout the day you spread your money over a wide range of trades, you're okay if one goes against you. For instance, if you purchase 500 shares divided among five stocks, and one bellies up, that's no problem. Once you start getting in rhythm with your stocks you can start buying 200-share blocks at a time ... but don't get ahead of yourself. I will soon be discussing this in greater detail in the Chapter 19, "Trading for Skill versus Trading for Income."

The harshest downside of leverage is when an amateur with no established system falls victim to his own temptation to put all his buying power on the line and buy just *one* security and will **hold** it. I've seen beginners come onto the floor and lose all $25,000 of their start-up cash, all on the very first day. They take the 20-to-1 leverage offered, which is $500,000 in buying power. They purchase 5,000 shares of a $100 stock and then watch the stock go against them, all day. In that situation, it only takes a $5 drop in the stock price to cause them to lose their shirts.

In that case, the risk manager scurries over to their desk and whispers: "You have to sell *now*."

Actually, the trader in that circumstance might not be an amateur. It could be someone well-seasoned in trading, but unaccustomed to so much buying power. Once again, it's all about self-limitation, or else the lack thereof.

I'll conclude this pay-per-trade versus pay-per-share tour by stating that it's essential to use both, to your advantage.

HANG ON TO YOUR PAY-PER-TRADE ACCOUNT

I still have my traditional pay-per-trade account. I still use that firm's site for all the market info and free data feeds. I also still use them for my banking—they have no ATM fees, worldwide. But the main reason I remain hooked up with pay-per-trade is in case of the extremely rare situation where I may want to **hold** for an extended period. Most pay-per-share firms won't leverage you if you're **holding** overnight. You can **hold** overnight with their system, but never with their money. If you have $25,000 in your account, the pay-per-share firms will only allow you to **hold** $25,000 worth of a security overnight.

I assume that you already have a broker, and it's most likely a pay-per-trade firm, and even though I've made it clear that you should eventually move on to pay-per-share, I suggest that for the reasons above, you never cancel your pay-per-trade account. Even if you have a zero balance, most pay-per-trade firms will keep your account open indefinitely. When you're ready to advance to a pay-per-share equity trading firm, you can simply transfer your money from one account to the other.

Be mindful of this, however, before you make the big switch: at pay-per-share firms your account must have a minimum of $25,000, and many require you to have a Series 7 license.

I suggest that you visit some pay-per-share firms in person. Ask those firms whether you can observe their trading floor. Go to each armed with the following questions:

- How much are the per-share commissions and monthly data-feed fee structures?

- Can I trade remotely from home?
- How often can I use withdrawal checks against my account?
- How flexible are you with leverage?
- What are the minimum account balance requirements and guidelines?
- What type of profit sharing programs do you offer?
- What percentage of the traders on the floor are professionals (trading per-share for at least one year)?
- Do you require a Series 7 license?
- What type of *free* group strategy classes or mentorship do you offer?
- What are my choices for trading stations? (For example: how many monitors, what working conditions and atmosphere, etc.).

 RULES TO REMEMBER

- Don't use a pay-per-trade broker if you're placing multiple trades and not **holding** overnight.
- Keep your pay-per-trade broker *only* for long-term trades and free resources.
- In pay-per-share trading, be extremely careful of how much leverage you use. Always start small (10-to-1).
- When searching for pay-per-share brokers, visit the actual trading floors and test their demos for at least a few days, and take note of their cost/fee structures.
- Trade remotely from home only after you've traded on their floor for a while.

CHAPTER 18

Paper-Trading Strategy

I'll begin with a formal description. Investopedia.com, a Forbes Media company, defines paper trading as "simulated trading that investors use to practice mimicking trades (buys and sells) without actually entering into any monetary transactions."

Paper trading is day trading without the loss or profit that results from using real money. You do everything you were trained to do when executing a real-time order, but this, of course, is just practice. You note the entry price in a log, on paper. It's all about getting your feet wet.

If you've ever attended a day trading seminar or training program for beginners, then chances are you've been shown how to paper-trade, but you haven't been *adequately* shown. You may not be aware that there are right ways and wrong ways to use this learning tool. There are pitfalls that must be avoided. When utilized properly, however, paper trading helps to maximize your real day trading performance.

In the intro to this book, I referred to my initial paper-trading experience. I painted a picture of the typical novice—me—just back from a three-day seminar. Part of my training had been paper trading. Now I was applying that method on my own. At home, I paper-traded for one straight month. My results were absolutely amazing. I made loads of fake money.

Then came the big transition, the morning I decided to start trading with real money. What happened on that day was pathetic.

I didn't sleep much that night.

You may be able to tell that I'm launching into another cautionary tale. In order to most clearly present to you my warnings and advice, I'll split paper trading into two distinctive stages, the *amateur* and the *advanced*. For each, there are different applications.

PAPER TRADING FOR THE AMATEUR

Most amateur day traders have been mentally armed with professional day trading strategies, but have very little practical experience. That's a dangerous situation. Add paper trading to the new guy's vulnerability, and things get even more dicey. That's especially true when he lacks adequate instruction in how to use that tool.

Here are the crucial things to remember: the method should *never* be understood as a test of strategy. Also, paper trading should *never* be used as lessons in how to day trade without incurring risk. Think about it: those reasons make no sense. How will it help you to *master* your strategies by way of *controlling your emotions* when you start trading with real money?

Most training programs don't stress that point. They bathe you in their proprietary strategies. They woo you with their system in a risk-free environment of paper trading or demo software programs. They give you $100,000 of monopoly money and let you go wild with it. This is how they seduce you to naively perceive that their system of trading works. This is basically a ploy to inspire the novice to sign up and fork over thousands in fees. I've learned to be sickened by that.

Let's compare that situation, for a moment, to a gambling scenario.

You walk into a casino. The floor manager comes at you with fake chips to play with, and sure, you go for it, why not? You've been given $100,000 in fake chips, and someone whispers strategies to you. You place $50,000 on the betting line, on the very first roll of the dice. You win three times in a row.

Wow, you think. *This system really works!*

Then you lose, and what does it matter? You walk away saying, *That was fun!*

My point is that after all that risk-free paper trading, day traders haven't adequately learned to be careful. They're so wowed by their successes with paper trading that they can't wait to strategize with real money. Like the gambler at the casino who's turned $100,000 in fake chips into $1 million in fake bucks, there's a good chance they're a little too confident.

With that human weakness in mind, I've devised a simple safeguard for amateurs to follow. Go get the poster board and markers out again, and find another space on your wall. My primary paper-trading rule is:

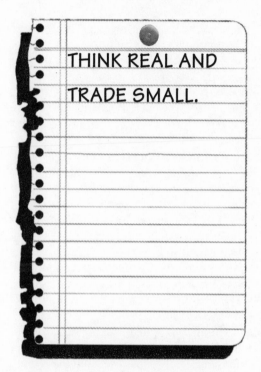

THINK REAL AND

TRADE SMALL.

By now you know the drill, the biggest maxim of all: even if you've learned to find a perfect stock to trade, until your skills have improved, you should only trade in 100-share blocks.

But it's just so easy to forget that precaution, whenever you paper-trade. It starts at the training program. The instructors there taught me their professional strategy. They put me on their demo software, and had me place paper trades.

At first, I did it all properly. I kept to 100-share blocks. So far, so good. But soon I was purchasing 1,000-share blocks and/or rashly averaging down, on each and every trade. I remember how gloriously stress-free it was, whenever a trade went against me.

No problem, I chuckled. *This is only practice.*

If I found myself in a bad trade, I would just average-down. It was only paper money, after all. I could simply buy more stock at lower levels. I did this every time the price dropped against my initial entry price. I would start off with a 100 shares, and if I was wrong on the entry price and the stock dropped precipitously, I would then buy an additional 100 shares, at a lower level. If it continued to drop further, I would buy even more shares at even lower price levels. The lower it went, the larger the share-block size I purchased.

This would go on until the price reversed in my direction. Because I had accumulated so many shares during that one trade—usually over a thousand—when the price went back up I would go into the green, and recognize a profit.

This scenario is very typical in paper trading. It sounds like a great strategy, right? Just keep on averaging down until the price reverses in your direction.

Sure.

If you're not sure why that strategy is foolish beyond belief, then refer back to Chapter 10, "Averaging-Down: Skilled Strategy."

The problem with paper trading that way is that two fundamental emotional issues are getting overlooked. First: each time you overexpose yourself with a too-large block of shares or average-down, you're not experiencing the real, raw fear that goes with your reckless risk with real money. Secondly, when averaging down you're assuming that the price will most likely retrace, and that's your own worst enemy coming around to get you; that's your own overconfidence. Too much lack of caution, combined with way too much nerve, are the hazardous day trading practices that paper trading can cause.

But take heart. There's a practical, simple mantra you can say to keep this from happening. Once again: Think real and trade small.

I know it seems hard, but just do it: convince yourself fake money is real. Paper-trade exactly the same way you would if you were trading for real.

If you fail to impose those mental measures on yourself, you may become much too complacent, not glued enough to the screen. That can make you lose focus. You might walk away for a few minutes, or have a long discussion on the phone. This may seem insignificant, but the trouble is, you're not preparing. You're failing to get accustomed to the concentration you'll need, when you start to trade with real money.

It's hard to just sit there, *all day*, watching the charts *every second*, especially when you're only pretending. But in real day trading, that's exactly what's required. That's why I'm pounding it into your brain to paper-trade like it's a real trade. For instance: when you enter into a paper trade, make sure that you're watching the Level 2 chart. Get into the pattern of noting the bid/ask price. *Never* use the *market* price as an entry price, because when you're trading for real, you'll have to pay the *ask* price when *buying*, and then the *bid* price when *selling*.

I've designed for you a practical tool for proper paper trading. See Table 18.1 for a data-entry form to use as a paper-trading log.

TABLE 18.1 Paper-Trading Log

Symbol Symbol	Number of Shares	Long/ Short	Price In	Time In	Price Out	Time Out	Stop Limit	Profit <Loss>

This form can be easily duplicated in the Excel program, or else you can have it photocopied. You need at least one fresh form for every trading day. Note that the form has all the important factors that must be logged for each trade, such as stock symbol, number of shares, price entry and exit, time of entry and exit, long or short position, and profit/loss amount.

The point of logging all that information is *not* to gauge your profits. You should be logging the info so that later, you can research each trade. You can always find things to learn from on the log sheet, whether you profit or lose.

With all the collected data, you can glean statistical trends. For instance, you may find that a certain stock is best traded after 1:00 P.M., or that some stocks take longer periods to hit price targets. You may find that certain stocks reverse before or after major support/resistance levels. You may also conclude that certain trades should have been **held** a bit longer, before stop/loss or profits.

As you can see, the trading log is a learning tool. It broadens your perspective and skills as a day trader. It should *not* be viewed as a proof of your profit-making abilities. Here's something to remember. Tack this motto up, too:

PAPER TRADING IS

NOT ABOUT

PROFITABILITY

VERSUS LOSSES

I can almost bet that you'll profit more in paper trading than real trading. It sure was that way for me. Don't be foolish like I was. I didn't bother to log the trades that would have wiped me out, had the trading been real. I chose to ignore the bad trades. That was typical amateur behavior.

I would enter into a trade with 5,000 shares, and then go to the store for lunch. I would come back and see that the stock dropped $2, so now I was down $10,000. I would blithely dismiss it as a botched trade, saying to myself, *If I'd been here watching it, I would have sold at a small loss* ... and then I didn't log it.

But if, on another occasion, the stock went up $2 and I profited by $10,000, then of course I proudly wrote it in there! Consequently, I learned nothing. All I did was acquire bad habits, like walking away during a trade, getting myself grossly overexposed, and getting myself overconfident.

Whenever paper trading, you should always disregard how much you're making. Focus instead on the underlying reasons for every aspect of your performance. You'll learn more from bad trades than good trades. Unless you're the superstar of all Wall Street day traders, you're going to trade like a normal amateur and make a lot of mistakes. You can count on that, but you can also learn from that.

Now I'll move on to the *advanced* stage of paper trading.

A WORD ABOUT ADVANCED PAPER TRADING

If an experienced day trader hasn't been consistently profitable, then some paper trading can help. Like an amateur he can use it to analyze his mistakes, and he can also use the method to safely test new stocks. As someone who's learned from his blunders as a greenhorn, he knows that you don't just dive headlong right into any new stock.

The seasoned day trader also knows that paper trading can be a great tool to get him through rough periods. He knows, for instance, that whenever the stock market gets extremely volatile, it's wise to take some days off.

But that doesn't mean he's on vacation. During the high-risk days, he takes time to paper-trade. That way he learns, in a zero-risk environment, how to trade in a high-volatility market.

Both amateurs and experienced traders can both get to a point where they simply need a break. During those periods, it's wise to paper-trade. It can be very therapeutic. Refer back to Chapter 5, "Knowing When to Take a Break," to review this vital point.

RULES TO REMEMBER

- Think real and trade small when paper trading.
- Paper-trade *exactly* the same way as you would when doing real trading.
- *Do not* construe paper trading as a way to gauge your profits.

CHAPTER 19

Trading for Skill versus Trading for Income

I f you're an amateur with no formal training, quit trying to go it alone. Quit day trading, right away. Review Chapter 16, "About Those Training Programs," pick a class or mentorship setting that best fits your level of skill, and get yourself there *yesterday*.

But if you're an amateur who's already experienced some training or mentoring, then by all means, please read on. I'll start with the most rueful, head-shaking confession that's made by professional day traders. They confide that as beginners, when they'd finished a class, they *immediately* traded for primary income. After spending all their savings on that pricey seminar, they were gung-ho to *immediately* make those bucks back.

Does that sound like you? Is that what you're doing? If so, then I repeat: *don't stop reading!*

The truth is, your biggest investment in know-how is *not* the training programs. It's the losses you're going to incur while developing into a pro. I highlighted the scary truth in Chapter 12, "Why Some Traders Make More Mistakes."

My goal in this chapter is not just to warn you, but to thoroughly and safely equip you. Here I show how you can minimize your post-graduate training fees—that is, your live-trading losses.

BUILDING A FOUNDATION OF TRADING SKILLS

For starters, you need to internalize this crucial, unshakable truth: as a greenhorn, you should be trading for skill. You should be focused on skill building, not money making. Trading for income comes later. You should remember that patience is paramount. You should never try to rush the process of becoming a professional day trader. If you thoughtfully read Chapter 1, you may have realized that you're definitely not highly skilled. Face it, you have a lot of learning to do, so you need to hang back like a student and sit there and take lots of notes.

Back when I was an amateur, I wish someone had grabbed me by the scruff of my neck and forced me to understand that. Back in the day, as a greenhorn, I would return from a training program, or finish a strategy manual, feeling pumped like a boxer on steroids. I was itching to throw down with the big boys. Didn't I possess the proprietary information that Wall Street traders commandeer? I was certain that I had just mastered the golden goose of day-trading expertise. I felt ready to make big moves, big trades.

The truth is I did have some great information. I'd been shown how to trade like a pro. The one thing I lacked, however, was applied experience. I also lacked an awareness of the deadliness of that shortcoming.

It was like I'd been watching a video on how to build beautiful houses. After the lights came back on, and I actually went to a work site and actually swung a hammer, I found that this wasn't as easy as I'd thought. I was miserably learning what the video couldn't teach me: that I needed not only to read blueprints and hammer, but I also had to deal with the relentless pressure of deadlines, and the deep-body stress caused by hot or cold weather. (That's why I respect carpenters, like my brave brother Adam in Buffalo, New York, who works outside all winter.)

The day trader's hammer is his finger tips. His nails are the keys on his keyboard. Like the builder, he needs to tread carefully, especially as a beginner. Though he won't smash his thumb or take a fall off a roof, or freeze or pass out from hot sun, he might hurt himself even worse . . . by the wallet.

It's not all bad news. On the contrary, I have some good news. I've worked out a system that allows you to *safely* train with real money, with minimal market exposure. Before I worked out my system, I was floundering in day trader hell. My problem was that I thought I was a pro. Just because I made several trades a day with tens of thousands of dollars, I thought I had it all figured out.

After my many losses, which were also painfully hard lessons, I found myself doing more homework and research. By necessity, I was becoming more patient. But I still hadn't yet realized my biggest misstep: I was trading to earn, not to learn.

You should only trade *to earn* if your profits are consistent.

You know by now mine were not.

One day I glumly just slumped there. My monitors glowered before me like unreachable, imperious gods. I'd been day trading for over five years.

I'd been having a very hard time. I felt like a pitiful loser, and it was the closest I'd ever come to throwing in the towel. But on that day I somehow managed to perk myself up, and continue. I figured I'd just have to change things. I'd have to redo my approach.

That was my moment of conception. Up to that point I'd had some really good trades, along with the really bad ones. Over time, I'd broken even. The reasons I'd survived those five years were my start with a healthy capital base, and my absolute will to improve.

(Warning: Please note that term above, *healthy capital base.* If you don't have one, or if you plan on investing more than half of your life savings, then by all means start highlighting in yellow.)

On that day I realized I should go back to the basics, back to square one, like in training. I should no longer stress myself to make money. I should focus on a method that creates consistency, and for now, just forget about earning.

Now maybe you're thinking: *That's crazy. It's absurdly counterproductive to* not *be focused on gains.* Well, profit is the end goal, of course, but crawling precedes walking and walking precedes running, that's a universal rule. So let's get even crazier. Let's make a crazy sign.

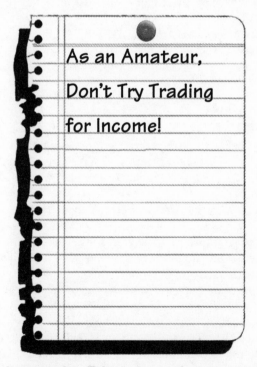

> ## As an Amateur, Don't Try Trading for Income!

Hang the sign up today. Take it down when your profits have been consistent for at least one straight month (20 full trading days).

I admit there's a downside to my system I will be explaining in a moment. It's the dismally miniscule profits. You won't make enough to call it income. It's true that you'll be trading with bucks, not with paper, but I'm talking about very few bucks. You'll need to be willing to gain satisfaction from the frequency of profitable trades—*not* from the dollar amounts.

But here's the point: Even if you only make two dollars on a trade (after commissions), what's important is that you'll be learning how to profit consistently. You must achieve that consistency. Then, and only then, should you budget for bigger trades. My system is a careful progression. You start off paper trading. Then you graduate to real money—just a little bit of money at a time.

My system consists of three levels. But before we launch into those levels, however, review the following chapters:

- Chapter 1, "Truths about Yourself to Know First"
- Chapter 4, "From Impatience to Cool, Calm, and Collected"
- Chapter 7, "How Overexposure to the Market Can Hurt"
- Chapter 8, "Knowing Your Financial Limitations: Budgeting"
- Chapter 14, "Stock Picking"
- Chapter 17, "Picking the Right Online Broker: Pay-per-Share versus Pay-per-Trade"
- Chapter 18, "Paper-Trading Strategy"

With that done, you're ready.

FIRST LEVEL

Assuming that you know how to read charts and how to place a trade, find a slow-moving, low-priced stock. That is, a stock with an average daily price range of 50¢ from the high of the day to the low, with stock price ranges from $10 to $30.

Paper-trade that stock for one week straight. Trade it throughout the day. Make enough on each trade to exceed your future commissions, when you trade with real money. In other words, if you're trading through a pay-per-trade broker, then you want to make at least a $20.00 profit on *each* trade. That more than covers the round-trip commission fees, usually $9.99 per trade. If you're trading through a pay-per-share broker, then to break even you only need to make $1.00 or so profit on the trade.

- You've seen this before: trade *only* in *100-share blocks*.
- Paper trade that stock consistently all week. Make *at least 10 trades per day*.

- Set proper stop/losses and limits. Don't worry about your intraday progress; just focus on trading for experience.
- At week's end, you should have five full days of active paper trading experience with just *one* familiar stock.
- Keep well-documented records of each trade. You should have notes explaining your reasons for entering and exiting each trade, and your state of mind in each trade.
- After this full week with one stock, if you feel confident to trade the *same* stock with real money, then the following Monday morning, you should begin real trading.
- Otherwise, you repeat one full week of paper trading.
- You switch stocks *only* if your research and experiences indicate the stock is a problem. (If you've read Chapter 14, "Stock Picking," however, it's doubtful that will happen.)
- If you choose to trade with real money, then take care to engrain these rules:
  - Do exactly what you did while paper trading.
  - If you're making mistakes that you didn't make while paper trading, *stop trading.*
  - Go back to paper trading until you get your confidence back.

Most likely you'll quickly get bored with the First Level, even when trading with real money, because you'll make or lose very little. Trading with 100 shares of a slow-moving, low-priced stock is very unexciting. This is where your patience comes in. During this time you learn valuable lessons, but thankfully, not by risking a lot.

As soon as you feel confident trading with real money during the First Level, now you have two choices: you can promote yourself to the Second Level, below, or you can increase a First Level stock by *100 shares at a time.*

If you choose the second option, then increase to 200 shares, then to 300, then to 400, and finally to a maximum of 500 shares per trade. Test each increase first with a full week of paper trading.

Your average First Level stock will only allow you *10* good trades per day. Each trade will take more time to reach your price levels than a Second or Third Level stock. This is why you have the option of increasing your shares per trade up to 500 shares.

When you trade in 100-share blocks, it may take the stock 30 minutes to move 25¢, so you'll either profit or lose $25 on each trade. The same trade with five hundred shares will still take 30 minutes to move 25¢, but you'll be profiting or losing by a factor of five. On average, with 500 shares you'll profit or lose $125 on the trade.

Again, it's all about baby steps and patience. *Always* start with 100 shares and gradually work your way up.

SECOND LEVEL

This procedure is identical to the First Level, except for one differential: your stock is in a different class. Find a medium-moving, medium-priced stock; that is, a stock with an average daily price range of $1 and stock price ranges from $30 to $50.

Paper-trade that stock for one week straight. Trade it throughout the day for at least 30 round-trip trades. Make enough on each trade to exceed your real-money commissions. Paper-trade that stock consistently all week. Make at least 30 trades per day, and of course, with only 100 shares at a time.

Set proper stop/losses and limits. Don't worry about your intraday progress; just focus on trading for the experience. At week's end, you should have five full days of active trading experience with just *one* familiar stock.

Keep well-documented records of each trade. You should have notes explaining your reasons for entering and exiting each trade, and your state of mind in each trade. After this full week with one stock, if you feel confident to trade the same stock with real money, then the following Monday morning, you can begin real trading. Otherwise, repeat one full week of paper trading. If you choose to trade with real money, then take care to engrain these rules:

- Do exactly what you did while paper trading.
- If you're making mistakes that you didn't make while paper trading, stop trading.
- Go back to paper trading until you get your confidence back.
- Increase the share size to 200 only after you've proven your performance with 100-share blocks, and you've tested the 200-share blocks for a full week of paper trading first.
- You can switch stocks *only* if your research and experiences indicate that the stock is a problem.

The Second Level differs from the First Level in that the stock you pick exhibits more movement and volatility. I set up those levels to create a gradual exposure to more risky trading experiences. When you trade at the First Level and then upgrade to the Second, I'm certain you'll see a huge difference. You'll find that the stock may move in one direction twice faster than you're used to.

This is why you should always start trading in 100-share blocks per trade. You should never trade a Second Level stock with more than 200-share blocks per trade. Remember to paper-trade it that way for one full week beforehand, and then move on to real money.

Your average Second Level stock will allow you more trades, per day, than a typical First Level stock. You should be able to execute at least *30 trades per day*. This is productive, yet scary. Before you increase your share size per trade, you should take more time getting to know your stock than you would with a First Level stock. I suggest that you trade it in 100-share blocks for at least one month, before you increase to 200.

When trading in 100-share blocks, it may take the stock *3 to 10 minutes* to move *25¢*; therefore, on each trade you chance to *profit or lose $25*. If you're in the same trade with 200 shares it will take the same time to move, but you'll be profiting or losing by a factor of two. With 200 shares you chance to profit or lose $50 on the trade. Therefore, if you're not ready for a Second Level stock, placing 30 trades per day can get very ugly.

Again, it's all about baby steps. With this Level, I repeat: *always* start with 100 shares and work your way up to 200, but *never exceed* 200 shares.

THIRD LEVEL

The Third Level is identical to the first two, but once again your stock is in a different type of class.

- Find a fast-moving, high-priced stock; for instance, stocks that have an average daily price range of $3, and price ranges of $50 to $100.
- Paper-trade that one stock for one week straight. Trade it throughout the day for at least 50 round-trip trades. Make enough on each trade to exceed your commissions.
- As always, your goal is to paper-trade consistently all week. Make at least 50 trader per day, and you know how few shares at a time.
- As always, set proper stop/losses and limits. Focus on the experience, not the progress.
- At week's end, you should have five full days of active trading experience with that one stock.
- As always, document your reasons for entering and exiting each trade, and your state of mind in each trade.
- After your one-week experience paper trading, start trading the same stock with real money, if you feel confident.

- If not, then repeat one full week of paper trading.
- If you choose to trade with real money, always remember the rules:
  - Do exactly what you do while paper trading.
  - If you're making mistakes that you didn't make while paper trading, stop trading.
  - If you're producing more losses than profits, go back to paper trading until you get your confidence back.
- As always, you can switch stocks only if the stock itself is the problem.

The Third Level is going to exhibit maximum exposure. *Never* trade with more than one hundred shares per trade, even when you've proven consistent. When overexposed to a Third Level stock, it's much harder to handle the swings.

You will never need to trade such stocks more than a hundred shares at a time. When trading a Third Level stock, you can easily profit or lose $25 every 10 seconds to 3 minutes! (Third Level stocks quickly move 25¢, and you have a 100 shares).

Because this level involves 50 or more trades per day, there's a potential of $1,250 in profits or losses per day (50 trades × $25 profit/loss).

So make sure you don't get greedy. Bad things happen when you get greedy. Stick to a maximum of 100 shares per trade, and *never* average down. If you follow that advice, you should be off to a great start when trading a Third Level stock.

SUMMARY

Paper trading is strictly for learning, but you shouldn't just do it randomly. I devised the levels with paper trading in order to slow you down and to condition you to research your mistakes. Your completion of each of the levels prepares you to trade live, armed with a risk-free experience in virtually every class of stock.

Always paper-trade any new stock that you've added to your stock list. You can always net profits with a First-Level stock while you paper trade and research a Second- or Third-Level stock. Eventually you'll be able to trade multiple stocks during the trading day. But hold off on that until you've proven that you can profit from one stock at a time. When you feel sufficiently ready, you can always increase the recommended share sizes (but stick to the maximum allowed), and/or start trading more than one stock in each level.

The key to the system is baby steps. Don't ever start trading in more than 100-share blocks without paper trading, first, the same amount for a

TABLE 19.1 Three Levels of Stocks

	Profile	Average Price Range	Average Intraday Price Range	Max. Shares Traded (Per Trade)	Duration of Each Trade (25¢ Moves)	Average Trades (Per Day)	Potential Profit/Loss (Per Trade)	Potential Profit/Loss (Per Day)
First Level	Slow moving, low priced	$10–30	$0.50	100–500	10–30 minutes	10	$25	$250 10 × $25
Second Level	Medium moving, medium priced	$30–50	$1	100–200	1–5 minutes	30	$25	$750 30 × $25
Third Level	Fast moving, high priced	$50–100	$3+	Max 100	10 seconds–1 minute	50	$25	$1250 50 × $25

week. And *never* trade a Third-Level stock with more than a 100 shares per trade—with no exceptions!

I want to stress that this system is not a complete day-trading strategy; it's not even close. All this system is designed for is to keep you in low gear. It's designed to give you a structured training mentality. It's not to be relied on for earning, but it *is* to be thoroughly relied on for the best chance of future success.

For your convenience, use Table 19.1 for reference.

The chart is designed to give a quick reference for all three levels of stocks. The "risk" is determined by how fast the stock price can move in a given period.

 RULES TO REMEMBER

- Always start with a First-Level stock, then progress upward from there.
- *Do not* trade with real money until you've been consistently profitable with your stock for a week straight in paper trading.

CHAPTER 20

The Perfect Trading Day

H ere's a list of the factors behind the perfect trading day, from the time you wake up until the evening.

- Your broker is pay-per-share.
- Your premarket prep has been thorough.
- All day you've been strategically consistent.
- At day's end you've closed all positions.
- You're not **holding** overnight.
- You're thoroughly prepared for tomorrow.
- ... And of course, you've made a good profit!

My goal in this chapter is to vividly illustrate the optimum day trading experience. To facilitate this, here's an in-depth description of an ideal day from my life.

EARLY MORNING ACTIVITIES

First I should mention that occasionally, I kick back and take a day off. It's never an impulsive decision; I've known since the day before. The reason is either the market conditions, or I've planned on a very late night.

Today I'm not taking off.

Depending on whether I'll be trading from home or going to my group-trading floor, I roll out of bed at either 5 A.M. or 7 A.M. (If I'll be heading out for the floor, which is located way down by Wall Street, I have to be up before dawn. The entrance to the subway is about three city-blocks away, and once I get down in that packed, massive cavern, finding a train with room to cram into can take up even more time.)

It doesn't matter what the clock says when I first open my eyes: I want a sweet rush of caffeine. Whether swarming humanity is where I'll end up, or just to my home-based quiet trading desk, the first thing I do, every day, is make coffee.

After I'm ramped from my hot liquid fix, I do my stretching routine. Then I check out the weather. If conditions in New York are inviting, or at least not intolerable, then I grab my mug of brew, exit my building, and take a brisk walk through a lovely little slice of the 843 acres of Central Park.

But if the weather is lousy, and it's wrecking my plan to enjoy some deep breathing in that gorgeous and grand green oasis, then I drop to my living room floor. I do multiple sets of sit-ups and push-ups.

This is all to get finely tuned. Such rigorous morning physical preps are indispensable. They boost mental clarity. They enable me to deal with the stress, at the market opening bell, when at 9:30 A.M. sharp, my heart jolts. They help me to keep myself calm through the day, when I'm hunched up and clenched, concentrating.

And now it's time for the cerebral part of my pre-market a.m. tuning.

Back while I was sleeping, the global money machines were not. I'm aware that momentous things could have happened, while I snoozed. Now that I'm awake and fully energized, I must make myself adroitly cognizant. Though my individual stocks may not be in the news, they can still be affected by global events, and I need to know all about those events, before I begin to trade.

So before I even brush my teeth, I boot up my computer. I begin the market news research. For my general market news, I use some major websites, like Bloomberg.com and the Yahoo Finance section.

Next I click on my TV. I tune into the CNBC business channel. I'm looking for breaking headlines—the stock-impacting kind.

Remember waking up to the shock that Washington Mutual (WM) was closed by the government, in late 2008? That was the largest bank failure in United States history. Its assets were sold to JPMorgan Chase & Co. at an absurdly low price, causing the stock price to plummet to pennies ... all in just one day. And I hate to make you do this, but as a day trader, you must: think also of the 9/11 attacks and their effects on the markets. I keep scanning for anything earth-shattering, hoping there's nothing out there.

As soon as I've seen that there isn't, and I've decided that today may be relatively normal, I begin a more focused news research. In the Yahoo! Finance section, the *Economic Calendar* is an extremely valuable resource.

It lists all the reports that will be released today, and about what time of day.

I just can't stress it enough. If you want to have a *perfect* day trading, you've got to glean beforehand what reports may hit the news wire, later when you're deep in your trades. And if you deem it news that just might affect your stocks, then already you know that during the day you'll need to approximate the time of that release, and close your positions a few minutes prior.

After my general market research, I begin to research my stocks. I focus on about ten. That doesn't mean, however, that I'll be trading them all; the reason for my eyeballing of that many stocks is to give myself plenty of options. I usually have at least one stock from each major market sector. This gives me flexibility. For instance, if the Financials are volatile today, I can choose my alternatives, Utilities and Energy.

I research each stock for a couple of minutes. I input each stock symbol and look for news info that might be relevant. I read through the articles and I try to discern whether news about my stock should concern me.

At this point I'm fully tuned in to the market. I switch from watching the news to preparing my entry/exit plans. Such planning is all about technical chart analysis. My system is crude, but effective. I go through each stock and I log the prior day's high, low, and closing prices. I'll say more about that later. For now I want to convey that those are the support and resistance levels to rely on for the time being.

I usually also have plenty of notes from the previous day's homework analysis. I go over them as well.

As soon as I'm armed with all the documented levels for each of my stocks of the day, I'm ready to start trading and/or monitoring the premarket trading activities.

PRE-MARKET TRADING

Pre-market is 8:00 A.M. to 9:30 A.M., before the opening bell. Most pay-per-share firms allow you to place trades (direct order executions) during that hour and a half. On the contrary, most pay-per-trade brokers (traditional online brokers) won't fill your order right away. Meaning, you can place an order at 8 A.M., but it won't get processed until after the bell.

You'll recall that I've stated that the factors that make the day *perfect* include a pay-per-share broker. The above is a big reason why. Imagine you've placed a market order during premarket trading, which won't get filled until later, and during the interim you can only sit and watch the price balloon!

Premarket trading is risky; you've seen me stress that before. In the past I've had ridiculous premarket losses, but at this point I know how to prevent the nail-biting caused by uncertainties. These days, if I do trade premarket, it's just to test the waters, and (you guessed it) I only use 100-share blocks.

You can easily predict what I'm going to say next: Don't trade premarket as a greenhorn! Just the same, however, you should definitely observe it, because it can teach you a lot.

I usually use this period not to trade, but to warm up. I continue my technical analysis and chart watching. As I've mentioned, I'm armed with my three important price levels, the previous day's high, low, and closing prices. Most important are the *high* and the *low*. I'm monitoring the volume levels as well, watching their affect on price directions.

Whenever you view this early a.m. trading, you'll notice larger than usual gaps between the bid and ask prices. You'll notice abnormal volatility. To make things even more confusing, the support and resistance levels are sometimes getting broken, with very little volume.

What the heck is going on here? Several different things. The overnight news from around the world is catching up to the market. Premarket economic reports are being released to the public. At the crack of dawn there was little, but now the news floods in.

Right now it's important to monitor how Wall Street reacts to this.

This is when I usually take a 15-minute break. It's time to just pause and watch the Street. You should always remember that Wall Street is smarter than your own intuition. After the release of a major report, let those guys decide what direction the stock should take. Don't ever try predicting it yourself. Ever!

After my break I might notice that one of my stocks has just broken through the previous day's high or low, with unusually high volume. The need for a new intraday resistance level or support level has just presented itself, and I'm glad that I caught it now, not later during regular trading hours.

The following is important to note and to remember.

The pre-market price levels are not logged on Level 1 and 2 charts for the present day's price movements. For instance, if your stock drops to $50 during pre-market trading, then rebounds to $51 by the opening bell, then the market indicators will only reflect the opening price level of $51. The low of $50 is not recorded, unless of course it hits again during regular market hours.

Meaning, if you're not paying attention to the premarket activity and taking notes, then you may be using the wrong intraday support and resistance levels.

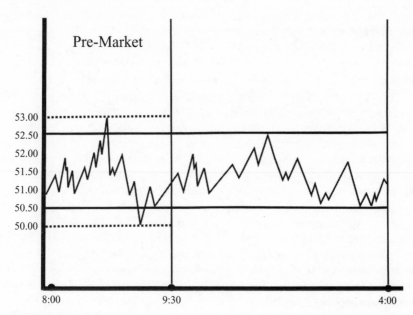

FIGURE 20.1 Intraday Chart

Refer to Figure 20.1, which shows a premarket low of $50, and a premarket high of $53. The price never hits either level throughout the entire day. The market indicators will only show actual low of $50.50, and actual high of $52.50.

At this point, at about 9:00 A.M., I'm honing in on the stocks that I plan to begin trading when the bell rings. The ideal situation is stocks that have been trading as usual during the premarket period. They display normal volume levels and react to the major support and resistance levels. They behave like tame tigers in cages. The animals are pacing back and forth, repetitiously wall to wall, rhythmic and predictable and tranquil.

Suddenly one tiger starts roaring at passers-by, and maniacally trying to gnaw its way out. In other words, one of my stocks is showing abnormal activity. That's usually a clear indication that I missed some important news, and my stock is now acting crazy, agitated like the beast.

The time to discover this is during premarket, before I've started to trade. So I utilize the premarket trading hours as a time to feel out the market, and to note what price action transpires.

Whether I'm home in my shorts or downtown fully dressed, during the final minutes before the opening bell I do one last stretching routine, and I get a fresh cup of coffee.

THE OPENING BELL

When the bell rings at 9:30 A.M. sharp, I'm fully prepared and calm. I know what price levels to watch for, on every stock I'll be trading.

This is all about focus and waiting.

Most training programs and manuals dictate to never trade during the first 15 minutes. That's an excessively risk-adverse advisement, but a rule to consider if you're new to this biz. As an amateur I suffered through many bad days because of botched trades in the very first minute.

The brief time that follows the opening bell is volatile and hectic. I've learned to trade during the first 15 minutes with only my most proven stocks. I know those stocks like I know my own face. I know how they are in the morning; I know all the ways they react; I know all their breaking points.

Trust me: if you're not in total rhythm with your stocks, then don't try to trade them at the opening bell. On certain days, during the first few minutes, I've seen stocks shoot over $10. Do you really want to pick bottoms or tops on stocks not familiar to you?

The opening bell is like the start of a horse race. The thoroughbreds ferociously blast from their gates, and each tries to head the stampede. The initial burst takes only a moment, and then a clear trend begins. Some horses are firmly in the lead, while others are lagging behind.

Horse racing is gambling. Day trading is not. At the track you're required to place your bets before the horses bust out, long before you can see what develops. Conversely, in day trading, you don't have to act beforehand. You can wait to see what trend your stock is setting for the day.

Because I'm no longer a rookie, usually I let myself enter a trade within minutes of the opening bell. But I never enter a trade until my predetermined price levels hit, and soon enough, they do. At least one of my stocks hits a price level that's making me lick my chops.

I also watch for new intraday trends. My initial predetermined price levels (calculated during my premarket research) usually only reflect what will be my first trade of the day. If I make a quick profit or loss (10¢ to 20¢ moves), then I'll continue trading that particular stock for the remainder of the day, but most likely I won't be reentering at the previous price level.

What matters is that each time I enter a trade, I have firmly in mind the price levels I've decided upon just before. I know the price to enter and I know the price to exit, whether it's a profit or a loss.

Having begun my trading, I'm now glued to the screens. I won't leave my station for anything. I will not take my eyes off the screens.

MIDDAY ACTIVITIES

By 10:30 A.M., I've executed about 30 trades. That's about 15 round-trip trades. That's a lot, and it's no accident, I like those high-energy launches; they build great momentum for the day.

I'm not yet concerned about how much money I've made or lost so far. I'm focused on control of my emotions. I'm busy with the mental concentration of finding quick intraday setups.

I usually enter and exit a trade about every one to five minutes. I'm looking for quick 10¢ to 20¢ moves. That translates to making or losing $10 to $20 on each trade, in the same amount of time. Per day, that's potentially 100 round-trip trades. I bang out most trades in the green, making $10 to $20 a trade, and losing $10 to $20 on a much smaller number of trades gone into the red.

Right about now you might wonder, how much capital do I need to purchase all those securities? The answer may surprise you. In previous chapters I mentioned that most pay-per-share firms require a $25,000 minimum balance. When you open your account with them, they usually give you buying power of $250,000 (depending on your skill level), which translates to 10-to-1 leverage.

Here's the part that may raise your eyebrows.

When I trade in hundred-share blocks, I usually only need $5,000 to $8,000 to purchase that security, because most of my stocks range from $50 to $80 per share. My multiple positions don't exceed 10, because I only watch 10 stocks per day. So at most I'm using $80,000 of my $250,000 leverage (10 stocks at $80 in 100-share blocks), at any given time throughout the day.

The point is I'm not trying to maximize my intraday buying power. Available capital doesn't mean that I should be using it all. You know I've learned that the hard way. In this book I've shown you can find trouble fast if you use all your buying power.

Think about it: If you're using more than 100,000 of buying power, a couple of things are going on: you're either buying stocks in 1,000-share blocks, or you have a lot more than 10 positions to trade, all at one point in time. Either way, you're seriously overexposed.

So there you have it, the quintessential truth about day trading stocks is to be a professional day trader, you don't need millions of dollars. All you really need is the minimum $25,000. And to those of you to whom $25,000 may seem like an awful lot, I would say think of this: it often costs people much, much more to get any small business started.

My trading style is called scalping. Scalping capitalizes on the numerous intraday price swings, on any given stock. I ferret out those quick 10¢ to

20¢ moves, ride them like a subway train, and get off at my predetermined stop.

And here I'll point out another reason why hitching up with a pay-per-share broker helps make for a *perfect* day. If you trade through a pay-per-trade broker, you can't afford to scalp only 10¢ to 20¢ cents without getting drastically overexposed. No such hazard will plague you when you trade the alternative way. I pay a commission of 35¢ for every 100-share block. That translates to about 70¢ for the entire round-trip trade.

So I can afford to make quick $10 to $20 profits on my intraday trades. If I profit $15 on a trade, with a pay-per-share commission structure I only lose 70¢ on the trade. Do you see how $15 per trade can seriously add up? I usually place over 100 round-trip trades per day. That's a potential for $1500 per day in profits. But, evevn on a perfect day you still lose on some trades, it's expected. Today is the usual perfect day for me. I will place 80 percent of my trades in the green. That means I can make about $1,200 in the green (80 trades at $15 profits) and I can lose about $300 (20 trades at $15 losses). So usually, on a *perfect* day, I net about $1100 in profit (after pay-per-share commissions).

During midday, I maintain a consistent profit by only trading 10 stocks, by knowing them very well, and by never trading a new stock either heavily or often. I remember the virtues of prudence (no matter how distasteful that word is). I don't stray from the system that works.

I quickly and decisively stop/loss. I enter each trade knowing when I'll sell at a profit or a loss. Without such self-disciplined, automatic reactions, I might start **holding** all day.

You lose some and you win more, that's the name of this game. My job is to log more green trades than red, and to almost never **hold**.

Emotions hurt your performance. They never help you win. I keep myself completely emotionally detached, even on a great day. I'm supposed to make money, that's my job, after all! Why should I get all excited? Don't get me wrong though, I'll celebrate later, when I've closed all positions, with a profit.

But at midday, I'm nose to the grindstone.

After sitting at my trade station for a few productive hours, I exit all my positions and gauge my performance. For the first time today, I look over my *profit/loss*. I already know I've made more green trades then red, but I want a little peek at the numbers.

Then I focus on which stocks are giving me trouble and which stocks are giving me love. I don't take my lunch break until I've determined the best stocks to focus on, when I get back. There are usually two or three. By best stocks I mean those that aren't in the news, are trading uniformly, and are reacting to intraday support and resistance levels almost as predictably as clockwork.

After lunch I do a quick chart analysis, especially of the best stocks. I adjust my screens so only their charts are showing. I'm digesting my food, it's 1:30 P.M., and the afternoon slump has set in; at this point I'm burned out, and I need to limit my stock watching, because my job gets a whole lot easier when I only watch a few.

This is when I allow myself a little more dicey risk. I'm tired, but I've narrowed my focus, and that makes things fairly safe. I start trading the predictable, reliable stocks in 200-share blocks, or I average-down, if that maneuver is needed.

By 3:00 P.M., the start of the final trading hour, I've usually logged close to 90 round-trip trades, or 180 executions. Most of the trades were in 100-share blocks; that's roughly a total of 18,000 shares traded.

At this point in the day I start to gauge my commission fees, feeling glad I don't do pay-per-trade. Do the math yourself. If I were using a pay-per-trade broker my commissions ($9.99 per trade) would be insane.

Once again I go to my net profit/loss calculations, and this time I eyeball them closely. Of my 90 round-trip trades, 75 were in the green and 15 were in the red. That translates to a gross profit of $900 (75 × $15 − 15 × $15). I subtract my commission fee of $63 (18,000 × $.0035 per/share), and I'm left with an intraday net profit of $837.

So it's late in the day and I'm up $837.

Not bad.

THE LAST HOUR OF TRADING

Now the market tends to pick up volume and volatility. During the last hour of trading, I'm always on high alert, just as I was in the premarket period.

Mostly I'm focused on making sure that I don't get caught up in any trades that may cause me to **hold** into after-hour trading. By the closing bell at 4:00 P.M. sharp, I want my positions closed out.

On a *not-so-perfect* trading day, right now I'd be struggling with my worst inner demons, greed or fear or both. The final hour is the time of day that can dramatically make you or break you, especially on a bad day, because on a bad day you might be tempted to spend it trying to make something back.

But on a *perfect* trading day like this one, with that $800+ profit, I'll spend the last hour cool, calm and conservative, which means without fear and greed.

I find myself in the green, right to the very last minute. On this day I would have placed an additional 10 to 20 more trades in the last hour, which lifts my intraday net profit to a lovely round number of $1,000.

This is how it goes on a day of *perfection*: one prudent strategy has led to another, and so on and so on.

During the final countdown, I'm looking to exit all my trades. I'll remain in a trade, however, if I want to **hold** until the final 10 seconds, or if I plan to sell it during after-hours trading.

In case you weren't aware, you can sell your positions in after-hours.

THE CLOSING BELL

Ding-ding-ding-ding!

Its 4:00 P.M. Eastern Standard Time, and all U.S equities markets are closed. The work day must be over.

Wrong!

I almost never stop working at 4:00—not unless I have a life-threatening emergency. There is so much left to do. I usually expect to be busy for at least a couple more hours.

I'm not in any after-hour trading positions. On a *perfect* day like this one, that very rarely happens. I take a quick break, about 15 minutes, to clear my mind and stretch. If I'm trading on the floor downtown with my fellow private equity traders, I slide over to them, and mingle.

Everyone's letting his guard down. Everyone's loosening up. After market is the only time I can approach the pros with my questions. I can always tell who wants to talk. Usually traders only like to talk when they've just had a great day.

Well, today *I* have a lot to say!

After the break, I have two choices. I can continue trading after-hours, or I can begin my homework. I usually make this decision within 20 minutes of the bell. I like to allow time for my stocks to show any signs of irregular activity. Most likely if they're heavily traded this late, it's because the traders are reacting to an after-closing news release. For example, a stock's after-market earnings release will create a high interest in trading after-hours.

AFTER-MARKET TRADING

If I've chosen to trade during after-hours, then soon I'm right back in the saddle. At most pay-per-share firms, after-hour trading ends at 8:00 P.M. EST. I never trade that late. For the most part I trade after hours if I messed up really bad, and I'm **holding** a large position. If that's the case, then I try to get rid of the remaining shares, quickly, by continuing to trade after four.

Sometimes the price retraces fast after-hours, and then I'm able to revive myself from a "near-death" trading experience.

That's depending on luck, of course. That's gambling. That's not how a *perfect* day ends. Once in a while there can be some great after-hours trades. In order to be worthwhile, the stock has to be trading with the same volume, or more, as it did during regular market hours. Again, this usually only happens if some major news is hitting the wire.

If I do enter such a trade, I'm looking for the same support and resistance levels that existed at the close. After-market trading usually stays active (worth trading) only until 6:00 P.M.. It really dies down after that. After the major news hits the wire, the stock will jump in either direction, but then it will level off and trade in a tight range until the final close, at 8:00 P.M..

Another reason why I never enter a trade after 6:00 P.M. is because it can be very difficult to exit before 8:00 P.M. The difference between the bid and ask prices can be very large, and simply not worth trading if the volume dies down.

Once I'm completely done trading for the day, and I've closed out all my positions, then I begin my homework.

HOMEWORK

Whether I'm actually home or working downtown, I like to call it homework. No matter where the location, when I'm done I need to recap.

I focus on the best and the worst trades of the day. I print out a list of all my trades for the day, or I simply view info on my screens. The list will include the following essentials:

- Stock symbol
- Amount of shares
- Long/short position
- Time of entry
- Time of exit
- Profit/loss
- Number of total trades

I keep both mental and written logs of what I've learned today. For instance, if I find that after 3:00 P.M. one of my stocks became extremely volatile and difficult to trade, then I note on paper to stop trading it the following day after three. I have a habit of keeping note pad reminders all over my trading station. Tomorrow when I begin my early-morning activities, I will see them there.

Taking time to recap is crucial. It makes me slow down and think about my trading style. Trading styles have to be constantly updated, just like a computer. If I'm not paying daily attention to my trading performance and trends, then I risk falling into that dark and murky place that I like to call spaced-out land.

In spaced-out land, *perfect* days like this one start to dwindle.

As an amateur I suffered due to lack of end-of-day recaps. Whenever I took big losses, I was so sick to my stomach that I didn't care to research the cause. I figured I simply entered the stock at the wrong price level, or I simply shouldn't have been trading that particular stock on that day. But in fact there were deeper lessons to be learned, lessons that would only be realized if I scrutinized my intraday activities. For instance, most likely I lost big because of overexposure. If, at the end of the day, I had gone over each trade, I would have noticed that I was string-trading and not waiting for proper set-ups. I would have realized I was trading on emotion, and letting it all slip between my fingers.

In order to be able to gauge your trading performance, you must go back and research what happened at the time you executed the order. These days I research my intraday trades and focus on a few essentials. I primarily like to know this:

- Which stocks was I trading the most, and why?
- Which stocks did I profit the most from on that day, and why?
- Which stocks did I lose the most on that day, and why?

Upon answering those three basic questions, I walk away feeling more in control of my trading style. Now I can relax and enjoy my evening, feeling better about my performance.

Homework is an investment in another *perfect* day.

CHAPTER 21

The Worst Trading Day

W hen you've started in the morning with no premarket preparation, you're trading on pure emotion, and your analysis and maneuvers are about as consistent as the capricious Northeastern weather, you're about to have your worst trading day.

I've had days like that as a greenhorn, and I've seen them happen to others. While trading near Wall Street I've witnessed lone rangers come onto the trading floor, and get wiped out in just a few hours. As incredible as that may sound, it happens all the time. It's possible to break every day trading rule in one single trading day, and I'm going to show you how.

One exemplary trader I saw especially sticks out in my mind. To me he's like the memory of a crazy car accident scene. Although he's an actual person, he and others like him remind me of the character called Quick-draw McGraw. Remember the Hanna-Barbera cartoon with that hyper, temperamental little gunslinger?

I'll call this trader Quick-draw McLoser.

The following is a description of what I'll assume has been a day in his life.

EARLY MORNING ACTIVITIES

It's dawn.

Quick-draw might be prostrate, balled up in bed, hiding deep under his covers. Or maybe he's wired and pacing his floor. Either way, this guy's a mess. He's so depressed and worried that he's sleeping way too much, or else he's insomniac.

Quick-draw has recently lost lots of money. The prospect of trading today makes him scared, and very rightly so; in his state of distraught exhaustion and fear, things will only get worse.

He'd be better off staying home, in bed, lying in a fetal position. He'd be better off sucking his thumb. That way he won't create any more damage than what he's already done.

Most likely his losses were yesterday, or over the past few days, because of huge over-exposure. Maybe last night he took a losing position and **held** it until this morning.

Maybe he's praying it will save him today by taking off like a shot.

Good luck, Quick-draw. You'll need it.

On days like this he completely abandons what the pros have all advised him to do. He doesn't even think about exercise. He doesn't care to scrutinize the market news. He doesn't even care to watch other stocks that can potentially gain him some profits. His only concern is whatever price his **held** stock will start to trade at, when premarket opens at 8:00 A.M.

If I'm wrong, and Quick-draw's not **holding**, then maybe his cliff-hanging, frayed-nerves condition is from trading for four days in the red. Today, which is Friday, is his last chance for the week, and even though he's fearful to day trade anymore, he's desperate to finally make a profit.

Can you see the gambling mentality emerging? It doesn't matter which strategic fiasco has caused Quick-draw's distress. What matters is that today, if he trades it will be on sheer emotion.

PREMARKET TRADING

It's a few minutes before premarket. I've arrived at the trading floor downtown. Quick-draw's already in position at his trading-desk, and he's noticeably nervous and pale. He looks even worse than he did yesterday, and yesterday he looked pretty bad. He always trades close to my station, so I observe him from time to time.

I'll return now to Quick-draw's perspective.

The hour of 8:00 strikes. The premarket data has started its dance across his glowering screens. He feels like he's watching a casino roulette ball bouncing on the spun wheel.

Then suddenly, the world's in slow motion. Quick-draw has just seen his death. Since the close of yesterday's after-market trading, his **held** stock has dropped three more dollars.

Quick-draw is in big trouble.

Should I buy more at these lower levels? That is, keep averaging down? Or should I cut my losses and stop/loss?

Quick-draw can't decide what to do. It's head-bashing hard to think straight. Panic starts biting all through him, just like a rabid dog. And then he goes numb. He just stares at the screen. He takes on the look of a zombie. He wants to plunge back into bed to the comforting escape of his sweet-dreams fortress. With a little bit of luck the stock just might retrace in his direction. But he's comatose, with no plan of exit.

Then a spark of adrenaline zaps him. Quick-draw snaps out of it. He straightens up in the chair. He realizes he needs a plan. At this point, any plan.

Like a typical gambler who's counting his chips, the only thing Quick-draw considers is the amount of his buying power. He checks out how much remains. His choice is quintessentially reckless: he'll average-down until the bell. With this ludicrous scheme he's desperately betting the price will retrace at 9:30 A.M.

And there we have it, folks: that's the hallmark casino decision.

The most notable issue is his judgment. It's taken a hike from his brain. Quick-draw is completely uninterested as to why this stock is dropping. He's ignoring the tell-tale signs of trending. He's failing to observe that the stock just broke through a major support level (30-day moving average), and with extremely high volume.

Quick-draw just doesn't care!

He's chosen to battle this out. He's going to stand and fight. The specter of the glazed-eyed Eternal Casino Addict is hovering over his shoulder.

So now he buys some more shares. He feels brave for showing up to his trading desk near Wall Street, and refusing to retreat to his bed.

His only hope is for the market to lend him mercy. What, has he forgotten?? The market has no mercy.

Let's assume that yesterday he bought XYZ stock, at an average price of $50 per share. He ended the day with 1,500 shares (total accumulated shares), and the price closed at $46.50. Then he **held** the losing positions overnight.

Next morning, today, at 8:00 a.m., the stock opened at $43.50, down another $3.00. So he's down $6.50 per share. That's equivalent to being in the red by $9,750 ($6.50 × 1,500 shares). Every $1 drop in price means he's losing $1,500!

With $250,000 leveraged buying-power, Quick-draw does the math. The fifteen hundred shares at $50 per share took only $75,000. On the bright side, he still has plenty of muscle.

But he's down almost $10,000!

Again Quick-draw considers his options. *I can go back home to bed and wait until the price goes back up later, I can stop/loss right now and take the $9,750 loss, or I can average this baby down, and rodeo-ride it back up.*

Quick-draw chooses the Wild Bill approach. *Eee-Hah!*

THE OPENING BELL

Its 9:30 A.M. There goes the bell. He's watching only that stock. He could care less what the rest of the market is doing. His only concern is riding that stock back to at least break-even.

He notices the stock price dropping further. So he purchases another 100 shares, and then another, and another. Now he has 2,000 shares of this stock, which is showing no signs of retracing.

Once again, Quick-draw feels the terror. The more he averages it down, it seems, the faster it wants to drop.

He now has roughly $150,000 of buying power left. He currently owns 2,000 shares at an average paid price of $49.75. The current market price is at $45.75, after hitting an earlier low of $42.75. So his updated *loss* is a little bit less; it's down to $8,000. By recklessly averaging down, it seems, he's actually gained something back.

Without a real plan of exit, however, those gains will be short lived. All it will take is an 80¢ cent move back down, and Quick-draw will be right back to his original $9,750 loss. And now he's **holding** 2,000 shares, instead of the original 1,500.

Overexposure has tightened the strangle.

MIDDAY ACTIVITIES

I get back from lunch and I notice that Quick-draw's in the exact same position he was in before I walked out the door. It's like he never got up for the break. I'm guessing he never ate lunch.

I'll return now to Quick-draw's point of view.

He refuses to acknowledge that his buying power is his worst enemy. He still has plenty of leverage that can sink him even further, or else pull him out of this mess. Well, he's trading on emotion, so he's flagrantly, crazily betting; he desperately believes that his buying power will sooner or later save him.

All afternoon he rides this stock, watching it go up and down. He's **holding** and frantically praying. Suddenly the stock goes all the way up to his break-even $49.75. "Oh, *yeah!*" he cheers, casino-style, startling every-one on the floor.

Then it rapidly retraces back down, to the low $47 range.

This has happened unbelievably fast—too fast for Quick-draw to react.

Quick-draw now gets very quiet, but I can see he's more agitated than ever.

He never sells any positions. The reason is he wants to make some money on this hell-ride. There's that, and then there are the destructive emotions of overconfidence and greed. He's allowed those emotions to make him believe that the price will move higher than the break-even point.

It hasn't.

Instead the price has continued to tank, and it begins to break through the original intra-day low of $42.75. Now he wishes he'd sold when it teased him, back when it reached his break-even $49.75.

Quick-draw feels beyond stupid. Oh, *yeah.*

But it's not over yet.

The price drops to $42.50, so he averages down some more. Quick-draw is stir-crazy now. He's laughing and crying all at once. He's getting a little delirious, convinced that the stock is an entity, aware, doing this to him with a vengeance.

He averages down some more, and then he does it some more.

It's near the last hour of trading. Quick-draw has ridden this roller-coaster since dawn. He has not once looked at the market indexes, or at any other stocks. He's been fixated on this one trade.

He just keeps on averaging it down.

LAST HOUR OF TRADING

It's 3 P.M. and Quick-draw has accumulated 5,400 shares. He's had to stop there, because he's reached his maximum buying power of $250,000.

At this point in the trading day, his average price paid has been $46.25. And the stock price is about to hit a new intraday low of $42.00.

Can you stomach doing the math? He's down $4.25 per share (on av-erage). That translates to an intraday loss of $22,950. There are 60 minutes left before the closing bell, and then there's after-hours. But Quick-draw is willing to wait this out. Isn't that all he's been doing?

Now enter the powers-that-be.

Recall how your pay-per-share trading firm deals with your leverage. The managers require your $25,000. Your money, upfront, is their cushion. It insures that they won't lose a dime on your negative trading activities. They don't mind lending (leveraging) you their $250,000, but as soon as you run deep into your collateral—the $25,000 you brought in—red flags go up at their monitors.

When there's only 10 minutes left to trade, and Quick-draw's own funds are gouged right down to a measly $2,000, the risk managers jump into action. What they do is called risk-management-intervention, or to put it more bluntly, forced selling.

(I'll never forget the sight of the risk manager walking over to Quick-draw's station. I felt his embarrassment as if it were my own. I knew that very soon my peer would be taking that miserable Walk of Shame.)

"We need you to sell all your positions right now," the risk-manager whispers discreetly.

It doesn't matter what the charts read or what price leap he thinks will happen; Quick-draw has to do what he's told. He's bought thousands of shares with the firm's money. The firm won't risk letting this stock plummet after-hours, or far worse, overnight. Not with *their* money, they won't!

So he miserably sells all 5,400 shares at an average of $42.25. The risk manager makes sure that he's done this, and then he pats him on the shoulder. Now the intervener walks away. The firm's assets are safe.

But all is not cool for our buddy. Quick-draw paid an average of $46.25 for all those thousands of shares. He sold all at $42.25. He lost $4 per share. His total loss on that trade—his *only* trade for the day—is $21,600.

THE CLOSING BELL

(I couldn't help peering at him. Having been there myself, I understood exactly how he felt. All of us pro traders can relate to what Quick-draw was experiencing).

For the rest of the trading session, he slouches. He's trying hard not to sob. He can't stop his mind from constantly replaying every maneuver he made. He feels like he;s going to puke.

AFTER-MARKET TRADING

Now Quick-draw can get some perspective. Even though he feels so low that he wants to crawl home to bed, he hangs around for a while.

He wants to keep an eye on the stock that just killed him, and only because he's curious. After getting mercilessly gutted and flayed, it's only natural to want to understand the dynamics of your destroyer.

Soon his curiosity turns into excitement. While he's watching the after-market price action of his money-munching XYZ stock, he notices a huge spike in volume and a major drop in price. It happens within mere seconds.

What in the world is going on?

It turns out that the stock has had its earnings release after the market just closed. The stock has reported miserable earnings, so it's dropped precipitously.

Quick-draw watches it tumble all the way down to a horrifying $34.50.

What if he were still **holding**?

He'd have lost an additional $8 per share!!!

I guess that means the risk manager really saved his ass.

You'll recall that when he woke up today, Quick-draw neglected some things. For one thing, he didn't check the news on his stock. If he had, he would have known that today it was releasing its quarterly earnings report.

Doesn't he know the ironclad rule? You *never* trade a stock on the day prior to or the day of a major news release! It must have slipped his mind.

HOMEWORK

The only homework for Quick-draw tonight is the attempt to budget himself out of this crater that he just sank himself into. He can't resume trading until the firm's group trading account gets a deposit of $22,000.

That's a lot of money for McLoser.

Parting Words

You'll recall that in Chapter 5, "Knowing When to Take a Break," I stress the importance of staying involved, even though you've briefly stopped trading. My writing of this book is an actual example of how I remained in the loop, during a hiatus of my own.

But why did you take a break? you might ask me. *Why did you stop and turn writer, when you were making so much money?*

I would respond with the reminder that day trading is a process that requires both rest and reflection. In that process, you can't skip steps. You can't be trading in hundred-share blocks, and on the next day start trading in thousands. You need some downtime in between that share increase, in order to study and learn, or you'll never become a professional, consistently profiting trader.

Even a pro needs some time off. It may be just to rest. It may be to play, to kick back, have fun . . . or even to brainstorm a book . . . but always with an ear on the market, every day, from the opening bell to the closing.

And the day trading process has setbacks, even for an expert. As usual I can best illustrate this by conveying my personal experiences.

Each time I advanced to a higher trading level, at first things always got rough. One such progression was my arrival at the conviction that I needed a pay-per-share broker. You'll recall that I'd been very actively trading with a traditional pay-per-trade broker, enduring prohibitive commissions. I cautiously traded in hundred-share blocks, looking for quick 10¢ to 40¢ moves, making $10 to $40 per trade. That was fine, because I was placing over 100 trades per day, but I was getting hit with a whopping $10 commission per execution!

So naturally I began seeking out firms with a pay-per-share commission structure. That was the logical and smart thing to do, but it also became a setback. Why? It was a whole new adjustment. There's the minimum $25,000 to become an associate pay-per-share trader. And then there's that move to New York.

After living in sunny San Diego for nine years, and day trading most of that time, I didn't go home to my cheap, familiar, easygoing western New York; I headed straight for the Big Apple. As you know, I had no choice. The pay-per-share day trading firms are concentrated there, most of them near Wall Street.

I was ready for that trading scenario, but I wasn't well-prepared for the hurdles. On the one hand, my ducks were expertly lined up: high leverage (20 to 1), a professional environment (trading floor), direct access (Level 2 and "fast-key" order execution), and of course my own extensive trading history. But the overall shock of moving, combined with the completely new system of trading, put a toll on my trading psychology. My comfort zone was obliterated. My normal rhythm got lost. My previous profit consistency dwindled. Basically, I had to learn how to day trade all over again. Though I was finally getting exposed to professional day trading and day traders, and I could see that my move to Manhattan was the best move for my career, it was going to take time to adjust.

During that time, I lost money. In an extremely expensive town!

The good side was working right next to some seasoned independent day traders. Those guys were mostly older, in their late 40s and 50s. They traded consistently profitably in 500-share blocks or more. They were what you call whale traders.

Taking peeks at their trading screens throughout the trading day, I was constantly blown away. Their daily profits (and losses) typically exceeded five thousand dollars.

What really got me, however, was all of their personal sagas. They emphasized their terrible trials while struggling to become professionals. As each and every one of them told similar horror stories, I listened with growing enlightenment. All of them had suffered great losses. For instance, most of them had remortgaged their houses—at least once—to recover. A few had to file bankruptcy. Many of them told me how they used to live like rats, eating peanut butter and jelly for a year.

Unfortunately, in this business, it can cost a lot to progress. They emphasized the importance of never losing your drive. They knew that each time they'd lost big, they'd also learned a huge lesson, something to add to their repertoires of growing expertise.

Their point, and the point that I'm making to you, is that this career isn't glorious, at least not right away. In accordance, I've refused to sugarcoat anything, because that would be criminal. The truth is you could lose both your mind and your shirt in the process of learning how to day trade as a pro.

My move to Manhattan involved sacrifice. In order to raise capital, I sold everything I owned. As I settled in the city, in the process of progressing, I suffered another round of agonizing losses. But now I can reap the rewards of the process. Now I'm a professional day trader.

For me, taking a break to write this book has been a fulfillment of the process. There's more to success than making money. I like being able to mentor. This book is an offering of rules and strategies that an amateur might forget. You have my blunders to learn from, and that makes my blunders worth something.

Rules to Remember

his final section is designed to be a quick reference list. I have simply gathered each rule from each chapter and placed them here. Also, it is crucial that you first read the entire chapter that corresponds to the rules. The rules by themselves are not meant to teach you, they are meant to remind you.

CHAPTER 1: TRUTHS ABOUT YOURSELF TO KNOW FIRST

- Increasing your skill level is a gradual process; never fast-track it without the help of professional mentorship or in-house training.
- A Series 7 license doesn't mean you're a professional day trader. You still need to be trained.
- Always remain active in day trading. That's the key to increasing skill.

CHAPTER 2: HOW EMOTIONS CAN DESTROY A TRADE

- If you feel yourself being controlled by your emotions—reduce your market exposure immediately.
- Stay consistent *all day* while trading—stick with 100-share blocks.
- Set realistic profit goals, and create a realistic budget.

CHAPTER 3: PREVENTING OVERCONFIDENCE

- Confidence is an emotional tool, and you must harness and control it.
- Never enter a trade without knowing your exit points.
- Once you've predetermined your exit points, always stick to them.

CHAPTER 4: FROM IMPATIENT TO COOL, CALM, AND COLLECTED

- Never pick entry or exits point when feeling out of control and impatient.
- Find stocks that move at least 25¢ cents every five-minute period.
- Do not trade more than 100-share blocks per trade until you become more advanced.
- Don't expect to make a lot of money in the beginning.
- Finish reading this book before you begin or go back to day trading.

CHAPTER 5: TAKING BREAKS

- Don't take time off just to get more cash.
- Gauge your performance at the end of each trading day.
- Log in the reasons why a trade went wrong.
- When things get consistently inconsistent, stop and take time off.
- During your time off, actively research your mistakes. Mentally prepare yourself for the return.
- Plan a budget for the inevitable—the times off.

CHAPTER 6: THE IMPORTANCE OF RISK MANAGEMENT

- Trade only the amount of shares, in one particular stock, that won't exceed the risk you can handle.
- If you're an amateur, always trade in 100-share blocks.
- If you're feeling stressed out, get out of the trade.
- Until you're highly skilled, don't trade until after 9:45 A.M.

- Practice learning your tolerance levels in low-risk (low-exposure) trades.
- Never overexpose yourself in any of the ways we've discussed.

CHAPTER 7: WHY OVEREXPOSURE TO THE MARKET CAN HURT

- Always trade stocks that are new to you in amounts no larger than 100-share blocks.
- Until you're consistently profiting during regular hours, avoid pre-market and after-market hours.
- When you're feeling completely lost and are most likely overexposed, stop/loss immediately.

CHAPTER 8: BUDGETING: KNOWING YOUR FINANCIAL LIMITATIONS

- If you're planning to train on your own, save up to prepare for three months of unemployment. If you're planning to be professionally mentored, save up for one month of unemployment.
- Don't try to trade for income until you're consistently profitable, after three months of training on your own or one month of mentoring.
- If you quit your day job, make sure you can get it back. Or, as an alternatiave safety net, bolster your day trading training with mentoring.
- Always have cushion money set aside for both your training and your active trading.
- Never keep your cushion money in your trading account.
- Use budgeting software to keep your accounting up-to-date and available.

CHAPTER 9: MINIMIZING YOUR RISK WITH STOP/LOSS

- Learning how to properly stop/loss is a process of trial and error. So again: trade in small hundred-share blocks.
- Never try gauging a stop/loss price until you've determined the support and resistance levels for that day.

- Before you even try to gauge what price level you want to sell at a stop/loss, know your financial limitations for that day.
- On every trade you enter, always stick to your predetermined stop/loss exit price.

CHAPTER 10: AVERAGING-DOWN: A SKILLED STRATEGY

- Never attempt to average-down until you're sufficiently skilled.
- Never average-down beyond your threshold for risk.
- Only average-down on your consistently profitable stocks.

CHAPTER 11: GAMBLING VERSUS DAY TRADING

- Learn risk management before you start day trading, or else you're just rolling the dice.
- Hone the skills of risk management during initial live-trading experiences. Always take advantage of the strategic options that day trading offers you—options you don't get in gambling.
- Never, ever ask yourself whether you're feeling lucky today.

CHAPTER 12: WHY SOME TRADERS MAKE MORE MISTAKES

- Never take your eyes off a trade!
- Log every one of your mistakes.
- Your mistake is another trader's profit, so understand what he did right.
- Focus on eliminating your chronic mistakes.
- Instead of shrugging them off, learn and grow from your errors.

CHAPTER 13: TRADING CONSISTENTLY ALL DAY

- Find your tolerance levels, and adjust your stop/loss and profit system accordingly.

- Discipline yourself to trade the same way, *all day long*.
- Never **hold** a losing position overnight!

CHAPTER 14: STOCK PICKING: SIMPLIFYING THE PROCESS

- Even with a good stock to trade, never lower your guard and/or trade in larger share blocks.
- Find stocks that have been trading consistently, over a three-month period, above 1 million shares in volume per day, on average.
- Never trade penny stocks.
- Only add stocks to your Watch List that are priced in the $10 to $100 range.
- Stay away from charts that exhibit intraday flat patterns.
- Don't trade stocks whose companies are dependent on regulations that can drastically affect their product sales.
- Don't be in a trade just before anticipated news hits the wire about it.
- Stay away from any stock that is even considering bankruptcy.
- Read this entire book before you trade stocks you've found.

CHAPTER 15: WHY NEWS CAN BE JUST NOISE

- Know which news will hurt your trade, and which news is just noise.
- Always know your stock's earnings announcement dates.
- Do not trade a stock on or before the day of an earnings announcement.
- If the news hits the wire midday, and it's immediately affecting the price of your stock, stop trading that stock for that day.

CHAPTER 16: ABOUT THOSE TRAINING PROGRAMS

- If you're a beginner day trader, go for some form of structured training.
- Go to training programs armed with questions.
- Don't expect to be a pro upon completion of any short-term program.
- Insist upon information about pay-per-per share brokers.
- If you're an advanced beginner, seek out mentorship programs.

CHAPTER 17: PICKING THE RIGHT ONLINE BROKER

- Don't use a pay-per-trade broker if you're placing multiple trades and not **holding** overnight.
- Keep your pay-per-trade broker *only* for long-term trades and free resources.
- In pay-per-share trading, be extremely careful of how much leverage you use. Always start small (10 to 1).
- When searching for pay-per-share brokers, visit the actual trading floors and test their demos for at least a few days, and take note of their cost/fee structures.
- Trade remotely from home only after you've traded on their floor for awhile.

CHAPTER 18: PAPER-TRADING STRATEGY

- Think real and trade small when paper trading.
- Paper trade *exactly* the same way as you would when real trading.
- *Do not* construe paper trading as a way to gauge your profits.

CHAPTER 19: TRADING FOR SKILL VERSUS TRADING FOR INCOME

- Always start with a First-Level stock, then progress upward from there.
- *Do not* trade with real money until you've been consistently profitable with your stock for a week straight in paper trading.

About the Author

J osh DiPietro has been day-trading stocks for 11 years. He operates a web site, www.daytraderjosh.com, and provides mentoring programs for aspiring day traders. His trading approach involves making many trades every day, taking small profits, exiting losing trades quickly, and minimizing commission fees. He is a critic of the educational paths offered by the established trading industry and is dedicated to providing an alternative education approach for aspiring traders.

Josh is 33 years old and resides in New York City.

Index